Lecture Notes in Computer Science   7161

Commenced Publication in 1973
Founding and Former Series Editors:
Gerhard Goos, Juris Hartmanis, and Jan van Leeuwen

Peeter Laud (Ed.)

Information Security Technology for Applications

16th Nordic Conference on Secure IT Systems, NordSec 2011
Tallinn, Estonia, October 26-28, 2011
Revised Selected Papers

 Springer

Volume Editor

Peeter Laud
Cybernetica AS
Ülikooli 2
51003 Tartu, Estonia
E-mail: peeter@cyber.ee

ISSN 0302-9743   e-ISSN 1611-3349
ISBN 978-3-642-29614-7   e-ISBN 978-3-642-29615-4
DOI 10.1007/978-3-642-29615-4
Springer Heidelberg Dordrecht London New York

Library of Congress Control Number: 2012935688

CR Subject Classification (1998): D.4.6, K.6.5, D.2, H.2.7, K.4.4, E.3, C.2

LNCS Sublibrary: SL 4 – Security and Cryptology

Typesetting: Camera-ready by author, data conversion by Scientific Publishing Services, Chennai, India

Printed on acid-free paper

Springer is part of Springer Science+Business Media (www.springer.com)

Preface

These are the conference proceedings of NordSec 2011, the 16th Nordic Conference on Secure IT-Systems. They contain the revised versions of the full papers that were accepted and presented at the conference, which took place during October 26–28, 2011, in Tallinn, Estonia.

The NordSec workshops were started in 1996 with the aim of bringing together researchers and practitioners within computer security in the Nordic countries, thereby establishing a forum for discussions and co-operation between universities, industry and computer societies. Since then, the workshop has developed into a fully fledged international information security conference, held in the Nordic countries on a round robin basis.

This year, the conference accepted contributions in the form of full papers, short papers, and posters. Full papers were solicited for mature results, short papers for ongoing work, and posters as a form of student contribution. We received a total of 51 valid paper submissions, among them 8 submissions as short papers. The Program Committee tried to give at least three reviews to all submissions. Out of the submitted papers, 16 were accepted as full papers and 8 as short papers. Also, some full submissions were accepted as short papers. In addition to the talks by the authors of accepted papers, we also had two invited talks by Estonian e-governance and security specialists. In their talks, they analyzed some of the most-used and highest-profile information systems for the Estonian e-government — the *X-road* middleware and the Internet voting system.

Since 2008, Nordsec conferences have been happy to welcome the participation of the Second-year students of the international Erasmus Mundus master's programme "NordSecMob" in security and mobile computing. The students are encouraged to participate in the conference by submitting posters reporting on work they have performed. This year, six posters were submitted and presented at the conference.

Even though NordSec is not a large conference, the efforts of many people are necessary for its successful organization. We would like to thank everybody who made the conference possible. We thank the Program Committee for reviewing the papers and discussing them, thereby creating the best possible program for the conference. We thank the subreviewers for the extra help they gave us with the reviews. We also thank the Poster Chair for helping the students to produce high-quality posters for the conference, and the invited speakers for agreeing to share their insights. And obviously, we are thankful to all the authors for submitting their papers for consideration of the program committee because, without those, there would not have been anything in the conference program.

We are especially grateful to the Organizing Committee of the conference. Making sure that all the tiny details are taken care of is a lot of work, and we heartfully thank Imbi, Liina, and Madeline for that.

We are also grateful to Cybernetica AS for agreeing to host the conference, and to the Estonian Centre of Excellence in Computer Science, EXCS (financed through the European Regional Development Fund) for providing financial support.

November 2011   Peeter Laud

Organization

General Chair

Peeter Laud   Cybernetica AS and University of Tartu, Estonia

Program Committee

Frederik Armknecht	University of Mannheim, Germany
Lizzie Coles-Kemp	Royal Holloway, University of London, UK
Mads Dam	KTH Royal Institute of Technology, Sweden
Simone Fischer-Hübner	Karlstad University, Sweden
Dieter Gollmann	Hamburg University of Technology (TUHH), Germany
Erland Jonsson	Chalmers University of Technology, Sweden
Svein Johan Knapskog	Norwegian University of Science and Technology, Norway
Igor Kotenko	St. Petersburg Institute for Informatics and Automation of Russian Academy of Sciences, Russia
Helger Lipmaa	University of Tartu, Estonia
Fabio Massacci	University of Trento, Italy
Chris Mitchell	Royal Holloway, University of London, UK
Kaisa Nyberg	Aalto University, Finland
Kai Rannenberg	Goethe University, Frankfurt, Germany
Heiko Roßnagel	Fraunhofer IAO, Germany
Andrei Sabelfeld	Chalmers University of Technology, Sweden
Jaak Tepandi	Tallinn University of Technology, Estonia
Dominique Unruh	University of Tartu, Estonia
Risto Vaarandi	Cooperative Cyber Defense Centre of Excellence, Estonia
Jan Willemson	Cybernetica AS, Estonia
Ender Yüksel	Technical University of Denmark, Denmark

Poster Chair

Margus Niitsoo   University of Tartu, Estonia

Organizing Committee

Madeline González Muñiz
Liina Kamm
Imbi Nõgisto

Reviewers

Table of Contents

Designing a Governmental Backbone

Arne Ansper

Cybernetica AS, Tallinn, Estonia

Abstract. The presentation is about the design of the backbone of the Estonian governmental information systems - X-Road. The system is already ten years old and has proven to be useful and reliable. The presentation describes the vision of the system, the requirements analysis process and the technical design decisions. The vision was to create a web-services based unified access to all governmental registries. The requirements analysis was guided by the existing legislation and organizational setup of the government. The technical design was pragmatic and based on some unorthodox solutions.

Keywords: case-study, eGovernment, web-services, digital signature, interoperability framework, distributed middleware, DNSSEC.

1   Introduction

X-Road is the backbone of the Estonian governmental information systems. It is a system for securing the inter-organizational data exchange. It is not a physical communication network, but more like a VPN with digital signatures and access control for web-services. We could call it "distributed middleware" or "distributed ESB (Enterprise Service Bus)".

2   History of the X-Road

It is already an old system - it has been in use for almost ten years now. There are more than 600 organizations connected to X-Road, offering more than 1500 services that were used more than 225 million times during 2010. The idea of the X-Road was born in the Department of State Information Systems, sometime at the end of last century. They wanted to offer unified data exchange environment that would reduce money and time spent on integration projects. The prototype was built and tested. The main idea was to use web-services, as a platform neutral protocol for inter-organizational communication and build a central hub that would mediate all service requests and perform access controls.

This was quite an innovative approach, because the web-services were just a couple of years old. The prototype was sound from the functional perspective - it provided unified access to different registries. But it did not address security concerns and did not take into account the legal and organizational framework - basically how the state is functioning.

P. Laud (Ed.): NordSec 2011, LNCS 7161, pp. 1–3, 2012.

3   Requirements for the System

The idea was to come up with a solution that would allow effortless access to the data in state registries, without compromising the security of the data, with minimal impact to the existing systems and without requiring major legal changes. The functions of the government are divided between agencies. They have a freedom to decide how they implement those functions - what are the procedures, systems, etc. On one hand this division creates redundancy and inefficiency. On the other hand, this creates stability and helps to ensure that the principles of the democratic government are followed. When we apply IT, we optimize the system. There is a danger that we over-optimize and create a system that puts too much power into someone's hands.

Each agency is authority in its field and responsible to ensure the rightful usage of its data. Centralization of the data or access to the data would violate this principle. Deployment of such a system would see a great resistance from the agencies. Creation of such a super-database would also create an inviting target for attacks and is bad from the security viewpoint.

The solution must be decentralized and based on collaboration. Central hub is not a solution. The data that is managed by one agency is needed to make some decision in another agency. The agency that makes a decision needs some evidence to prove later why such decision is made. We need a system that would preserve the authenticity, integrity and evidentiary value of the data. If we have such a system in place, it will be used more and more. Many business processes that used to be independent will start using external services. The system must ensure the high availability of the services.

Finally, some data is confidential. It must be protected against external and internal attackers. It is important to notice that the security requirements are prioritized. When people normally talk about "security" they think about confidentiality. In reality, the other properties are more important. In fact, this is pretty standard set of security requirements. Indeed, we can use standard security measures to satisfy them. The important question is how to make all this technology and procedures available to all organizations that need to exchange data. Most of the organizations are very small and without IT and security management capabilities. The solution must be very easy to deploy, maintain and use.

4   Architecture of the System

We designed a distributed system. Each organization runs a security server. Security server is a mono-functional self-contained GNU/Debian based server that implements all security related aspects of the inter-organizational communication. It is an appliance. Security servers are communicating with each other directly. The data flow between organizations is direct.

Security server is basically an application level firewall for SOAP + digital signature creation and verification device for SOAP messages + highly available VPN device.

Local applications see the security server as a provider of all web services offered by other organizations. Remote service requests by local application will be proxied by security server. Security server will sign all the outgoing SOAP messages (requests and responses). Security server will verify the signatures of all incoming SOAP messages, will time-stamp them and archive them. Security servers contain full history of communication. Digital signature mechanism together with archiving ensures the authenticity, integrity and evidentiary value of the exchanged data.

Security servers also control access to the web-services at the organizational level. The organization receiving the service must ensure that only right people can use this service, by using whatever technical means it sees appropriate. This obligation is enforced by service provisioning contract between the organizations. Two level access control isolates the details of organizational authentication and access control mechanisms and minimizes the impact to the existing systems. The balanced use of technical and organizational security measures was an important success factor of the X-Road.

The availability of the system is increased by having a minimal number of central services: only time-stamping and secure directory. Time-stamping is used in a way that makes it non-time critical. The time-stamping is performed asynchronously in the background. Directory service is based on the Secure DNS (DNS-SEC). All the information that needs to be shared is put into DNS zone: IP-addresses, valid certificates, names of the organizations and groups, etc. Well-proven DNS protocol and implementation provide robust, scalable directory service with built-in caching and redundancy. Security extensions ensure that the data cannot be tampered. All X-Road servers run a local caching DNS server that performs strict validation of zone signatures and ensures the availability of directory information during network outages.

There are also mechanisms against DoS attacks. Critical resources (i.e. CPU time, file handles) are shared between different clients in a fair manner. Security servers provide also meta-services that help to discover the structure of the system: what organizations are connected, what are the services, download the WSDL descriptions of the services, etc. Meta-services are used by portals to automate the generation of the user-interfaces for invocation of services.

5   Organization and Procedures

X-Road has central agency that ensures its operation. X-Road central agency was created in parallel with the system development. The operating procedures of the agency, security regulations and rules for organizations that connect with the system were all aligned with the technical solution.

Central agency ensures the legal status of the X-Road and the information exchanged via it, by enforcing the stated policies. It is responsible for steering the further development of the X-Road and ensuring its consistency and integrity. It provides central services like certification, time-stamping, secure directory and monitoring and resolves the potential disputes between communicating parties.

Internet Voting in Estonia

Priit Vinkel

Estonian National Electoral Committee,
Lossi plats 1a,
Tallinn, Estonia
priit.vinkel@vvk.ee

Abstract. Estonia was the first country in the world to introduce Internet Voting pan-nationally in binding elections in 2005. Although Internet Voting is only one of many ways of voting in Estonia, the number of voters has grown exponentially. The short paper explores the topic of Internet Voting based on the six-year experience of the pioneer country Estonia. The factors of success in the process include for example the relative small size of the country and the positive experiences with previous government e-services. The role of a secure online authentication token — ID-card — would also be crucial in implementing the idea of remote voting in an uncontrolled environment.

Voter's right to change the I-vote with another I-vote or with paper-ballot and the supremacy of the paper ballot serve as main strongholds against vote buying and other infringements of the principle of free elections.

Possible future developments and expansion of technical platforms will be addressed.

Keywords: Internet Voting, elections, e-government, e-services, remote authentication.

1   Introduction

Estonia is a parliamentary democracy, the 101 members of the unicameral parliament Riigikogu are elected under proportional electoral system, the governing coalition usually comprises of two or more political parties. Head of state is the President with mainly representative duties. Estonian reform-readiness might be explained with the state history (after Soviet occupation and being part of the Soviet Union, Estonia regained its independence in 1991 and had to rebuild an effective governance under rule of law, restore private property and market economy etc). Since 2004 Estonia is member of European Union and NATO[1].

In 2005, Estonia was the first country in the world to have remote voting over the Internet in pan-national binding elections. Since then the number of Internet voters has risen more than 14 times. This short paper looks at the building blocks

---

[1] More about history, culture, society etc in an encyclopedia about Estonia: http://www.estonica.org/en/

P. Laud (Ed.): NordSec 2011, LNCS 7161, pp. 4–12, 2012.
© Springer-Verlag Berlin Heidelberg 2012

of the Estonian Internet Voting system, addresses some emerged problems and future plans. Most likely Internet Voting in Estonia is there to stay as already a quarter of voters vote over the Internet. However, the constant struggle of improving the system and the surrounding processes is crucial in preserving the trust of the voter in online voting.

2   The Estonian Internet Voting System

2.1   Pillars of Success

Using Internet Voting for national elections is not a very widespread practice. Only Switzerland, Estonia and Norway allow legally binding remote Internet Voting [1]. Therefore, the understanding of the factors that help for implementing this concept is quite important. The current concept of Internet voting that has been used for voting in two general elections (2007 and 2011), in two local elections (2005 and 2009) and one European Parliament election (2009). The number of Internet Voters has grown sharply from less than 10,000 in 2005's local elections to over 140,000 in the 2011 general elections. The latter account for 24.3% of all votes cast and 56.4% of the advance votes [2]. And one red line has always followed through all these years — accepting Internet Voting relies heavily on the trust of the voters. Without a doubt, trust is a key factor for almost all crucial e-solutions, but the direct connection with remote Internet Voting has been reiterated in according scientific surveys [3]. The three most important factors of keeping and building this trust could be summarized as put on figure 1.

Open Receptive Society. The Republic of Estonia currently has about 1.35 million inhabitants, dispersed over 45,227 km². According to The Global Information Technology Report 2009-2010 [4], in the category of government success in

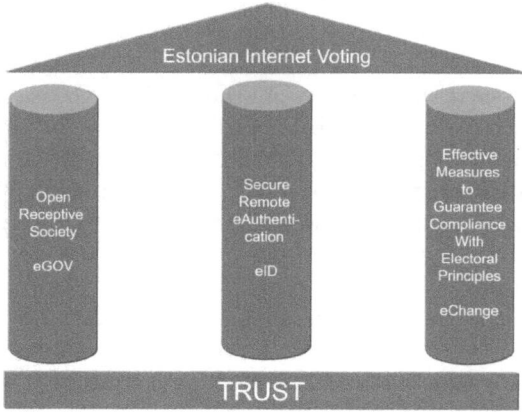

Fig. 1. Three pillars of Estonian Internet Voting

ICT promotion Estonia lies on 11th place forerunning such IT giants as US, Korea or Japan. In the field of providing quality online public services Estonia shares the positions 26–28 with Hungary and Ireland. In the category of presence of ICT in government agencies, the top three countries are Singapore, Sweden and Estonia. Since 1st June 2010 even the official publication of legal acts — The State Gazette — is entirely electronic, it means the legal acts are published only on the Internet[2].

An important factor explaining the possibility to launch totally new solutions like the official virtual identity or Internet Voting is the smallness of the country. Lennart Meri, the late president of the Republic of Estonia compared in his speech at St. Olaf College in Minnesota on 6 April 2000 Estonia with a small boat: "A super tanker needs sixteen nautical miles to change her course. Estonia, on the contrary, is like an Eskimo kayak, able to change her course on the spot."

Therefore, as the number of actual voters is around 1 million and there is generally a positive notion towards innovation, such ideas as Internet Voting could be addressed more easily.

Secure Remote e-Authentication. The cornerstone of Estonian e-services, public as well private, is eID[3]. Since 2002, ID card as the new generation's mandatory primary identification document. The ID cards are issued by the Government and contain certificates for remote authentication and digital signature. All Estonian citizens and resident aliens above 15 years old must have ID-card.

Each ID card contains two discrete PKI-based digital certificates — one for authentication and one for digital signing. The certificates contain only the holder's name and personal code and have two associated private keys on the card, each protected by a unique user PIN. The certificates contain no restrictions of use: they are by nature universal and meant to be used in any form of communications, whether between private persons, organizations or within the government. The eID card can be also used for encryption of documents so that only the person intended to view the document can decrypt it. This is an efficient means for secure transfer of documents using public networks. In addition to that, each ID card contains all data printed on it also in electronic form, in a special publicly readable data file.

The number of issued ID-cards has in June 2010 exceeded 1.1 Million. Over 2/3 of cardholders have used the eID card for remote personal identification and over 1/3 for digital signature. Here has to be noted, that Internet voting has strongly promoted electronic use of ID card. Another important promoting factor has been the agreement between banks to allow Internet banking only with ID-card or PIN-calculator. The old password-cards can be used only for very small transactions.

In order to use the ID card, the smart-card reader and a computer with relevant software (free to download); an Internet connection and Windows, Mac or Linux operating system are needed. A couple of years ago a new solution was brought to the market: m-ID, where a mobile telephone acts as an

---

[2] The Estonian State Gazette. https://www.riigiteataja.ee/tutvustus.html?m=1
[3] More info about the Estonian ID-card can be found at http://www.id.ee/?lang=en

ID-card and a card reader at the same time. In addition to functionality of an ordinary SIM, a Mobile-ID SIM also holds a person's mobile identity that enables providers of internet services to identify the person and to give digital signatures. Personal identification and digital signature functionality are secured by up-to-date security technology and corresponding Personal Identification Numbers. What makes the solution more convenient is the fact that an ID-card reader in the computer is not needed any longer- instead, it enables making electronic transactions, just like an ID-card: it makes it possible to log into databases, internet banks etc and sign various contracts digitally.

Parliamentary debate over eID card raised several privacy and security questions, but the parties supporting compulsory eID commanded over majority of votes. The most controversial questions were possible risk of identity theft and the general IT security. To prevent the use of the ID-card issued to another person, respective provisions were added to the Penal Code. According to the law fraudulent use of the ID-card is punishable by a pecuniary punishment or up to three years of imprisonment.

Effective Measures to Guarantee Compliance with Electoral Principles. The secrecy of voting has traditionally been viewed in Estonia as the right and obligation to cast one's vote alone in a voting booth. In the case of the Internet voting, the state is not in a position to secure the privacy aspect of the procedure. Legislators proceeded from the interpretation of the Constitution according to which secrecy of voting, drawing on its two sub-principles — the private proceeding of voting and the anonymity of the vote — is required to ensure free voting and is not an objective per se. Consequently, instruments aimed at securing secrecy can be adapted, provided that voters are given the opportunity to vote freely for their preferred party without fearing condemnation or expecting moral approval or material reward [5].

The voter's right to anonymity during the counting of the votes is guaranteed to the extent to which it can be secured in the case of absentee ballots by mail; the so-called "system of two envelopes" (see Figure 2), used for absentee ballots by mail, is both reliable and easy to understand for the I-voters.

A double-envelope scheme known from the postal voting in some countries guarantees the secrecy of the vote. The voter's choice is encrypted by voting application (i.e. voter seals the choice into an inner blank envelope) and then signed digitally (i.e. he puts the inner envelope into the bigger one and writes his name/address on it). The signed and encrypted votes (outer envelopes) are collected to the central site to check and ensure that only one vote per voter will be counted. Before counting, digital signatures with personal data (outer envelopes) are removed and anonymous encrypted votes (inner envelopes) are put to the ballot box for counting.

The scheme uses public key cryptography that consists of a key pair — a private and a public key. Once the vote is encrypted with a public key then it can only be decrypted with the corresponding private key. The National Electoral Committee, holding the private key, collegially opens the encrypted I-votes on Election Day [6].

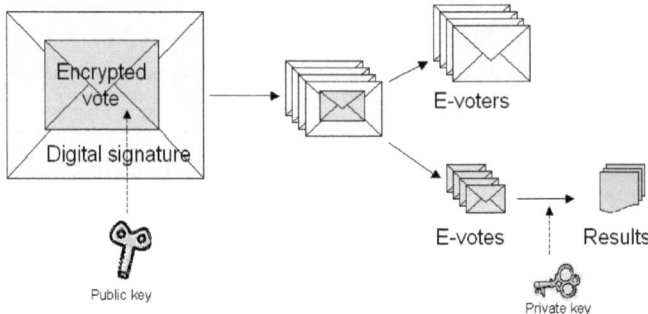

Fig. 2. Double envelope system used in Internet Voting

In order to guarantee the freedom of voting, I-voters have been granted the right to re-vote electronically an unlimited number of times and replace the vote cast on the Internet by a paper ballot. However, this can only be done within the advance polling days. In case of several I-votes the last one is counted; in case of contest between an I-vote and a paper ballot, the paper ballot is counted. If several paper-ballots are cast, all votes are declared invalid. Thus, the "one vote — one voter" principle is ostensibly guaranteed.

In case of the Internet-based voting, the possibility to change a vote is not just permissible; it is a constitutional obligation. According to the opinion of the Supreme Court of Estonia [7], the principle of the freedom of vote gives rise to the obligation of the state to protect voters from persons attempting to influence their choice. With regard to that principle, the state has to create necessary prerequisites in order to carry out free polling and to protect voters from undesired pressure while making a voting decision.

2.2   System Architecture

The main components of the Estonian I-voting system (seen on Figure 3) are the Voter Application; the Vote Forwarding Server and the Back-office, which is divided in two: the Vote Storage Server and the Vote Counting Application. The Voter Application is a stand-alone application in voters' personal computers to cast and encrypt votes.

The processes of the Vote Forwarding Server (a network server) are authentication, the checking of franchise, sending a candidates' list to voters, receiving signed and encrypted ballots. The network server immediately transfers the received encrypted ballots to the Vote Storage Server and transposes the acknowledgements of receipt from the Votes Storage Server to the voters. The network server completes the work when the I-voting period finishes. The Vote Storage Server receives encrypted ballots from the network server and stores them until the end of voting period. The Votes Storage Server has also a responsibility of votes' managing and cancelling. The Vote Counting Application is an offline app which summarizes all encrypted ballots. The encrypted ballots are transferred from Vote Storage Server to Vote Counting App by using offline data carriers.

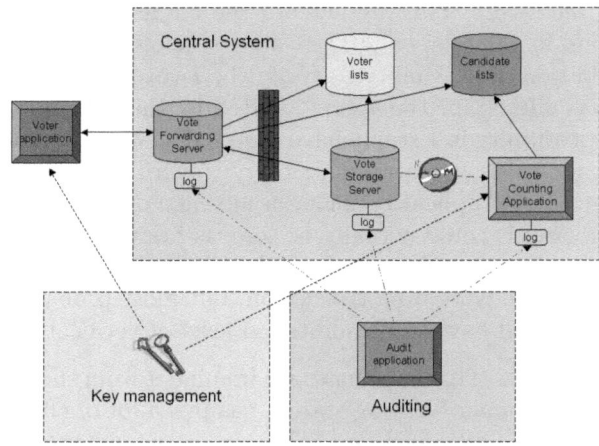

Fig. 3. The general architecture of the Internet Voting system

Vote Counting Server does not receive voters' digital signatures and so, does not know voters' personal data.

Additionally, the I-voting system delivers independent log files, which consist of trace of the received encrypted ballots from the Vote Forwarding Server, all annulled encrypted ballots, and all encrypted ballots sent to the Vote Counting App and all counted encrypted ballots. The used cryptographic protocol links all records in the log files. The National Electoral Committee has the right to use the log files to resolve disputes. Hence, there is an independent audit trail to verify the I-voting process and help solve problems should they appear [8].

3   Emerged Issues and Future Trends

3.1   Main Issues After Five Elections

Security. It is impossible to prove security, but only the opposite. This popular IT proverb has kept its ground in the Estonian Internet Voting case. As a matter of fact e-enabled elections from 2005 to 2009 have had quite little publicly exposed concerns regarding security issues tied explicitly to one way of voting — over the Internet. The usual topics: why I-voting, compliance with principles of free and fair voting, the possible impact on the election results etc were discussed in the parliament and in scientific circles, less in the media. The National Electoral Committee had no complaints presented and the overall notion had been fairly positive. However, after 2011 general elections, discussions about the possible the infringement of principles of security flared up again. Most probably the growingly prominent position of Internet Voting among other voting methods has played a significant role in this fact. A thorough discussion about the technical issues emerged in 2011 has been covered by Heiberg *et al* [9].

Verification of the I-vote. Norway entered the circle of countries providing e-enabled elections in September 2011 by introducing Internet Voting in local elections. In addition, a possibility to verify the I-vote by using SMS and paper polling cards was offered for the voters[4]. Lifted by this example the discussions of offering this possibility in Estonia have emerged as well. To date, the Estonian system has not foreseen a separate possibility to verify the I-vote. Only in case of re-voting the Voter Application shows a message of the fact that the person has voted before and it could actually be seen as first lever verification (stating the receiving of the vote). Nevertheless, the discussions currently held in the parliament have yet to come to a conclusion, but most probably the 2013 local e-enabled elections will have some additional level of verification used.

Uniformity of elections. This issue has been imminent from the very beginning of the concept. The Estonian I-Voting system has put a lot of effort in fulfilling all universal principles of election. Nevertheless, the very fact that Internet Voting is fundamentally different from traditional voting is grounds enough to have doubts in equal conduct of matters. The actual conundrum is that Internet Voting can never have all the same characteristics as paper voting. The main issue within the complex of uniformity is whether changing the vote should be exclusively an e-matter. As already stated before, changing the I-vote is not about changing the ticket but rather voting again in order to be free. Therefore, constitutionally, I-voting even has to be conducted in a non-uniform manner [10].

Role of soft laws. Not all provisions fit in the narrow limitations of a legal act. There are some principles concerning I-voting that need to be agreed upon by the players — the parties. The soft laws include things like prohibiting I-voting parties or encouraging voters to change their vote for other reasons than guaranteeing the secrecy of the vote[5]. However, there were some parties that did not agree with these soft provisions and started a discussion of integrating the agreement further into hard law. To date the discussion is still in process.

3.2 Future of I-Voting — Where to?

Finally, some points considering future development in the field of Internet Voting in Estonia.

To replace paper voting. As stated before, Internet Voting is only one of many possibilities of voting in Estonia and at the moment it can be said that it shall be so also in the nearer future. The purpose of e-enabled voting has always been supplementary. It offers new possibilities but does not take away existing ones. Although the eID rollout has been completed, only roughly a half of the population has ever used the ID-card electronically. So, I-voting will most probably stay a successful e-government service meant to keep existing voters and offer a

---

[4] Norwegian Internet Voting Project http://www.regjeringen.no/en/dep/krd/prosjekter/e-vote-2011-project.html?id=597658
[5] Good Practice of Internet Voting:
http://www.ega.ee/files/Good%20Practice%20of%20E-voting%202009.pdf

convenient voting method for possible new ones. It will not replace paper-ballot, at least in the near future, and if at all, it would probably replace postal-voting from abroad.

To have e-kiosks in polling stations. There might be questions of as having implemented one e-solution, why not a similar one. Most probably Estonia will not enable electronic voting in polling stations (in form of voting machines). We have a simple and fairly linear ballot, few questions and quite small electorate. All this indicates that Internet Voting will be sufficient for our needs. Moreover, as the concept of Internet Voting is not limiting the place and environment of voting, so offering Internet Voting in polling station grounds during advance voting might be possible.

To match the voting periods. At the moment Internet Voting is possible during advance voting for 7 days, traditional voting for 3 days. This discrepancy has been seen as an infringement of uniformity since adopting the provisions. The main problem is seen in the political environment the voter makes his or her decision. Moreover, the voting situation is already different during the long advance voting period compared to voting Sunday. Therefore, I-voting and traditional voting periods shall be equalized. The effects of shortening the I-voting period have been also discussed in the 2011 EUI report [3].

To move to smart phones. At the moment the Internet Voting Application is a stand-alone program designed for use in a computer environment (Windows, Mac and Linux platforms supported). Voting with a smart phone is not possible. Although there have been some ambitious ideas from some political parties of entering this uncharted territory, the most likely scenario will not include smart phones in Internet Voting. The relative lack of a strong cost benefit factor is underlined by the broad heterogeneity of smart phone platforms. For the foreseeable future Internet Voting will stay exclusively with computers.

4 Conclusions

Being a sparsely populated Northern state with few strong traditions when it regained independence in 1991, Estonia was and still is able to benefit from excellent opportunities for successful exploitation of new ideas. The unique chance to rebuild the state has offered wide opportunities to take contemporary, functional and logical decisions. Internet Voting is on the one hand an essential public e-service in the Estonian information society, on the other hand an innovation in electoral administration which impact deserves permanent attention and scientific research.

The Estonian Internet Voting system stands literarily speaking on three pillars. First, the Estonian eID — a secure and widely accepted way of remote e-identification. Second, e-services are widely accepted in the Estonian society. And third, we have managed to build the Internet Voting system as similar to the traditional voting logic as possible, incl. means to guarantee secure and anonymous voting (the virtual voting booth or possibility to change the I-vote) and a virtual twin-envelope system. Internet Voting is not a separate concept but prominently seen as just another e-service for the citizen for communicating with the government (state), as part of the modern information society.

In all of the five elections e-enabled voting has been implemented, the factor of trust has been of the upmost importance. Without a doubt, trust will stay the most important factor of choosing Internet Voting also in the future and building and stabilizing this trust is the most important but also one of the most difficult tasks of the election administration.

References

1. Competence Center for Electronic Voting and Participation. E-voting database, `http://db.e-voting.cc/`
2. Estonian National Electoral Committee. Internet Voting — Voting Methods in Estonia, `http://www.vvk.ee/voting-methods-in-estonia/engindex/`
3. Trechsel, A.H., Vassil, K.: Internet Voting in Estonia: A Comparative Analysis of Five Elections since 2005. Report for the Estonian National Electoral Committee, European University Institute (October 2011).
   `http://www.vvk.ee/public/dok/Internet_Voting_Report_20052011_Final.pdf`
4. Dutta, S., Mia, I.: The Global IT Technology Report 2009–2010: ICT for Sustainability. World Economic Forum (2010)
5. Drechsler, W., Madise, Ü.: Electronic Voting in Estonia. In: Kersting, N., Baldersheim, H. (eds.) Electronic Voting and Democracy. A Comparative Analysis, pp. 97–108. Palgrave Macmillan, Basingstoke (2004)
6. Estonian National Electoral Committee. E-Voting System: General Overview (2010),
   `http://www.vvk.ee/public/dok/General_Description_E-Voting_2010.pdf`
7. Constitutional Review Chamber of the Supreme Court of Estonia. Constitutional Judgement 3-4-1-13-05 (September 1, 2005), `http://www.nc.ee/?id=381`
8. Madise, Ü., Maaten, E., Vinkel, P.: Internet Voting at the Elections of Local Government Councils on October 2005. Report for the Estonian National Electoral Committee (2006), `http://www.vvk.ee/public/dok/report2006.pdf`
9. Heiberg, S., Laud, P., Willemson, J.: The Application of I-voting for Estonian Parliamentary Elections of 2011. In: Kiyaias, A., Lipmaa, H. (eds.) Postproceedings: 3rd International Conference on E-voting and Identity, Tallinn, September 29-30, 2011. LNCS. Springer, Heidelberg (forthcoming, 2012)
10. Madise, Ü., Vinkel, P.: Constitutionality of Remote Internet Voting: The Estonian Perspective. In: Juridica International. Iuridicum Foundation, vol. XVIII (forthcoming, 2011)

A Ring Based Onion Circuit for Hidden Services

Hakem Beitollahi and Geert Deconinck

Katholieke Universiteit Leuven, Electrical Engineering Department,
Kasteelpark Arenberg 10, Leuven, Belgium
{Hakem.Beitollahi,Geert.Deconinck}@esat.kuleuven.be

Abstract. The capability that a server can hide its location while offering various kinds of services to its clients is called hidden services or location-hiding. Almost previous low-latency anonymous communication systems such as Tor, MorphMix, etc. that can be used to implement hidden services are vulnerable against end-to-end traffic analysis attack. In this paper, we introduce a novel architecture for implementing hidden services which is robust against end-to-end traffic analysis attack. Moreover, our scheme is more robust against various traffic analysis attacks than previous low-latency anonymous communication architectures.

1   Introduction

The capability that servers can hide their location (IP address) while offering various kinds of services (e.g., web pages) to their clients is called hidden services or location-hiding. Hidden services were introduced to resist distributed DoS attacks since these attacks depend on the knowledge of their victim's IP addresses[7]. A server that is accessible but hidden can resist a variety of threats (both physical and logical) simply because it cannot be found. Location-hiding has also been recommended for preserving the anonymity of the services which need to resist censorship such as for dissidents or journalists publishing information accessible from anywhere [13].

Most activities in anonymous communications offer sender and relationship anonymity (see Section 2). However, recent years have provided little literature on hidden services such as Tor [5]. In fact, although almost low-latency anonymous communication systems such as MorphMix [12], Tarzan [6] and Freedom [3] can be used to enable hidden services through the rendezvous point protocol, only Tor [5] has deployed hidden services. In Tor, the security of the hidden server is only as strong as the position of the last node (exit node) is compromised in the circuit. In fact, if an adversary could monitor traffic of the exit node, then it can find the location of the hidden service immediately. This is not only the problem of Tor, but the problem of all other anonymous communication systems [1,6,12] that are based on linear onion circuits.

A linear (serial) onion circuit is a circuit that starts from an entry node (entry onion router), continues through some cascade middle onion routers and closures in an exit node (exit onion router). The entry and exit nodes are called endpoints in these circuits (figure1). The clients' traffic enters the circuit at the

P. Laud (Ed.): NordSec 2011, LNCS 7161, pp. 13–30, 2012.

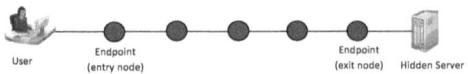

Fig. 1. A linear onion circuit

entry node, routes through middle onion routers and finally reaches the exit node. The exit node delivers traffic to the destination (e.g., the hidden server). Tor [5], MorphMix [12], Tarzan [6] and Freedom [3] are examples of linear onion circuits.

Previous works [9,10] show that, upon compromising (e.g., hacking or eavesdropping) the entry and exit points of a linear circuit, it is possible to compromise the anonymity of a connection via traffic analysis. This is well-known as an end-to-end traffic analysis attack; thereby linear onion circuits are vulnerable against end-to-end traffic analysis attack. Now the question is: can we design an architecture to implement the hidden services that resist end-to-end traffic analysis attack?

In this paper, we introduce a novel architecture to enable hidden services that withstands end-to-end traffic analysis attack. The Ferris wheel architecture is a ring-based onion circuit that lackes any exit node; thereby spontaneously is robust against end-to-end traffic analysis attacks. The hidden server constructs a ring of onion routers, including itself; i.e., the hidden server also acts as an onion router and it is a part of the ring. Our architecture looks like a Ferris wheel, because suppose there is a Ferris wheel that all people (regardless of their sex) sat on the Ferris wheel's seats have the same clothes, same color and same appearance (node homogeneity). One of these people is the target (e.g., HS). The Ferris wheel is rotating and adversaries want to find the target person, but whom of them?

The rest of the paper is structured as follows: section 2 reviews the related work. Section 3 describes the attack model. Section 4 presents the design of the Ferris wheel architecture. Section 5 discusses directory services. Section 6 discusses security analysis of Ferris wheel. Section 7 shows robustness of our architecture against traffic analysis attack and finally Section 8 concludes the paper.

2   Related Work

Anonymous communication networks first time were introduced by David Chaum in 1981 [4]. He described a network that distributes trust across multiple nodes (aka mixes) that carry the communication. The design is of a public key based, high-latency anonymous communication network such as might be appropriate for emails, but it cannot be used for bidirectional, low-latency communications such as web-browsing, chat or remote login. The first published, as well as the first deployed, distributed and circuit-based system for low-latency anonymous communications was onion routing [11] and then followed by MorphMix [12], Tarzan [6] and Tor [5]. All of these architectures work by passing traffic through multiple onion routers that have composed a linear circuit. At each onion router (OR) the traffic changes its appearance by adding or removing a layer of encryption to/from the traffic, depending on whether it is traveling from the circuit initiator to responder or vice versa.

All of the above architectures are fundamentally based on linear onion circuits but differ in some details such as implementation procedure, types of onion routers (overlay node vs. trusted mixes), type of keys (public keys vs. symmetric keys) for nested cryptography, utilizing the dummy traffic, etc. Although all the above architectures can be used to implement hidden services via rendezvous protocol, only Tor [5] supports hidden services. In Tor, any user to connect the hidden server must select its rendezvous point and informs the contact information of this node to the hidden server through the introduction points (introduction points are the nodes that listen to users' connections on the behalf of hidden server). Next, the hidden server constructs a linear onion circuit toward the rendezvous point; thereby the user can communicate with the hidden server while does not know the location of the server.

The common security problem in all the above architecture is that all of them are vulnerable against end-to-end traffic analysis attack. If an attacker could monitor traffic of the exit node of the circuit,he can immediately disclose the location of the hidden server.

3 Attack Model

Like all practical low-latency anonymous architectures such as Tor [5], MorphMix [12] and Tarzan [6] we assume adversaries can only monitor some fraction of network traffic and have control over some fraction of overlay nodes. By control we mean adversaries can operate malicious onion routers of their own. So, like all practical low-latency anonymous communication architectures, our architecture does not protect against global adversaries who can monitor all network traffic.

4 The Architecture of Ferris Wheel

Ferris wheel is composed of a set of overlay nodes. Any overlay node is identified by its IP address. In addition, each overlay node has a key-pair consists of a private key PrK and a public key PuK. This key-pair is generated locally when a node runs for the first time. Each overlay node acts as an onion router (OR) and relays data. Each OR maintains two symmetric keys: a link encryption key and an onion key. The link encryption key is set up locally between any two adjacent ORs. This key is used to encrypt/decrypt the header of packets. A unique onion key takes place between the hidden server and each OR along the circuit; i.e., the hidden server shares a unique onion key with each OR of the circuit. The onion key is used for nested encryption and decryption of the payload of packets.

The hidden server (HS) is an overlay node that wants to give hidden services to clients while its location remains secret. To achieve this goal, the hidden server constructs a ring of onion routers including itself, i.e., HS also acts as an onion router. All ORs including HS, locate logically on a ring. Each OR on the ring has a parent and a child. The parent and child of an OR are determined by HS when circuit is initiating. The parent of each OR is its adjacent node on the ring in the anticlockwise direction; while the child of each OR is its adjacent node on the ring in the clockwise direction. Figure 2.a shows the parent and child of node A. Each OR knows only the contact information of its parent and child. Traffic circulates in the ring in both directions: clockwise and anticlockwise.

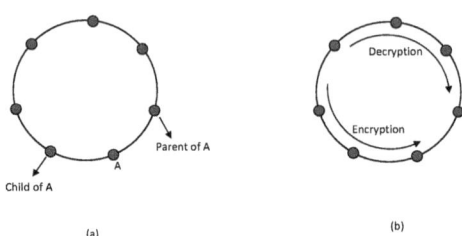

Fig. 2. a) The parent and child of node A, b) Encryption and decryption directions

Rule 1: when a packet circulates (rotates) in the clockwise direction, any OR of the ring when receives the packet, decrypts the packet with its onion key and then forwards the packet to the next OR of the ring in the clockwise direction, i.e., its child.

Rule 2: when a packet circulates in the anticlockwise direction, any OR of the ring when receives the packet, encrypts the packet with its onion key and then forwards the packet to the next OR of the ring in the anticlockwise direction, i.e., its parent.

Figure 2.b shows direction of encryption and decryption. In this paper, the traffic that rotates in the clockwise direction is called clockwise traffic and the traffic that rotates in the anticlockwise direction is called anticlockwise traffic. The ring has an entry node which traffic of clients is entered the ring via this node.

Rule 3: the entry node of the ring periodically generates a constant number of Query packets and Response packets and rotates them in the ring in the anticlockwise and clockwise direction, respectively.

The frequency rate of packet generation and exact number of them is determined by HS. Note that Query packets (with capital Q) differ from clients' query packets. They are dummy packets that are generated to cover clients' query packets. Similarly, Response packets (with capital R) differ from HS's response packets to clients. The former is dummy traffic to cover the later. Clients' query packets enter the ring though the entry node of the ring. The entry node replaces sufficient number of Query packets by clients' query packets and rotates them in the ring in the anticlockwise direction. All peers of the ring see traffic, but only HS can understand the traffic; other peers cannot distinguish Query packets from clients' query packets. When HS whishes to respond to a client, it replaces the sufficient number of arrived Response packets by its response packets to the client. The packets rotate in the ring in the clockwise direction and reach the entry node; then the entry node delivers the response packets to the client.

HS controls flows of the Query and Response packets in the ring through the fingerprint test and inappreciably observers the behavior of the ring. To achieve this goal, at each round, both HS and the entry node of the ring generate fingerprints for the packets; then in the next round, HS compares fingerprints that have been generated by itself with the fingerprints that have been generated by the entry node of the ring. In case of inconsistency, HS notices malicious behavior in the ring. Below, we explain the architecture of Ferris wheel step by step.

4.1   Setting Up the Link Encryption Key

As pointed above, the link encryption key is a symmetric key and is used to encrypt/decrypt the header of packets. Each OR, upon knowing its child creates a link encryption key with it. The procedure of creating the link encryption key is as follows: when node x wants to set up the link encryption key with its neighbor y, it first establishes a TCP connection with y. Then x generates a packet that containing the first half of the Diffie-Hellman handshake (g^x) and a nonce. Node x encrypts the packet with y's public key (node x can acquire the public key of node y by referring to the directory servers) and sends it to y. When node y receives the packet, generates the second half of Diffie-Hellman handshake (g^y) and encrypts the nonce with the created link encryption key (g^{xy}). Then node y encapsulates both of them in a packet, encrypts the packet with x's public key and sends it to node x. Hence a symmetric link encryption key (g^{xy}) has been established locally between two adjacent nodes: x and y.

4.2   The Format of Packets

All packets have the same size. Each packet is 1024 bytes and consists of a header and a payload. There are two types of packets: Query packets and Response packets. The format of both types is the same. Clients' query packets and response packets to clients also have the same format as Query (Response) packets. Figure 3 shows the format of packets. Packets are composed of two parts: header and payload. The header part includes CircID (2 bytes) and Len (2 bytes). CircID indicates circuit identifier that specifies which circuit the packet refers to, because a node may participate in several rings. Circuit identifiers are connection-specific, i.e., a ring circuit has different CircID names in each OR-to-OR connection. In other words, each portion of the ring (the portion of the ring between a parent node and its child) has a different CircID name and this name is determined by the parent node when the ring is created for the first time. Len indicates length of the payload. The header part of control packets is encrypted/decrypted according to the link encryption key between the parent node and child node.

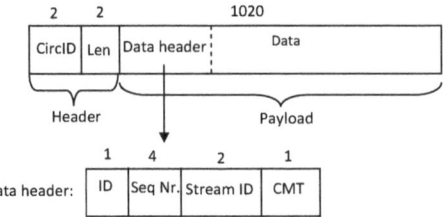

Fig. 3. The format of packets

There is an additional header (the data header) at the beginning of the payload's body. It contains ID, sequence number, StreamID and CMT. ID (2 bytes) is a unique number that indicates node identification. Sequence number (4 bytes) is a unique random number and is used to counter replay attacks. StreamID (2 bytes) indicates the stream identification because many streams can be multiplexed over a ring. CMT (1 byte) indicates comment and shows what the packet is about. The comment "Dummy" means the packet is a dummy packet. The comment "Fingerprint" means that the packet includes the fingerprints of the packets of the previous round. Data (1012 bytes) is the data part and determines the content of the packets. The payload part (data header + data) is encrypted/decrypted by the onion keys.

4.3   Constructing a Ring Onion Circuit

To construct the first ring onion circuit, the hidden server uses a guardian node; thereby, let us first look briefly at the guardian nodes.

Guardian Nodes. A guardian node is a honest and healthy node that is not under the control of attackers and its traffic is not monitored by attackers. The using of guardian nodes in our architecture is not in contradiction with our attack model, because we assume that attackers can monitor and control only a fraction of the network. We only need one guardian node to construct only the first ring. Other rings are constructed without using guardian nodes (see 4.8). Previous works [9,14] also use guardian nodes. A big difference between using guardian nodes in our architecture and those works is that we use only one guardian node for a short time merely to construct the first ring. Whereas in other works [9,14] guardian nodes participate in the circuit and permanently are used.

Construction Procedure. HS constructs a ring onion circuit incrementally, one hop at a time. HS always tells the last negotiated node in the circuit to extend one hop farther. For simplicity, let's construct a small ring with 4 ORs and let's HS uses one guardian node. Figure 4 shows the ring that we want to construct. We construct the ring step by step.

HS randomly selects the first OR (OR1) and constructs a packet. The packet includes the address of OR1, a random bit-string that serves as a symmetric

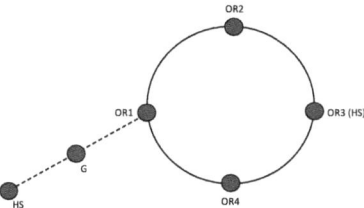

Fig. 4. Constructing a ring onion circuit with 4 ORs

onion key (K_{o1}), a nonce (nonce1), the timer value of t_l and a tag equaled to "$head_{r1}$". K_{o1}, nonce1, t_l and the tag are encrypted with the public key of OR1. The timer value of t_l represents the lifetime of a circuit (see 4.9). HS encrypts the whole packet with the public key of the guardian node G and then sends it to node G. In the following relations, $E_K(.)$ is encryption with key K and | is concatenation.

$$HS \rightarrow G: \ E_{PuK_G}(ID_{OR1}|E_{PuK_{OR1}}(K_{o1}|nonce1|t_l|tag = head_{r1})) \qquad (1)$$

Node G decrypts the packet with its private key, discovers the address of OR1 and then sends the remainder of the packet to OR1 (relation 2).

$$G \rightarrow OR1: \ E_{PuK_{OR1}}(K_{o1}|nonce1|t_l|tag = head_{r1}) \qquad (2)$$

If OR1 does not accept to participate in the circuit, then HS tries another node. In the remaining, suppose all nodes accept to participate in the circuit. OR1 accepts the onion key K_{o1} and then encrypts nonce1 with K_{o1} and sends it to node G. Node G encrypts the packet with its private key and returns the packet to HS. HS decrypts the packet with the public key of G and K_{o1}, respectively, and discovers nonce1; thereby notices that OR1 has accepted to participate in the circuit. Now the symmetric onion key K_{o1} has been shared between HS and OR1. Meanwhile, the "$head_{r1}$" tag indicates to OR1 that it is the head (entry point) of a ring which the ID of the ring is r_1.

To extend the circuit to the next OR, HS randomly selects the next OR (OR2), generates a random bit-string that serves as the symmetric onion key K_{o2}, constructs a packet, specifying the address of OR2, K_{o2}, nonce2 and t_l. K_{o2}, nonce2 and t_l are encrypted with the public key of OR2. HS encrypts the packet with the public key of G and K_{o1}, respectively, and sends it to node G. Node G decrypts the packet and sends it to OR1. OR1 decrypts the packet with its onion key and discovers the address of OR2, then establishes a local link encryption key with OR2, chooses a CircID (e.g., C_1) for the packet that it is not currently used on the connection between it and OR2 and sends the remainder of the packet to OR2 (relation 3).

$$OR1 \rightarrow OR2: \ E_{PuK_{OR2}}(K_{o2}|nonce2|t_l) \qquad (3)$$

OR2 accepts the onion key K_{o2}, encrypts nonce2 with K_{o2} and sends it back to OR1. OR1 encrypts the packet with K_{o1} and sends it to node G and finally node

G encrypts the packet with its private key and returns it to HS. HS decrypts the packet with the public key of G, K_{o1} and K_{o2}, respectively and discovers nonce2. Now the circuit has been extended to OR2 and the symmetric onion key K_{o2} has been shared between HS and OR2. Meanwhile, OR1 knows OR2 as its child and correspondingly OR2 knows OR1 as its parent.

HS acts as OR3 and extends the circuit to OR3 (itself). To achive this goal, HS generates a random bit-string K_{o3}, constructs the following packet (relation 4) and sends it node G.

$$E_{PuK_G}(E_{K_{o1}}(E_{K_{o2}}(ID_{OR3}|E_{PuK_{OR3}}(K_{o3}|nonce3|t_l)))) \tag{4}$$

Node G, OR1 and OR2 decrypt the packet, respectively. OR2 discovers the address of next OR (OR3), establishes a link encryption key with OR3, sets up CircID between itself and OR3 to a new CircID (e.g., C_2) and sends the remainder of the packet to OR3. Meanwhile OR2 knows OR3 as its child. OR3 (HS) encrypts nonce3 with K_{o3} and sends it back to OR2. OR2, OR1 and G encrypt the packet respectively and finally node G delivers the packet to HS. Now the circuit has been extended to OR3.

To extend the circuit to a fourth, fifth or beyond, HS proceeds as above, always telling the last negotiated node in the circuit to extend one hop further. In our example, OR4 is the final node; suppose the circuit is extended to OR4 as explained above and the symmetric onion key K_{o4} is shared between HS and OR4. To finish the constructing the ring, HS must fasten the circuit, i.e., it should extend the circuit to OR1; thereby the ring is created. To achieve this goal, HS creates a packet as follows (relation 5) and sends it through the chain $G \to OR1 \to OR2 \to OR3 \to OR4$ to OR4.

$$E_{PuK_G}(E_{K_{o1}}(E_{K_{o2}}(E_{K_{o3}}(E_{K_{o4}}(ID_{OR1}|E_{PuK_{OR1}}($$
$$tag = tail_{r1}|nonce5|ID_1|seq1|seq2|N_Q|N_R|T_Q|T_R)))))) \tag{5}$$

Each node of the circuit removes a layer of encryption and finally OR4 discovers the address of the next OR (OR1), sets up a link encryption key between itself and OR1, chooses a new CircID (e.g., C_4) between itself and OR1 and sends the remainder of the packet to OR1. Meanwhile, OR4 knows OR1 as its child. OR1 decrypts the packet, discovers from "$tag = tail_{r1}$" that it is the tail of the same ring that already had been selected for its head. Hence, the construction of the ring is complete and OR1 is the entry node of the ring. OR1 encrypts nonce5 with its onion key K_{o1} and sends it back to OR4. The chain $OR4 \to OR3 \to OR2 \to OR1 \to G \to HS$ returns the packet to HS as explained above. ID_1 is a unique and secret ID for the entry node of the ring that is determined by HS. Seq_1 and seq_2 are used for initializing the counters that are used for generating sequence numbers for Query and Response packets (see below). N_Q and N_R indicate the number of Query and Response packets, respectively, that the entry node should generate periodically with the period of T_Q and T_R, respectively.

4.4   Operational Phase of the Ring

The entry node of the ring should periodically generate N_Q Query packets and N_R Response packets and then circulates them in the anticlockwise and clockwise directions, respectively. To generate a Query and a Response packet, OR1 fills out the fields of the packet as follows. CircID is filled out with the common CircID between itself and its parent or its child appropriately based on whether the packet is Query or Response. The ID field is filled out with ID_1. The sequence number is filled out with a unique random number (OR1 initializes two counters with seq_1 and seq_2, the former is used for generating Query packets and the latter is used for generating Response packets. When OR1 creates a Query or a Response packet, increases the corresponding counter by one; then the output of the counter is used to fill out the sequence number field). StreamID is filled out with a random number because StreamID is only meaningful for clients' query packets or HS's response packets to clients. CMT is filled out with "Dummy". The data field is filled out with a random value and finally Len is filled out accordingly.

Circulation of Query Packets. When OR1 generates Query packets, it should circulate them in the ring in the anticlockwise direction. Hence, OR1 first encrypts the Query packets with K_{o1} and then forwards them to its parent (OR4 in figure5). Any OR in turn when receives packets from its child encrypts the packets with its onion key and then forwards them to its parent. When the packets reach to HS, HS first records a copy of each packet for inspection and fingerprinting phases (see below), encrypts the packets with its onion key and then forwards the packets to its parent. The Query packets rotate in the ring in the anticlockwise direction until reach again to the entry node of the ring (i.e., OR1). Figure 5.a shows a Query packet (M_Q) when rotates in the ring.

Inspection phase by HS: HS removes all encryption layers from the Query packets with onion keys of the ORs that have been located between it and the entry node of the ring in the correct order (remember that HS has all onion keys); for instance, in figure 5, when a Query packet (e.g., M_Q) reaches HS, it has the following state: $E_{K_{o4}}(E_{K_{o1}}(M_Q))$. HS obtains the plaintext of M_Q as follows: $M_Q = D_{K_{o1}}(D_{K_{o4}}(E_{K_{o4}}(E_{K_{o1}}(M_Q))))$

HS checks ID of each packet to be sure that the packet has been generated by the entry node. HS also checks sequence number of the packets to be sure that (1) they are not duplicate and (2) have correct sequence number. If packets are duplicate packets or have bogus sequence numbers or bogus ID, HS notices that the ring has malicious behavior.

Fingerprinting phase by HS: For generating the fingerprint (a digest) for a Query packet, HS encrypts the packet repeatedly with all onion keys of ORs located respectively in the anticlockwise direction started from the onion key of the entry node of the ring (OR1) and finished with the onion key of the child of OR1 (i.e., OR2 in figure 4). For instance in figure 5.a, the Query packet of M_Q is encrypted as follows: $E_{K_{o2}}(E_{K_{o3}}(E_{K_{o4}}(E_{K_{o1}}(M_Q))))$. After encrypting each

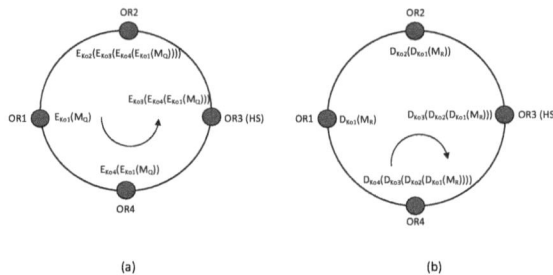

Fig. 5. a) State of a Query packet when rotates in the ring, b) State of a Response packet when rotates in the ring

Query packet as above, HS generates a 32 bits digest for the payload of the packet as the fingerprint for that packet and then records digests in the memory for future judge. It is worth noting that the digest only is generated for the payload part of the packet and the header part is not included. Any hashing function such as SHA-1 or MD5 can be used for generating the digests.

When Query packets again reach the entry point of the ring: When Query packets circulate full round of the ring and again reach the entry node, the entry node generates the fingerprint (digest) for each packet. We note that when a Query packet circulates full round in the ring and reaches again to the entry node, it has been encrypted repeatedly with all onion keys of the ORs located respectively in the anticlockwise direction started from the onion key of the entry node and finished with the onion key of the child of the entry node (see figure 5.a); thereby the fingerprint for a Query packet that is generated by the entry node should be equal to the fingerprint that has already been generated by HS. After generating the fingerprint for a Query packet, the entry node drops the packet from the ring. Now, the entry node concatenates all digests, encapsulates them in data field of a Query packet(s), sets the CMT field of the packet(s) to "Fingerprints" and then circulates the packet(s) within other anticlockwise packets in the next period (remeber rule 1).

Comparing fingerprints: In the next period, when the packet(s) containing fingerprints of the packets of the previous period reaches HS, HS compares the fingerprints generated by the entry node with the fingerprints that have already been generated by itself. If at least one case is not match, the HS notices malicious behavior in the ring.

Circulation of Response Packets. When the entry node generates Response packets, unlike Query packets, it decrypts Response packets with its onion key (e.g., $D_{k_{o1}}(M_R)$) and then forwards the Response packets to its child. Any OR when receiving Response packets from its parent, decrypts them with its onion key and forwards them to its child. When the packets reach to HS, HS first records a copy of each packet for inspection and fingerprinting phases, decrypts the packets with its onion key and then forwards the packets to its child. The Response packets rotate in the ring in the clockwise direction until reach again to the entry node of the ring (i.e., OR1). Figure 5.b shows a Response packet (M_R) when rotates in the ring.

Inspection phase by HS: To obtain the plaintext of Response packets, HS repeatedly encrypts the packets with the onion keys of the ORs between it and the entry node of the ring in correct order, i.e., started from the onion key of its parent and finished with the onion key of the entry node. For example in figure 5.b, when a Response packet reaches HS, it has the following state: $D_{K_{o2}}(D_{K_{o1}}(M_R))$. HS obtains the plaintext of M_R as follow: $M_R = E_{K_{o1}}(E_{K_{o2}}(D_{K_{o2}}(D_{K_{o1}}(M_R))))$. After obtaining the plaintext of Response packets, HS checks ID and sequence number of packets to be sure that they have been generated by the entry node and also they are not duplicate or bogus packets. The next phase is to generate fingerprints for the packets.

Fingerprinting phase by HS: For generating the fingerprint for a Response packet, HS decrypts the Response packet repeatedly with the onion keys of all ORs of the ring according to their position in the clockwise direction started from the onion key of the entry node (OR1) and finished again with the onion key of the entry node. For instance in figure 5.b, the Response packet of M_R is decrypted as follows: $D_{K_{o1}}(D_{K_{o4}}(D_{K_{o3}}(D_{K_{o2}}(D_{K_{o1}}(M_R)))))$. Below, you can see why a Response packet is decrypted two times (one in the first and one in the end) with the onion key of the enry node. After decrypting each Response packet as above, HS generates a 32 bits digest for each Response packet as the fingerprint and keeps the fingerprints in the memory for future judge.

When Response packets again reach the entry point of the ring: When Response packets circulate a full round in the ring and reach again the entry node, the entry node first decrypts the packets with its onion key and then generates the fingerprint for each packet. We note that when a Response packet circulates a full round in the ring, reaches again the entry node and the entry node decrypts the packet, the packet is decrypted repeatedly with the onion keys of all ORs as their positions on the ring in the clockwise direction. It means that the fingerprint generated by the entry node for a Response packet is equal to the fingerprint generated by HS for the Response packet. After generating fingerprints for all Response packets, the entry node drops all of the packets. The entry node concatenates all digests, encapsulates them in a Response packet(s), sets the CMT field of the packets to "Fingerprints" and then rotates the packet(s) within other dummy Response packets in the clockwise direction in the next period (remember rule 2).

Comparing fingerprints: When the Response packet(s) containing all fingerprints reaches HS, HS compares fingerprints generated by the entry node with the fingerprints that have been generated by itself. If the ring operates normally, there should be no inconsistency betweens the fingerprints generated by OR1 and the fingerprints generated by HS.

4.5   Communication between Clients and HS

Relaying Clients' Query Packets to HS. A client to send its packets to HS, sends the packets to a rendezvous point (RP). The RP point delivers them to the entry node of the ring. In order to forward clients' query packets to HS, the entry node replaces the sufficient number of Query packets by clients' query packets at each period time and rotates them in the anticlockwise direction. We note that the number of packets that rotate anticlockwise at each round is a fixed rate of N_Q; thereby if the number of clients' query packets is greater than $N_Q - N_f$, the entry node sends $N_Q - N_f$ of them in the current period and the remainder of them in the next period(s). Suppose that at each period N_f packets are used to send fingerprints of the packets of the previous period.

Relaying HS's Response Packets to Clients. To respond to clients, HS (1) creates the appropriate packets, (2) generates the fingerprint for each packet, (3) iteratively encrypts the packet with the onion keys of the ORs located between the entry node (including the entry node) and itself in the anticlockwise direction starting with the onion key of the entry node and finalizing with the onion key of its child. Next, HS (4) replaces the sufficient number of arrived Response packets[1] by its response packets to clients and then (5) forwards them to its child. Any OR on the route decrypts the packets with its onion key and then delivers them to the next node of the ring in the clockwise direction. When packets reach the entry node, the entry node first decrypts the packets with its onion key and then generates the fingerprint for each packet. Afterward, if some packets are for clients, the entry node delivers them appropriately to the clients through rendezvous points and drops the rest of packets. When the number of response packets to clients is greater than N_R, HS sends N_R of them in the current round and the remainder of them in the next round(s). As can be seen HS responds to clients while nobody knows which node was HS.

4.6   The Rendezvous Point Protocol

Clients must know how to access a hidden service. Hence, hidden servers must provide a mechanism that clients know how to connect to them. We use a protocol which is called the rendezvous point protocol. In this protocol, a set of rendezvous points listen to users' connections on the behalf of hidden servers. The contact information of these nodes is clear for public. There are multiple numbers of RP nodes that are shared between all hidden servers. Any time a RP node was attacked by the adversary, it is replaces by a new node. However, as there are multiple numbers of RP nodes, the probability that the adversary could bring down all nodes is negligible.

---

[1] HS only generates fingerprint for the remaining of Response packets. It does not generate fingerprint for dropped Response packets.

4.7   Constructing the Next Rings

As discussed above, HS constructs the first ring with the help of a guardian node. HS locates behind a guardian node and anonymously constructs a ring that itself participates in. If HS does not use the guardian node, then if the entry node of the ring and one of the neighbors of HS (HS's child or HS's parent) are malicious or their traffic is monitored by the adversary, the location of HS is disclosed immediately because the adversary can conclude that HS is constructing the ring. However, HS does not need the guardian node to construct other rings.

HS constructs the next rings through the current ring. As in the ring, HS can anonymously respond to its clients, it can anonymously construct other rings through the current ring. To achieve this goal, HS selects a rendezvous point, generates an appropriate packet to construct a new ring, encrypts the packet appropriately (as discussed above) and then replaces an arrived dummy Respond packet by the generated packet. When the packet arrives to the entry node of the ring, the entry node delivers the packet to the rendezvous node. The rendezvous node decrypts the packet, discovers the IP address of the next node (which is the entry node of the new ring) and forwards the packet. The new ring is constructed incrementally as explained in 4.3.2. During the construction procedure of a new ring, the response packet of the nodes of the new ring which contains the nonce (see Section 4.3.2) enters the entry node of the ring through the rendezvous point. Then, the entry node replaces a dummy Query packet by the packet. The packet circulates in the anticlockwise direction and reaches HS. We note that neither the entry node, nor rendezvous node, nor other nodes of the ring know that a new ring is being constructed.

4.8   Tear Down a Circuit

Any circuit has a short lifetime in the range of few minutes (e.g., 3 minutes). How much should be the lifetime for a circuit is an open question. A ring is destroyed automatically. As discussed earlier, during the circuit's construction, HS introduces the timer value of t_l to each node which represents the life time of the circuit (e.g., $t_l = 3$ minutes). When the ring is initialized and a node receives the first set of data packets in the ring, then the node sets a timer to t_l. Any second, the timer is decreased by one. When the timer reaches zero in a node, the node closes all streams on that circuit, deletes contact information of its neighbor nodes (its parent and child) and erases the circuit's history.

4.9   Changing Parameters of a Circuit

The values of N_Q, N_R, T_Q and T_R for a circuit are determined based on several factors such as the number of clients, the requirements of clients, the amount of bandwidth that ORs assign to a circuit, etc. Always HS can anonymously change the parameters for a circuit. To achieve this goal, HS creates a packet, inserts new values of N_Q, N_R, T_Q and T_R in the data field of the packet, encrypts the packet appropriately as discussed above, and replaces a dummy arrived Response packet by the generated packet. When the packet arrives to the entry node, the entry node discovers the new parameters and changes value or frequency rate of Query or Response packets.

4.10   Reply to Clients through Multiple Rings

An HS constructs multiple rings in parallel. HS does not have to reply to a user only through one particular ring. In fact, HS can reply to a client through different rings; i.e., anytime, it can choose a different ring and reply to the client through it.

5   Directory Servers

Directory servers are servers that keep information of overlay nodes that includes: IP addresses, public keys, network bandwidth and the aliveness status of these nodes. Any node when joins the overlay network publishes and registers its signed information (above information) in the directory servers. In this paper, the directory servers are assumed to be **trusted**.

6   Security Analysis

Below we summarize some active attacks and discuss how well our design withstands them.

Detecting malicious rings

If malicious ORs participate in a ring, they can actively (1) drop all packets or some packets, (2) replace the packets with bogus packets and (3) replace the packets with old packets (replay attacks). HS can detect all types of malicious behavior. Suppose {OR1, OR2, OR3, OR4(HS), OR5, OR6} have composed a ring and have located on the ring in the clockwise direction respectively. Assume that OR5 is the hostile OR. If OR5 drops all anticlockwise packets or some of them, then HS can detect malicious behavior in the ring because on the period time, it does not receive N_Q anticlockwise packets. If OR5 drops all clockwise packets or some of them, then in the next period, HS does not receive all fingerprints of N_R clockwise packets. If OR5 replaces anticlockwise packets with bogus packets, then HS detects malicious behavior in the ring through inspection phase, because it does not retrieve correct ID and sequence numbers of the packets. If OR5 replaces clockwise packets with bogus packets, then HS detects this by fingerprint test, because the fingerprints generated by HS do not match with the fingerprints generated by the entry node of the ring. If OR5 replaces anticlockwise packets with old anticlockwise packets (replay attacks), then HS detects this in inspection phase through sequence numbers. If OR5 replaces clockwise packets with old clockwise traffic, HS detects this in fingerprinting comparison phase, because the fingerprints generated by HS do not match with the fingerprints generated by the entry node of the ring. In the all above cases, when HS detects malicious behavior in the ring, it drops the ring and switches to a new ring.

Malicious entry node

If a malicious node is selected for the entry node of a ring, then the malicious node can block communication between HS and clients. The only node that can distinguish clients' query packets from Query packets is the entry node; thereby, the malicious entry node can regularly generate Query and Response packets, while drop clients' query packets. The malicious entry node can generate wrong fingerprints for packets and any other malicious activity. However, the malicious entry node cannot break anonymity of HS. The solutions against malicious behavior of the entry node of the ring are as above solutions. For instance, if it generates wrong fingerprints, or any other malicious activity, HS tears down the circuit. If the entry node blocks clients' query packets while regularly send Query and Response packets, then HS can notice this by testing the entry node: HS regularly through another node tests the entry node of the ring by sending query packets and making sure to receive them.

7   Traffic Analysis Attacks

One fundamental attack against anonymous systems and hidden services is based on traffic analysis [10]. In this section, we look at how well Ferris wheel withstands traffic analysis attacks.

Information leakage in the overlay network

Mix-based systems (Mix-net) that consist of few and well-known mixes hide traffic of a user among traffic of other users by mixing and reordering traffic from different users. It is clear that in these architectures a system with fewer users provides less anonymity. Unlike the mix-based systems, circuit-based systems hide relay nodes of the circuit among pool of nodes. It is clear that a quiet overlay network or an overlay network with few nodes is more vulnerable to traffic analysis attack than a busy overlay network with many nodes. In a system, if most of overlay nodes have little activity, in an adversary's view, the nodes with most activities are suspicion to be part of the circuit. To thwart this problem we assume several different hidden servers use the same overlay network to implement their circuits, the adversary cannot easily find the nodes of a particular circuit because most of overlay nodes will be busy and they belong to different circuits and moreover a node may participate in several circuits. This is similar to mix-based systems when we say more users, better anonymity.

Useful properties of the Ferris wheel architecture

Node homogeneity: All ORs of the ring are equal and have exactly the same behavior. The hidden server itself is an onion router and a part of the ring. Its position can be anywhere on the ring. HS is not distinguishable from other ORs. In fact, in an adversary's view any node can be HS.

Traffic homogeneity: Clients' query packets are not distinguishable from Query packets. The HS's response packets to clients are not distinguishable from

Response packets. In fact, the homogeneity of traffic does not allow distinguishing legitimate traffic from cover traffic (Query and Response packets).

Secure against end-to-end traffic analysis attack

In a linear circuit, the entry node of the circuit knows the sender (user) and the exit node knows the receiver (e.g., HS); thereby, if an adversary controls both entry and exit nodes of a linear circuit, he can break the anonymity of the system and discover both sender and receiver. If the adversary controls (or monitors) only the exit node of a circuit, he can discover only the receiver (e.g., HS) and if the adversary controls (or monitors) only the entry node of a circuit, he can disclose only the sender (user). All linear onion circuits such as Tor, MorphMix, Tarzan, Freedom, Web MIXes are vulnerable against this attack. Our architecture simply withstands end-to-end traffic analysis attack due to lack of any exit nodes in the architecture. Traffic originates from one node (the entry node), circultaes in the ring and again comes back to that node; thereby there is no exit node in the architecture that an adversary wants to use end-to-end traffic analysis techniques to break the anonymity of the hidden server. In fact, simply because of no exit nodes in the architecture, our architecture is spontaneously robust against this attack. Although an adversary may own the entry point of the ring, it does not help the adversary to discover the hidden server because the important node to discover the location of HS is the exit node that the ring does not have it.

Robust against packet counting

In some architectures, simple packet counting attack can effectively confirm the endpoints of a stream. However, as there is no exit node in the Ferris wheel architectureour, the packet counting attack cannot help attackers to break the anonymity of the hidden server. Moreover, in the Ferris wheel architecture, a constant number of same-sized packets per time unit are exchanged between any two nodes; thereby an adversary cannot use the packet counting attack to break the anonymity of the architecture.

Timing pattern attack

The reference [8] sets up a timing pattern attack against Tor such that an attacker pretends itself as a legitimate user and sends traffic between times t_0 and t_1 and then stops sending traffic between t_2 and t_3. Next, the attacker can repeat this timing pattern attack. Through this timing pattern attack, the attacker could notice which nodes are being used to relay a specific stream. This attack model can be applied to other anonymous communication architectures such as MorphMix [12] and Freedom [3]. Thanks to Query and Response packets that make the Ferris wheel architecture robust against this attack. In the Ferris wheel architecture a constant number of packets is exchanged between nodes; thereby if a user stops to send traffic between t_2 and t_3, the dummy Query and

Respond packets travel in the ring and always the attacker sees the same shape in the network.

Thwarting the distance attack

An adversary can compute the latency between any two ORs (sometimes it is known as latency attacks [1,10]). Then the adversary sends a query to the hidden server and waits for response. The adversary times the period that he gets response, i.e., round trip time. This round trip time enables the adversary to estimate the distance between himself and the hidden server; thereby, he can estimate how many nodes are between it and the hidden server. This attack can be easily thwarted in the Ferris wheel architecture, if HS does not respond to clients immediately after receiving their query packets, but responds to clients after a random delay. The random delay should be as enough as the clients' query packets circulate full round in the ring. As discussed earlier, HS replaces the sufficient number of dummy Response packets by its response packets to clients and as Response packets are initiated from the entry node and circulate the ring in the clockwise direction and pass through all nodes of the ring, the adversary is confused to understand which OR has respond to him. Therefore it cannot guess the distance between itself and the hidden service.

Preference of the Ferris wheel architecture in peer selection over linear circuits such as Tor

There are two methods to select onion routers of a circuit: a) routers are randomly selected regardless their quality such as high bandwidth and uptime, b) routers are selected based on their quality. The former is more secure and provides better anonymity; however the performance of the circuit might not be good. The latter provides better performance; however, the security and anonymity of the circuit is degraded. Bauer et al [2] show that selecting onion routers based on their quality noticeably impact on the anonymity of circuits such as Tor, Morphmix and Tarzan. They show that in a network with 66 nodes which 6 nodes of them is malicious, if nodes are randomly selected for a circuit the probability that two malicious nodes occupy endpoints of the circuit is 0.7%, while if nodes are selected based on their quality, this probability would be about 47%. The interesting point is that, the Ferris wheel architecture has more flexibility to choose routers of a ring from the nodes that have high quality because even if malicious ORs are selected for the ring, the anonymity of HS is not broken as the ring has no exit point. However, in linear circuits such as Tor, Morphmix, Trazan, Freedom, it is possible that a malicious OR is selected for the exit node; hence, the anonymity of HS is broken.

8   Conclusion

This paper proposes the Ferris wheel architecture, a novel architecture to enable hidden services in the overlay networks that resist against end-to-end traffic analysis attack. Ferris wheel is a ring onion circuit that the hidden server, itself, is a part of the ring. Traffic rotates at both directions: clockwise and anticlockwise. Ferris wheel has three major properties: (1) lake of exit node, (2) node homogeneity and (3) traffic homogeneity that make it robust against variety of traffic analysis attacks. The hidden server notices any malicious behavior in the ring through the fingerprint test.

References

1. Back, A., Möller, U., Stiglic, A.: Traffic Analysis Attacks and Trade-Offs in Anonymity Providing Systems. In: Moskowitz, I.S. (ed.) IH 2001. LNCS, vol. 2137, pp. 245–257. Springer, Heidelberg (2001)
2. Bauer, K., McCoy, D., Grunwald, D., Kohno, T., Sicker, D.: Low-Resource Routing Attacks against Tor. In: Proceedings of the 2007 ACM Workshop on Privacy in Electronic Society (WPES 2007), Virginia, USA (2007)
3. Boucher, P., Shostack, A., Goldberg, I.: Freedom Systems 2.0 Architecture. White paper, Zero Knowledge Systems, Inc. (December 2000)
4. Chaum, D.: Untraceable Electronic Mail, Return Addresses, and Digital Pseudonyms. Communications of the ACM 24(2), 84–88 (1981)
5. Dingledine, R., Mathewson, N., Syverson, P.: Tor: The Second-Generation Onion Router. In: Proceedings of the 13th USENIX Security Symposium (August 2004)
6. Freedman, M.J., Morris, R.: Tarzan: A Peer-to-Peer Anonymizing Network Layer. In: Proceedings of the 9th ACM Conference on Computer and Communications Security, Washington, USA (November 2002)
7. Keromytis, A., Misra, V., Rubenstein, D.: SOS: An Architecture for Mitigating DDoS Attacks. IEEE Journal on Selected Areas in Communications 22(1) (2004)
8. Murdoch, S., Danezis, G.: Low-Cost Traffic Analysis Of Tor. In: Proceedings of the 2005 IEEE Symposium on Security and Privacy, pp. 183–195 (May 2005)
9. Øverlier, L., Syverson, P.: Locating Hidden Servers. In: Proceedings of the 2006 IEEE Symposium on Security and Privacy, CA, USA, pp. 100–114 (May 2006)
10. Raymond, J.-F.: Traffic Analysis: Protocols, Attacks, Design Issues, and Open Problems. In: Federrath, H. (ed.) Designing Privacy Enhancing Technologies. LNCS, vol. 2009, pp. 10–29. Springer, Heidelberg (2001)
11. Reed, M.G., Syverson, P.F., Goldschlag, D.M.: Anonymous Connections and Onion Routing. IEEE Journal on Selected Areas in Communication Special Issue on Copyright and Privacy Protection 16(4), 482–494 (1998)
12. Rennhard, M., Plattner, B.: Introducing MorphMix: Peer-to-Peer based Anonymous Internet Usage with Collusion Detection. In: Proceedings of the Workshop on Privacy in the Electronic Society (WPES 2002), Washington, DC, USA (2002)
13. Waldman, M., Mazieres, D.: Tangler: A Censorship-Resistant Publishing System Based on Document Entangnlements. In: Proceedings of the 8th ACM Conference on Computer and Communication Security, pp. 126–135 (November 2001)
14. Wright, M., Adler, M., Levine, B.N., Shields, C.: Defending Anonymous Communication Against Passive Logging Attacks. In: Proceedings of the 2003 IEEE Symposium on Security and Privacy, California, USA, pp. 28–43 (May 2003)

User Tracking on the Web via Cross-Browser Fingerprinting

Károly Boda, Ádám Máté Földes, Gábor György Gulyás, and Sándor Imre

Department of Telecommunications, Budapest University of Technology and Economics,
Magyar tudósok krt. 2., H-1117 Budapest, Hungary
bodakaroly88@gmail.com, {foldesa,gulyasg,imre}@hit.bme.hu

Abstract. The techniques of tracking users through their web browsers have greatly evolved since the birth of the World Wide Web, posing an increasingly significant privacy risk. An important branch of these methods, called fingerprinting, is getting more and more attention, because it does not rely on client-side information storage, in contrast to cookie-like techniques. In this paper, we propose a new, browser-independent fingerprinting method. We have tested it on a data set of almost a thousand records, collected through a publicly accessible test website. We have shown that a part of the IP address, the availability of a specific font set, the time zone, and the screen resolution are enough to uniquely identify most users of the five most popular web browsers, and that user agent strings are fairly effective but fragile identifiers of a browser instance.

Keywords: web privacy, user tracking, user identification, profiling.

1 Introduction

In the very beginning of the creation of the Web, users could be effectively identified by the IP addresses of their computers [2]. Later on, as the use of dynamic IP addresses and Network Address Translation became widespread, this piece of information alone was no longer enough; instead, tracking the browsing habits of a user could be performed by storing an identifier in a cookie in the web browser, so that it would supposedly identify the user for every HTTP response containing the cookie. This technique has two significant disadvantages: the cookie can only identify a single browser application, and the cookie database can be wiped, destroying the identifier. However, these techniques still seem to be widely used, albethey somewhat aged [9], [10].

Although there are cross-browser storage techniques that avoid the aforementioned problem (e.g. Local Shared Objects or LSOs, also known as Flash cookies [6]), active tracking methods (i.e. those that rely on client-side storage) all share the shortcoming of the possibility of destroying the identifier, which fueled the research of passive methods. These techniques do not store anything on the user's computer; instead, they query certain parameters that are accessible through the web browser, e.g. time zone and screen resolution.

P. Laud (Ed.): NordSec 2011, LNCS 7161, pp. 31–46, 2012.
© Springer-Verlag Berlin Heidelberg 2012

Passive techniques include history stealing attacks [3], [4], and browser finger-printing algorithms [1]. With history stealing, the attacker website tries to extract unique history entries from the browser – usually by exploiting unpatched vulnerabilities or misusing API functions. Browser fingerprinting checks certain properties of the browser and the computer it is run on, and tries to calculate a unique identifier from the gathered information. The first major fingerprinting experiment was Panopticlick [1], which has amassed more than 1.5 million records; it identifies users based on the so-called User Agent String (UAS, i.e. a line of text that includes the most important information about the system and the browser), parameters from the HTTP request, the list of plugins, the time zone, the screen resolution, the set of installed fonts, and the availability of some cookie-like storage techniques.

Switching browsers might provide some protection against fingerprinting, but it is unlikely that somebody would install several versions of multiple browsers to avoid being tracked. However, one version each of multiple types of browsers installed on a single computer is not uncommon. (Although defeating tracking techniques is presumably not the main motive; reasons could range from platform-exclusive extensions to selectively optimised webpages.). Furthermore, browser extensions that allow spoofing certain settings (e.g. the UAS) can also be effective means of defence. It must be noted, however, that these measures are completely ineffective against cross-browser fingerprinting techniques, which rely on other parameters, for instance, on the detection of installed font types or plugins. In order to cross-browser fingerprint a user, a website operator has to choose some browser-independent features as a basis of identification. These are likely to include a set of, but are not limited to, the following browser- and system-dependent properties:

- Networking information. Since HTTP requests are sent via TCP/IP, the server always sees the IP address (and hostname), and the TCP port number. The location of the client can also be inferred from the IP address in most cases.
- Application layer information. The user agent string is a standard HTTP header, and is sent with every request. It contains the type and version of the browser; the name and version of the operating system; the type and version of the layout engine (e.g. Gecko for Firefox); and the names and versions of certain extensions. It must be noted that some browsers (e.g. Opera) are extremely verbose about their version, so even minute patches change their UASes. Finally, the HTTP request usually contains a language preference code (e.g. 'en-us'), too.
- Information gained by querying the browser. JavaScript programs have access to the list of fonts, plugins (along with their version numbers), screen resolution, and the time zone. Additionally, some vulnerabilities may allow access to browser history [3] or to other client-side databases that are otherwise inaccessible for the visited website.

In this paper, we discuss a new browser-independent fingerprinting technique as our main contribution, and provide the analysis of the collected data in regard to a related experiment. Our most important contribution is the analysis of font detection via JavaScript from the viewpoint of using the detected fonts as input for fingerprinting. Furthermore, we analyse other browser-related information sets, such as the UASes, which were eventually not incorporated into the aforementioned fingerprinting algorithm, but were collected during the same experiment; we have shown that these may also be of interest for a tracker with different goals than ours.

The paper is structured as follows. In Section 2, we briefly discuss the evolution of techniques that aim to track the browsing habits of users. Then, in Section 3, we describe our own browser fingerprinting experiment, and compare the gathered results to the Panopticlick dataset. Subsequently, in Section 4, we analyse the results which we collected by it. Finally, we discuss improvements to the algorithm in Section 5, and then conclude our work in Section 6.

2   Brief History of Web Privacy

The goal of tracking one's browsing habits is usually to amass as much information about her from as many sources as possible. Such an extensive collection of data about somebody is called profiling.

Profiling has several approaches [11]. First, 'information superpowers' provide an extensive set of services (e.g. mail, calendar, social network) that cover most needs of average users, effectively making them profile themselves; Google can be taken as an example. Second, publicly accessible sources of personal data (e.g. social networks, microblogging services) can be used to get information about somebody with minimal effort. Finally, one can use tracking techniques, which comprise cookie-based methods and fingerprinting alike.

The technique of evercookies [5] combines multiple persistent storage spaces of the browser – including traditional HTTP cookies, LSOs, and HTML5-based databases – to mark the browser with a virtually indestructible identifier. If the evercookie script detects the absence of the identifier from any of the exploited storage spaces, it can recreate any of them from the remaining ones. The method can track the user across browsers hosted on the same computer if plugins that are shared by multiple browsers are installed (e.g. Adobe Flash and Microsoft Silverlight). However, evercookies are still vulnerable to deleting local storages, and furthermore, cross-browser storages may not be supported forever.

Another, local storage-independent, but more or less defunct technique of identification is history stealing [8]. It checks for the presence of popular websites in the browsing history, and identifies the user with the set of hits. In order to do this, the tracker embeds a set of invisible hyperlinks into a website, and queries their colours from a script. By default, all popular browsers mark already visited links with a different colour from that of uncharted ones. However, current browsers (e.g. Firefox 5.0) no longer allow checking such properties of hyperlinks from JavaScript code; therefore, CSS-based history stealing does not seem to be an effective means of tracking anymore [7]. But stating that the history stealing-like attacks are completely finished is untimely: besides other methods [12], history stealing inspired the algorithm of 'whitelist stealing', which works with the combination of Firefox and the NoScript plugin, and guesses whether well-known sites have been whitelisted by the user or not [4].

To the best of our knowledge, the Panopticlick fingerprinting experiment is the first major attack in the literature [1]. This project has a publicly accessible webpage[1] where users can generate their fingerprints and get an understanding about how unique their software configuration is. More than 1.5 million users have submitted their browser fingerprints to the database so far. The identification is based on the UAS, the ACCEPT header of the HTTP request, the screen resolution and colour depth, the time zone, the presence and, if applicable, the version number of plugins and extensions; the list of fonts available on the computer; information whether JavaScript is enabled or disabled; and information whether certain persistent storage requests ('supercookies') are accepted by the browser.

Panopticlick has several merits. First, its runtime – which manifests itself only on the client side – is minimal. Secondly, it does not rely on persistent storage techniques, which means that even disabling all cookies is an ineffective defence measure. And finally, it is extremely precise, according to their results – browsers enabling Flash or Java can be identified at an accuracy rate of 94.2% [1].

The disadvantages of Panopticlick include being dependent of the browser instance. The reason for this is that the UAS and the complete font and plugin lists are taken into consideration. Moreover, either Adobe Flash or Java must be enabled to query the font list. To avoid this shortcoming, we propose a novel method, a cross-browser fingerprinting algorithm that is based solely on JavaScript, and incorporates font detection as its core technique. Our preliminary experiments showed promising results, and to prove the viability of such a technique, we started to build a fingerprint database for further analysis.

It must be mentioned that Panopticlick and our method share a common drawback, namely the inability to distinguish instances in a set of identically configured computers, as is the case when multiple users browse the web in a computer room at the same time. We argue, however, that this obstacle cannot reasonably be overcome by passive techniques; persistence is a must for identifying almost completely identical computers.

3   Harvesting Method and the Fingerprint Dataset

3.1   Collecting Fingerprints on the International PET Portal and Blog[2]

The goal of our fingerprinting technique is to create a unique identifier from specific browser data using JavaScript and server-side algorithms. Therefore, the following factors are taken into consideration: *system features* (e.g. operating system, screen resolution), *list of installed font types*, and the *first two octets of the IP address*. The chosen system features can be easily queried from the well-known global variables, but to acquire the list of installed fonts, we use custom JavaScript to test each font in a given database if it is installed on the client machine.

---

[1] http://panopticlick.eff.org/
[2] http://pet-portal.eu/fingerprint/

We wanted to achieve the following goals: browser independence, plugin independence, and cross-domain tracking. Browser independence is granted by using general attributes, and we found a set of fonts that makes the font detection algorithm work equally well in all major browsers. Since we do not check installed plugins, our technique is plugin independent (for plugin detection see Section 4.6). Finally, cross-domain tracking is achieved by using only the first two octets of the IP address, which remains constant in many cases even if the IP address of the client changes dynamically. It must be noted that this concept may not work in general, as the first two octets may change after switching to a different ISP or another service (e.g. from wired to 3G data) of the same ISP; the success depends on many factors (e.g. the size of the country where the user resides or the assignment scheme of IP addresses for that country). However, this is a relatively small source of entropy for our generated user ID, and may be left out in future experiments. We do not further discuss this possibility in this paper; we leave it as future work.

Table 1 shows a list of attributes in the database structure. The meaning of most variables is clear, but there are a few to explain. The first one is 'basic fonts'; it is a specialized font list which contains thirty selected fonts that can be recognized in all major browsers (this is included in the fingerprint). The user ID is the script-generated identifier, derived from the first two octets of the IP address, the screen resolution, the time zone, and the 'basic fonts' variables; we stored its hash under the name 'short user ID'. We also store the full font list for researching a better feature set.

Table 1. Database structure: field names and their content

locality	Hungarian or international
short user ID	user ID in a shorter, hashed format
created	time of fingerprint creation
ip	visitor IP address in a hashed format
UAS	the user agent string of the browser
os	operating system
screen	screen resolution
timezone	time zone
basic fonts	standard font list for user ID generation
all fonts	all detected installed font list stored for analysis

Later during the research, we extended this structure with some extra variables in order to be able to make more complex queries, and get more detailed results. We added 'universal font list', which is derived from 'all fonts', but it contains only those fonts that are recognised equally well by all browser versions and types (and therefore could be included in a future feature set). Finally, we also added an extra browser version field called 'browser version', derived from the 'user agent string'. It has two parts; one is the browser name (Firefox, IE, etc.), the other is the major version number (3.6, 3.9, etc.). This field helps to make simpler and more precise browser-specific queries.

3.2   Database Statistics

The dataset under examination was collected for six months from September, 2010. For each user who clicked the 'Start the test: I want my fingerprint!' button, we recorded all data above, and displayed the fingerprint generated by the server-side script.

During the six months' data collecting process we had 989 test runs from 615 different IP addresses, which generated 662 different user IDs. These numbers suggest that most of the identifiers have been created by different computers. However, there are some IP addresses which belong to more than one ID, which can occur in two situations: either the same tester tried various settings or browsers, or there were multiple testers who connected with the same IP address (we conjecture that the former is a more likely occurrence).

The database allowed us to make some interesting observations. There are 450 different UASes, which means that nearly half of the browsers in our database are unique just by the UAS. The number of different font lists (i.e. all fonts) is 588, which suggests that it is a quite unique identifier for browser instances. There were 649 visitors with Hungarian national, and 340 visitors with international language settings. This information is not enough to infer anything significant, but it should reflect the proportions of the nationalities of our testers.

Before the analysis, we assumed that the font lists are in conjunction with the operating system; to prove this, we ran a specialized query. The result is that for Windows and Mac, the number of different font lists are close to the number of different user identifiers (slightly in excess of it in the case of Windows), and for Unix-like systems, the number of different font lists is much smaller than the number of different user identifiers. This suggests that, in the case of Unix-like systems, the font list is not a relevant factor, in contrast to other OSes.

The testers used 68 different screen resolutions; the most popular was 1280x800 with 18%, followed by 1280x1024 with 16% of the testers. The majority of the testers used a widescreen resolution, especially specific to notebook screens. The count of the most popular combination of (basic fonts, screen resolution, time zone) is 26 from 9 different IP addresses, which is a quite small set to maintain anonymity.

The script ran in 26 different major browser versions the preferred one being Mozilla Firefox 3.6 with 44% of the tests. The tests showed that the system- and browser-related features can greatly vary; we depicted these on Fig. 1. (We would like to mention that the graph is very similar in shape to that of the Panopticlick project [1].) After analysing the dataset, we can state that 72% of the users tested the fingerprinting algorithm only once, and, within the group that tried multiple times, 28% certainly tried multiple types or versions of browsers.

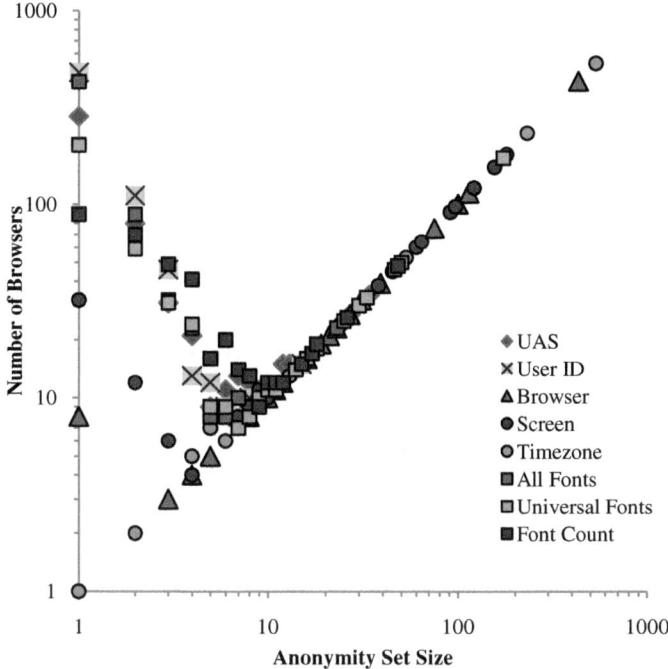

Fig. 1. The number of identical values for different attributes

3.3 Comparison with the Panopticlick Dataset

Since the number of entries in our fingerprint database is relatively limited, we verified the quality of the data by comparing the entropy of the attributes of the entries to their counterparts in the Panopticlick dataset [1]; the current values of the entropy of the latter are publicly available on their website. The comparison is summarised in Table 2. The fields marked with an asterisk were added during the analysis of our dataset (when comparing the results, it must be taken into consideration that the Panopticlick database had more records than ours[3]).

Table 2. Comparison of the entropy of values in our database and that of Panopticlick

	Our	Panopticlick
User agent string	8.095	10.0
Timezone	2.22	3.04
User ID	9.03	-
All fonts	8.57	13.9
Universal fonts*	6.83	-
Detected fonts*	7.63	-
Plugins	-	15.4

---

[3] We compared the datasets in April-May, 2011.

We would like to highlight two variables having high entropy: these are the user IDs in our experiment, and plugins in that of Panopticlick. Based on the comparison of the two values, we conjecture that the entropy of the user ID could be even higher (around 12-14 bits) for a bigger data set. The current fingerprint in our experiment does not incorporate the 'plugins' variable due to the fact that we did not attempt plugin detection; in the future, it might prove to be advantageous to include it, too. Furthermore, according to the entropy of the fonts in the Panopticlick database, a more precise user ID generation could be done with a greater dataset (and with more font types included).

4   Lessons Learned: Analysis of the Dataset

4.1   Capabilities of the New Fingerprinting Method

An interesting finding in our research was the correlation of font lists and UASes: the results show that the font lists provide a solid base for unique identification under the Windows and Mac OSes (see the graph on the left-hand side of Fig. 2). We have made another important discovery on the correlation of UASes and the generated user IDs, even though the latter did not incorporate the UAS (only the OS type). This means – if we assume that UASes are more or less unique per user – that the generated user IDs can also be assumed to be a precise identification method for all OSes (see graph on the right-hand side of Fig. 2 and Section 3.2).

Therefore, similarly to the algorithm of Panopticlick, it seems that our method can efficiently track changes in the dynamic IP address (e.g. when a user reconnects or roams between networks), and distinguish between different PCs behind a NAT (e.g. computers in an office). However, in contrast to the method of Panopticlick, our fingerprint is resistant to updates to the computer and the browser; switching browsers, (un)installing plugins, and, due to the exclusion of the UASes, emptying local storage spaces are ineffective against an attacker using it, as is explained in Section 3.2.

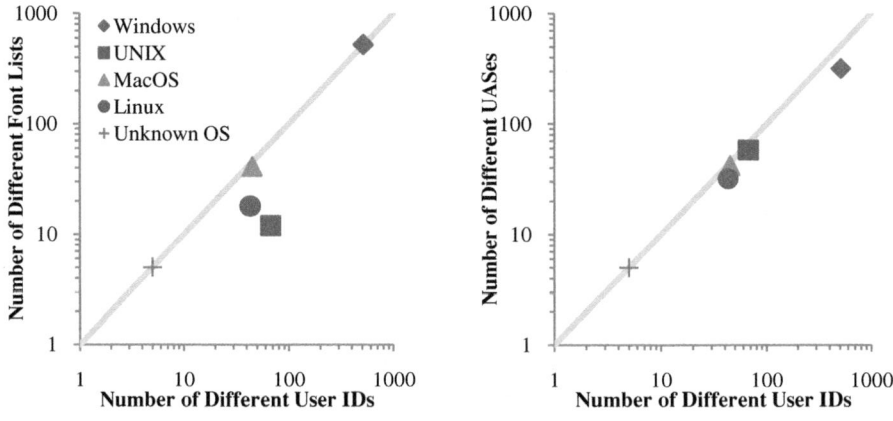

Fig. 2. Correlation between the number of font lists, UASes, and generated user IDs for different OSes

However, there are several important lessons learned from the analysis. We have discovered system- and browser-specific weaknesses: we have identified a number of operating system-specific weak spots, e.g. the verbosity of the .NET framework version number and the massive quantity of different fonts under Windows, and the detailed version number of the OS under Linux (see Table 3 for examples). Some browser-specific weak spots also facilitate fingerprinting, the verbose browser build codes and toolbar version numbers being the most characteristic examples.

Through the analysis of the UAS, we have got to know the properties of its components, and concluded that it was a unique identifier for many users (see Section 4.3). We have determined, for each browser version, the degree of uniqueness of the UAS, i.e. the percentage of unique UASes for further analysis. Besides, the font list is also quite unique; the introduction of a universal font list (i.e. a list of fonts that a browser is limited to choose from for rendering) could make fingerprinting harder (see Section 4.4).

Our results have allowed us to define a new combination for better identification. We have got to know that the various identifiers, e.g. user ID, UAS, IP address, and font list, can be used to track changes in the fingerprint, largely due to the correlation between them being almost zero for the most popular OSes. For instance, if one of these changes while the other three remain constant, then the signatures pertaining to a user can be grouped together even if they are in an office behind a NAT router (see Section 4.6 for some proposals). However, we have not yet written a proof-of-concept program for this idea, and leave it as future work.

4.2   Special Cases

Fingerprinting allows the correction of failures in identification in some cases. By visual inspection, we have successfully identified some of the returning visitors, who:

- used more than one browser,
- tried multiple combinations of screen resolution and time zone,
- or changed their IP addresses dynamically.

Besides comparing different attributes in the records, the stored UASes helped also in matching these records, being sources of additional entropy. Based on these observations, we can track the changes in attributes, naturally within certain limits; these correction techniques can be automatised, but this is out of the scope of this paper. (We would like to mention that the Panopticlick project defined a very simple correction technique that would allow precise monitoring of changes in fingerprints [1].)

However, there were certain errors, i.e. where the algorithm produced failures, indicating weaknesses to be improved in future research. Here we give three examples of these. The first one was a user getting multiple IDs after trying multiple browsers. There were 28 such cases, all of which can be accounted to erroneous font detection, i.e. not all fonts being browser independent. The use of the universal font list decreased this number to 6, which is the same result as in the second type of error; therefore, this can be corrected by using fonts for fingerprinting from the universal font set.

In the case of the second type of error, despite most factors being identical in the analyzed records, different fonts (and OSes) were detected, resulting in different IDs. This was the issue for 6 records, from which 4 had identical UASes, 5 of them had Linux, and 1 had Windows 98 (allegedly). However, this does not necessarily mean an error, e.g. the user might have installed some fonts between the two fingerprinting attempts, and/or used a tool for spoofing the UAS.

For the third type of error, everything was identical within the records (including the UAS and the user ID), but the algorithm detected different basic fonts (used in the fingerprinting feature set). Despite our efforts, we could not reproduce this phenomenon.

4.3   Anonymity Sets

The sets of different identifiers can be distributed into many small anonymity subsets. In the following, we examine the anonymity sets of the current font lists and UASes, and the means of influencing them under the current circumstances. Unfortunately, we have a large number of small subsets in each identifier. On the graphs, we denoted with AF (Arbitrary Fonts) if clients were allowed to use arbitrary fonts, and with UF (Unified Fonts) if they were allowed to only use a limited set of fonts (however, the viability of using a unified font set on the web may be questionable).

Figure 3 demonstrates how much the anonymity set of the ideal UAS alone (i.e. with JavaScript off) grows in contrast to the current UAS. It is pleasantly surprising to see that, when using the ideal UAS with JavaScript on but no font detection, the anonymity sets are bigger than with the current UAS and JavaScript off.

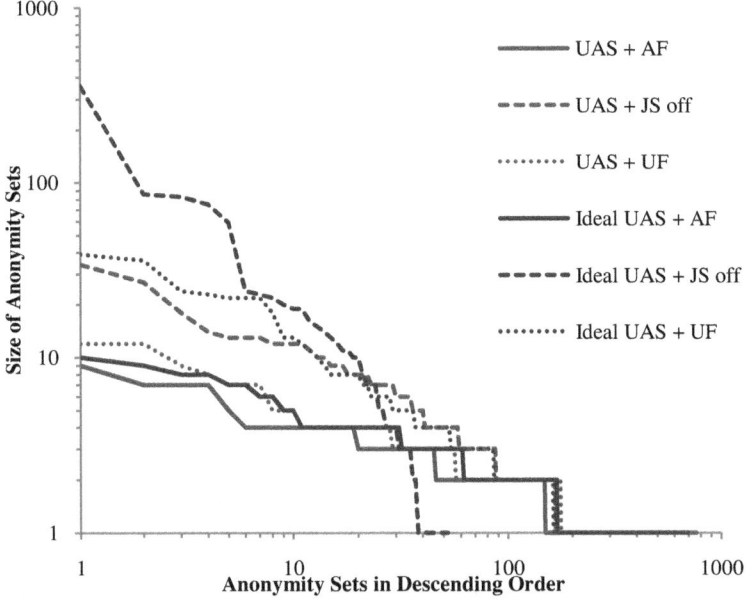

Fig. 3. Anonymity set sizes in decreasing order for different UASes with different parameters, and for different font sets (no fonts detected if JavaScript is turned off)

In the case of Linux users, the ideal UAS has a bigger impact on the anonymity sets, since the UAS does not incorporate the entire operating system version string (see the UAS analysis for more details), which results in greater anonymity sets. With JavaScript on, the situation is much worse: the curve is almost flat, i.e. all from the first 10 anonymity sets contain only a single user.

In reality, the UAS is much too detailed, and the variety of font combinations is abundant. Figure 3 also describes the anonymity sets of the current UAS with AF, UF, and JavaScript off. It can be seen that the introduction of a universal font set would improve the results, but, for now, JavaScript off results in the largest anonymity sets.

Under ideal circumstances (i.e. an uncommunicative UAS and either a universal font set, or a completely disabled font detection), the results are better than with the current UAS and JavaScript off.

4.4 Font Lists

It is important to mention that in our test we also included some special font types especially used by graphic designers, not only the widespread ones. There were a few tests with these special font types, too, which may have affected the results.

We have plotted the frequency of the different font types used by the testers in descending order, and it gives a cascade curve (see Fig. 4). The source of the font types (i.e. the application whose installation package includes them) suggests that each interval between adjacent dips in the graph characterises a software package.

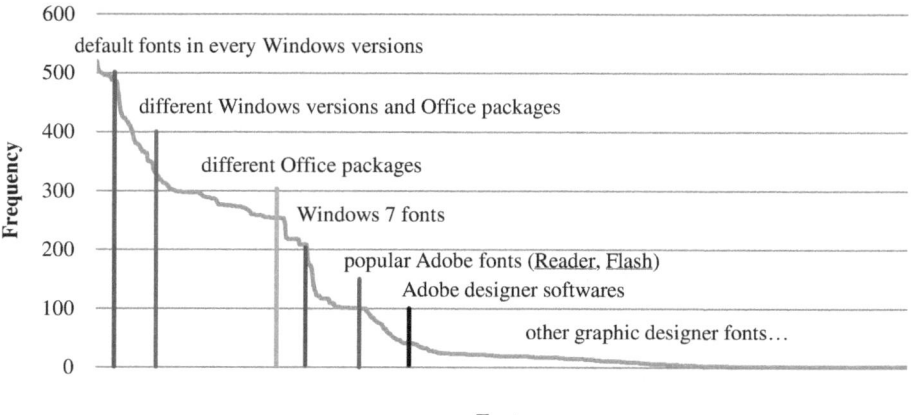

Fig. 4. Number of different font lists in descending order of the latter. (Under Windows OS)

There were multiple cases where, if the types of browsers for one tester differed, so did the font lists. This is caused by the different browser implementations. Firefox performs font replacement: if a font type is missing, it replaces it with another one from the same family (for example, if Helvetica is missing, it uses Arial as a substitute); Opera, however, does not do this, and, what is more, it does not even recognise all fonts.

This means that font type detection is not a browser-independent technique with the inclusion of all the fonts, so we had to create a font list in which all the fonts can be recognised by the five main browsers – a font list that is a partial feature set for the fingerprinting. This is what we call 'universal font list', which is created by listing the top recognized fonts by all browsers in descending order.

Eckersley suggests that browsers should only confirm the existence of fonts and plugins rather than enumerating all in a list, and queries should be answered with an exponential backoff in order to prevent exhaustive searches by malicious JavaScript code [1]. However, this would not work against the discussed font detection algorithm, since it checks the offsetWidth and offsetHeight DOM variables instead of the mere existence of a font in the system; as such, the only effective defence would be to remove these attributes from the JavaScript API.

4.5   Analysis of the User Agent String

While collecting our dataset, we recorded some browser-related values that eventually did not become parts of the cross-browser user identifier. The UAS is a highly interesting example of these, since its structure is complex (see Fig. 5 for an example), and this diversity leads to a very large number of possible combinations. It can be seen that verbosity can be increased by certain plugins, which further increases the uniqueness of the UAS.

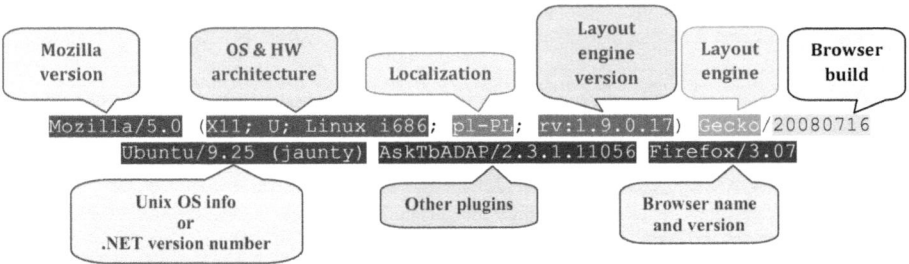

Fig. 5. Structure of the UAS

Based on the list of recorded UASes, we can state that the most popular browser is Firefox 3.6, which sends a different UAS in 40% of its total number of occurrences in our group of testers; this is a very high percentage. For Windows systems, a major distinctive factor is the version number of the .NET framework because of its verbosity. The same versions may also differ in appearance either because of a space character before the dot, or due to multiple version numbers being shown, as you can see at Table 3. Moreover, there are some cases when a plugin or toolbar causes the difference between the same versions.

The browser build dates can also cause differences. Opera is updated so often that the version number makes a lot of browsers unique. Similarly, nearly 70% of Linux users are unique by the system's distribution name and version number, which are known to be frequently updated. Many different variations are caused by the combination of the distribution version, browser build date, layout engine version, and plugin and toolbar versions.

The UAS could be shortened easily by using less detailed version numbers, thereby decreasing the probability of its uniqueness. (It must be mentioned that the Panopticlick project had a similar proposal, too. [1]) For example, the UAS could only include the family of the operating system, and exclude the full version. Likewise, only the major browser version numbers, which can be one or two digits, should be disclosed. The parts that refer to the build date, layout engine and plugins could be entirely omitted. We argue that the ideal UAS would contain the following items: OS family, localization, browser name, and major version number, e.g. 'Opera/10 (Ubuntu; hu)'.

Most of the people use one browser at a time, and use the same browser at least for months, but most for years. This means that multiple users from one IP address (for example family members or office workers) can be differentiated just by the UAS if they do not use the same browser with the same version (and the same OS version, toolbars, and .NET version). Therefore, the UAS can be used as a local ID, but there are some cases when it seems to be globally unique (see Table 3 for examples). It must be noted, however, that current UASes are simpler, and therefore contain less information than the ones obtained during our database building period.

Table 3. Examples of unique attributes in UASes. (We have slightly mixed the actual data tuples, lest we violate our test users' privacy, but each value is taken from our database)

.NET version	Toolbar version	Build date	Browser version	Linux version
(.NET CLR 3.0.04506.648)	GTB7.1	20100513	9.0.597.15	Ubuntu/10.10 (maverick)
(.NET CLR 3.5.30729)	GTB7.0	20100611	9.0.597.19	Ubuntu/9.10 (karmic)
(.NET CLR 3.5.30729)	AskTbPLTV5/3.8.0.12304	20100722	9.0.597.44	SUSE/3.6.12-0.7.1

4.6   Tests: Private Browsing Mode and Anonymous Browsing

Using TOR or any other proxy against the fingerprinting attempt is futile. These techniques modify the IP address only, and therefore the other parameters could still be used to track the user. We have run special queries on our database to verify this, and found 9 pairs of records where everything but the IP address was identical, and the close timestamps suggested that the user did not change her location significantly. In 2 cases, the user changed another parameter in addition to the IP address, but these records clearly belong to the same user due to the changes in the IP address. There was 1 single hit where we can reasonably assume a change in the user's location based on the big difference (i.e. more than an hour) between the timestamps; we conjecture that this was caused by the same user visiting from her laptop.

In general, disabling cookies is recommended as an extreme defence measure against tracking. The private browsing feature, which can be found under a different name in all modern browsers, aims to delete the tracks of the user's browsing activity by wiping the cache, history, cookies and other local storage spaces. However, it does not protect against passive fingerprinting, because it does not disable JavaScript, and the IP address and the UAS are still visible. Therefore, unless the browser reports a unified and uncommunicative attributes, fingerprinting will work in private browsing mode, at least to some extent.

In certain newer browsers, the user may tick a checkbox under the privacy settings configuration window to signal that she does not want to be tracked; however, this setting is not enforced, i.e. the server may choose not to honour it. This may work for honest website operators, but nonetheless, it is still up to them to decide if they stop tracking the user or ignore the request.

4.7 Increasing the Robustness of Fingerprinting

There are some values that remain constant or rarely change after the installation of the system. Because of the diversity of the values, the generated user ID has the largest entropy in our database. Dynamic IP address change does not cause any problem, because we only use its first two octets, but the modification of the supposedly constant parameters (screen resolution, time zone, and basic system fonts) makes the generated ID fail. However, the changes would be detectable using the remaining data (IP address, all fonts, and UAS).

Adding plugin detection could also increase the robustness of our fingerprinting algorithm, since there are many different plugins with different versions and a variety of combinations. The entropy of plugins was outstanding in the report of the Panopticlick project, so it is worthwhile to develop a browser-independent method for plugin detection, similarly to the font list. We argue that one should rely on those plugins that are rarely updated, and not under control of the browser; some examples of these are the Java runtime environment, Silverlight and Flash.

5 Discussion and Future Work

We are aware of certain spots to be improved in our experiment, namely that we should identify users with a cross-checking identifier (e.g. a nickname or a cookie), and we should explicitly encourage testing with multiple browsers on the same computer. For this reason, connecting related records was somewhat harder, albeit successful in most cases; however, the number of multiple-browser tests is not convincingly high. In a new experiment, we would like to avoid these issues, and focus especially on cross-browser data collection. This way, the experiment would be conducted within narrower bounds, but it would be more precise, and allow explicit identification of the client. Furthermore, plugin detection would also be included to improve the fingerprinting algorithm.

Besides the aforementioned proposal, there are several other ways of improving the algorithm. For example, a hybrid technique (i.e. one that combines fingerprinting with persistence) would likely increase the robustness of our method. One could, for instance, store an evercookie with the identifier generated by the fingerprinting algorithm, and use it to identify a user if she installs some previously absent fonts in the basic font set.

The inclusion of persistence in the method would have several other advantages. First, it would increase the accuracy of the algorithm in corporate environments, where computers are configured identically. Secondly, a persistent identifier would allow us to verify the results of the fingerprinting experiment, i.e. observe how frequently identifiers change.

In order to get a picture of the characteristics of the anonymity sets, we would need a larger data sample with several different devices and systems. It would be desirable to acquire more results with international visitors, too, to get a more nuanced data set. Moreover, as mobile devices (e.g. smartphones and tablets) spread rapidly, it would be interesting to see how our fingerprinting algorithm performs on them. We expect that such devices would have a more fixed parameter set: the screen resolution normally cannot be altered on most of them, and – supposedly – so is true for the set of supported fonts. In addition to these, there are certain other parameters that we expect not to change frequently, such as the version of the Flash plugin. Considering all these aspects, we assume that the fingerprinting of mobile devices can be carried out effectively. It must be noted, however, that one could also face some obstacles; for instance, some devices could have limited JavaScript capabilities, and certain plugins, such as Flash, might be unavailable on some models.

Finally, it would be interesting to see how well users can be identified based on the history of their IDs. Let us suppose that an attacker records the 'course' of the parameters of a certain user, e.g. by means of a persistent identifier. Then, the adversary could observe some traffic on a network, and attempt to identify the victim in the mass based on a probabilistic model. This should be defined in such a way that it tolerates some change in the fingerprint, and should be independent of the presence of the persistent identifier. Such a technique could significantly boost the power of the attacker, and constitute a serious threat to privacy.

6   Conclusion

In this paper, we have presented and analyzed a new method providing effective identification of browser instances. The latter is true largely due to the fact that the list of fonts is easily accessible through the JavaScript API. Therefore, if resistance of identification is to be secured with the web browsers of today, the only option seems to be to disable such scripts. That way, one's anonymity set can be greatly increased.

Users of computers in a set of identically configured machines are likely to have the best odds against our fingerprinting algorithm. If such computers are centrally managed, it is unlikely that any of them has a unique feature based on which it could be identified. Therefore, passive methods are insufficient in such a context.

Our research has some important implications regarding the user's behaviour. We have provided recommendations about browser types and versions that are likely indistinguishable from other such browsers. Furthermore, it can be seen that resistance to identification is easier achieved with popular system settings. It must be noted, however, that these measures are not necessarily easy to carry out without causing inconvenience to the user.

We have also given some guidelines for developers to make their browsers resist our fingerprinting algorithm. In particular, the verbosity of the UAS and the plugin versions should be decreased, and a standard 'substitute font set' – preferably supported by all browsers – should be introduced. Furthermore, users should be able to set fake system properties in the browser in order to hide their real operating system, time zone and screen resolution.

Finally, we have proposed some improvements for our method, and defined certain directions for future experiments; an explicitly cross-browser experiment would provide a high-precision dataset.

Acknowledgement. We would like to thank the Eötvös Károly Institute (http://www.ekint.org) for supporting our research. Furthermore, we would like to thank the High Speed Networks Laboratory for financially supporting our work.

References

1. Eckersley, P.: How Unique is Your Web Browser? In: Atallah, M.J., Hopper, N.J. (eds.) PETS 2010. LNCS, vol. 6205, pp. 1–18. Springer, Heidelberg (2010), doi:10.1007/978-3-642-14527-8_1
2. Gulyás, G., Schulcz, R., Imre, S.: Comprehensive analysis of web privacy and anonymous web browsers: are next generation services based on collaborative filtering? In: Joint SPACE and TIME International Workshops 2008, Trondheim, Norway (June 2008)
3. Wondracek, G., Holz, T., Kirda, E., Kruegel, C.: A Practical Attack to De-anonymize Social Network Users. In: Proc. of the 2010 IEEE Symposium on Security and Privacy, pp. 223–238 (2010), doi:
   http://doi.ieeecomputersociety.org/10.1109/SP.2010.21
4. Mowery, K., Bogenreif, D., Yilek, S., Shacham, H.: Fingerprinting Information in Java-Script Implementations. In: W2SP 2011: Web 2.0 Security and Privacy 2011 (2011)
5. evercookie – virtually irrevocable persistent cookies,
   http://samy.pl/evercookie/ (retrieved on August 3, 2011)
6. Soltani, A., Canty, S., Mayo, Q., Thomas, L., Hoofnagle, C.J.: Flash Cookies and Privacy (2009), SSRN http://ssrn.com/abstract=1446862
7. Mozilla Firefox 4 Release Notes, http://www.mozilla.com/en-US/firefox/4.0/releasenotes/ (retrieved on August 5, 2011)
8. Grossman, J.: I know where you've been,
   http://jeremiahgrossman.blogspot.com/2006/08/i-know-where-youve-been.html (retrieved on August 5, 2011)
9. Gomez, J., Pinnick, T., Soltani, A.: KnowPrivacy. Technical Report 2009-037, University of California, Berkeley (2009)
10. What They Know – WSJ, http://blogs.wsj.com/wtk/ (retrieved on August 5, 2011)
11. Paulik, T., Földes, Á.M., Gulyás, G.G.: Blogcrypt: Private Content Publishing on the Web. In: Fourth International Conference on Emerging Security Information, Systems and Technologies, SECURWARE 2010, Venice, Italy (July 2010)
12. Weinberg, Z., Chen, E.Y., Jayaraman, P.R., Jackson, C.: I still know what youvisited last summer. In: Proc. of the 2011 IEEE Symposium on Security and Privacy, pp. 147–161 (2011), doi: http://dx.doi.org/10.1109/SP.2011.23

Comparison of SRAM and FF PUF in 65nm Technology

Mathias Claes[1], Vincent van der Leest[2], and An Braeken[1]

[1] Industrial Sciences and Technology, Erasmus University College,
Nijverheidskaai 170, 1070 Brussels, Belgium
[2] Intrinsic-ID, High Tech Campus 9, Eindhoven, The Netherlands

Abstract. Hardware security is an essential tool in the prevention of cloning, theft of service and tampering. This security is often based on cryptographic primitives, which use a key that is securely stored somewhere in the hardware. The strength of the security is therefore dependent upon the effort required from an attacker to compromise this key. Since the tools used to carry out attacks on hardware have increased significantly over the years, the protection provided by simply storing a key in memory has decreased to a minimum. In order to protect devices against attacks on their keys, Hardware Intrinsic Security (HIS) can be used. One of the best known types of HIS primitives are Physically Unclonable Functions (PUFs). PUFs are primitives that extract secrets from physical characteristics of integrated circuits (ICs) and can be used, amongst others, in secure key storage implementations. This paper describes the results of our study on two important types of intrinsic PUFs, based on SRAM and D flip-flops. Both memory types present a specific start-up pattern (when powered up), which can be used as a PUF. For secure practical applications, a PUF should possess enough reliability for a single device and enough randomness between different devices. In this paper, a general test framework is proposed for measuring this reliability and randomness of both PUF types. Based on this framework, tests have been performed on PUFs in 65nm ICs and results are presented and compared between PUF types. From these results it can be concluded that SRAMs are slightly outperforming D flip-flop memories when it comes to usage for PUF implementations.

Keywords: Physical Unclonable Function, Hardware Security, SRAM, D flip-flop.

1 Introduction

One of the main assumptions in cryptography is that participants possess a secret key, in order to differentiate themselves from potential attackers. As a consequence, encrypted messages can only be read by the person knowing the key. However it is not easy to store a secret key. Many devices operate in environments where physical attacks can be applied. By opening the unit, an attacker is able to "easily" read the digital key.

P. Laud (Ed.): NordSec 2011, LNCS 7161, pp. 47–64, 2012.

To guarantee the secrecy of keys, even if an attackers has physical access to a system, a promising technique called Physical Unclonable Function (PUF), has been introduced by Pappu in 2001[1]. PUFs are based on the internal randomness present in physical systems. The basic idea is that the keys are not stored in the system, but can be dynamically generated as the response on a physical stimulus, called the challenge. Even if an attacker knows all the details of the system, it is impossible to generate the same key or to clone the device. When an attacker tries to intercept the key, he will destroy with high probability the PUF during the physical attack. Another advantage of using a PUF is that additional physical security is achieved without any special manufacturing steps. Moreover, since the process variations are beyond the control of manufacturers, no two systems are equal.

1.1   Related Work

Many different PUF instances are known today. A large class of PUFs consists of the delay based PUFs, like the ring oscillator PUF described by Gassend et al. [2] in 2002 and the Arbiter PUF described by Lee et al. in 2004 [3]. In 2007 SRAM based PUFs were introduced by Guajardo et al. [4], followed by Butterfly PUFs introduced in 2008 by Kumar et al. [5], and finally D flip-flop PUFs in 2008 by Maes et al. [6]. Implementations exist for dedicated Integrated Circuit (ICs), programmable logic devices such as Field Programmable Gate Arrays (FPGAs), and also for programmable ICs such as microcontrollers. Besides these examples, there are also a number of other constructions, some of which are purely theoretical.

Since 2002, the concept of PUF has received lots of interest in literature, especially with respect to aspects related to design and applications. We refer to [7] for an overview of the latest evolutions in these areas.

1.2   Our Contribution

In this paper, we focus on Static Random Access Memory (SRAM) and Data-flip-flop (FF) PUFs implemented on application-specific integrated circuits (ASICs). D-FF, or shortly FF, PUFs have a real security advantage over SRAM PUFs against invasive attacks such as probing attacks, since they can be distributed across an integrated circuit. It is much harder for an attacker to locate them. SRAM and FF PUFs consist of standard Complementary Metal Oxide Semiconductor (CMOS) components, and thus do not require an extra fabrication process. The choice for ASIC implementations follows from the fact that these are more secure than implementations in reconfigurable logic.

In order to be able to exploit these PUFs for practical purposes, they should possess high reliability and uniqueness/randomness. In order to test both properties, we present a general framework. For measuring the reliability, we describe the behavior of our devices under varying environmental conditions. Measurements are taken from 20 different devices, fabricated in 65nm technology. An estimate of the uniqueness of the device is obtained by two different tests.

The physical strength of the PUF was mostly only theoretically proven or very limited tested, i.e. without evaluation under external stress conditions and over time. The most complete test framework on PUFs has been presented in [8]. These tests were performed on a 90nm SRAM PUF. In this paper, we extend the list of tests and evaluate them on SRAM and FF PUFs in a 65nm technology. It is the first time that both types of PUFs are compared using the same test setting on the same chip.

1.3   Organization

In Section 2 we provide a description of the test framework. A brief system description is given, followed by the testing strategy. In Section 3, we show the results of the different reliability tests and in Section 4 the uniqueness tests. We end in Section 5 with conclusions and future work.

2   Test Framework

Biometric measurements and PUFs share the same property, exhibiting noise. As a result, PUF responses and biometric measurements are not fully uniformly distributed, which is undesirable for security applications. In order to use PUF responses in cryptographic applications like secure key storage mechanisms as described in [9], processing by means of a fuzzy extractor or helper data algorithm needs to be applied. We do not address these algorithms in this paper as this can be achieved using well-known methods based on secure extractors [10,9]. It is clear that smaller noise percentages in the PUF responses allow the use of more efficient error correcting codes requiring less redundant information.

The strength of a PUF is expressed in two basic properties, reliability and uniqueness. We explain both concepts more into detail, together with the corresponding tests that give an estimate of their strength. But first, we shortly give the system description.

2.1   System Description

For each IC, we evaluate two commercial SRAM memories and one FF memory that are integrated in 65nm CMOS technology. The so called PUFPUF ICs were designed by IMEC The Netherlands and produced on a Multi-Project-Wafer (MPW) at TSMC. The commercial SRAM memories, NXP (nxp_mem1kx64) and TSMC (TS1N65LPA1024X64M8), are organized as 1024 × 64 bits, while the FF memory is organized as 256 × 64 bits. Consequently, we examine two types of memory based PUFs without fuzzy extractor and other processing steps.

2.2   Reliability Tests

The first important property for PUFs to be studied, is reliability. It measures the consistency or stability when the environment (such as ambient temperature, supply voltage, etc.) varies. Environmental changes will contribute to temporary or permanent variations in the desired properties. These variations are determined by the main parameters of transistors such as threshold voltage, leakage current, delay, etc. The effect of these variations should be minimized as much as possible because of two reasons. The device should be in the first place resistant since it can be naturally subject to environmental changes. On the other hand, it should not be possible for an attacker to leak information from the device by simply changing, for instance, the temperature.

We have identified six different tests for evaluating the reliability of the PUF. First of all, the behavior under varying temperature should be studied. As chips operate at higher frequencies, the temperature of the die rises. Higher operating temperatures degrade the performance of transistors and inter-connections. High temperatures and temperature gradients can cause delays to change, which may cause transient or permanent failure.

Secondly, the effect of voltage variation is studied. It is well known that a decrease in supply will slow down a circuit. Moreover, the performance loss is not linear, which affects different parts of the circuit and therefore the reliability of the PUF.

To see the effect of power dips on the initial state of the PUFs, the data retention test was carried out. If a dip in the power voltage occurs, a threshold should be set, so the state of the PUFs are not influenced.

The fourth test is a voltage ramp-up test, which is performed at different temperatures. When different ramp-ups are applied, the stability and the present randomness could change.

In the fifth test, called the voltage dip test, the required dip time for properly resetting the memories is studied. It is well known that data remanence gets steadily longer at lower temperatures. For instance static RAM contents below $-20°$ C can persist from seconds to minutes after the power supply is removed. Therefore this test is also performed at different temperatures.

Finally, the last test for measuring the reliability of the PUF is called the ageing test. Silicon will gradually degrade over time, which will have repercussions on the PUF. Several mechanisms stand out: time-dependent dielectric breakdown (TDDB), hot carriers, negative bias temperature instability (NTBI), electro migration, stress migration and soft errors. Some of these failure mechanisms target transistors, while others come from interconnect.

2.3   Uniqueness Tests

The other important security parameter for PUFs is uniqueness. This entails the following two aspects:

- Each device should be unique, meaning that the probability for two devices having a PUF response close to each other is negligible.
- Each PUF response is random and unpredictable, meaning that bits in a PUF response can only be predicted with negligible probability.

Two important measurement distances are respectively related with these two property.

- Intra class distance (within-class distribution) is the Hamming distance (HD) between the responses from the same challenge of one PUF instance.
- Inter class distance (between class distribution) is the HD between the responses from the same challenge of two different PUF instances.

In our measurements, we mainly use the fractional Hamming distance (FHD), instead of the HD, which is the HD divided by the total length. As μ_{intra} represents the average noise of one PUF, it is clear that μ_{intra} should be as small as possible. On the other hand, μ_{inter} measures the average distinguishability (how well are we able to distinguish two different devices) of two systems based on their PUF responses. Consequently, μ_{inter} should be ideally equal to 50%.

We have distinguished two different tests for evaluating the uniqueness of PUFs. The first test is called the between-class uniqueness test in which μ_{inter} values are measured, which give a good first indication of the randomness of our PUFs.

The second test is an entropy test which estimates the present entropy in the PUF responses. Although μ_{inter} is a good indication of the uniqueness of the response, it can not be used to assess the true independent entropy. In order to find the independent entropy, we will check the ability to compress the response strings and calculate the min-entropy.

3   Reliability Test Results

We here describe the test set-up, together with the observations and the conclusions that can be drawn from the six reliability tests, as described above. Since the two SRAM memories, NXP and TSMC, give approximately the same results, we do not show the exact results for both but instead restrict to one of them. We refer to [11] for a detailed description of both.

3.1   Temperature Test

In order to test the effect of varying the temperature 20 PUFPUF ICs were placed in a test set-up. These ICs were powered up repeatedly and after each power up the contents of the memories were read (and stored into a file). During the test, each IC was read 20 times at 5 different ambient temperatures (-40°C, -10°C, 20°C, 50°C, 80°C), resulting in 100 files per memory per device. One measurement at an ambient temperature of 20°C is used as enrollment, to which all other measurements are compared. Comparison between measurements is based on the FHD between the start-up patterns of the chip.

The resulting FHD values of the NXP SRAM are plotted in Fig. 1 on the top side. The number of measurements per device is set to the horizontal axis, while the vertical axis present the FHD between start-up patterns and enrollment of the chip. At the top of each graph, the current condition (in this case: the different temperatures of the measurements) is specified. Various ICs are marked with colored lines. A similar representation for all the other test results is used in this paper.

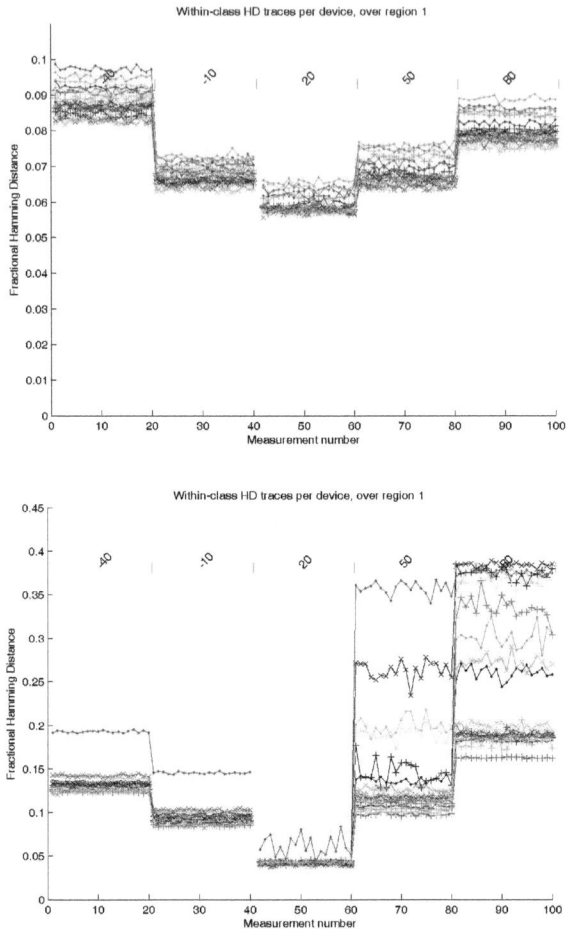

Fig. 1. FHD vs. temperature for 20 SRAM memories (top) and FF memories (bottom)

From this graph we deduce that the noise levels steadily remain below 10% (in comparison to enrollment at 20°C), no matter at what temperature the measurements are taken. This means that the reconstructed values are extremely stable and consequently allow very efficient error correction codes in the fuzzy extractor.

The FHD of the FF memories are shown in Fig. 1 on the bottom side. Variation in temperature shows a maximum deviation of 0.4 measured for the FFs, which will require additional processing in the fuzzy extractor for these FF memories to be usable as PUFs. Hence the fuzzy extractor used for the FFs will be more complex (and therefore require more hardware resources) than the one used for SRAM. Furthermore, results of FF memories vary considerably from chip to chip.

Consequently, we can conclude that SRAM memories have a better performance in this test than the FF memories, since the FHD in regard to enrollment is low.

3.2 Voltage Variation Test

In order to find out the consistency of the start-up values of the memories under slight variations of the power voltages, 10 PUFPUF ICs were placed in a test set-up. These ICs were powered up repeatedly and after each power up the contents of the SRAM and FF memories were read (and stored into a file). During the test, each memory was read 10 times at 5 different core voltages (90% of Vdd, 95%, 100%, 105% and 110%), resulting in 50 measurement files per memory per device. One measurement (at 100% of Vdd) per memory per IC is used as enrollment, to which all other measurements are compared. Comparison between measurements is based on FHD between start-up patterns of the memories.

From this test, we conclude that there are no remarkable variations in FHD between the different core voltages. The FHDs are approximately constant over all supply voltages. A maximum deviation of 0.07 is measured for both types of memories, which is very good.

3.3 Data Retention Test

To investigate the effect of power dips on the initial state of the PUFs, the Hamming Weight HW (number of bits in a string with value 1) is used, more specifically the fractional FHW (HW divided by the string length).

At the beginning of the test, the memories of the ICs were filled with 0xFF (FHW = 1). Next, the supply was lowered to a certain percentage (from 100% to 10% in steps of 10%) of Vdd for 1 second. Then, the supply was set to Vdd again and the contents of the memories are read out. For each supply value, this test was performed 10 times. During the test, the FHW of the measurement of three PUFPUF ICs were monitored. If the FHW drops below 1, the memories lose their content.

When the supply voltage lowered to 20% of Vdd, some bits flip to zero. However, the FHW still remains approximately 1. At 10% of Vdd, we measured a FHW of 0.2 for the FFs and 0.5 for the SRAMs. Consequently, the results from this test are very good since the voltage must be very low (20% of Vdd) in order for the memories to lose their values. Together with the results of the voltage variation test, we conclude that the devices are very resistant to variations in supply voltage.

3.4 Voltage Ramp-Up Test

The test set-up consisted of 10 PUFPUFs ICs. These ICs were powered up repeatedly at 8 different ramp-up times. After each power up, the contents of the memories were read (and stored into a file), resulting in 80 files per memory per device. One measurement with a ramp-up time of $1\mu s$ at 20°C is used as enrollment. Comparison between the measurements is based on FHD between the start-up patterns of the memories.

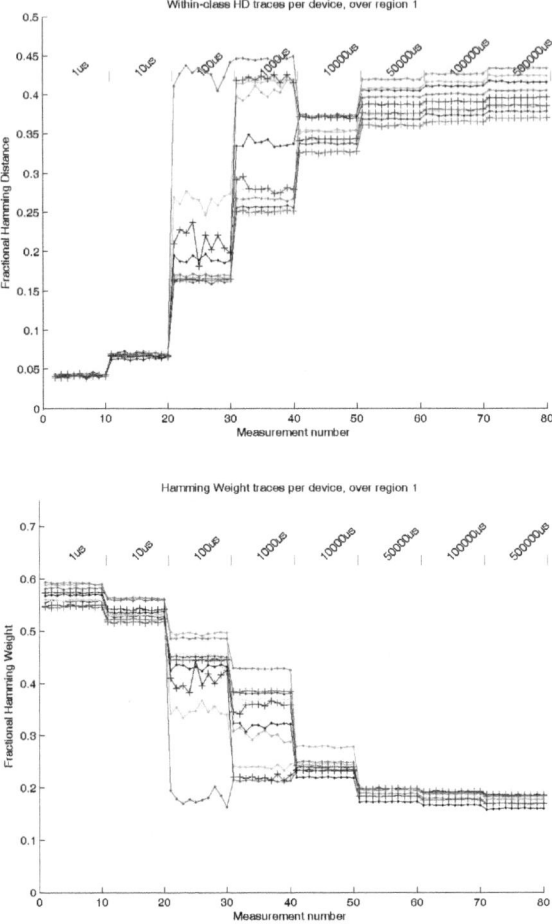

Fig. 2. FHD (top) and FHW (bottom) vs. ramp-up time for 10 FF memories at 20°C

When the ramp-up time of the supply becomes longer, the FHD with regard to enrollment becomes larger. In Fig. 2 (top) it can be seen that the response of the FF memories change rapidly (unstable) when the ramp-up time becomes longer ($10\mu s$ to $100\mu s$). At 500ms the FHD of the SRAMs is less than 0.2, as can be seen in Fig. 3 (top), while the FHD of the FF is almost 0.45 (Fig. 2 top). When we look at the FHW of the FF in Fig. 2 (bottom), we see a strong biasing towards zero at slow ramp-ups. This is not the case for SRAM memories, as can be seen in Fig. 3 (bottom).

Therefore, a ramp-up time of the supply should always be kept sufficiently short in any set-up. When the ramp-up time is kept below $100\mu s$, this will not cause problems (FHD < 0.1). Based on this observation, a ramp-up time of

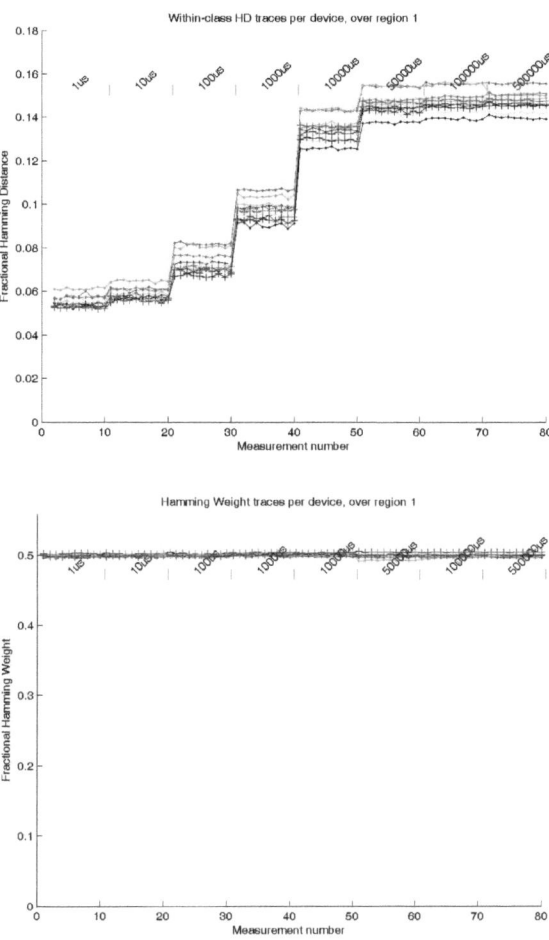

Fig. 3. FHD (top) and FHW (bottom) vs. ramp-up for 10 SRAM memories at 20°C

$25\mu s$ at 20°C is used as enrollment for the voltage ramp-up test at different temperatures (-40°C to +80°C).

The FHD graphs at different temperatures (like -40°C, represented in Fig. 4) show that the SRAM memories do not experience a significant impact when combing temperature and ramp-up variation. The FF memories behave normal over ramp-up times at low temperatures, but change rapidly at high temperatures. If the ramp-up time at low temperatures is less than $100\mu s$, the distance is kept below 15%. Less steep ramp-ups at low temperature seem to be closer to enrollment, due to decrease in propagation delay with operating temperature.

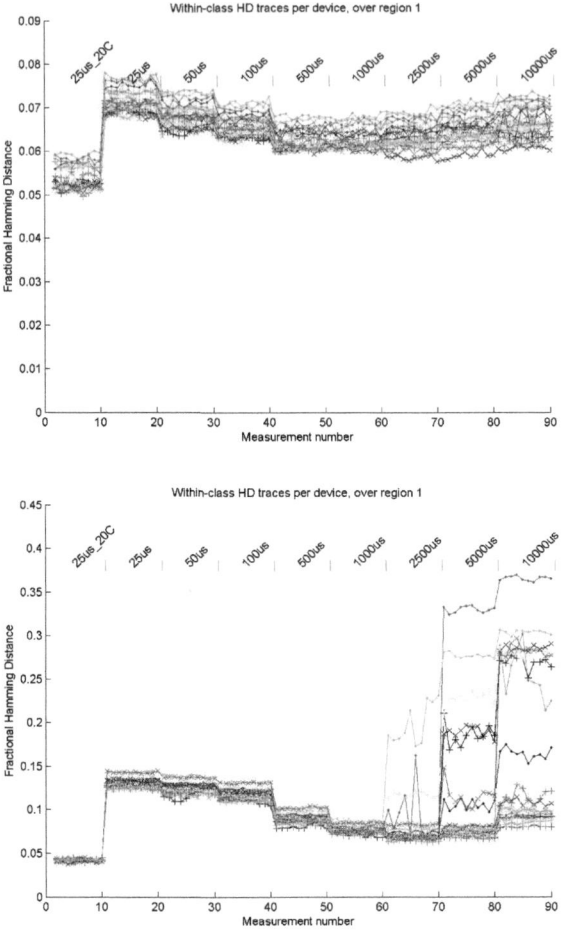

Fig. 4. FHD vs. ramp-up time for 20 SRAM (top) and FF (bottom) memories at -40°C

3.5   Voltage Dip Test

Remanence is tested by placing PUFPUF ICs in a test set-up, which is suitable for asserting a dip on the core voltage of the IC. At the beginning of the test the memories of 10 ICs were filled with 0xFF (all 1s). Then the ICs were powered down for a certain amount of time (voltage dip). After the ICs were powered up, the contents of the memories were read. As data remanence gets steadily longer at low temperatures, the dip test is performed at 20°C and -40°C. Each memory was read 10 times at 8 different dip times and compared to enrollment where dip time of 1s was used, which is long enough for a proper reset of all the memories.

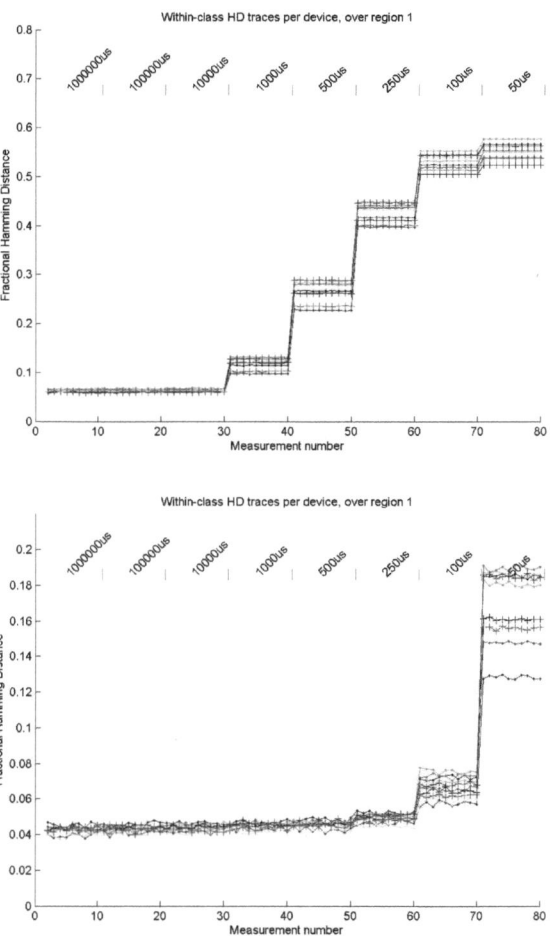

Fig. 5. FHD vs. dip time for 10 SRAM memories (top) and FF memories (bottom)

From Fig. 5 we conclude that when the dip time of the supply voltage becomes shorter at 20°C, the FHD with regard to enrollment becomes larger. In order to have a FHD below 0.15, a proper reset should take at least 1ms for the SRAM memories and only 100μs for the FF memory. At -40°C, as shown in Fig. 6, the reset should take at least 1s for the SRAM memories and 50ms for the FF memory.

3.6   Ageing Test

For the ageing tests, one PUFPUF IC was placed in an oven at 80°C with a supply voltage of 110% Vdd (1.32V). Under these conditions, we accelerate the ageing effect of a chip. The total acceleration factor [12] is computed as the

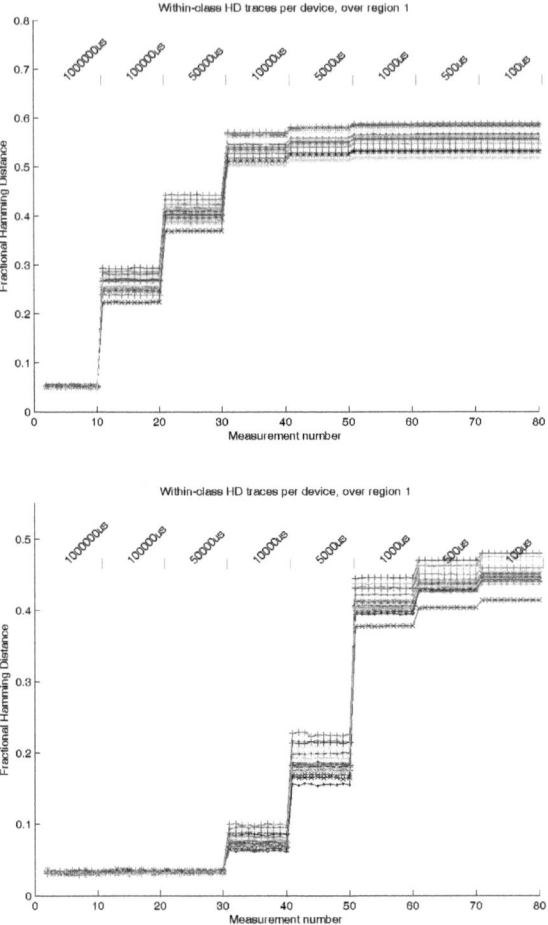

Fig. 6. FHD vs. dip for 10 SRAM memories (top) and FF memories (bottom) at -40°C

product of the thermal acceleration factor (TAF) and the voltage acceleration factor (VAF), which are computed as:

$$TAF = e^{\frac{E_a}{k}(\frac{1}{T_{op}} - \frac{1}{T_{stress}})}$$

$$VAF = e^{\gamma(V_{stress} - V_{op})}$$

The factor E_a (0.5 eV) is the activation energy, k (8,62 10^{-5} eV/°K) is Boltzmann's constant, T_{op} (313°K (40°C)) is the normal operating temperature, T_{stress} (353°K (80°C)) is the temperature used in the stress test, γ (2.6) is the voltage exponent factor, V_{stress} (1.32V) is the core voltage under stress conditions and V_{op} (1.2V) is the core voltage under normal operating conditions. This results in a total estimated acceleration factor of TAF×VAF = 8.17×1.37 = 11.2.

Every few days the ambient temperature was lowered to +20°C and the SRAM start-up values were measured (and stored in a file). Afterwards, the temperature was increased back to +80°C. One measurement at an ambient temperature of 20°C before starting the ageing test was used as enrollment, to which all other measurements are compared. Comparison between measurements is based on the FHD between the start-up patterns of the memories.

The ageing test has been running for 111 days . With the estimated acceleration factor of 11.2, we simulate an effective ageing of around 41 months , hence almost 3.5 years. The results show that within this time frame the ageing is quite limited. The maximum FHD remains below 10%. The results furthermore show that the SRAM memories experience less influence from ageing than the FF memories. Hence SRAM is more resistant to ageing than FFs.

3.7   Summary of the Reliability Tests

Table 1 summarizes the reliability tests. The notation used in the table represents mainly the relative strength between the different memories.

Table 1. Summarization of test results for measuring PUF reliability

Memory	Temperature	Voltage	Retention	Ramp-up	Dip time	Ageing
NXP SRAM	++	++	++	+	+/−	+
TSMC SRAM	++	++	++	+	+/−	+
FF	+/−	++	++	+/−	++	+/−

The results with respect to the ramp-up and dip time tests can be used for defining the system parameters. The ramp-up time is stricter for a FF than for an SRAM memory. On the other hand the required dip time is smaller for a FF than for an SRAM memory.

However, the results of the temperature test will have the largest consequences on the required efficiency of the fuzzy extractor. For the SRAM memories, there is only a 10% deviation for the different temperature measurements. This number is far below the acceptable boundaries (approximately 25% errors) for efficient error correction within the fuzzy extractor, where the efficiency is measured in terms of required hardware resources [13]. The FF reaches a maximum deviation of 40%, which will require extra processing and therefore more complex fuzzy extractors.

4   Uniqueness Test Results

We here describe the test set-up, together with the observations and the conclusions that can be drawn for the two uniqueness tests, as described earlier.

4.1 Between-Class Uniqueness Test

When performing uniqueness tests, we are interested in finding out whether it is possible to distinguish between different devices given their PUF responses. This is mandatory when considering PUFs for authentication purposes or applications requiring unique identifiers. In order to create a between-class distribution, the response on one specific challenge of a particular device is compared to responses on the same challenge from different devices. The intra-class distribution is computed by calculating the FHD for different responses on a specific challenge from one particular device. Both histograms can be approximated by a Gaussian distribution and are summarized by providing their means, respectively, μ_{inter} and μ_{intra}, and their standard deviations, respectively, σ_{inter} and σ_{intra}.

In other words, the between-class uniqueness test measures the average distinguishability of two systems based on their PUF responses, i.e. μ_{inter}. For this reason μ_{inter} should be close to 50%. The calculation of μ_{inter} is based on 20 different ICs. It can be concluded that μ_{inter} of the 3 different memories are concentrated around 0.5. We refer to Table 2 for the exact values of μ_{inter} and σ_{inter}.

As μ_{intra} can be considered as the average noise on the response, it should be close to 0. The results of the tests are also very good for all three memories, as can be seen in Table 2.

Table 2. Summary of estimated means and standard deviations

Memory	μ_{inter}	σ_{inter}	μ_{intra}	σ_{intra}
NXP SRAM	0.4927	0.0035	0.0597	0.00270
TSMC SRAM	0.4970	0.0029	0.0536	0.00259
FF	0.4992	0.0039	0.0434	0.00512

From the between-class results, it can be concluded that it is possible to distinguish between different devices given their PUF responses.

4.2 Entropy

To estimate the entropy we use two compression algorithms (to estimate an upper bound for the entropy) and calculate the min-entropy, which leads to a lower bound on the entropy. Context-Tree Weighting (CTW) [14] is an optimal compression method for stationary sources and shows a good estimator of the available entropy. ZIP compression is the most common compression method.

Both algorithms are used to check the ability to compress response strings, as shown in [15]. The amount of compression will give an estimation of the upper bound of the entropy from our PUF responses. When the algorithm is capable of compressing the PUF responses, the responses do not have full entropy. This test was carried out by first concatenating all PUF responses into one string of 163840 bits respectively (8192×20) for the SRAM (NXP and TSMC) and 40960 bits (20×2048) for the FF. As can be seen in Table 3, the three types of memories turn out to have good compression resistance.

Table 3. Compression results of a concatenated string of 20 different devices

Memory	Response	CTW	ZIP	CTW ratio	ZIP ratio
NXP	163840	162525	163207	99,1%	99,6%
TSMC	163840	164171	164002	100%	100%
FF	40960	41173	41087	100%	100%

Besides the compression factor, it is also possible to estimate the min-entropy of these memories. Min-entropy is the worst-case (i.e., the greatest lower bound) measure of uncertainty for a random variable. For this purpose we will be using the method that is described in NIST specification 800-90 [16] for binary sources. The output values of these sources have a probability of occurring p_0 and p_1 respectively (the sum of these two probabilities is 1). When p_{max} is the maximum value of these two probabilities, the definition for min-entropy of a binary source is:

$$H_{min} = -log_2(p_{max})$$

Assuming that all bits from the PUF start-up pattern are independent, each bit of the pattern can be viewed as an individual binary source. For n independent sources (in this case n is the length of the start-up pattern) the definition below holds, which is a summation of the entropy from each individual bit.

$$(H_{min})_{total} = \sum_{i=1}^{n} -log_2(p_{i\ max})$$

For our calculations we take the enrollment patterns that we have used during the temperature test. These patterns are bitwise added together to calculate a HW per bit, which can have a value between 0 and the number of enrollment patterns (m). Based on this HW, p_{max} can be calculated for each individual bit of the start-up pattern:

$$\text{if } HW_i > m/2 : p_{i\ max} = HW_i/m,$$
$$\text{else: } p_{i\ max} = (m - HW_i)/m$$

Based on these values for p_{max}, the min-entropy of each individual bit (source) as well as the total min-entropy of the start-up pattern can be calculated using the formulas above. Finally, the average min-entropy per bit of a memory is calculated by dividing $(H_{min})_{total}$ by the length of the pattern n.

Fig. 7 displays how the average min-entropy per bit of the NXP memory develops over an increasing m. It can be seen that after using 20 devices for this min-entropy test (the total number of chips measured for this paper), the average min-entropy per bit is still rising. This means that the values found by this test for the different memories are still conservative estimates, since these values would increase with more devices. Hence, the min-entropies from Table 4 are a conservative lower bound of the total entropy per bit for these memories.

Based on the results from this section, it can be concluded that the entropy per bit for all tested memories is a value somewhere between the 0.75 (from

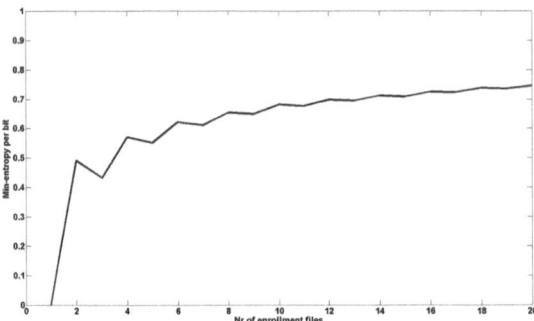

Fig. 7. Min-entropy development over the number of enrollment files (m)

Table 4. Conservative min-entropy estimate per bit based on 20 enrollment files

Memory	Min-entropy
NXP	0.75
TSMC	0.76
FF	0.77

min-entropy) and 1 (based on the compression test). This is a very high entropy, especially considering the fact that the lower threshold is based on a very conservative estimate. We therefore conclude that the amount of entropy indicates that these memories are sufficiently unique to be used as PUFs.

4.3   Conclusions of the Uniqueness Tests

Table 5 summarizes the results from the uniqueness tests.

Table 5. Summarization of test results for measuring PUF uniqueness

Memory	between-class	compression	min-entropy
NXP SRAM	++	++	++
TSMC SRAM	++	++	++
FF	++	++	++

From these results, we conclude that there are no significant differences between SRAM and FF memories regarding PUF uniqueness. Both memory types perform very well in the uniqueness tests, since their entropy is high and μ_{inter} is close to 50%. These results show that it is possible to distinguish between different devices given their PUF responses.

5   Conclusions and Future Work

In this paper, we first defined a test framework for measuring the reliability and uniqueness properties of a PUF. This framework is used for comparing two types of intrinsic PUFs, the SRAM and FF PUFs, in 65nm technology. By means of six reliability tests, we have evaluated the strength of the PUFs under several external stress conditions. The SRAM PUFs turn out to have a shorter ramp-up time but a larger reset time, compared to the FF PUF. However, the most important difference is the resistance against temperature variations which is much better for the SRAM PUFs than for the FF PUFs. This results in a more efficient fuzzy extractor (being an implementation with less hardware resources) required for the SRAM PUF. From the results of the uniqueness tests, we conclude that both PUF types possess a sufficient amount of randomness.

Future work will be the evaluation of other types of PUFs following the proposed test framework of this paper. Using more devices (than the 20 used for this paper) for future tests will result in better statistics which would allow for even more confidence in test results. Secondly, it is also interesting to study the behavior of the PUF in combination with its processing algorithms, like the fuzzy extractor.

Acknowledgements. The authors would like to thank IMEC The Netherlands for supplying the PUFPUF chips that have been used for the study as described in this publication.

All work preformed by Vincent van der Leest in this study has been supported by the European Commission through the FP7 program under contract 238811 UNIQUE.

References

1. Ravikanth, P.S.: Physical one-way functions. PhD thesis, AAI0803255 (2001)
2. Gassend, B., Clarke, D., van Dijk, M., Devadas, S.: Silicon physical random functions. In: ACM Conference on Computer and Communications Security, pp. 148–160. ACM Press, New York (2002)
3. Lee, J.W., Lim, D., Gassend, B., Suh, G.E., Dijk, M.V., Devadas, S.: A technique to build a secret key in integrated circuits with identification and authentication applications. In: Proceedings of the IEEE VLSI Circuits Symposium, pp. 176–179 (2004)
4. Guajardo, J., Kumar, S.S., Schrijen, G.-J., Tuyls, P.: FPGA Intrinsic PUFs and Their Use for IP Protection. In: Paillier, P., Verbauwhede, I. (eds.) CHES 2007. LNCS, vol. 4727, pp. 63–80. Springer, Heidelberg (2007)
5. Kumar, S.S., Guajardo, J., Maes, R., Schrijen, G.J., Tuyls, P.: The Butterfly PUF: Protecting IP on every FPGA, pp. 67–70 (2008)
6. Maes, R., Tuyls, P., Verbauwhede, I.: Intrinsic PUFs from Flip-flops on reconfigurable devices. In: 3rd Benelux Workshop on Information and System Security (WISSec 2008), Eindhoven, NL, p. 17 (2008)
7. Sadeghi, A.-R., Naccache, D.: Towards Hardware-Intrinsic Security: Foundations and Practice, 1st edn. Springer-Verlag New York, Inc., New York (2010)
8. Selimis, G.N., Konijnenburg, M., Ashouei, M., Huisken, J., de Groot, H., van der Leest, V., Schrijen, G.J., van Hulst, M., Tuyls, P.: Evaluation of 90nm 6T-SRAM as Physical Unclonable Function for secure key generation in wireless sensor nodes. In: ISCAS, pp. 567–570 (2011)

9. Tuyls, P., Skoric, B., Kevenaar, T.: Security with Noisy Data: Private Biometrics, Secure Key Storage and Anti-Counterfeiting. Springer-Verlag New York, Inc., Secaucus (2007)
10. Dodis, Y., Ostrovsky, R., Reyzin, L., Smith, A.: Fuzzy extractors: How to generate strong keys from biometrics and other noisy data. SIAM J. Comput. 38, 97–139 (2008)
11. Claes, M., van der Leest, V.: PUFPUF test results. Tech. rep., Intrinsic-ID (2011)
12. Altera, Reliability report 49 q1 2010, Tech. rep.
13. Bösch, C., Guajardo, J., Sadeghi, A.-R., Shokrollahi, J., Tuyls, P.: Efficient Helper Data Key Extractor on FPGAs. In: Oswald, E., Rohatgi, P. (eds.) CHES 2008. LNCS, vol. 5154, pp. 181–197. Springer, Heidelberg (2008)
14. Willems, F., Shtarkov, Y., Tjalkens, T.: Context-Tree Weighting: Basic properties. IEEE Transactions on Information Theory 41, 644–653 (1995)
15. van der Leest, V., Schrijen, G.-J., Handschuh, H., Tuyls, P.: Hardware intrinsic security from D flip-flops. In: Proceedings of the Fifth ACM Workshop on Scalable Trusted Computing, STC 2010, pp. 53–62. ACM, New York (2010)
16. Barker, E., Kelsey, J.: NIST Special Publication 800-90: Recommendation for random number generation using deterministic random bit generators (revised), NIST, Tech. rep. (March 2007)

Modular Anomaly Detection
for Smartphone Ad Hoc Communication

Jordi Cucurull, Simin Nadjm-Tehrani, and Massimiliano Raciti

Department of Computer and Information Science, Linköping University,
SE-581 83 Linköping, Sweden
{jordi.cucurull,simin.nadjm-tehrani,massimiliano.raciti}@liu.se

Abstract. The capabilities of the modern smartphones make them the
obvious platform for novel mobile applications. The open architectures,
however, also create new vulnerabilities. Measures for prevention, detection, and reaction need to be explored with the peculiarities that
resource-constrained devices impose. Smartphones, in addition to cellular
broadband network capabilities, include WiFi interfaces that can even be
deployed to set up a mobile ad hoc network (MANET). While intrusion
detection in MANETs is typically evaluated with network simulators, we
argue that it is important to implement and test the solutions in real devices to evaluate their resource footprint. This paper presents a modular
implementation of an anomaly detection and mitigation mechanism on
top of a dissemination protocol for intermittently-connected MANETs.
The overhead of the security solution is evaluated in a small testbed
based on three Android-based handsets and a laptop. The study shows
the feasibility of the statistics-based anomaly detection regime, having
low CPU usage, little added latency, and acceptable memory footprint.

Keywords: intrusion detection, resource footprint, ad hoc networking.

1 Introduction

With the expected replacement of the majority of phone handsets with smartphones the need for addressing security issues on Internet-connected devices
becomes more urgent. Strengthening the security of handsets, specially on open
platforms on which the owner is allowed to make unrestricted downloads and
create potential threats to the platform or applications is a major concern of the
research community. Measures to enhance security through both prevention and
detection need to be explored and the peculiarities of the resource-constrained
handsets compared to earlier platforms is an exciting field of research. In this
paper we explore the impact of one such security mechanism in terms of the
resource claims on a modern smartphone platform.

Smartphones add the possibility of WiFi-based Internet connections to the
cellular communication. However, the phones also enable the peer-to-peer mode
of communication that has been subject of studies in the mobile ad hoc networks (MANET) research for over a decade. With the increased connectivity

P. Laud (Ed.): NordSec 2011, LNCS 7161, pp. 65–81, 2012.

provided by the infrastructure-based technologies there are no major deployments of ad hoc networks in every day scenarios. However, experience shows that when disaster strikes the existing infrastructures are severely overloaded, or rendered useless due to damages. Thus, message dissemination in disaster area networks using a phone-to-phone mode of communication is a potential means for establishing situational awareness. Our earlier work, among others, has been focused on studies of energy and bandwidth constrained communication using specially devised protocols for such scenarios [1,2]. This work is part of the larger context of the Hastily Formed Networks project supported by Swedish Civil Contingencies agency [3].

While imposing policies and methods for preventing threats from malware and adversary actions on modern smartphones is a subject attracting a lot of attention [4,5,6,7,8,9], to our knowledge there is little earlier work that addresses intrusion detection with a focus on the resource footprint. There is, of course, a large body of research on intrusion detection techniques for MANET [10], including our own earlier evaluation of a distributed statistical anomaly detection system [11]. However, these techniques are commonly evaluated in simulation platforms due to the difficulty of performing large scale evaluations on physical testbeds. This can act as a proof of concept for a protocol or a proposed defence mechanism, but will not be able to answer questions on the resource claims.

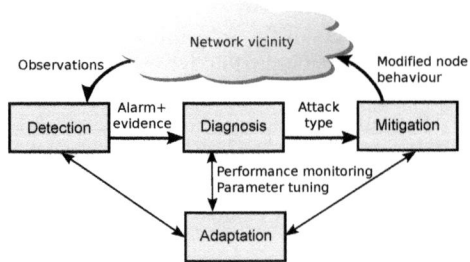

Fig. 1. General Survivability Framework (GSF)

Some approaches based on intrusion detection combine misuse and anomaly detection and one or more techniques for mitigation. An approach we have adopted, called General Survivability Framework (GSF), combines four modules that can be independently developed for various communication protocols (see Figure 1). The detection module is an anomaly detector. It detects deviations from normality by observing the traffic pattern in and out of the observed node. The diagnosis module, reminiscent of a misuse detector, matches the observed anomalous patterns with known attack patterns in order to aid a more direct and focused mitigation. The mitigation module has an action to curb the effects of each known attack, to be performed in the node that detects that attack. It also has a generic mitigation for unknown attacks, e.g. acting in a more careful mode with respect to peer communication. Finally, the adaptation module is intended to adjust the GSF by inducing changes in the other algorithms to adapt to changes in the operating conditions, including the handset's monitored features. In this paper we provide a modular design and partial implementation (detection and mitigation boxes) of the GSF on top of an implementation of an opportunistic dissemination protocol over the Android smartphone platform.

The design and implementation has been carefully devised to care for modularity. This allows convenient replacements of the detection-diagnosis-mitigation modules as well as the ad hoc communication protocol. This should provide a basis for evaluating other detection engines and separate the effects of the GSF from the underlying protocol that provides the means of communication. The design has been realised on two modern Android smart phone platforms with the goal of evaluating and isolating the added overhead imposed by the GSF.

The contributions of the paper are as follows (1) We have implemented Random Walk Gossip (RWG) [1], a manycast algorithm for resource-efficient dissemination in disaster area (infrastructure-less) networks on top of an Android platform. (2) We have implemented an instance of the modular GSF, a statistical-based anomaly detection and a mitigation module, thus enabling the study of its performance overheads on a physical device, which extends the earlier NS3-based simulations [11] of the proposed technique. (3) We perform experiments on a small testbed with 3 handsets and a laptop which indicate that the resource overhead of anomaly detection and mitigation, in terms of CPU, memory and latency, is quite low when the load in the network is within a measured operating range.

The paper is organised in the following sections: Section 2 provides the background on the existing GSF and RWG, Section 3 explains the design and implementation for Android, Section 4 details the evaluation done with the real smartphones, Section 5 briefly describes the related work, and Section 6 concludes the paper.

2 Background

2.1 General Survivability Framework

GSF is a generic framework in which arbitrary detection, diagnosis, mitigation, and adaptation elements can be introduced. In this paper we base our implementation and evaluation on certain instances (detection and mitigation) of the components named in Section 1. The detection component is based on the statistical anomaly detection algorithm proposed in Cucurull et al. [11]. A statistical approach is chosen due to its small footprint, ideal for the resource-constrained nature of smartphones. The GSF periodically captures the network state, an observation, which is represented by a vector of numerical values called features. An observation is composed of network statistics, such as packet rates, estimation of number of neighbour nodes, and so on. Each observation is taken every a certain time defined by the *evaluation period* parameter. The detector algorithm calculates the Euclidean distance between an observation and a normality model local to the smartphone. The normality model of the system is generated in a two-step process during a training period. First, a vector which is the average of many observations is created. Second, a number of observations is taken to calculate the threshold, which is the mean of the distances plus three times their standard deviation. An observation is categorised as anomalous if the distance is above a threshold. When an anomaly is detected a general mitigation, or specific one if the attack is identified, is engaged. Earlier work [11] and an extension of it for multiple mitigations and known attack classifications has provided a proof of concept for feasibility of this approach in a distributed ad hoc communication setting. This paper will elaborate on realisation of some instances in a real handset deployment.

2.2   Random Walk Gossip

RWG [1], the routing protocol chosen in the implementation, is a message dissemination protocol for intermittently connected ad hoc networks. The protocol copes with intermittent connectivity, scarcity of bandwidth, and energy, as well as unknown and unpredictable network topologies with partitions. RWG is a manycast protocol, which means that a message is intended to reach a given number k of nodes, with no knowledge of the node IDs in the topology. RWG is based on a store-and-forward mechanism, i.e. each node keeps the messages to forward in a local buffer until it realises they are *k-delivered* or they expire. The protocol follows a three-way packet exchange (see Fig. 2).

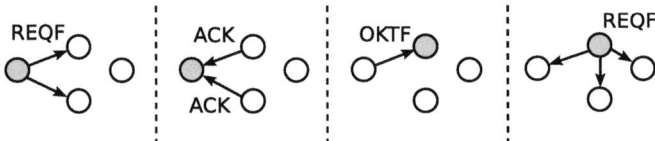

Fig. 2. Random Walk Gossip

First, a Request to Forward (REQF), that includes the message payload, is sent by the current custodian of the message (grey nodes in the picture). The neighbouring nodes hear the REQF reply with an acknowledgement packet (ACK). The custodian randomly chooses one of these nodes and sends an OK to Forward (OKTF) indicating the next custodian. The other nodes retain the message without actively disseminating it. Partitions can be overcome by the movement of nodes. Thus, new uninformed nodes will be informed by some node that keeps the message as *inactive* and restarts to disseminate. In order to keep track of which nodes have seen a given message, each packet header contains a bit vector, *informed*. Each position of the vector maps to one encountered node ID, using a hash function. This is also used to indicate whether a current encountered node has seen the message earlier. The vector enables the protocol to know when a message is k-delivered (when k bits are set). Finally, when a node realises that a message is k-delivered it sends a Be Silent (BS) packet to its vicinity.

3   Layered Communication and Anomaly Detection

This section proposes a layered modular design for the implementation of the described GSF and RWG services in Android smartphones with an emphasis on component independence and interchangeability.

3.1   Overall Architecture

The communication and anomaly detection services described in this paper are offered over arbitrary point-to-point ad hoc network connections and for any set of applications. An organisation based on a stack of loosely coupled services, such as the well-known IP network stack, is therefore the most appropriate. The service stack is composed of three layers, each one implementing one possible service. Figure 3 details the layers and each implemented service.

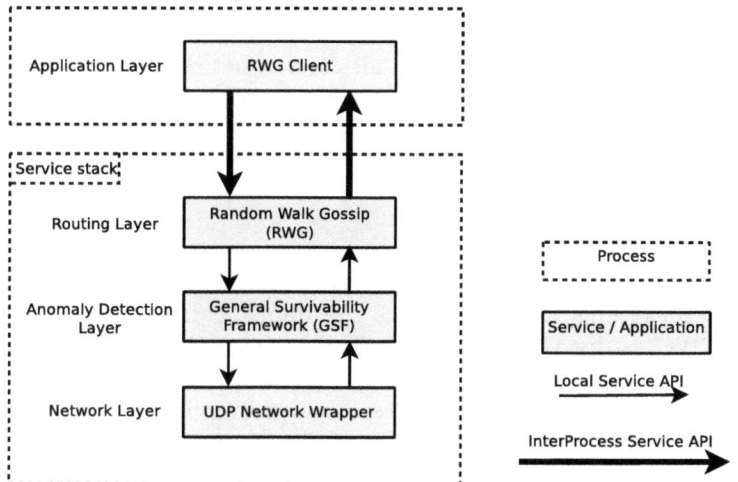

Fig. 3. Layered communication and anomaly detection structure

The network, routing, and anomaly detection layers compose a block that provides the main communication and anomaly detection service. The layers interact among themselves with a well-defined and generic inter-layer service API, which allows to easily exchange, aggregate, or bypass them. For example, the anomaly detection layer is optional and can be bypassed. The application layer comprises the applications that use the service. A specific API to interact with the applications is provided by the topmost layer of the service stack.

In Android we have implemented each of the lower three layers as locally bound services running all of them in a single process. At the same time, the topmost layer of the stack offers the main service via inter-process communication open to the applications, which run as independent processes.

The inter-layer and inter-process service APIs support send, receive, and other control operations. In the inter-layer service API the receive operation is implemented with an event listener, provided by the upper layer, that is invoked when a packet is received. The inter-process API provides the same operations, but they are invoked by inter-process messages. The network packets are exchanged among the layers as raw byte arrays, allowing the abstraction of the APIs from the specific type of packet and communication protocol.

3.2   Network Layer

The network layer provides an abstraction of the network over which the routing protocol will actually run. It includes basic services to initialise the network interface, set up an ad hoc network, and send and receive packets. As defined by the inter-layer service API there is an operation to send packets and a listener, provided by the upper layer, for notifying their reception. A dedicated thread calls the listener each time a packet is received.

In the present implementation the packets are encapsulated within UDP datagrams, which are present in virtually all current network stacks. Furthermore, this guarantees compatibility with an earlier implementation of RWG for the Symbian platform [2].

3.3   Routing Layer

The routing layer provides the service to route the messages sent by the application layer. This layer also provides the inter-process service API to interact with the applications. This paper describes the implementation of manycast routing using RWG as described in Section 2. However, other protocols can also be implemented since the inter-layer interface is generic enough to support them.

The realisation of the protocol is based on a former implementation for Symbian OS [2]. Due to the extensive use of timers, the architecture follows an event-oriented approach implemented with a task scheduler. The architecture, depicted on Figure 4, includes the following components:

- **Data Storage:** data buffer that stores control information and payload of the messages sent and received to and from the network.
- **Task Storage:** data buffer that stores tasks pending to execute. The tasks may include sending specific types of packets or deletion of expired messages.
- **Task Dispatcher:** thread that executes the tasks present in the task storage at the scheduled time.
- **Wake One Packet:** thread that regularly sends a packet when there is no network activity, to discover neighbours.
- **Application Handler:** method that initiates the transmission of a message sent from the application layer. It creates an entry to the data storage and the required new task to execute.
- **Packet Receiver:** method that processes a packet received from the underlying layer, i.e. network or anomaly detection layers. It creates or updates entries to the data storage and new tasks to execute.

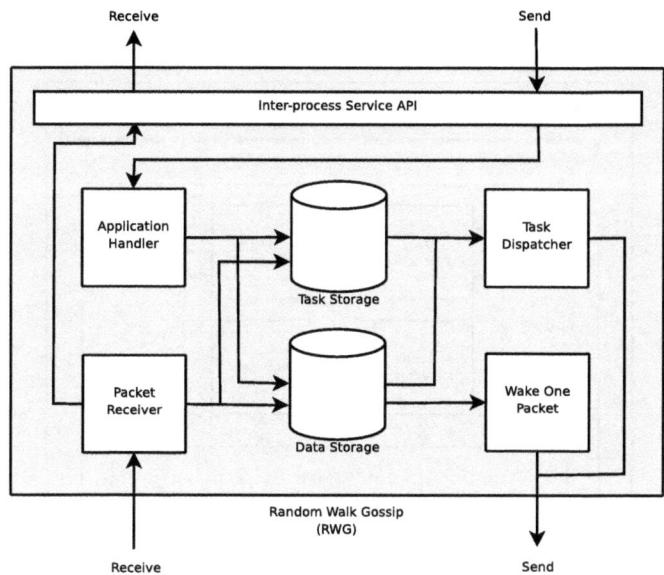

Fig. 4. Random Walk Gossip architecture

The packets sent and received to and from the network are encapsulated in objects of a class called *RWGPacket*. This class provides access to the packet headers and payload. Since the service APIs only support arrays of bytes, the object also provides methods to marshall and unmarshall the packets.

3.4   Anomaly Detection Layer

The anomaly detection layer provides a service to detect anomalies at network routing level. It is placed between the routing layer and the network layer to intercept the packets sent and received. Thus, it is able to detect anomalies and apply a response without any modification to the other layers' code. The architecture of the service, depicted on Figure 5, includes the following components:

– **IDS Engine:** main thread that governs (and periodically runs) the steps of the intrusion detection loop, i.e. data collection, anomaly detection, diagnosis, and mitigation.
– **Data Source:** component that processes each packet received or sent to generate statistics for further analysis. It returns the statistics generated, as a vector of doubles, when they are requested.
– **Anomaly Detector:** implements the detection box of GSF. This component periodically analyses the statistics created by the data source to detect anomalies. It returns alarms if an anomaly is detected.
– **Diagnoser:** implements the diagnosis box of GSF. This component diagnoses a specific attack when a detected anomaly matches a known attack. It returns a code that indicates the diagnosed attack.

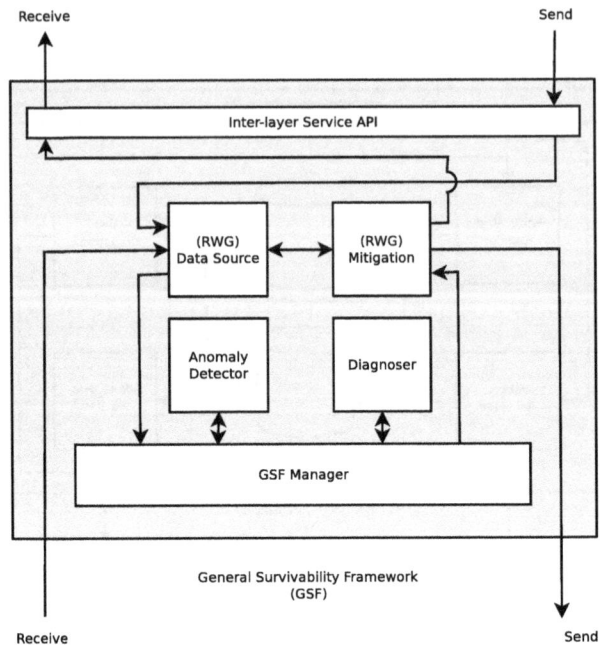

Fig. 5. General Security Framework architecture

– **Mitigation:** implements the mitigation box of GSF. This component applies mitigation measures, such as modifying or rejecting the flow of packets sent and received, when an anomaly is detected.

The service requires the RWGPacket class of the routing protocol to read and manipulate the packets received. The Data Source and Mitigation components are the only ones dependant on this class and the routing protocol present in the routing layer. Hence the replacement of the routing protocol only requires the modification of these two components.

3.5   Application Layer

The application layer comprises all the applications that use the main communication and anomaly detection service. It communicates with the service stack through the inter-process service API. Many applications connected at the same time to the service and running on different processes are supported.

3.6   Implementation on Android

This section discusses the implementation details of the communication and anomaly detection service. It describes the decisions taken during the implementation, and the configuration of the system. Java has been the language used for most of the project, with the exception of a few tools used for configuring the network. Since the service is intended to run on resource-constrained handheld devices, performance has been a main criteria for the implementation decisions.

UDP Network. This module is implemented as a local Android service. It runs on the main thread of the service stack and has an additional thread that monitors the reception of packets, calling the listener provided by the upper layer when a message is received. This component also initialises the ad hoc network. A rooted phone is required for this purpose, since the network ad hoc mode is not supported by the Android API and a set of native tools must be run with administrator rights.

Random Walk Gossip. This module, implemented as a local service, runs on the main thread of the service stack and includes two additional threads for the Task Dispatcher and Wake One Packet components. These two threads only wake up when new tasks or actions are scheduled or ready to be executed by using signals and a timer respectively. This saves up resources spent on polling lists or checking the state of the system. Other aspects optimised are frequent protocol operations, such as the sending, reception, and management of messages, which involve:

1. *Creation, search, and elimination of packet entries in the Data Storage*: the Data Storage has a doubly-indexed organisation based on a HashMap and a TreeSet. The HashMap provides constant access to the entries by the ID of the message, operation repeated each time a packet arrives. The TreeSet provides fast sequential access, $O(n)$, to the entries sorted by the time-to-live parameter of the message to speed up the deletion of expired messages.
2. *Creation, search, and elimination of tasks in the Task Storage*: the Task Storage has a two-indexed organisation also based on a HashMap and a TreeSet. In this case the hashmap organises sets of tasks by message ID, which provides fast access, $O(\log n)$, to all the tasks related to a message, e.g. to remove them when the message expires. And the TreeSet provides fast creation and access, $O(\log n)$, to the tasks ordered by their release time.
3. *Marshalling and unmarshalling of packets to/from byte array*: the marshall and unmarshall methods of the RWGPacket class have been implemented minimising the creation and destruction of objects. It is also worth mentioning that special classes have been created to support unsigned integers and binary operations to deal with the headers of the network packets.

General Survivability Framework. This module, implemented as a local service, runs on the main thread of the service stack and includes one additional thread for the IDS Engine component. This thread is waken up following the evaluation period of the IDS. The value chosen for this period is a trade-off between the IDS performance and the CPU utilisation.

Each of the four components (as described in Figure 5) that are part of the IDS loop have a well defined interface (IDataSource, IAnomalyDetector, IDiagnoser, and IMitigation) and are easily replaceable. This facilitates the implementation and evaluation of different detection and diagnosis algorithms and mitigation techniques. Other aspects that have been considered are:

1. *Anomaly detection frequency*: in earlier versions of GSF, the anomaly detector was triggered each time a packet was received, and later the alarm were aggregated to issue a verdict. In this implementation, the anomaly detection is triggered periodically, and when a packet is received, only the statistics to feed the detector are updated, reducing the number of operations performed.
2. *Marshalling and unmarshalling of packets to/from byte array*: the Data Source and Mitigation components of the IDS unmarshall the packets using the RWGPacket class. The IDataSource and IMitigation interfaces are independent of the routing protocol and oblivious to this class. Hence, a generic IPacket base class was created to ease the exchange of generic packet objects among the components. Thus, packets are unmarshalled by the Data Source and forwarded in this state to the Mitigation component, avoiding the need to do the operation twice.

4   Performance Evaluation

This section describes the evaluation of the performance of the implemented services by testing over a simple setup with three Android smartphones. The main phones are a LG P990 Optimus 2x and a Samsung I9100 Galaxy S2, both with dual core ARM Cortex-A9 processors at 1Ghz and 1.2Ghz, 512MB and 1GB of RAM, and Android v2.2 and v2.3, respectively. The Samsung and LG phones, with implementations of RWG and GSF, were used to set up an ad hoc network. An application to generate load, which creates messages periodically, were installed in the LG phone. An HTC G1 smartphone and a regular laptop were used to create an attack and monitor the network respectively.

Four tests were performed with different network loads, half of them with GSF enabled and half of them with the drain attack [11]. This attack sends ACK packets with random non-existing identities that trigger the retransmission of the messages that the neighbours store in their buffers. A flood of packets sent to the network and processed by the receivers is created. The generic mitigation described in Cucurull et al. [11] has been implemented. Hence the ACK, OKTF, and BS packets coming from unknown nodes during an alarm period are rejected (known nodes are the ones that sent at least one REQF packet during non alarm periods). This mitigation also includes a limited forwarding of the information contained in the *informed* vectors exchanged, although in this particular case without effect. The mitigation is strictly applied during periods in which an alarm is raised.

All the tests lasted 10 minutes, plus one minute for network initialisation. The last 5 minutes of each test contained the drain attack. The normality models were trained during 5 minutes with each network load. The rate of the attack was set to 2 ACK packets/second. The parameters used for the routing protocol are the ones described in Asplund et al. [1], except the time the protocol waits for ACK messages after sending a REQF. This parameter was set to 0.3 seconds following further studies on the Symbian platform [12]. To keep compatibility with previous implementations, the chosen size for the *informed* vectors was limited to 16 bits each. The time to live of the packets was set to 60 seconds, which scales it to be consistent with earlier simulations. The main parameter of GSF is the evaluation period, which is also used to derive the packet statistics. The value used was 5 seconds, that is enough to get relevant statistics in the network created and provide reasonable attack detection delays given the explained setup.

4.1 Evaluation Scenario

The scenario comprised one phone (LG) sending messages and another one (Samsung) receiving and retransmitting them. The main purpose of these tests is to analyse the overhead of the GSF implementation and demonstrate its function.

The performance tests use four metrics: the CPU usage, the memory usage, the *propagation latency* for a message, and the Packet Transmission Rate (PTR) in the network. The CPU and memory usage were obtained with a small C application installed in the Samsung phone that monitored the process of the service. The CPU usage is read every 250ms and the values shown in the next sections are the average of all the observations. The CPU usage covers both CPU cores, i.e. when only one core is used at 100% the metric shows a total CPU usage of 50%. The propagation latency has been calculated in the LG phone. It is the average time elapsed starting from the time a message is sent until it is received back again because of its dissemination by the other phone. The PTR, which shows the total number of packets exchanged per second in the network, has been calculated with a laptop sniffing the traffic with the Wireshark application.

The tests have been performed in four different settings which are the product of enabling and disabling the GSF and applying or not applying the drain attack.

4.2 CPU and Memory Usage

The system was evaluated for different network loads up to 16 messages per second. The average CPU usage obtained, depicted in Figure 6, shows that:

- The GSF functionality only imposes a slight increment to the CPU usage. GSF, by the virtue of its design, has been optimised to consume as little resources as possible despite the fact that the evaluation interval is kept short for a faster detection latency.
- When GSF is enabled and an attack is introduced, the CPU usage is kept to levels similar to the case without an attack, except for the load of 16 msgs/sec. Instead, when an attack is introduced and GSF is not enabled, the CPU usage easily exceeds the 40%.

The *maximum* CPU usage for the three network loads applied (4, 8, and 16 msgs/sec) with GSF enabled, but without attack, was found to be 20%, 25%, and 84% respectively.

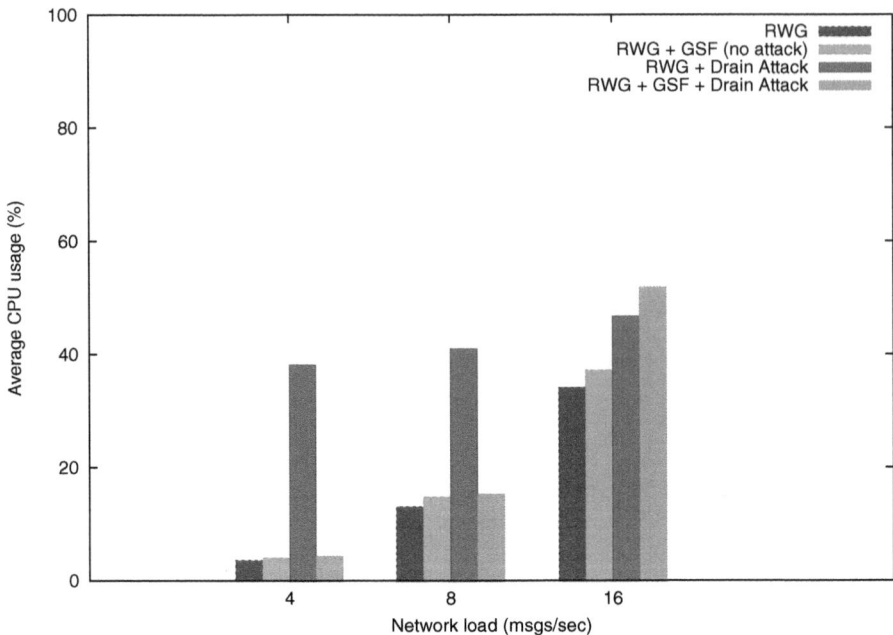

Fig. 6. Average CPU Usage

The CPU usage increase during the attack is a consequence of the high number of packets produced. The packets saturate the service causing message retransmissions that produce more saturation. When the load is set at 16 msgs/sec, the attack produces a cascading chain of retransmissions that saturate the system before giving any chance to GSF to completely mitigate the effects of the attack. Due to this increase of packets (around twice the normal rate) and the overhead of GSF processing them, the CPU usage is a bit higher than when GSF is not enabled.

Another aspect observed is that, although the service stack is composed of many threads, the CPU use is not well-balanced. Only one thread takes care of the received packets, and too many resource consuming operations are assigned to it. When the number of packets exceed a certain limit, one core is used at 100% while the other is idle. It is worth mentioning that most of the CPU usage is due to the cost of processing each packet received in the routing layer.

Regarding the memory, in all the cases the service stack used between 21 and 27 MB. No significant changes were observed either when enabling the GSF or in presence of the drain attack.

4.3   Latency

The propagation latency was evaluated for the same network loads. The results, depicted in Figure 7 with logarithmic scale, show that:

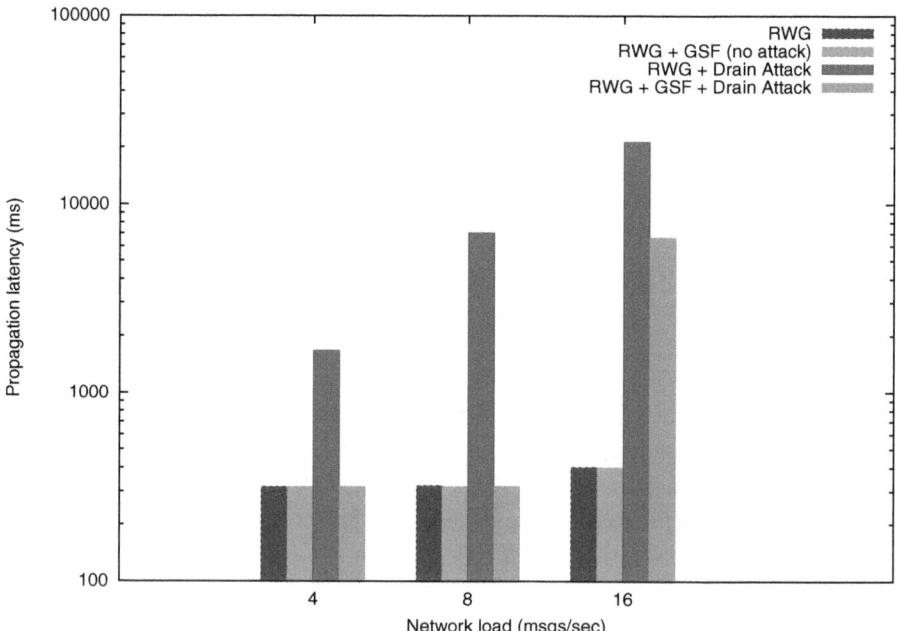

Fig. 7. Message propagation latency

- GSF does not impose an increment to the message latency when it is enabled.
- Similar to observations on the CPU usage, when GSF is enabled and an attack is introduced, the latency is kept close to the one without attack except in the high load case (16 msgs/sec). Instead, if GSF is disabled the latency increases exponentially, because the attack saturates the network with unnecessary packets.

As mentioned before, with the 16 msgs/sec load the whole network is destabilised before GSF can mitigate the attack.

4.4 Packet Transmission Rate

The PTR was also evaluated for the above three loads with similar effects. When measuring PTR we are considering the total load on the network, both data (embedded in the REQF packet of the protocol) and signalling (ACK, OKTF, BS). Figure 8 shows a segment of a curve that represents the packet rate observed under different loads of data with the GSF enabled and the drain attack.

The behaviour is analogous to the one observed in simulation studies [11]. The normal rate without attack, until 360 seconds when the attack starts, is around 16, 30, and 100 pkts/sec for the loads of 4, 8, and 16 msgs/sec respectively. When the attack starts it increases to 400, 750, and 800 pkts/sec respectively. But, after 5 seconds when the attack is detected, and matching with the evaluation interval, the rate decreases to around 20, 40, and 200 pkts/sec because of

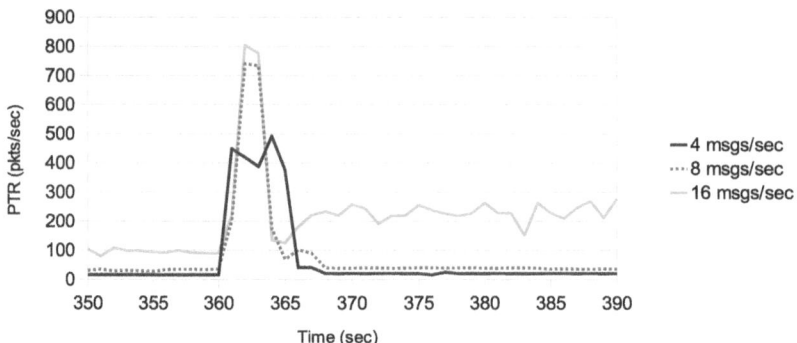

Fig. 8. Packet transmission rate

the mitigation applied. These rates, after around 60 seconds, go down close to the initial levels, except for the 16 msgs/sec load. This difference of rate before the attack and during mitigation is inherent to RWG and due to some retransmissions of messages lost during the traffic peak produced by the attack in the first 5 seconds.

5   Related Work

With the large number of smartphones sold [13], the security aspects have become matter of concern. Recently, many studies [4,14,15] are devoted to the analysis of smartphone security. Shabtai et al. [15] study the security mechanisms integrated in the Android devices. They also include a taxonomy of the identified threats and possible types of solutions. These include network malicious activity and draining mobile device's resources as threats and anomaly detection as a potential solution among others. In Android most of the intrusion detection work is devoted to malware detection (for an overview see [16]). Nevertheless, the mechanisms applied share many characteristics with the ones applied for mobile ad hoc networks.

Cheng et al. [5] present SmartSiren, a collaborative mechanism for virus detection and mitigation on smartphones. The system detects viruses spread via SMS/MMS and Bluetooth by monitoring the messaging activity.

Bose et al. [6] propose a behaviour-based malware detector for smartphones. It monitors the behaviour of the applications, taking into account the temporal patterns of the system calls and events, creating behaviour signatures. The signatures are compared and classified against a database that contains samples of fair applications and malware.

Schmidt et al. [7] present a technique for malware detection for smartphones. The work is focused on the selection and management of features to monitor the phone. The system is composed of a client (for Symbian S60 and Windows Mobile 6), installed in the phone. It periodically collects and sends a number of features to a server that analyses them with existing knowledge-based learning algorithms.

Kim et al. [8] describe a misuse detection approach based on monitoring the power consumption of smartphones. A database is populated with power signatures of fair applications and malware. They propose a two component approach that includes a client in the phone that collects the signatures and a data analyser, which can be in the phone or in a server, that performs the detection. The system is implemented over Windows Mobile 5.0.

Shabtai et al. [9] present Andromaly, a behavioural host-based malware detection system for Android devices. The system is composed of many components grouped as feature extractors, processors (for detection and analysis), main service, and graphical user interface. They perform extensive tests with six different machine learning classification algorithms and three feature selection algorithms to study the obtained detection performance. This paper shares the philosophy of our work, but it is applied to malware instead of network attacks.

Our approach, compared to Cheng et al. [5] and Schmidt et al. [7], is not dependent on external servers and, as opposed to Bose et al. [6], it is fully implemented within the smartphone. These two characteristics are very important in an ad hoc environment in which communications are not reliable. The approach also includes mitigation, usually not present in other works [7,8,6,9]. As shown in Section 4 the cost of our solution is not expensive in terms of CPU or memory overhead. A complete resource usage evaluation, as covered by our work, is not usually provided [5,6,7,8].

6   Conclusions

This paper described the design of an intrusion detection service for Android smartphones applied to network routing level. The design emphasises the modularity of the service to facilitate its implementation with different routing protocols and with different detection algorithms and attack mitigation techniques.

An implementation of the service on top of a dissemination protocol for intermittently-connected networks was developed. Its performance was tested and analysed using several metrics, such as the CPU and memory usage, the rate of packets exchanged in the network, and the latencies to propagate the messages. These tests demonstrated that the intrusion detection service produces a low overhead on the phone and the network, and confirmed the reduction of the impact of attacks. The code for the implementation can be shared in the context of research cooperation. However, due to reuse of some parts of the code in a critical infrastructure project, the code is not public.

Further work can be done along two different lines. While the implementation has provided evidence for the feasibility of the deployment of a survivability framework, a more comprehensive implementation would need to address diagnoses of different known attacks and mitigations thereto. At the same time larger testbeds, with tens of smartphones, can be created to evaluate the capacity of the GSF to detect and mitigate attacks on a more realistic testbed. Further work could also include more detailed studies of the energy consumption and energy profiling of the whole service.

Acknowledgements. This work was supported by a grant from the Swedish Civil Contingencies Agency (MSB) within the project "Hastily Formed Networks" [3], and the national Graduate school in computer science (CUGS). We want also thank Ekhiotz Jon Vergara and Mikael Asplund for cooperation based on earlier works.

References

1. Asplund, M., Nadjm-Tehrani, S.: A partition-tolerant manycast algorithm for disaster area networks. In: IEEE Symposium on Reliable Distributed Systems, pp. 156–165. IEEE Computer Society, Los Alamitos (2009)
2. Vergara, E.J., Nadjm-Tehrani, S., Asplund, M., Zurutuza, U.: Resource footprint of a manycast protocol implementation on multiple mobile platforms. In: The Fifth International Conference on Next Generation Mobile Applications, Services and Technologies, NGMAST 2011. IEEE (September 2011)
3. Hastily Formed Networks, `http://www.ida.liu.se/~rtslab/HFN`
4. Landman, M.: Managing smart phone security risks. In: Information Security Curriculum Development Conference, InfoSecCD 2010, pp. 145–155. ACM, New York (2010)
5. Cheng, J., Wong, S.H., Yang, H., Lu, S.: SmartSiren: virus detection and alert for smartphones. In: Proceedings of the 5th International Conference on Mobile Systems, Applications and Services, MobiSys 2007, pp. 258–271. ACM, New York (2007)
6. Bose, A., Hu, X., Shin, K.G., Park, T.: Behavioral detection of malware on mobile handsets. In: Proceeding of the 6th International Conference on Mobile Systems, Applications, and Services, MobiSys 2008, pp. 225–238. ACM, New York (2008)
7. Schmidt, A.D., Peters, F., Lamour, F., Albayrak, S.: Monitoring smartphones for anomaly detection. In: Proceedings of the 1st International Conference on MOBILe Wireless MiddleWARE, Operating Systems, and Applications, MOBILWARE 2008, pp. 40:1–40:6. ICST (Institute for Computer Sciences, Social-Informatics and Telecommunications Engineering), Brussels (2007)
8. Kim, H., Smith, J., Shin, K.G.: Detecting energy-greedy anomalies and mobile malware variants. In: Proceeding of the 6th International Conference on Mobile Systems, Applications, and Services, MobiSys 2008, pp. 239–252. ACM, New York (2008)
9. Shabtai, A., Kanonov, U., Elovici, Y., Glezer, C., Weiss, Y.: Andromaly: a behavioral malware detection framework for Android devices. Journal of Intelligent Information Systems, 1–30 (2011)
10. Xenakis, C., Panos, C., Stavrakakis, I.: A comparative evaluation of intrusion detection architectures for mobile ad hoc networks. Computers & Security 30(1), 63–80 (2011)
11. Cucurull, J., Asplund, M., Nadjm-Tehrani, S.: Anomaly Detection and Mitigation for Disaster Area Networks. In: Jha, S., Sommer, R., Kreibich, C. (eds.) RAID 2010. LNCS, vol. 6307, pp. 339–359. Springer, Heidelberg (2010)

12. Vergara, E.J.: Implementation of a manycast protocol for intermittently connected mobile ad hoc networks in disaster areas, Master Thesis. Linköping University (2010), http://urn.kb.se/resolve?urn=urn:nbn:se:liu:diva-58603
13. IDC: Press Release (June 2011),
    http://www.idc.com/getdoc.jsp?containerId=prUS22871611
14. Enck, W., Ongtang, M., McDaniel, P.: Understanding Android security. IEEE Security Privacy 7(1), 50–57 (2009)
15. Shabtai, A., Fledel, Y., Kanonov, U., Elovici, Y., Dolev, S., Glezer, C.: Google android: A comprehensive security assessment. IEEE Security Privacy 8(2), 35–44 (2010)
16. Burguera, I., Zurutuza, U., Nadjm-Tehrani, S.: Crowdroid: Behavior-based malware detection system for Android. In: Workshop on Security and Privacy in Smartphones and Mobile Devices, SPSM 2011. ACM (October 2011)

Mental Voting Booths

Jérôme Dossogne[1] and Frédéric Lafitte[2]

[1] Université Libre de Bruxelles, Department of Computer Science,
Boulevard du Triomphe - CP212, 1050 Brussels, Belgium
jdossogn@ulb.ac.be
[2] Royal Military Academy, Department of Mathematics,
Renaissancelaan 30, 1000 Brussels, Belgium
frederic.lafitte@rma.ac.be

Abstract. In this paper, we introduce the notion of mental voting booths, i.e., a building block for voting schemes that provides remote voters with similar protection as that offered by physical voting booths, essentially protecting them from over-the-shoulder coercion attacks (shoulder-surfing). We introduce a framework to model voting booths and formulate a property of the modelled booths that is sufficient to ensure over-the-shoulder coercion resistance. Next, we propose an example of mental booth that is simple enough to be used by any voter without prior training and show that an execution of the remote booth in the presence of the adversary is equivalent to that execution in his absence (e.g., inside a physical booth). The only cost lies in the use of an untappable channel in order to transmit a piece of information before the voting phase. Mental booths also allow for the voter to safely delegate his own voice to an untrusted person while still being able to verify that the untrusted person followed his instructions while voting.

Keywords: remote voting, i-voting, e-voting, home-voting, shoulder surfing, over-the-shoulder, coercion resistance, voting booth.

1 Introduction

Electronic voting (e-voting) is a growing trend [34] and a growing concern. A key issue slowing the adoption of such technologies, in particular remote e-voting [32,15](e.g. Internet voting [20,24]) is trust. The security of the different proposed schemes often relies on cryptographic primitives and protocols which are not easily understood by the majority of the designated users. This lack of understanding and errors occurring in the implementation of proven protocols can lead to a growing mistrust. However, these are not the only factors slowing the deployment of e-voting. Indeed, factors like the lack of physical voting booths protecting the user from coercion[1] while he votes is also a recurring argument against remote e-voting [20]. The fact that electoral authorities do not have control over all the equipment used by voters is perhaps the main challenge faced

---

[1] Nowadays, a physical voting booth does not prevent a voter from using his cellphone to take a picture of his vote in order to sell it afterwards.

P. Laud (Ed.): NordSec 2011, LNCS 7161, pp. 82–97, 2012.

by remote e-voting schemes. In this paper, we present a technique allowing for a voter to be protected from coercion [22,14] by creating what we call a mental voting booth which compensates for the lack of physical voting booths in the context of remote e-voting. The idea is to create a voting interface for the user such that no attacker can distinguish between a vote for candidate 1 from a vote for candidate 2 by observing the voter's interactions with the interface (over-the-shoulder attacks [11], also known as shoulder surfing [33]) or by operating the computer system on behalf of the voter.

Separation of duty. In any scheme where a voter is associated to an anonymous identifier, and the votes are encrypted, it is obvious that an authority who owns both the decryption key and the identity of the voter has the possibility of coercing the voter. Therefore, it is imperative to use the separation-of-duty concept in order to distribute the different responsibilities between different authorities and to limit the required communications between them as much as possible. This would force the authorities to collude in order to coerce the voter. A rapid separation-of-duty could be the following:

1. Key generation office: generates the secret keys and anonymous identifiers for the voters and the counting office. Transmits the keys and the associated identifier to each party.
2. Polling office: gathers all the votes and corresponding identifiers, transmits them after the election to the counting office.
3. Counting office: establishes the result of the tally using the data sent by the polling office and from the key generation office.
4. The voter(s): uses his identifier and his key given by the key generation office to vote.

With this separation of duties, neither the key generation office nor the polling office can learn for which candidate a particular user voted for (unless authorities collude). As mentioned earlier, the purpose of this paper is to present techniques allowing a better protection against shoulder surfing that could be reused in other voting scheme lacking this property.

Mental booths. In the following, we restrict security analysis to the security of the voting booth. We define a voting booth simply as an interface that offers limited actions to the voter, each action generating a feedback. Our goal is to show that remote voting can be made as secure as voting from a physical booth. This assertion is formally established using behavioural equivalence between two executions: a honest execution of the interface inside a physical booth, and an adversarial execution of the same interface from a remote location. A voting booth that satisfies this requirement offers over-the-shoulder coercion resistance against an adversary that monitors executions of the interface during the entire voting procedure: honest executions are indistinguishable from executions that pretend to be honest. The technique and security analysis are rather simple and easy to understand.

Related work. None of the following schemes JCJ/Civitas [12,22], Helios [1,2], protects voters against over-the-shoulder attacks by a visible attacker (a relative or a coercer watching or influencing the voter during the voting phase) or an invisible one (malware such as keyloggers [20]). The recent Selections [11] does provide over-the-shoulder coercion-resistance against a visible attacker by establishing panic passwords between the voter and the authority once with an untappable channel. In our case, we aim to protect the user also against an invisible attacker (e.g. malicious code) and currently require the same use of an untappable channel. Grünauer[2] provides a scheme stated as keylogger resistant and based on TAN (transaction numbers) which requires that the users memorizes a number associated to each choice. Their solution, as the paper indicates, is acceptable only for small organizations where the number of voters and the number of candidates is small. Compared to the approaches mentioned above, our solution is scalable, protects against a stronger adversary, and requires less effort from the voter. Our proposal could reminisce of independently developed systems such as CodeVoting (see SureVote [9,10,21]), maybe of Bingo Voting [7] or more exactly as an evolution of a combination of both systems. The following paragraphs describe those techniques.

SureVote. SureVote is based on the idea of supplying the voter with a list of "sure codes" and "vote codes" per candidate in a polling place, then the voter uses the vote code associated to the candidate of his choice to vote and receives back the associated sure code. Therefore, the voter is ensured that his ballot has been correctly lodged, regardless of any actions performed by any intermediary between voter and authority. In other words, this system ensures only the voter's ability to detect modifications made to the ballot he sent and does not protect him from coercion against an over-the-shoulder adversary: the attacker could very well request the printed list and observe him while he votes. If the list is never printed, then the voter has to remember two random values per candidate, which prevents the scheme from being scalable.

CodeVoting. CodeVoting is introduced in [21] as an extension of SureVote that offers to distribute the codes via a physical "code card" (which is common for certain netbanking services [17]) and to use a smartcard reader in order to translate the codes on the code card into vote codes. However, their system suffers several drawbacks. Since a code card is involved, their system does not provide any protection against shoulder surfing (the attacker might read the card). Moreover, their system requires an infrastructure for the management of Code-Cards, VoteCard (the smartcard), and also a smartcard reader per voter and a certified ad hoc smartcard reader-printer (that could be shared in a public place). The authors state that the trust in the machine is moved to the smartcard / smartcard-reader. A smartcard could very well be easier to check than a computer, but would still require a very high level of expertise for the average voter and would force him to trust experts. Another drawback is the possibility of a successful "mistrust attack" regardless of the countermeasure proposed in

---

[2] http://easyvote-app.sourceforge.net

[21]. Indeed, the authors argue that in order to create mistrust and confusion, malware could make the user believe that the procedure failed (while it did not) which would lead the voter to retry. The server would then refuse the new vote since a vote was already received, thus damaging the trust placed in the voting system. The authors then state that if the system allows the voter to cast several votes this attack would not be a problem. However, firstly nothing prevents the malware to continue lying to the voter and to state that the procedure failed, and secondly the malware could very well simulate the behavior of a voting system where the voter can only vote once. Since such an attack aims for trust, a voter would have either to believe that the voting system works fine and that he is under attack or that the system fails to behave correctly. Since both situations are possible, this ambiguity is already a successful attack on trust. Basically, our approach can also be seen as a code sheet, but unlike [21], has the following properties: it is scalable, does not require dedicated hardware nor user training, and most importantly allows for creating an over-the-shoulder coercion free voting environment.

Bingo Voting. Our proposal also appears to have common grounds with Bingo Voting, a voting scheme where the user receives one dummy random number per candidates and later, at the moment he votes in a physical voting booth, an additional effective random number. The voter then associates all the dummy numbers to the candidates, except for the candidate of his choice. For that candidate, the effective number is used, which is distinct from all the dummy numbers. The voter then leaves the voting booth with a receipt for his vote, free from coercion from an attacker since the latter cannot know which of the numbers is the effective one. Then, the list of all unused dummy values is published along with zero knowledge correctness proofs used during the protocol. To summarize the common grounds, both approaches rely on the use of cryptographically secure random number generation, both have an available implementation in Java, and both associate a number to each candidate in each ballot. On the other hand, Bingo Voting was created for local e-voting protocols while our proposal is designed for remote e-voting (and thus also works in the local case), therefore, Bingo Voting did not have the need and thus does not protect against over-the-shoulder attacks. The correctness of the proposal in [7] is ensured only if each voter verifies a cryptographic proof in order to dismiss fake ballots. The biggest difference is that in order to provide coercion protection, the scheme relies on the voting machine. It must not be tampered with and must guarantee the secrecy of votes. Likewise the voting booth has to be secured, e.g. no hidden cameras may be able to monitor the voting while our technique is designed on purpose to prevent such requirement, considered as an unrealistic hypothesis. In our case, the voting machines sanity is not important to protect the voter from coercion. Furthermore, due to the lack of such a requirement our scheme is immune to all the attacks allowing coercion on the voter due to a tampered voting machine or booth described as effective against their scheme in [7]. Also, Bingo Voting requires additional devices such as a trusted and certified printer.

Contribution. The purpose of this paper is to present a building block used to create a coercion-free voting environment that can be combined to existing electronic voting schemes. The environment is coercion-free even if the coercer is allowed to monitor the entire voting procedure (over-the-shoulder). Protection against this strong opponent is based on the assumption that the voter and the authority distributing the secret keys are allowed to communicate once via an untappable channel, before the voting phase (e.g., at registration). In order to allow the voter to dispute the published results of the voting procedure, a signed receipt of his ballot should be transmitted by the polling office to the voter at the end of the voting phase. Obviously, in order to create an acceptable remote voting platform, other techniques should also be used to provide other required properties [31] such as the possibility to vote anonymously [16] or verifiability [5]. As with the other mentioned schemes, the technique we propose does not protect the user from an attacker denying him access to a computer or rendering his ballots void by entering random values as input to the voting system. Also, obvious as it is, it does not protect from an attacker deducing that a coerced voter did not follow his instructions if, for example, not a single voter did vote for the attacker's choice. In such case, if the results are published, the attacker will obviously know that the voter cheated him or that the system did malfunction. To summarize, our mental booth has the following properties:

- The voter obtains the guarantee (i.e. receipt) that his vote has been correctly received by the polling office.
- The voter cannot convince the adversary of whom he voted for by using his receipt.
- The coercer cannot force the user to cancel a vote, nor to vote for a particular candidate, even if the user reveals his secrets and lets the adversary vote on his behalf. That is, the adversary cannot tell apart fake and valid secrets.
- If for some reason (e.g., disability) the voter is unable to vote, he can safely delegate his voice.
- Mental booths can be plugged into existing e-voting schemes in order to achieve remote voting with equivalent security.
- The only effort required from the voter is to remember a number in $\mathbb{Z}_n$ where n is linked to the security parameter.

As suggested in section 4, one can come up with many enhancements of this proposal in order to increase usability by using, instead of numbers in $\mathbb{Z}_n$, representations such as pictures, sounds, etc. and requiring from the user only his ability to remember the chosen secret after seeing (or hearing) it among others. An implementation of an i-voting scheme using a variant of the presented technique (and more to provide other desirable properties such as anonymity and verifiability) is available at `http://qualsec.ulb.ac.be`.

Outline. Section 2 starts by over-viewing definitions of coercion-resistance. Next, the notion of mental booth is introduced and a property necessary for over-the-shoulder coercion resistance is formulated. Section 3 proposes a simple example that is shown to be over-the-shoulder coercion-resistant, according to the definition given in section 2. A variant of this scheme is proposed in section 4 with the aim to increase usability. Section 4 also discusses the possibility of vote delegation. Finally, section 5 concludes and discusses to what extent our solution also applies to non-remote voting.

2 Definitions

Examples of security requirements for e-voting protocols are privacy, accuracy, fairness, robustness, universal verifiability, incoercibility and receipt-freeness [30,28]. In this work, we focus on coercion-resistance, a property that is linked to receipt-freeness [6] and for which different definitions can be found in the literature. We start by over-viewing some current definitions and notice that they do not capture over-the-shoulder coercion resistance. Then, we formulate a property of remote booths that is necessary for protection against over-the-shoulder coercers. A *mental booth* is simply a remote booth that satisfies this property, thus offering coercion resistance against an adversary that monitors and influences the honest voter at any point of the protocol (possibly during the whole execution). This allows to protect the voter from malware that might be present in his machine, but also against an adversary who uses the machine on behalf of the voter.

Coercion-resistance. Several definitions for coercion resistance have been proposed in the literature. Juels *et al.* define coercion resistance as the following four requirements [5,22].

1. Receipt-freeness. A coercer cannot force a voter to cast a certain vote and to provide a receipt that would certify his vote.
2. Immunity to simulation attacks. A coercer cannot exploit secrets revealed by the voter since he cannot tell apart real and fake secrets.
3. Immunity to forced abstention attacks. A coercer should not be able to tell whether a particular voter has voted or not, so that he cannot force the voter to abstain.
4. Immunity to randomization attacks. A voter cannot be forced to divulge or nullify his vote by using random messages chosen by the coercer.

However, they assume a remote voting setting where the machines used to cast a vote are not compromised [22]. On the other hand, they take into account forced abstention attacks. As noted in [29], anonymous channels are necessary to achieve immunity to forced abstention since monitoring the (lack of) activity of a non-anonymous channel allows the adversary to make sure that the voter did abstain as instructed. Moran and Naor [29] define receipt-freeness based on an ideal voting functionality, building upon the definition of coercion proposed by Canetti and Gennaro in the context of multiparty computation [8]. However, their solution is tailored for settings where a physical booth is available: they assume the existence of an untappable channel between voter and authority during the voting phase. This assumption is also made in [14] where the authors formally define coercion-resistance and receipt-freeness in terms of process algebra (applied π-calculus).

The difference between their two definitions lies in the ability of the adversary to interact with the voter during the voting phase. That is, in [14], both notions capture the property that a voter cannot cooperate with a coercer in order to prove which candidate he voted for. But in the weaker notion of receipt-freeness, the adversary can only interact with the user before and after he voted but not during the voting phase. The intuition that receipt-freeness is necessary to achieve coercion-resistance has been formally confirmed in [14].

Over-the-shoulder coercion-resistance. In the case of remote voting, in particular Internet voting, an additional security requirement arises: resistance against shoulder-surfing [20]. To the best of our knowledge, very few schemes [11] deal with this class of attack. In [11] the voter chooses a password and also a set of *panic passwords* allowing the voter to fake a session when coerced by a visible adversary. As stated in [11], this solution requires some user training and also requires the voter to remember a *set* of passwords. Finally, one major drawback of this solution is that if the voter is unaware of the presence of the adversary (e.g. keylogger), he will use his actual password and allow the adversary to replay it.

Assumptions. The only secret involved in the use of the voting interface is a symmetric key $k \in \{0,1\}^\eta$ where $\eta \in \mathbb{N}$ is the security parameter. This key could be chosen by the key generation authority and communicated to the voter via an untappable channel. The authority then associates an anonymous identifier to the key and communicates it to the user. In practice, the exchange can be done physically upon registration of the voter. In order to provide over-the-shoulder coercion-resistance against the adversary described above, we base our scheme on the requirement that if a user reveals his key k, it is impossible for him to convince the adversary that it is the right one. That is, no matter how the adversary interacts with the voting booth, he must not be able to determine if a revealed key is correct, thus preventing vote selling. The adversary can still guess the key with negligible probability $2^{-\eta}$.

Modeling the booth. We model a voting booth as an interface that offers limited actions to the voter (e.g. vote, re-vote, verify, etc.) each generating a feedback. This definition can be instantiated rigorously using different formalisms. In the next section, we model the booth as a finite state machine whose state transitions are triggered by the available actions. It is assumed that the user successfully identified himself to the interface using his anonymous identifier. This opens a new session between the voter and the interface that can be secured according to the underlying voting scheme (we focus on the voting booth that can be built on top of this scheme). For any set of actions, the corresponding feedbacks must be chosen so that no adversary can tell if the voter followed his instructions or if he just pretended to do so. If so, the resulting interface is coercion resistant against over-the-shoulder adversaries. This leads to the following security definition.

Security definition. The security definition is based on the following intuition. Any *dishonest* execution starting from any *honest* state of the system, should be indistinguishable from an *honest* execution starting from the initial state (i.e.

first use of the interface). The set of dishonest executions is modeled by requiring that the actions do not make use of the secret k. On the contrary, the set of honest executions are defined such that all actions use k. That is, we assume a honest user always uses the correct key when voting. This approximation of honest vs. dishonest executions is sound: an honest execution cannot be considered dishonest, and a dishonest execution is considered honest with probability negligible in the security parameter. The rigorous meanings of "indistinguishable", "execution", and "state" can be adapted to the formalism underlying the proof. In the next section, the proposed system is modeled as a labeled transition system and "indistinguishability" is established by means of trace equivalence in a rather exhaustive manner.

3   Example of Mental Booth

We propose a simple mental booth for the case of "choose 1 out of l" elections. Before defining the interface, we start by describing the different phases of the voting procedure (see figure 1). Keeping in mind the objective and scope of this paper, we will not provide the same amount of detail for each phase.

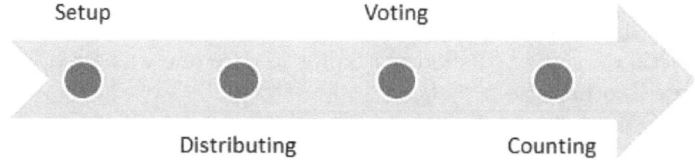

Fig. 1. Phases of a voting procedure

- Set-up: The key generation office creates random pairs of the form (id, k) where id is an anonymous identifier and k a secret integer in $\mathbb{Z}_n$.
- Distributing: the random pairs are (encrypted then) transmitted to the poll office. Upon registration of a voter, the key generation office picks at random a pair (id, k) and transmits it to the voter using an untappable channel. This phase is the only moment when the voter should not be observable from the attacker. Using designated verifier signatures [16,13,26], it is possible to provide an additional signed receipt. This signature should be verifiable only by the voter and a judge (or by extension a (group of) witness(es) considered as legitimate support to the eyes of a judge) in order to provide the voter with a proof in case of dispute later on. Of course, by doing so, the witness gains the same power of coercion against the voter as the authority of distribution.
- Voting: during this phase, the voter goes and identifies himself to the interface (e.g. a website). The voter is asked to associate a distinct number from $\mathbb{Z}_n$ to each candidate. If the voter wishes to select candidate 2, he associates k to that candidate and random numbers to other candidates. By doing so the polling office is able to determine which candidate the anonymous voter id voted for. On reception of the vote, the polling office provides a signed receipt of the casted ballot.

– Counting: the tally is created based on the casted votes, the associated anonymous identifiers, the secret keys and associated identifiers.

Let us now describe the actions in more detail. We assume without loss of generality that the list of candidates is ordered, so that a vector of l numbers is sufficient to make the ballot unambiguous.

newvote($k_1, \ldots, k_l$) In order to cast a ballot, the voter associates one integer $k_i \in \mathbb{Z}_n$ to each candidate. If $k_i = k$ for some i in $\{1, \ldots, l\}$, then the vote is validated for candidate c_i. Otherwise, the vote is discarded. In the case of a malformed ballot (e.g. vectors do not have the same length, or some components are equal), the user receives a feedback $\otimes$, otherwise, he receives a feedback $\top$ meaning that the message was successfully sent and the corresponding vote received and saved (possibly overwriting a previous vote).

receipt($k_1, \ldots, k_l$) This function can be used to terminate a session. The input must again be a vector of l integers in $\mathbb{Z}_n$. If the vector contains k, the message is considered honest, otherwise dishonest. In the case of an honest action, the interface checks if an honest ballot has already been received and replies either with a signature (receipt) r if the ballot was found and with a feedback $\perp$ otherwise. Similarly, if the action is not honest, the interface returns either a signed (dishonest) ballot in case one was already received or a message $\perp$ otherwise.

Practical considerations. Clearly, it is unlikely that users left on their own will enter values appropriately. For example, a user unaware of the attacker's presence might start assigning his secret number to the selected candidate, and only then assign the number zero (for example) to all the other candidates. This issue can be prevented using an appropriate implementation of the interface. For example, the implementation must forbid duplicated values and must allow the user to associate a number to the next candidate only when numbers have already been assigned to all previous candidates.

Concrete values for the security parameter can only be given according to a specific application. However, in our case, using brute force to guess-determine the secret is not a threat since the attack cannot be carried off-line. On-line guessing are easy to prevent using an exponential backoff/delay. Furthermore, the interface is built so that it is impossible to determine whether a guess is correct or not. Therefore, depending on the election, the secret to memorize could be shorter than a PIN code.

Remark. In order to illustrate what could possibly go wrong, let us assume an attack where the voter told the adversary his number is k' when in fact it is k. Assume the adversary sends the ballot $(k', 22, 38)$. Then a message receipt($k', 1, 2$) should return r' whereas a message receipt($22, 1, 2$) should return $\perp$. However, the interface is unable to know which of the numbers $k', 22$ or 28 the adversary is using as k. This would allow the adversary to identify a user that pretended to reveal the correct secret k. In order to exclude this possibility, the interface must reply with r' if any of the numbers in a message **receipt** were associated to the ballot. Therefore, it is necessary that the interface adopts the same behavior when receiving an *honest* ballot. That is, after sending the ballot (k, k_1, k_2), a call to the function **receipt** with argument k should yield the same result as with argument k_1 or k_2, even if the interface does know which integer is the correct one. This requirement implies that the probability of an adversary using the secret number moves from $2^{-\eta}$ to $l2^{-\eta}$.

Defining the interface. The feedbacks returned by the interface are determined by the following pseudo-code where it is assumed that the interface uses variable hb (db) to store the last received honest (dishonest) ballot. We abuse somewhat the notation by writing $v \cup w$ ($v \cap w$) for the set containing all components of vectors v, w (common components of v, w). Also, for the sake of clarity, we omit the pseudo code for indicating a malformed ballot (feedback $\otimes$). This has no impact on the proof since the interface does not use k to realize that a ballot is malformed.

- Procedure **newvote** on well formed input $K \in \mathbb{Z}_n^l$:
    1. if $k \in K$ then
       hb $= K$; return $\top$
    2. if $k \notin K$ then
       db $= K$; return $\top$
- Procedure **receipt** on well formed input $K \in \mathbb{Z}_n^l$:
    1. if $k \in K$ then
       if hb $\neq \emptyset$ and $K \cap$ hb $\neq \emptyset$ then return r
       else return $\perp$
    2. if $k \notin K$ then
       if $K \cap ($hb $\cup$ db$) \neq \emptyset$ then return r'
       else return $\perp$

Security Proof

According to the pseudocode above, the interface can only be in one the following states.

- A initial state, no ballots received
- B received honest ballot but no dishonest one
- C received dishonest ballot but no honest one
- D received both honest and dishonest ballots

The interface can be defined by a labeled transition system, i.e., a directed graph whose nodes correspond to states and edges are labeled by actions that trigger state transitions. Our interface uses the following actions and feedbacks.

Actions	Feedbacks
v honest vote (with k)	$\top$ vote received
v' dishonest vote (without k)	$\perp$ no vote received
c honest check (with k)	r receipt for honest vote
c' dishonest check (without k)	r' receipt for dishonest vote

In order to comply with the formal definition of trace equivalence (e.g. see [27]), the transitions should be given in the following form.

$$(A, v) \xrightarrow{\top} \{(B, v), (B, v'), (B, c), (B, c')\}$$
$$(A, v') \xrightarrow{\top} \{(C, v), (C, v'), (C, c), (C, c')\}$$
$$\text{etc.}$$

Based on those transitions, two graphs can be defined, one representing all honest executions, the other all dishonest ones. The two graphs are then trace equivalent if all paths (transitions) have the same labels. However, for our purpose it is convenient to assume that the feedback is part of the state (see figure). For example, performing action v from state $(A, \bot)$ yields the observable feedback $\top$ and executing c from the same state returns feedback $\bot$. Thus, equivalence holds when honest and dishonest paths generate the same feedbacks.

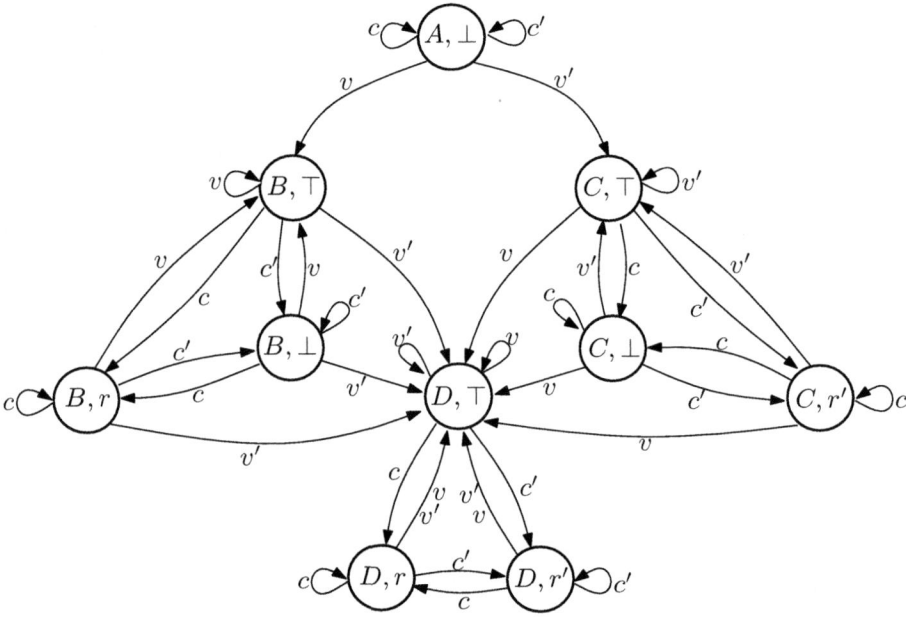

In the graph, adversarial (honest) executions follow arcs labeled with actions v' or c' (v or c). The initial state of a dishonest execution can be any honest state and that execution must be equivalent with an honest execution that starts at state $(A, \bot)$. That is, for any honest initial state s and for any sequence of actions a' in $\{v', c'\}^*$, the execution of a' from state s produces the same feedbacks as the corresponding honest actions a in $\{v, c\}^*$ executed from state $(A, \bot)$. This equivalence can be tested exhaustively in $O(H \cdot L \cdot 2^L)$ where H is the number of honest states and L the length of the longest cycle that visits each node once. The probability of the adversary using k is $xl/2^{-\eta}$ where x is the number of actions executed, l the number of candidates, and η the security parameter

$(\eta = \log_2(n))$. In this rather small example, one can check manually that the executions are trace equivalent.

4   Increasing Usability

Electronic voting must be accessible to the widest possible range of users. Keeping this in mind, this section proposes an alternative version of the mental booth introduced in the previous section. In this version, the interface displays m values in $\mathbb{Z}_n$ that the voter has to bind to candidates, including the secret value k. Actually, the integers in $\mathbb{Z}_n$ can be mapped to representations that are easier to remember (e.g. pictures). The voter would only have to associate the given representations to the given candidates in order to vote. This has several implications:

1. The probability of an attacker submitting a ballot supporting his choice is now $1/m$, where m is the number of values displayed by the interface. Also, the probability of casting a valid ballot for the wrong candidate is l/m.
2. It is likely that, in the previous version, a user would introduce "fake values" that are not distributed uniformly over $\mathbb{Z}_n$. Forcing him to choose values among truly random ones might actually increase security.
3. Since the user only has to associate values with choices, there should not be any type (word, number, picture, music) of value unusable.
4. The user must not memorize his secret value, he is only required to identify it among other values.

An attacker could ask the voter to reveal his secret value before interacting with the booth. If afterwards the revealed value is not displayed by the interface, the adversary would know that the voter lied. Therefore, it is imperative to always display a fixed set of values and to ask the voter to memorize one of those values in addition to his secret k. By doing so, the voter has the possibility to reveal one of the $m - 1$ values that will appear on the webpage. If the adversary asks the voter to reveal both remembered values, the voter can safely argue that he only memorized the correct one.

Description. We will now describe this variant by describing each phase of figure 1 for an election with l choices.

- Set-up: For each voter, the authority chooses m random values and selects one of them as the voter's secret value. This value will form the shared secret key. This authority has to transmit the list of values for each voter to the authority in charge of the website who would then not learn any more information than the attacker would.
- Distributing: This phase is the same as the corresponding phase in section 3.
- Voting: During this phase, the voter goes and identifies himself with the website of the election and is shown the list of candidates along with m values. He is then asked to associate one different value to each candidate. He will associate his secret value to his choice and if and attacker is trying to

coerce him, he will associate one of the other values to the attackers choice. Then, the voter submits his vote. By doing so the polling office associates the casted vote and the anonymous identifier of the voter. On reception of the vote, the polling office provides a signed receipt of the casted vote.

– Counting: This phase is the same as the corresponding phase in section 3.

Absentee ballots. A property of mental booths is that it offers the possibility to delegate votes. This property offers an appropriate alternative when one does not wish to trade security against usability. An absentee could reveal his secret value to an honest person and ask that person to vote on his behalf. The receipt would convince an honest absentee that his vote is in the ballot box. Furthermore, using the scheme from section 3 or 4, a voter could ask someone to cast a vote on his behalf without revealing the selected candidate. Of course, a vote buyer cannot exploit this vote delegation, since the buyer has no guarantee that the vote is valid (i.e. it is not worth buying). This feature could be an important improvement over existing electronic voting systems (remote or local) for disabled persons currently forced to rely on the honesty of a helper.

Remarks. In order to prevent a user from voting (forced abstention), the attacker has to keep him under his surveillance during the whole voting period in order to ensure that the voter does not choose any of the values to associate to candidates. Even then, the attacker would still not be able to make him vote for a particular candidate but only to deny him the right to vote. As mentioned earlier, we do not consider forced abstention attacks also because it would require the use of an anonymous channel. The mentioned technique requires an untappable channel once during a brief period of time. If such a channel could be materialized by a permanently stationed distribution booth available to any citizen in the case of a regional election, such a channel would require a real identity and presence (by opposition to a virtual one) and thus could not suit the needs of virtual communities and their elections. Finally, if a voter forgets his secret, he should restart the distribution procedure. This should not have any impact in legislation where every voter is legally obliged to vote (e.g. Belgium) since only voting without using his secret would be considered as a legitimate blank vote.

5   Conclusions

In this paper, we present a technique that allows a voter to cast a ballot in front of an attacker without allowing the latter to learn information about the selected candidate nor to force the voter to vote for the attacker's choice. It turns out that the technique also allows a user to delegate his vote: by instructing someone how to complete the ballot and asking him to return a receipt, the voter is ensured that his instructions were followed without revealing the selected candidate.

Perhaps the proposed techniques might improve the security offered by physical booths: an adversary might not enter a physical booth with the voter, but he can force the voter to enter the booth with an inconspicuous camera (for example) and ask him to record the procedure. In fact, mental booths also offer protection against electromagnetic eavesdropping (van Eck phreaking), an attack that applies to *non-remote* electronic voting [25] or against the new man-in-the-middle attacking the Diebold voting machines revealed by the VAT team of the Argonne National Lab recently in [19,18,3] (and earlier to the Sequoia AVC Voting Machine [4]).

Usability of mental booths can be largely improved either by a careful choice of actions/feedbacks or by using representations of the secret integers that are easier to remember. The framework for proving over-the-shoulder coercion resistance of voting booths is also subject to improvement. In particular, approaches that are more efficient than exhaustive state space exploration would allow to guarantee the security offered by very elaborated interfaces. In any case, the general approach can be used as a sound guarantee that adding functionalities (i.e. actions/feedbacks) to the interface will not jeopardize over-the-shoulder coercion resistance.

We did not consider to what extent security holds over multiple sessions. The proposed scheme requires from the voter to register once per election, or to remember a sequence of numbers, one number for each session.

References

1. Adida, B.: Helios: web-based open-audit voting. In: Proceedings of the 17th Conference on Security Symposium, pp. 335–348. USENIX Association, Berkeley (2008)
2. Adida, B., De Marneffe, O., Pereira, O., Quisquater, J.J.: Electing a university president using open-audit voting: analysis of real-world use of helios. In: Proceedings of the 2009 Conference on Electronic Voting Technology/Workshop on Trustworthy Elections, EVT/WOTE 2009, p. 10. USENIX Association, Berkeley (2009)
3. Argonne National Laboratory, The Brad Blog: "Man-in-the-middle" remote attack on Diebold touch-screen voting machine by Argonne national lab (video) (2011), http://www.youtube.com/watch?feature=player_embedded\&v=DMw2dn6K1oI
4. Argonne National Laboratory, The Brad Blog: Remote vote tampering attack on a sequoia avc voting machine by argonne national lab (2011)
5. Backes, M., Hritcu, C., Maffei, M.: Automated verification of remote electronic voting protocols in the applied pi-calculus. In: Proceedings of the 21st IEEE Computer Security Foundations Symposium, pp. 195–209. IEEE Computer Society (2008)
6. Benaloh, J., Tuinstra, D.: Receipt-free secret-ballot elections (extended abstract). In: Proceedings of the Twenty-Sixth Annual ACM Symposium on Theory of Computing, STOC 1994, pp. 544–553. ACM, New York (1994)
7. Bohli, J.M., Mueller-Quade, J., Roehrich, S.: Bingo Voting: Secure and coercion-free voting using a trusted random number generator (2007), http://eprint.iacr.org/2007/162
8. Canetti, R., Gennaro, R.: Incoercible multiparty computation. In: Annual IEEE Symposium on Foundations of Computer Science, p. 504 (1996)
9. Chaum, D.: SureVote: Technical Overview. In: Preproceedings of the Workshop on Trustworthy Elections. In: WOTE 2001 (2001)
10. Chaum, D.: SureVote: How it works (2011), http://www.surevote.com/

11. Clark, J., Hengartner, U.: Selections: An internet voting system with over-the-shoulder coercion-resistance. In: Financial Cryptography and Data Security (2011)
12. Clarkson, M.R., Chong, S., Myers, A.C.: Civitas: Toward a secure voting system. In: IEEE Symposium on Security and Privacy, pp. 354–368. IEEE Computer Society (2008)
13. Dall'Olio, E., Markowitch, O.: Voting with designated verifier signature-like protocol. In: International Conference WWW/Internet, pp. 295–301. IADIS (2004)
14. Delaune, S., Kremer, S., Ryan, M.: Coercion-resistance and receipt-freeness in electronic voting. In: IEEE Computer Security Foundations Workshop, pp. 28–42. IEEE Computer Society, Los Alamitos (2006)
15. Dill, D.L., Castro, D.: Point/counterpoint: The u.s. should ban paperless electronic voting machines. Commun. ACM 51, 29–33 (2008)
16. Dossogne, J., Markowitch, O.: A tripartite strong designated verifier scheme based on threshold rsa signatures. In: International Conference on Security & Management, pp. 314–317. CSREA Press (2009)
17. Dossogne, J., Markowitch, O.: Online banking and man in the browser attacks, survey of the belgian situation. In: Goseling, J., Weber, J.H. (eds.) Proceedings of the 31th Symposium on Information Theory in the Benelux (WICSITB 2010), Rotterdam, The Netherlands, pp. 19–26 (2010)
18. Friedman, B.: Diebold voting machines can be hacked by remote control (September 27, 2011), http://politics.salon.com/2011/09/27/votinghack/
19. Friedman, B.: National Security Lab Hacks Diebold Touch-Screen Voting Machine by Remote Control With $26 in Computer (September 27, 2011), http://www.bradblog.com/?p=8785
20. Jefferson, D., Rubin, A.D., Simons, B., Wagner, D.: Analyzing internet voting security. Commun. ACM 47, 59–64 (2004)
21. Joaquim, R., Ribeiro, C.: CodeVoting protection against automatic vote manipulation in an uncontrolled environment. In: Proceedings of the 1st International Conference on Evoting and Identity, pp. 178–188. Springer, Heidelberg (2007)
22. Juels, A., Catalano, D., Jakobsson, M.: Coercion-resistant electronic elections. In: Proceedings of the 2005 ACM Workshop on Privacy in the Electronic Society, WPES 2005, pp. 61–70. ACM, New York (2005)
23. Juels, A., Catalano, D., Jakobsson, M.: Coercion-Resistant Electronic Elections. In: Chaum, D., Jakobsson, M., Rivest, R.L., Ryan, P.Y.A., Benaloh, J., Kutylowski, M., Adida, B. (eds.) Towards Trustworthy Elections. LNCS, vol. 6000, pp. 37–63. Springer, Heidelberg (2010)
24. Kenski, K.: To I-Vote or Not to I-Vote?: Opinions About Internet Voting from Arizona Voters. Social Science Computer Review 23, 293–303 (2005)
25. Kuhn, M.G.: Electromagnetic Eavesdropping Risks of Flat-Panel Displays. In: Martin, D., Serjantov, A. (eds.) PET 2004. LNCS, vol. 3424, pp. 88–107. Springer, Heidelberg (2005)
26. Laguillaumie, F., Vergnaud, D.: Multi-designated verifiers signatures: anonymity without encryption. Information Processing Letters 102(2-3), 127–132 (2007)
27. Laroussinie, F., Schnoebelen, P.: The State Explosion Problem from Trace to Bisimulation Equivalence. In: Tiuryn, J. (ed.) FOSSACS 2000. LNCS, vol. 1784, pp. 192–207. Springer, Heidelberg (2000)
28. Magkos, E., Burmester, M., Chrissikopoulos, V.: Receipt-freeness in large-scale elections without untappable channels. In: Schmid, B., Stanoevska-Slabeva, K., Tschammer, V. (eds.) Towards the E-Society. IFIP, vol. 74, pp. 683–693. Springer, Boston (2002)

29. Moran, T., Naor, M.: Receipt-Free Universally-Verifiable Voting with Everlasting Privacy. In: Dwork, C. (ed.) CRYPTO 2006. LNCS, vol. 4117, pp. 373–392. Springer, Heidelberg (2006)
30. Qadah, G.Z., Taha, R.: Electronic voting systems: Requirements, design, and implementation. Computer Standards & Interfaces 29(3), 376–386 (2007)
31. Sampigethaya, K., Poovendran, R.: A framework and taxonomy for comparison of electronic voting schemes. Computers & Security 25(2), 137–153 (2006)
32. Sanford, C., Rose, J.: Characterizing eparticipation. International Journal of Information Management 27(6), 406–421 (2007)
33. Tari, F., Ozok, A.A., Holden, S.H.: A comparison of perceived and real shoulder-surfing risks between alphanumeric and graphical passwords. In: Proceedings of the Second Symposium on Usable Privacy and Security, SOUPS 2006, pp. 56–66. ACM, New York (2006)
34. Weldemariam, K., Villafiorita, A.: A survey: Electronic voting development and trends. In: Electronic Voting, pp. 119–131 (2010)

Methods for Privacy Protection Considering Status of Service Provider and User Community

Kazutomo Hamamoto, Yasuyuki Tahara, and Akihiko Ohsuga

Graduate School of Information Systems, University of Electro-Communications,
1-5-1 Chofugaoka, Chofu-shi, Tokyo 182-8585, Japan
{hamamoto,tahara,ohsuga}@ohsuga.is.uec.ac.jp

Abstract. Protecting personal privacy is going to be a prime concern for the deployment of ubiquitous computing systems in the real world. That becomes serious especially when a user receives user centric services from a service provider by offering personal information, because the service can be of a higher quality if the user provides more personal information despite the increase of privacy violation risk. Therefore, this paper proposes a privacy protection method that realizes avoidance of unwanted information disclosure by controlling disclosable attributes according to the results from monitoring two elements: user background information of the provider and user community status. The monitoring is done before disclosing individual attributes corresponding to the privacy policy (i.e., the required anonymity level) by each user. The validity of the proposed methods was confirmed by a desk model.

Keywords: Privacy, Anonymity, Lifelog.

1 Introduction

When a user receives personal services, such as content recommendation service or action support service, from a service provider by supplying personal information including one's lifelog, preference, age, etc., privacy protection is essential. If the information given to the provider is generally large and detailed, the received service quality increases although the anonymity level lowers. For example, when receiving recommendation of the guide to good eating about 'food', if you offer even more personal information such as place, price, gender, age, etc. in addition to such preference as European/Japanese?, favorite dish? and so on, you can get good recommendation with accuracy. However, for privacy protection, the offered information should be reduced as much as possible to prevent the anonymity level from lowering. This indicates that a trade-off exists between privacy protection and service quality [1], [3].

When the service quality from the provider is not satisfactory, it is possible to increase it by increasing the offered information quantity, at the cost of lowering the anonymity level. However, in some critical situations, a dilemma whether to increase the information quantity or prioritise anonymity arises. In such cases, the demand of the withdrawal of information that has been disclosed unwillingly is meaningless

P. Laud (Ed.): NordSec 2011, LNCS 7161, pp. 98–113, 2012.

because it is almost impossible to withdraw or cancel information once disclosed. Thus, it can be said that this trade-off control is one-way and has a so-called 'No Entry Area', as shown in Fig.1, namely in that area it is impossible to increase the anonymity level once lowered such as from (1) to (2).

Considering these circumstances, this paper proposes a method that realizes avoidance of unwanted information disclosure by controlling openable attributes (i.e., the attributes disclosable as per required anonymity level) according to the results from monitoring two elements: the user background information of the provider (i.e., the information that the service provider already possesses about the user) and the user community status (i.e., head count etc. of the community including the user) that influences the anonymity level. This monitoring is done before disclosing individual attributes corresponding to the privacy policy (hereafter the required anonymity level) set by each user. This paper aims to propose such privacy protection methods to enable service acquisition corresponding to the offered information without any unintended personal information leakage.

The typical target service is ubiquitous service to an ad hoc user group or crowd, so called 'community' benefitting from same service; thus, for example, information recommendation service to people who are in an air port lounge or in the waiting room of a hospital and so on.

This paper is organized as follows: in Section 2, the related works are described, and different problems are analysed in Section 3. The proposed methods are described in Section 4. In Section 5, evaluation and validity verification are discussed, followed by an outline of future works in Section 6. Finally, Section 7 concludes this paper.

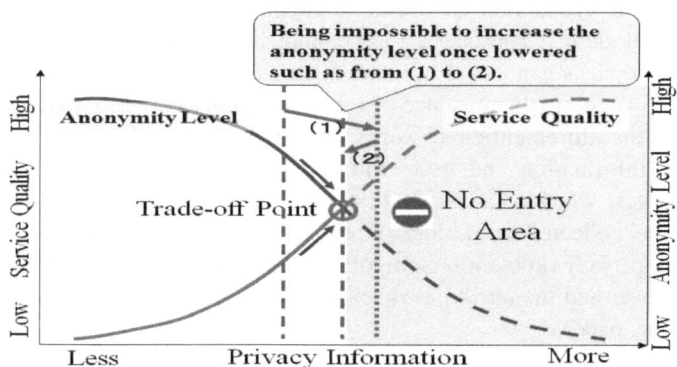

Fig. 1. One-way Trade-off Control

2   Related Works

Relevant works [1-15] were analysed on the basis of the following three viewpoints.

Storage Location of Personal Information and Disclosing Condition. In many cases, personal information of each user is stored in a secure server located between users and providers, and then batch processing such as data analysis or anonymization, is carried out in bulk [4], [5], [9], [12], [13]; this architecture concept is adopted in this paper. The privacy policy that includes the purpose of the use of personal information or the required anonymity level (i.e., identifying probability) is collated from users and providers, and on satisfying certain conditions, personal information is disclosed [3], [4], [5], [10], [11], [14]; disclosing condition of this paper is original such as to be proposed afterwards.

Privacy Protection Methods and Specific Individual Identification. For policies having different aforementioned collations, it is impossible to disclose information, although some ways such as obeying the dictates of the user are taken to make progress [1], [2], [6], [7], [12], [13]. Techniques that make information granularity blunt or rough, except the K-anonymity method, are used to manage anonymity [3], [5], [10]; the concept of K-anonymity method is adopted in this paper. Specific individual identification is possible in systems that handle information such as name [1], [8], [12], [14]; however, in many cases it is impossible because of various privacy protection techniques [2], [7]. To prevent specific individual identification by proposed methods is the final goal of this paper; although there is a related work such as to identify an unique individual by using a technique called 'shadow attack' that monitors the behaviour of the user of the services given from the service provider [11].

Explicit Trade-Off Control. Although almost all related works do not refer to the trade-off between anonymity and service, some works explicitly consider it. One trade-off is the balance between the received services and the offered attributes achieved via user hands-on control [1], [4], [6], and the other is a system that searches for the type and granularity of openable attributes automatically using the machine learning technique [3]. The user's load cannot be neglected in the former and in the latter, some services cannot be utilized. A research on the trade-off between privacy and trust [15] suggests the presence of inherent affinity between trust and service.

Although the aforementioned works discuss the trade-off, very few describe user background information and user community status that influences the anonymity level. However, when considering that various new services and applications that utilize lifelogs collected from blogs or social network services spread and circulate in the network, privacy protection is important. This is achieved by careful control of the anonymity level and the attributes disclosed from the trade-off standpoint, and that is the aim of this paper.

3   Problem Analysis

3.1   Prerequisite Framework

When considering prerequisite framework based on user, server and provider, the best way to protect personal information is to handle all informations on only serverside without passing those informations to the provider; however, it is necessary to move some provider's functions to serverside in proper form [2], [7]. Namely it is not realistic in omnipresent environment of provider because of excessive load concentration

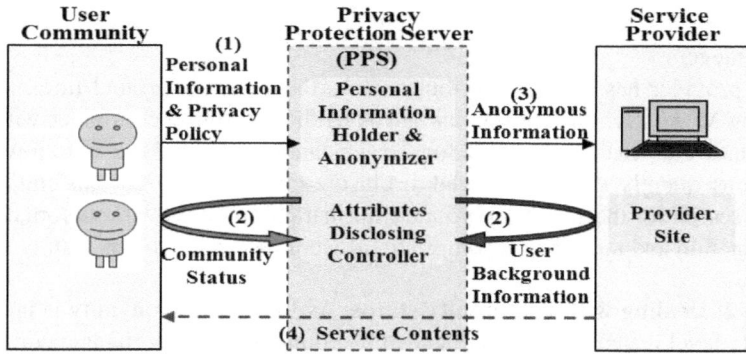

Fig. 2. Prerequisite Framework

on server. Precisely it is almost impossible to move certain service exclusive DB to serverside each time, consequently some services are not available.

Accordingly the prerequisite framework describing the two elements: the user background information of the provider and the user community status, can be considered to be similar to that found in the literature; this framework includes a secure server between users and providers to store personal information and perform various processes such as anonymization, and pass the processed information to the provider like broker. In order to establish realistic secure server adaptive to real world, it is necessary to solve not only relating technical issues but also governmental or statutory matters involving various institutions; thus, it is not so easy then consider it as prerequisite condition out of the scope of this paper despite key issue to realize this paper's goal.

The secure server is called the privacy protection server (PPS) in this paper and performs maximum privacy protection on the basis of careful trade-off control by considering the two elements. It uses the concept of K-anonymity [10] that ensures anonymity by controlling the number of people having the same attribute that is more than the K constant. Fig. 2 shows this framework.

3.2   Two Problems

In the process from (1) to (4) in Fig. 2, the problem regarding monitoring the two elements i.e. user background information and community status in step (2) exists. Another problem is the interpretation of the results obtained from monitoring, in the anonymizing and disclosing processes. The basic ideas for coping with and solving those problems are described as follows.

Problem 1: Dealing with user background information. Here, let numerical value L be the required anonymity level, a set of attributes R be the openable attributes corresponding to L and function f (L) = R. In order to avoid careless entry of unintended information disclosure in the 'No Entry Area' shown in Fig.1, it is possible, without any careless disclosure of all R, to gradually increase the openable attributes from R´ (f (L + α) = R´) to R (#R = #R´ + β) by lowering the anonymity level stepwise from L + α to L with monitoring the service quality [18]. Here, α and β are positive integers.

If the provider has a set of attributes M as the user background information, by combining M with R´, the substantial attributes disclosed to the provider will be M + R´. This indicates that it is possible for the substantial anonymity level to lower below L, and consequently such unintended disclosure could happen. To this end, it is necessary to search for the user background information of the provider before disclosing the information and take some appropriate measures according to the results.

Problem 2: Dealing with community status. As long as K-anonymity is applied, the anonymity level is unavoidably influenced by community status change; consequently it happens for the worst that the required anonymity level cannot be defended. Even if a moving average or some regularized indicator is applied to reduce the influence of the change, it is not completely eliminated. Therefore, in this paper, disclosing control of the openable attributes is performed along with informing the user about the openable attributes in advance by sensing such changes. Thus, it is possible to reflect the user's intention in disclosing control of attributes beforehand. It resembles an advanced demand signals scheme (ADS) [19] that controls the signals beforehand by measuring traffic flow towards the intersection.

4   Proposed Methods

4.1   Anonymizing and Disclosing Control

The K value cannot be used as the anonymity level for each user because it changes according to the community scale. Therefore, the required anonymity level L, the same L as the previous section, is introduced that has four different levels that decrease in the order of 3, 2, 1 and 0. The value of K corresponding to each level of L is appropriately determined depending on the community scale. For instance, for six persons group in Table 1, K = 2, 3 and 4 correspond respectively to L = 1, 2, and 3, although K = 2, 4, and 6 correspond to the same L in eight persons group in Fig. 6 (Section 4.3). The PPS shown in Fig. 2 determines the openable attributes according

Table 1. Personal Information of a Group of Persons

Name	Att 1	Att 2	Att 3	Att 4	Att 5
	Gender	Job	Blood	First Trip	Goal
Alice	F,0.33	Stu,0.53	A,0.46	Yes,0.46	USA,0.33
Bob	M,0.53	Stu,0.53	AB,0	Yes,0.46	USA,0.33
Mike	M,0.53	Busi,0.33	A,0.46	No,0.46	UK,0
John	M,0.53	Busi,0.33	O,0	No,0.46	Fra,0.33
Hanak	F,0.33	Stu,0.53	A,0.46	No,0.46	Ita,0
MikeJ	M,0.53	Stu,0.53	B,0	Yes,0.46	Fra,0.33

(Notes) Att: Attribute, F: Female, M: Male, Stu: Student, Busi: Business,
      USA: United States of America, UK: United Kingdom,
      Fra: France, Ita: Italy

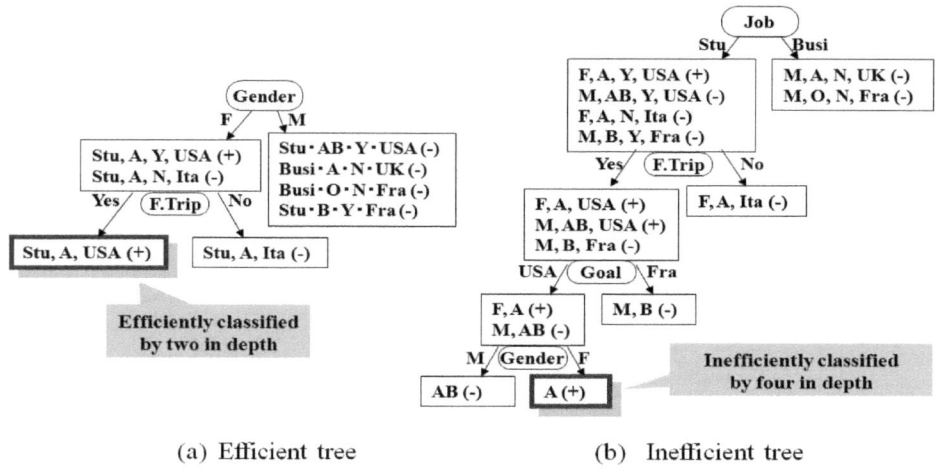

(a) Efficient tree   (b) Inefficient tree

Fig. 3. Decision Trees of Alice

to L of each user by monitoring consolidated personal information, and then discloses them to providers after proper processing as proposed afterwards. The decision tree learning algorithm is applied to control the disclosing attribute group and order [4].

In general, a selective attribute in the decision tree learning algorithm is identified for efficient classification and fast access to the target object by choosing attributes such as information gain that generates big entropy. However, on the contrary, in this paper, an inefficient decision tree is generated for the unintended disclosure of the target object (i.e., privacy protection object) by using such attribute because the entropy is relatively low; as a result, by using this tree, privacy is protected. Hereafter, a specific case is described.

Table 1 shows the personal information of a group of people in an airport waiting room, where users receive services such as contents recommendation from providers through PPS. The figures in the table show the entropy when classified according to each attribute value. For the case of Alice, when classified by gender, the entropy is calculated from the definition referring to Fig. 3 (a) as follows:

$$-\sum_{i=1}^{k} p_i \log p_i = -\{2(\frac{1}{2}\log\frac{1}{2} + \frac{1}{2}\log\frac{1}{2}) + 4(\frac{4}{4}\log\frac{4}{4})\} / 6 \cong 0.33$$

Thus, as shown in Fig. 3, although the efficient decision tree needs only two in-depth attributes to specify the object, the inefficient tree needs four in-depth attributes for the same. The inefficient classifying tree is used for privacy protection. The attributes are individually disclosed from such an attribute because the object is not easily specified. In particular, 'Job: Student → First Trip: Yes → Goal: USA' becomes a disclosing order. However, in order to avoid complex processing, all openable attributes determined by L are not disclosed individually but simultaneously in the following section.

4.2   Proposed Method 1 (Against Status of Service Provider)

Technique to Avoid the Influence of User Background Information. Fig. 4 shows a situation where the provider has some user background information. The user discloses the attributes 'a' and 'b' that are determined to be openable by the required anonymity level L = 2. If the provider already has the user background information equivalent to attribute 'c', the substantial anonymity level lowers from L = 2 to L = 1 by combining 'a' and 'b' to 'c'.

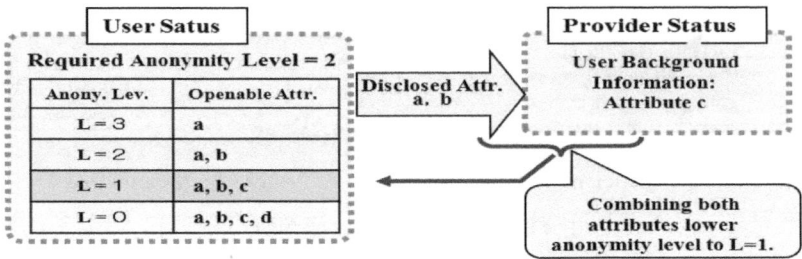

Fig. 4. Influence of user background information

Using Table 1, the following situation can be assumed.

(1) For Alice, the openable attributes corresponding to the required anonymity level L = 2, indicating K = 3, are 'Job: Student,' 'Blood: A' or 'First Trip: Yes'. These are disclosed to the provider independently.

(2) Because the concerned provider is located in the airport, it is possible to acquire in advance the required information such as boarding members list including name, nationality, destination and first-time overseas travellers etc..

(3) The provider can select three people Alice, Bob and MikeJ using the 'First Trip: Yes' attribute when received at Step (1). If the provider acquires information that MikeJ was in a French embassy three hours ago from a location service provider, MikeJ's 'Goal' is possibly France. Thus, the target person having attributes such as 'Job: Student,' 'Blood: A' or 'First Trip: Yes' is Alice or Bob, which indicates that the substantial anonymity level lowers from the initial level L = 2 (K = 3) to L = 1 (K = 2), then the required anonymity level cannot be defended.

In order to avoid this, this paper proposes a certain method (*Proposed method 1*) that appropriately changes disclosing control of attributes according to the results obtained from monitoring the user background information before disclosing openable attributes corresponding to the required anonymity level. Contents and procedures are shown in each step in Fig. 5. This, together with Table. 1 or Fig. 4, illustrates the conditions of the selected sample as follows:

In step (1), the candidate provider is appropriately searched for by the query words composed of attributes common to all users. An example of a query is '(Gender: Man, Female), (Job: Student, Business), (Blood: A, AB, O, B), (First Trip: Yes, No), (Goal: USA, UK, France, Italy)' like LCM (least common multiple).

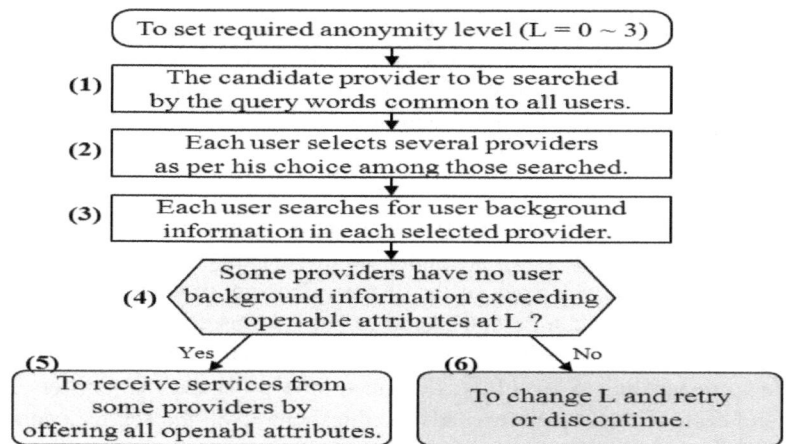

Fig. 5. User background information search flow

In step (2), each user selects several providers, each denoted by H, of his/her choice among the providers that were searched for (e.g., Alice selects an USA provider such as supplier giving supportive information for female students to live in USA).

In step (3), the appropriate pages of each selected provider site are downloaded and are to be searched for the same attributes of each user from the viewpoint of how much of each user's attribute information is included in the pages. For the case of Mike, instance of such attributes is 'Gender: Man, Job: Business, Blood: A, First Trip: No, Goal: UK'.

In step (4) and (5), the service is received by disclosing openable attributes corresponding to required anonymity level L from the provider that is considered not to have attributes exceeding the range of the openable attributes corresponding to the L level. For example, if L = 2 in Fig. 4, only the provider that does not have 'c' and 'd' attributes will be able to provide some services.

In step (6), as for the other providers, it is possible that they may not maintain the L level when disclosing openable attributes corresponding to the L level, and therefore retry after changing the L level, or the service itself should be cancelled; this is one procedure to realize the trade-off between privacy protection and service quality.

Technique to Search for User Background Information. Considering all attributes of each user that have already been registered in PPS, the target is to find the number of the same attributes in the provider site. In particular, by using the pair of words of the attributes and its values, the co-occurrence frequency of the pair is measured. As for the co-occurrence level of a pair of words, two typical coefficients are used as the index of relativity between the pair: the Jaccard coefficient and the Simpson coefficient [16]. In this paper, the Jaccard coefficient is used considering that the paired words have a tendency to appear simultaneously and it is important to determine whether the target site also has this tendency. Jaccard coefficient functions properly in such case.

If the number of such pairs offered from the user and the chosen providers in step (2) in Fig. 5 are assumed to be P and H, respectively, co-occurrence level $\boldsymbol{J}$ (the Jaccard coefficient) of each pair of words is shown as a two-dimensional array. Assuming P and H for the first and second dimensions, respectively, $\boldsymbol{J}$ is defined as follows.

$$\boldsymbol{J} = [[J_{11}, J_{12}, \ldots, J_{1p}], [J_{21}, J_{22}, \ldots, J_{2p}], \ldots, [J_{h1}, J_{h2}, \ldots, J_{hp}]]$$

Among P pairs, if the number of the pair that can be disclosed by level L is assumed to be R, the number of the pair that cannot be disclosed is Q = P – R. For a certain provider, if any J_{hp} value of each of the Q pairs does not exceed a certain threshold level T, such a provider can be considered to not have user background information regarding Q, and then the service can be received by only offering the attributes R, openable corresponding to level L, as described in step (4) and (5). Conversely, if any J_{hp} value of each of the Q pairs exceeds the threshold level, the service cannot be received from such provider.

4.3 Proposed Method 2 (Against Status of User Community)

As stated in Section 3.2, required anonymity level L cannot be defended because of the community status change. Therefore, to defend L, it is necessary to control the disclosing attributes according to the current anonymity level. Fig. 6 shows this situation considering the case of Mike as an example. Fig. 6 (a) shows the initial situation

(a)

Name	Req.Ano.Lev	Att1 Gender	Att2 Job	Att3 Blood	Att4 FirstTri	Att5 Goal
Alice	L=1 0.33,2	F 0.33	Stu 0.53	A 0.46	Yes 0.46	USA 0.33
Bob	L=1 0.33,2	M 0.53	Stu 0.53	AB 0	Yes 0.46	USA 0.33
Mike	L=2 0.46,3	M 0.53	Busi 0.33	A 0.46	No 0.46	UK 0
John	L=2 0.46,3	M 0.53	Busi 0.33	O 0	No 0.46	Fra 0.33
Hana	L=3 0.53,4	F 0.33	Stu 0.53	A 0.46	No 0.46	Ita 0
Mike	L=3 0.53,4	M 0.53	Stu 0.53	B 0	Yes 0.46	Fra 0.33

Req.Ano.Lev. Entropy, K

Similar additional members increase the anonymity level, then some attributes may be added.

Unlike additional members make anonymity level down, then some attributes should be dropped.

(b) (*) : Additional member

Alice	L=1 0.25,2	F 0.25	Stu 0.41	A 0.45	Yes 0.35	USA 0.25
Bob	L=1 0.25,2	M 0.49	Stu 0.41	AB 0	Yes 0.35	USA 0.25
Mike	L=2 0.41,4	M 0.49	Busi 0.41	A 0.45	No 0.45	UK 0.35
John	L=2 0.41,4	M 0.49	Busi 0.41	O 0	No 0.45	Fra 0.25
Hana	L=3 0.49,6	F 0.25	Stu 0.41	A 0.45	No 0.45	Ita 0
Mike	L=3 0.49,6	M 0.49	Stu 0.41	B 0	Yes 0.35	Fra 0.25
X(*)		M 0.49	Busi 0.41	A 0.45	No 0.45	UK 0.35
Y(*)		M 0.49	Busi 0.41	A 0.45	No 0.45	UK 0.35

(c)

Alice	L=1 0.25,2	F 0. 41	Stu 0.49	A 0.35	Yes 0.45	USA 0.25
Bob	L=1 0.25,2	M 0.41	Stu 0.49	AB 0	Yes 0.45	USA 0.25
Mike	L=2 0.41,4	M 0.41	Busi 0.25	A 0.35	No 0.35	UK 0
John	L=2 0.41,4	M 0.41	Busi 0.25	O 0	No 0.35	Fra 0.41
Hana	L=3 0.49,6	F 0.41	Stu 0.49	A 0.35	No 0.35	Ita 0
Mike	L=3 0.49,6	M 0.41	Stu 0.49	B 0.35	Yes 0.45	Fra 0.41
Z(*)		F 0.41	Stu 0.49	B 0.35	Yes 0.45	Fra 0.41
T(*)		F 0.41	Stu 0.49	B 0.35	Yes 0.45	Fra 0.41

Fig. 6. Changes of Anonymity

in which Mike has L = 2 (K = 3) and the three attributes, 'Male', 'A' and 'No' can be disclosed. Fig. 6 (b) shows that the anonymity level increases because two members having same attributes as those of Mike join the group; thus, another attribute 'Busi' can be disclosed. Fig. 6 (c) shows the opposite situation; therefore, the openable attribute should be limited only to 'Male' to defend L.

In order to simplify the influence of community change, there are some methods such as using regularized entropy in the anonymity level calculation [4] or a certain attribute disclosing index considering lifelog statistics and community character. In spite of these methods, the influence cannot be easily simplified, and thus cannot be considered as a suitable solution.

We propose an advance agreement attribute disclosing controlling method (*Proposed method 2*), namely reflecting the user's intention in advance. It is outlined as follows: the method senses momentarily information in advance such as the number of people moving toward the service area or the attributes associated with those people; forwards those sensed data to the server in the service area whenever just after sensed; forecasts instantly the anonymity level change and the openable attributes by analyzing those gathered data; listen to the user's intention about attributes to be disclosed beforehand; and determines whether to disclose additional attributes by obtaining user consent. Fig.7 illustrates such essence as the described above. Thus, appropriate real time disclosing control can be performed according to the current conditions. Details are shown in Section 5 by simulation.

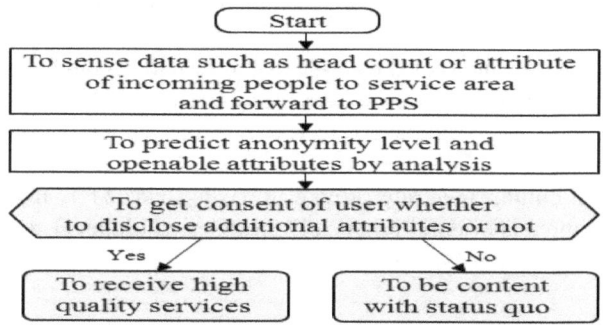

Fig. 7. Predicting process Flow

5   Evaluation and Validity Verification

5.1   Evaluation and Validity Verification for Proposed Method 1

By using the case group shown in Table 1, it is verified that the proposed method 1, described in Section 4.2 (Fig. 5), is appropriate when treating user background information and anonymity level and disclosing attributes from two evaluation aspects:

(#1) There is no risk in disclosing unintended personal information,
(#2) There is no sacrifice of the unintended anonymity level.

Table 2. Jaccard Coefficient Value

Provider	Attr1 Gender Male	Attr 2 Job Business	Attr 3 Blood A type	Attr 4 FirstTrip No	Attr 5 Goal UK
(a)	0/4 (0)	2/22 (0.09)	2/7 (0.29)	0/1 (0)	0/0 (0)
(b)	0/0 (0)	0/0 (0)	1/1 (1)	0/1 (0)	0/7 (0)
(c)	0/21 (0)	0/6 (0)	2/12 (0.17)	0/16 (0)	0/2 (0)

· Figures show Jaccard Coefficient $(|A \cap B|) / \sum (|A \cup B|)$.
· Marked cells show openable attributes corresponding to Required Anonymity Level $L = 2 (K = 3)$.

In step (1) in Fig. 5, the query words used are common to all users, so the anonymity level is the highest and each user consents the disclosure of such personal information beforehand by understanding the purpose of the use. Thus, aspects (#1) and (#2) can be realized. In steps (2) and (3), while processing only one-sided download of the contents of the related page of the provider site takes place; thus, aspects (#1) and (#2) can be realized. In steps (4) and (5), only when any J_{hp} value of each of the Q pairs does not exceed threshold T, all openable attributes R corresponding to L are disclosed and receive the service; thus, aspects (#1) and (#2) can be realized. In step (6), the processing is performed from the user's standpoint; thus, aspects (#1) and (#2) can be realized. Therefore, the proposed method 1 is verified to be appropriate from both evaluation aspects.

Table 2 shows an example of the result of the provider searching experiment for user background information in step (3) assuming the case of Mike in which $L = 2$ (K = 3). Here, 'Provider' means the site selected by Mike among all sites searched and hit by Google in step (1). If the threshold T is set to 0.1, because any attribute of the Q pairs (non-marked columns) of any provider does not exceed T, the services can be received from all three providers. Practically, such threshold level should be carefully determined based on various system conditions.

5.2   Evaluation and Validity Verification for Proposed Method 2

As in the previous section, it is verified that the proposed method 2, described in Section 4.3, is appropriate by simulation using a multi-agent simulator [17], [20]. In particular, the possibility of real time disclosing control based on an advance agreement attribute is considered. That is, acquiring personal information of the people moving towards the service area beforehand, informing the user in the service area of the change of openable attributes and negotiating with the user as to which attribute is to be opened with high priority may be achieved. Fig. 8 and Fig. 9 show the simulation status.

In Fig. 8, pedestrian agents assuming customers move toward the boarding gate in the airport after passing A area, receive services at B area (service area) and pass C area toward exit. Various sensing are performed at A area. Key parameters are A_t

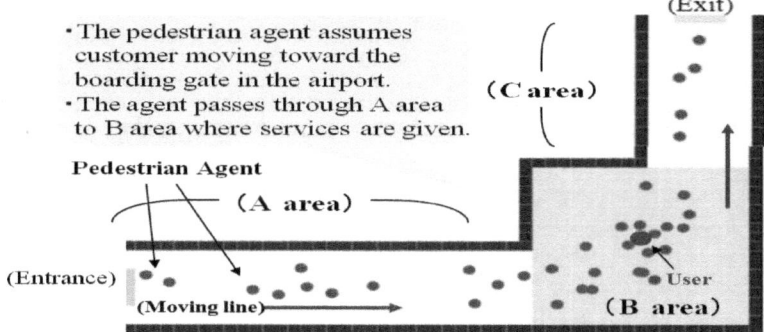

Fig. 8. Simulation by Pedestrian Agents

and B_t, that are the average time for an agent to pass A area and the average time to receive the service at B area, respectively, unit time being a step. Other parameters are commonsensibly and properly decided by the simulator. The value of the anonymity level is defined to be the number of agents in A or B area having the same attribute as the marked agent (user) locating in B area to receive services.

Fig. 9 shows the simulation by assuming $A_t = 40$ steps and $B_t = 80$ steps; therefore, $\alpha = 2$ such that $B_t = \alpha \times A_t$. The upper and lower graphs show the situations of the A and B areas, respectively. A(t), A1(t) and A2(t) show the number of people, the anonymity level of attribute 1 and the anonymity level of attribute 2, respectively, at Time = t steps in the A area. Similarly, B(t), B1(t) and B2(t) correspond to the number of people, the anonymity level of attribute 1 and the anonymity level of attribute 2, respectively, in the B area.

From the graph, $B(120) \fallingdotseq A(40) + A(80)$, $B(160) \fallingdotseq A(80) + A(120)$,
       or $B1(440) \fallingdotseq A1(360) + A1(400)$, $B1(480) \fallingdotseq A1(400) + A1(440)$,

can be read, which suggests that the situation in the B area can be predicted from the situation in the A area. This is because $B(40n) \fallingdotseq A(40(n - 1)) + A(40(n - 2))$ can be obtained by the average value because of $B_t = 2 \times A_t$, where n is a positive integer.

That is, the anonymity level of B1(t) in Fig. 9 shows that it can be predicted at Time = 440 steps that the value of B1 at Time = 480 steps exceeds the required anonymity level beforehand. Then, at Time = 440 steps, it is possible for the user to negotiate and decide whether to disclose additional attributes; thus, an advance agreement disclosing control is possible. However, considering the actual time consumption in negotiation and confirmation, it appears reasonable to forecast the present conditions just when disclosing using relevant past data. This suggests that it is verified from the evaluation aspect (#1) viewpoint. In contrast, in the situation in which the number of already disclosed attributes should be decreased by forecasting, it is possible to discontinue disclosing as soon as possible by prior notification, and thus the sacrifice of the anonymity level can be minimized as per the user's consent. Therefore, aspect (#2) can be achieved.

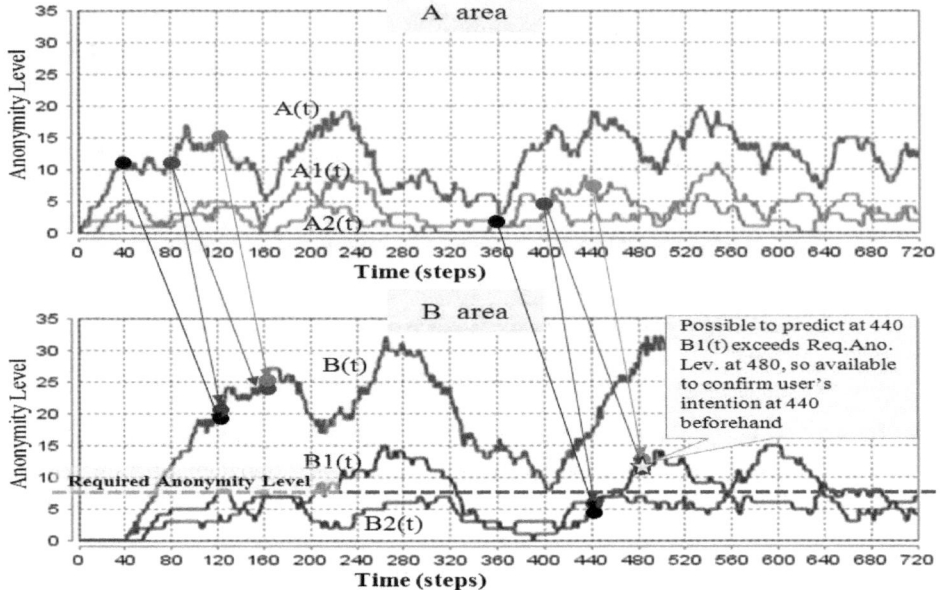

Fig. 9. Simulation of Anonymity Change

5.3   Evaluation of the Proposed Methods for Trade-Off

Apart from the aforementioned evaluation, the proposed methods should be evaluated from the viewpoint of the contribution to an effective trade-off between service and anonymity from the following two aspects: (a) easy and rapid acquiring the balance point between service and anonymity and (b) no unintended information disclosure and availability of a slightly higher service level.

First, this paper aims to introduce the required anonymity level (L) that can be set by each user and notify such users of the openable attributes determined by L; thus, the mechanism that a phased adjustment is enabled is considered. Moreover, although it is usual to individually disclose openable attributes in order [3], [18], in this paper, all openable attributes are disclosed simultaneously; therefore, the balance point can be efficiently attained. This suggests that the evaluation of aspect (a) is clarified.

Second, unintended information disclosure can be avoided by the proposed method 1 in case the provider has some user background information; it is possible to raise the service level by increasing information disclosure intentionally by the proposed method 2 in case the community status changes. This indicates that the evaluation aspect (b) is also clarified.

Because of the aforementioned explanation, the technique proposed in this paper is appreciable from the viewpoint of contribution to an effective trade-off.

6   Future Works

Although some experimental evaluating tests for validity verification and specific architecture need further investigation, two proposed methods were evaluated from two viewpoints by using the desk model or simulation and described to be appropriate from the viewpoint of 'Contribution to an effective trade-off'. When these methods are actually applied, the decision of using either one application or two applications together depends on the actual conditions such as service content, provider status and system condition. For instance, when it is apparent that there is no community change, only searching for user background information is necessary. However, in particular it is future work to pursue how to combine and coordinate these two applications.

In the proposed method 1, the threshold by which a provider is considered to have user background information and the technique choosing the most appropriate page of the provider site are the key problems to be pursued and could be solved in the future. In the proposed method 2, in the simulation, although the example of airport was assumed, given the average speed in the approach area (A area) or average travel time B_t at the service area (B area), α and A_t can be defined; therefore, the application of this method becomes possible to locations such as a shopping street or an amusement park. However, there are problems because of the differences between simulation and reality or the limitation of the simulation itself, and this is also an area for future work.

Eventually, when lifelogs increase in number, privacy violation by the secondary use of other providers becomes a big problem. Fig. 10 shows an example of privacy violation by such secondary use; that is, if some lifelogs acquired by a separate provider are linked and analysed, the individual image becomes clearer. A key to prevent such analysis is, when personal information is offered from one provider to another, to ensure the anonymity level required by the original owner of the information based on the idea of the proposed methods; however, it is a future task.

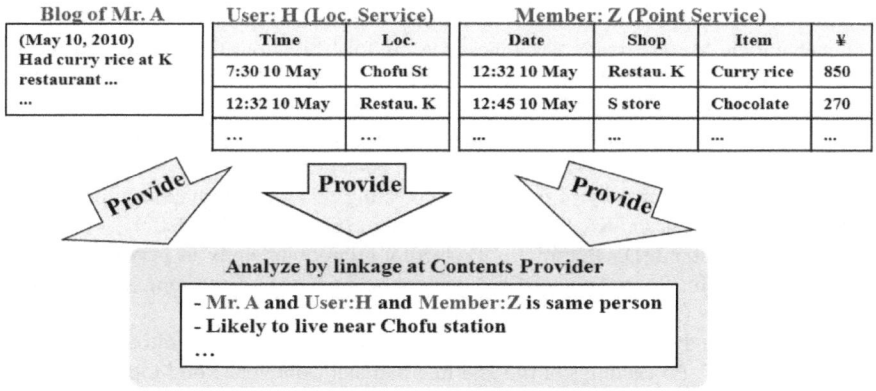

Fig. 10. Inference by Linkage Analysis

7   Conclusion

The trade-off existing between privacy protection and service quality was discussed. Two problems associated with appropriate trade-off control, namely those with user background information of the provider and community status, were treated and two counter-measures were proposed. Careful anonymity level control through phased adjustment and advance agreement attribute disclosing controlling methods considering user background information and community status are crucial to prevent unintended privacy information disclosure.

References

1. Yamabe, T., Fujinami, K., Shoji, T., Nakamura, N., Nakajima, T.: PENATES: Privacy Protection Architecture for Context-Aware Environments. In: Computer Symposium, Tokyo, pp. 55–64 (2004)
2. Tamaru, S., Iwaya, A., Takashio, K., Tokuda, H.: An application Framework for Personalized Public Space Considering Privacy. IPSJ report in Japan, pp. 49–56, 2003-OS-93
3. Miyamoto, T., Takeuchi, T., Okuda, T., Harumoto, K., Ariyoshi, Y., Shimojo, S.: Proposal for profile control mechanism considering privacy and quality of personalization services. In: DEWS 2005, Japan, 6-A-01 (2005)
4. Imada, M., Takasugi, K., Ohta, M., Koyanagi, K.: LOOM: A Loosely managed privacy protection method for ubiquitous networking environments. IEICE Journal B in Japan J88-B(3), 563–573 (2005)
5. Nakanishi, K., Takashio, K., Tokuda, H.: A concept of location anonymization. IPSJ Journal in Japan 46(9), 2260–2268 (2005)
6. Hirotaka, N., Nobuhiro, N.: Service platform for privacy Controllable Tag. IPSJ report in Japan, 2007-UBI-16, pp. 57–63 (2007)
7. Sanda, T., Yamada, S., Kamioka, E.: Proposal for a method of privacy protection in ubiquitous computing environments. IPSJ Journal in Japan 2003(93(MLB-26)), 45–51 (2003)
8. Langheinrich, M.: A Privacy Awareness System for Ubiquitous Computing Environments. In: Borriello, G., Holmquist, L.E. (eds.) UbiComp 2002. LNCS, vol. 2498, pp. 237–245. Springer, Heidelberg (2002)
9. Myles, G., Friday, A., Davies, N.: Protection Privacy in environments with location-based Applications. IEEE Pervasive Computing 2(1), 56–64 (2003)
10. Sweeney, L.: K-anonymity: a model for protecting privacy. International Journal on Uncertainty, Fuzziness and Knowledge-based System 10(5), 557–570 (2002)
11. Pareschi, L., Riboni, D., Bettini, C.: Protecting users' anonymity in pervasive computing environments. In: Sixth Annual IEEE International Conf. on Per. Com. and Communications, pp. 11–19 (2008)
12. Hong J. I., Landy, J.A.: An architecture for privacy-sensitive ubiquitous computing. In MobiSYS 2004, Proceedings of the 2nd International Conference on Mobile Systems, Applications and Services, pp. 177–189 (2004)
13. Sato, K.: Life-log: About the Profit Use of the Cellular Phone Behavioral Data that Considers the Privacy Protection. IPSJ Magazine in Japan 50(7), 598–602 (2009)
14. P3P, http://www.w3.org/P3P/

15. Seigneur, J.-M., Jensen, C.D.: Trading Privacy for Trust. In: Jensen, C., Poslad, S., Dimitrakos, T. (eds.) iTrust 2004. LNCS, vol. 2995, pp. 93–107. Springer, Heidelberg (2004)
16. Matsuo, Y., Tomobe, H., Hasida, K., Nakajima, H., Ishizuka, M.: Social Network Extraction from the Web information. JSAI Journal in Japan 20, 46–56 (2005)
17. ArtiSoc, http://mas.kke.co.jp/
18. Hamamoto, K., Tahara, Y., Ohsuga, A.: Proposal for Profile Opening Method Considering Privacy by Anonymization. In: JWEIN 2010 Symposium in Japan, Proceeding 2010 (August 2010)
19. Kato, Y., Hasegawa, T.: Effect of Advanced Demand Signals scheme. In: IEEE VTS 54th Vehicular Technology Conference, VTC 2001 Fall, pp. 708–712 (2002)
20. Kaneda, T.: Kozo Keikaku Engineering Inc., Nagoya-Ins.of Tech. Univ.: Pedestrian Simulation by Artisoc, Japan, pp. 79–114 (2010) ISBN 978-4-904701-17-1

The Security and Memorability of Passwords Generated by Using an Association Element and a Personal Factor

Kirsi Helkala and Nils Kalstad Svendsen

Gjøvik University College, Norway
{kirsi.helkala,nils.svendsen}@hig.no

Abstract. A well-established truth regarding password authentication is that easily remembered passwords are weak. This study demonstrates that this is not necessarily true. Users can be encouraged to design strong passwords, using elements associated with a given service, together with a personal factor. Regulatory bodies and information security experts are often asked the question: "what is a good password?" We claim that this is not the right question; it should be: "how can one design multiple passwords that are strong and memorable at the same time?" This paper presents guidelines for password design that combine a Personal Factor with an element associated to the login site. Analysis of the passwords generated by a group of volunteers and their ability to recall multiple passwords at later moments in time show that one can actually achieve good memorability of strong and unique passwords.

1 Introduction

It is a general assumption that secure passwords are difficult to remember, and as a consequence, users tend to create and use passwords that are weak (e.g., dictionary words), reused, or passwords that they write down [1, 15, 18]. In spite of these well-known short comings, passwords are likely to remain one of the top authentication mechanisms in the future [3, 14]. This is due to the users acceptance, the low initial cost of password systems and the complexity and costs of alternative authentication methods [20].

One approach to solve the problem of poor-passwords is the use of one-time password generators to create secure passwords that the user does not have to remember. However, these generators always have to be carried along in order to be usable and are therefore vulnerable to theft [11, 22]. *A second* solution is the application of different techniques to design memorable and yet, strongly textual passwords. An example is the mnemonic password, which uses a long sentence, transformed by various substitutions, rotations and the removal of patterns, to create a meaningless string of characters [15, 23]. Although these techniques produce strong and memorable passwords, they do have a problem of scalability. Because passwords should not be reused [12], users still have to remember different passwords for each and every account they have. Using these

P. Laud (Ed.): NordSec 2011, LNCS 7161, pp. 114–130, 2012.

techniques, instead of remembering n passwords, they have to remember n sentences and a modification style. Instead of changing the techniques used to design passwords, a change of authentication scheme has been proposed as a *third alternative*: challenge-response protocols. A user and the machine share secret(s) and the users identity is verified by the correct answers to random challenges, based on the secret(s). The challenge-response can be done by numerical computations, for example, as [16] or by visual authentication schemes, such as, [17]. Visual authentication schemes are based on the idea that humans are better at remembering objects than strings of letters or characters [13]. Examples of these recognition-based systems are random image recognition (e.g., Deja Vu [4]), graphical password (e.g., Draw a Secret [13]), and cognitive authentication schemes that rely on a secret set of pictures (e.g., [22]). Again, scalability could be a problem for both the systems and the users. In the case of cognitive passwords, the prevention of re-use of a password would require a unique set of questions for every site [15]. The creation of a set of images, unique to each site could be made manageable by using site-dependent seeds, but the main question still relies on the user. Finally, when multiple, visual password schemes are in use, it is not a given that the user would be able to recognize all of the visual passwords correctly, especially if the schemes are similar.

Based on previously reported work [9], we present an approach that gives the user a tool or a methodology to facilitate the design of good, strong passwords. We have sought a new set of guidelines for generating passwords that would work in large scale. Our main criterion has been that the method should be able to use easily remembered input to produce a high quality password. Users would no longer have to memorize multiple passwords, but instead, would memorize a generation style and learn how to use it. In this paper, we present a two-level guideline for generating memorable and secure passwords. *The first level* is general and takes care of the input part, such as, an Association Element and a Personal Factor. *The second level* deepens the security by providing targeted guidelines for three different types of passwords: word, mixture and non-word passwords. We present the results of an experiment that we ran, using the suggested guidelines, and we investigate the properties of the generated passwords. Of particular interest for our research are the uniqueness, strength, and memorability of these passwords.

The remainder of this paper is structured as follows. Section 2 gives an overview of related approaches used to strengthen the security of passwords. Our suggested methodology and an empirical study are presented in Section 3. Section 4 gives a high-level description of the collected data, investigates how the participants have interpreted and applied the guidelines, and quantifies the memorability and strength of the passwords generated. Finally, Section 5 concludes the paper and briefly outlines ongoing and future work.

2   Related Work

Strategies to obtain scalable password-authentication mechanisms were addressed by Gehringer [5], who has based his recommendations upon a strategy proposed by Craig Busse: An anagram of the site name was suggested, embedded with user's initials and digits. A user would design his or her own human, computable, embedding-strategy. This technique would give a memorable and different password for each site. However, a password designed in this manner would be breakable by an adversary who could gather enough passwords to solve the pattern.

Halderman et al. [7] have a similar approach. They proposed a password-strengthening technique that uses a cryptographic hash function to arbitrarily compute a password for many accounts. The only thing a user has to remember is a short master password. In their scheme, a site password is calculated in two steps. In the first step, a variable V is set as $V = f^{k_1}$(username : master_password), where $f(x)$ is a hash function. Here, the username can be any unique identifier chosen by user and it is used as salt to defend against listed hash-value attacks. This step is site-independent and can, therefore, be stored for further use. In the second step, the site password is computed as site_password = f^{k_2}(site_name : master_password : V). The computations in this scheme are not humanly computable. The scheme was designed to be used with a web browser.

The username and site information is also used in the approach of Stubblefield and Simon [19]. They proposed an authentication scheme that resembles human-computable hash functions and graphical approaches. In their solution, inkblots are generated based on information about the user, the authentication target and a random seed. In order to generate a $2n$-length password, a user is shown n inkblots. From each inkblot the user associates a word, and from that word, two letters are selected to be part of a password. Users can use different selection and modifying methods, (e.g., capitalization or substitution) in each selection of a letter. However, it was noted that users who used only one human computable hash function in each selection achieved better rates of recall.

Vu et al. [21] focused on the capabilities of human memory for remembering passwords. According to them, generation has an important role in recalling passwords. Humans remember passwords that they have generated by themselves better than passwords that are given to them. These authors have used association as a basis for the password in two of their methods. However, these associations are not related to the account they have used. They mentioned that account-related association might have given even better results.

3   Empirical Study

Based on the ideas and the results of the related work discussed in Section 2 this paper explores a new idea and provides guidelines for the generation of passwords. A person who has to generate a password is encouraged to combine an Association Element and a Personal Factor. The Association Element can be something he or she receives from a site or service on the Internet, while the Personal Factor can be either something strictly personal or something that is personally related to the service provided. The guidelines do not say how these two elements are to be combined or mixed, because the participants themselves know what kind of passwords they are most likely to remember. This aspect is combined with a second set of guidelines, which is based on previously published work [9, 10]. In these studies, passwords were divided into three categories and a set of guidelines was derived for each category: word, mixture and non-mixture passwords. Non-word passwords are character strings, which do not contain any words. However, they can contain letters. Mixture passwords are character strings containing both a word and a non-word part(s), e.g., "2Glibrary" has a non-word part ("2G") before the word part ("library"). Word passwords are strings, which are either pure dictionary words, e.g., "library", or readable modifications of them, e.g., "L1br@ry". By following the guidelines for the respective category, good passwords, in terms of password-strength, can be generated.

In order to see if the combination of an Association Element and a Personal Factor used in the process of designing a password is practical at large scale, we asked each participant to design one password for each of ten different Internet services. Over a period of two months, questionnaires were used to document whether the passwords produced according to the guidelines were easier to recall than other passwords. The collected data was also used to analyze the security of the password structures generated by our association-design process.

3.1   Experiment

The data collection was carried out in the spring of 2011, using B.Sc. students of engineering. The experiment was divided into three different phases. In the *first phase* the participants received guidance on how to generate good, associated passwords. In the *second phase*, students were asked to generate passwords for ten different services on the Internet. The *third phase* was the recall phase, in which participants were asked to recall their passwords after several days, after one week, and after one and half months. 51 participants designed passwords, 49 took part in the first recall test, 39 returned the second recall form, and 29 returned the third recall form. Before the results were analyzed, one participant was excluded because he or she had not understood the task and generated a new password each time, instead of recalling the original ones. Participants were aged nineteen to twenty-five and most were male.

Selection of Internet Service Sites. The selection of the Internet services for which the participants were asked to generate passwords, was selected based on the following criteria: (1) we avoided Internet services that are frequently used by Norwegians in order to reduce the risk of the participants disclosing real passwords for these services; (2) the service provided by the cite were known among the participants, in order to ease the associative process; (3) the set of presented sites contained languages that are both known and unknown to the participants, in order to stimulate other associations than linguistic ones. Based on these criteria, the following services were selected: a Publisher of Scientific Journals, a Jeweler, a Bookstore, a Music Store, an Outdoor Sport and Hunting Store, an E-mail Provider, a Doctor, a Flight Company, a Bank, and a Clothing Store.

Fig. 1. Example of selected Internet services, screenshot from a Finnish bookstore (`www.akateeminenkirjakauppa.fi`)

An example of a site and how the sites were presented to the participants is shown in Figure 1. The data collection revealed that some of the selected services were used very little or not at all by the participants (the Publishers website and the Jewelry Store) and some were used a lot (the Music Store, the Clothing Store and the E-mail Provider). However, the participants were not customers or users of any of the firms, whose websites were used in this study. Also, the language used on sites varied: two sites were in Norwegian, three in English, three in Finnish and two in Swedish. Most of the participants had Norwegian as their mother tongue, and the known languages were English and Swedish. Finnish was foreign language for all participants.

Phase 1: Education. In the instructional phase, the participants were gathered in an auditorium to hear and discuss the general design guidelines and the specially targeted guidelines for each category of password. Participants had received the instructional material beforehand in printed form and the same material was reviewed in the auditorium. The material also contained practical examples as well as the guidelines.

General Guidelines. The main, general guideline explained how to combine the Associated Elements and the Personal Factors. We introduced the term *Associated Element*, an element that has been chosen by looking at the login site of the service on the Internet. Participants were told that the Associated Element could be, for example, "easily picked", such as the IP address, some text on the

1. Identify element associated to the service
2. Identify Personal Factor
3. Create password in one of the listed categories
   (a) Word password:
       i. Minimum 13 characters
       ii. Use many short and modified words
       iii. Remember special characters when modifying
       iv. The longer the password, the less modification is needed

   (b) Mixture password:
       i. Minimum 11 characters
       ii. Use several short (not the same length), modified words together with extra characters from large character set
       iii. Remember special characters when modifying

   (c) Non-word password:
       i. Minimum 9 characters
       ii. Use characters from all character sets but in such way that there are many special characters

Fig. 2. Design guidelines for different password categories

site, colors, or "personal associations", such as, feelings and memories related to the service itself or related to the site layout. In other words, this element could be whatever the user associates to or with on the site. Secondly, we introduced the *Personal Factor*, something very personal, for example, the name of a dog. The participants were encouraged to avoid any public information, e.g., their addresses or phone numbers or any critical secrets (such as, social security numbers), as this would facilitate social engineering attacks and could also compromise the participant.

Password Category Guidelines. The guidelines for design of word, mixture and non-word passwords, which were used in this study, are based on those presented in Helkala [10]. However, due to translation (the participants received all instructions in Norwegian), and usage of a more common language, these guidelines were somewhat shorter than the originals. The reformulated guidelines are shown in Figure 2.

Example of Designing Process. The participants were provided with examples of the designing process for each category. Taking the Book Store presented in Figure 1 as a selected site, the design process could proceed as follows:

1. Association: Triangle and circle in a logo (in a password one can use forms, for example, V for "triangle" and O for 'circle")
2. Personal factor: Princess with a golden ball, 1984 (the first book one of the authors had read)
3. Examples of passwords for each category:

- Word: Tri@ngleCirclePricessWith@GoldenB@ll
- Mixture: V&O/Princess_With_a_Golden_Ball84
- Non-word: V&O/Pwagb_84 or VP&rOi8n4cess

The principles for categorization and evaluation of the quality of the designed passwords can be found in Helkala [8].

Phase 2: Password Design. The day after the instructional session, the participants were asked to design one password for each of ten different services found on the Internet. The participants were shown the picture of the login site for each service (similar to the example in Figure 1), and they had thirty minutes to complete the task of generating a password for all the sites. The participants were allowed to use whatever style they wanted to, in order to make a memorable password, under the condition of including an Association Element. The designed passwords were collected using a paper-based form. The paper-based solution was selected in order to minimize the risk of leakage of the generated passwords to the Internet, in case some of the participants, against the given recommendations, had chosen to actually use some of the passwords on some of their user accounts. Furthermore, in order to minimize the risk of leakage of information, only meta-password information was in contact with networked devices.

Phase 3: Recall. Three recall sessions were carried out. In each recall session, participants were again shown the pictures of the login sites of the services and they were asked to write down the passwords they had earlier designed on paper. The first recall session was two to three days after the designing session, the second recall session took place one week after designing session, and the third session took place one and half months after password-generation session. The passwords were not in use between the sessions.

4 Analysis and Results

In each step of the experiment, the participants were asked to complete a paper-based questionnaire. Subsequently, the meta information of the generated passwords was digitalized for further analysis. This section first gives a description of the collected data. We then looked into how the participants interpreted the guidelines by categorizing the applied Association Elements and Personal Factors. We also investigated the semantics of the passwords generated to see if there was any trend in the way that the participants combined the elements. Finally, we explored the memorability of the passwords generated with the suggested guidelines by quantifying the effect of the Association Element on memorability, tracing the memorability over time and analyzing how password-strength influences memorability.

Table 1. Examples of good passwords

Category	Password	Description	Score
Word	$K@1#y@H0$f@R	4 words: "skal øya hos far" modified with 3 uppercase letters 2 digits, and 6 special character	749
Mixture	EeSn# &S0l3!	based on 'Jeg elsker snø og sol" 2 words: modified with 2 uc, 1 d and 1 sc non-word: 1 lc, 1 uc, 1 d, and 2 sc	808
Non-word	2(3+4i)=A	9 characters, all character groups	945

4.1 Description of the Collected Data

The collected passwords were categorized according to the guidelines in Figure 2 and the strength of each password was evaluated with the password-quality tool previously published in [8]. This tool computes a quality-score, based on the search-space entropy of the structure of a certain password within a category of password. The quality score is computed based on password meta information, meaning that the password itself does not have to be disclosed. Similarly, the structural information is obtained from password meta information and the analysis done by the password-quality tool. Passwords obtaining more than 735 points are considered good ones (in entropy measures, this equals 47 bits). Examples of good passwords within each password category are given in Table 1.

The distribution of the collected passwords is shown in Table 2. The general problem with the passwords collected in this experiment is that they were too short (not satisfying the first rule in guidelines) and they also lacked special characters. Most of the word and mixture passwords were modified, but not sufficiently to make the passwords strong. Only 10.4% of the word-parts were modified with special characters and 22.7% with digits. Capitalization was the most commonly used modification tool, appearing in 60.0% of the passwords generated.

From a linguistic point of view, 60.0% of the passwords were generated using only Norwegian. 19.9% of the passwords were based on English, and 9.3% were based on Finnish words. 8.9% were bilingual passwords. Most bilingual passwords were Norwegian-English. This indicates that participants are most comfortable to use words that they understand.

Table 2. Overview of the collected data

Category	Percent	Modified	Good ones, score>735	Good ones of those which satisfy min. length
Word	21.3 %	90.6%	8.5%	12.3%
Mixture	47.4 %	91.1%	25.4%	30.9%
Non-word	31.3 %	-	46.8%	59.7%

4.2   Association Elements

All of the passwords generated contained an Association Element. We divided these elements into three main categories: Primary, Secondary, and Tertiary. By *primary association*, we mean Association Elements that can be found on the site itself, such as text on the site, the name of the site, the IP-address, or logos. *Secondary association* contains elements that are related to the service itself, such as the book titles (the Bookstore), geographical names (the Flight Company), or medical operations (the Doctor). *Tertiary association* means a new association based on the primary or secondary association. An example of a tertiary association used by one of the participants for a music store password is the following: the first association is a band called Metallica and the tertiary association is the astrological sign of the drummer in the band. The distribution of the categories of association is shown in Table 3. From the table, it can be observed that there is a clear preference for primary Association Elements, but the fraction of secondary and tertiary associations is noticeable. This shows that the participants had understood the concept of the use of Association Elements and were able to use this in the process of generating passwords.

From the point of view of information security, the primary association is the most vulnerable because this can be perceived as the public part of the password. An adversary can make a list of possible primary associations, based on observation of the Internet site, and can use these in an attack. However, in most cases, the participant had associated sites differently, and in cases in which the primary association element was the same, e.g., the Internet address or the colors used on the site, they had been used differently in the actual passwords. Secondary and tertiary associations differed from one participant to another, and the logic behind these associations would be difficult to follow for a person who does not know the participant.

4.3   Personal Factors

Similar to the Association Elements, the Personal Factors were divided into four categories: No factor, Service-related, Site-related and Not related. No factor means that the participants had not used a personal factor at all. Service-related factors were associations of the services, such as names of relatives or friends who work for similar companies, favorite books or artists, travel plans, names of the TV-series, movies or games. Site-related factors included association with the site layout, such as, opinions of the site, notation of the coloring or language of the site. The largest proportion of the factors were not related to either the service or the site. These factors included various number series (personal records, shoe sizes, lucky numbers, timestamps or dates), word games and jokes, names of

Table 3. Association Elements

Category	Primary	Secondary	Tertiary
Percent	56.8 %	25.7%	17.5%

Table 4. Personal Factors

Category	No Factor	Service-related	Site-related	Not related
Percent	15.1 %	13.9%	4.6%	66.5%

friends, spouses, relatives and pets, brands of cars, bicycles, weapons and clothes, and hobbies.

The distribution of the Personal Factors over the categories is shown in Table 4. Although 15.1% of the passwords did not contain a Personal Factor, a large majority of the participants had seen the benefit of using a Personal Factor. It is also interesting to observe that in as many as in 66.5% of the passwords, this factor was actually personal and independent of the service. Looking beyond the numbers in Table 4 it is evident that even if most of the participants had used different personal factors for all passwords, as many as 40% of participants had decided to use the same personal factor in all ten passwords.

The Personal Factors varied considerably, and most of them were based on information that is rather difficult to find. None of the participants selected or created the same Personal Factor. Even though several participants used their favorite books or artists as their Personal Factors, these favorites were not same.

4.4 Password Semantics

Passwords also differed in structure. Participants used several different ways to combine Association Elements and Personal Factors. These have been categorized into ten main categories, described in Table 5. Among these categories, the participants also used the password guidelines in order to transform pure word associations into stronger, modified word-passwords, mixture passwords or non-word passwords. 36% of participants used the same positioning of Association Elements and Personal Factors for all of their passwords. However, in these cases, either the Personal Factor was different each time, or the Association Element was not primary. The use of the Personal Factors and Association Elements made the passwords unique. Finally, the strategy selected was found to be a key factor in ensuring the uniqueness of the generated passwords.

From a security point of view, the most vulnerable situation occurs when a user applies a similar primary association, the same Personal Factor and the same structure in each password. Examples of similar primary associations are the site address and the name of the service. If a user designs passwords with similar primary associations, the same Personal Factor and the same structural style, the revealing of one password will reveal other passwords as well. In our study, 12% of participants used same Personal Factor, the same structural type and a similar primary association. This is a weakness that should be taken into account when teaching this particular technique for the design of passwords, and is similar to the weakness of users using the same password for multiple accounts.

Table 5. Positions of Association Element and Personal Factors in passwords

Category	Percent
1. Pure Association Element	12.6%
2. Association Element + Personal Factor	8.4%
3. Personal Factor + Association Element	25.9%
4. Written among others either as words or syllabus, starting with Association Element	11.6%
5. Written among others either as words or syllabus, starting with Personal Factor	6.8%
6. Written Personal Factor between words or syllabus of the Association Elements	6.8%
7. Written Association Element between words or syllabus of the Personal Factor	3.4%
8. Sentence where Association Element and Personal Factor are combined with other words	10.8%
9. Letters and symbols from the sentence of Association Element and Personal Factor	3.0%
10. Other methods	10.4%

4.5   Memorability of Passwords

As discussed in Section 1, the difficulty of remembering good passwords is one of the main criticisms of the use of passwords as an authentication mechanism. Therefore, in our analysis, we were particularly interested in exploring the effect of the Association Element on the memorability of passwords. Further, we investigated the memorability of association passwords over time. Finally we investigated the collected data to see if the suggested guidelines can break the Catch 22 of the poor memorability of strong passwords.

Effect of the Association Element on Memorability. In order to determine whether the association has an effect on the memorability of passwords, we compared the data collected in this particular study to an earlier study previously reported in [9], in which the same password guidelines were used. In the previous work, the participants received similar instructions on how to make good passwords in three password categories. After the instruction session, each participant was asked to design one new password with the style they found best suited to them. After a week, the participants were asked to recall the password. In other words, from the previous study, we have one group of good passwords, which have been generated without an Association Element, and from the current study, we have another group of good passwords generated using an Association Element. The data shows that the current study gives a recall percentage of 49%, while the study in [9] had a recall percentage of 31%. ANOVA analysis shows that, at a significance level of close to 5%, the data provides sufficient evidence to conclude that use of an Association Element has positive effect on the memorability of the password ($F - value = 3.7$ and $Pr(> F) = 0.05562$).

Memorability of Association Passwords over Time. In general, association passwords were recalled well. Not everybody who started the study returned all of the questionnaires. 49 persons returned the first recall test (after several days). This means that 490 different passwords were generated. The rate of fully recalled passwords was 51.7%. 39 persons participated in the second session, which took place after a week, and resulted in 390 passwords. The recall-rate among these passwords was 49.5%. The third recall session took place one and half months after the designing session, and the recall-rate was 32.1%. Twenty-nine persons answered the last questionnaire. To estimate the effect of drop outs on the recall-rate, we computed new recall-rates for two first recall sessions, using only the data from those twenty-nine persons who returned all three questionnaires. The recall-rates were similar, respectively 52.5% and 54.6%. The participants did not use these passwords during test period, meaning that passwords were only recalled three times during the two-month test period. The large number of drop outs was due to the difficulty of finding a suitable time to meet with the participants at the same time.

Figure 3 shows the Forgetting Curve for association passwords in this study. The curve has similarities to the shape of a negative exponential or Pareto function which is described by Averell and Heathcote [2] as characteristic for Forgetting Curves. We are not aware of similar Forgetting Curves for other guidelines to the design of passwords. Our results have similarities to those of Zviran and Haga (although their participants were asked to remember only one or two passwords). While studying the memorability of cognitive passwords, Zviran and Haga used self-generated and system-generated passwords as a control group. The recall-rates for one self-generated password after three months were 31%, and for system-generated, 24% [24]. In [25], Zviran and Haga further report a 35% recall-rate for self-selected passwords after three months, and 23% for random passwords. The recall-rate for associative items was 69%, fact-based items, 89% and opinion-based items, 72% [24]. These studies already indicate that associative passwords are easy to remember. Our results show that the design guidelines suggested in Figure 2 can bring the memorability of ten designed passwords up to the memorability of one self-generated password.

Memorability vs. Password Strength. It is often stated that a memorable password cannot be a strong one and vice versa. In order to classify the passwords as strong or weak, we used the principles for categorization and evaluation reported upon in [8] as classifiers. Table 6 shows the respective results at the first recall session (two to three days after the passwords were generated). These early numbers give us an indication that the proposed guidelines may break the password myth, because it is clear that the rate of fully recalled, good passwords is significantly higher than the respective rate for weak passwords. It is also interesting to observe the high proportion of weak passwords that are not remembered.

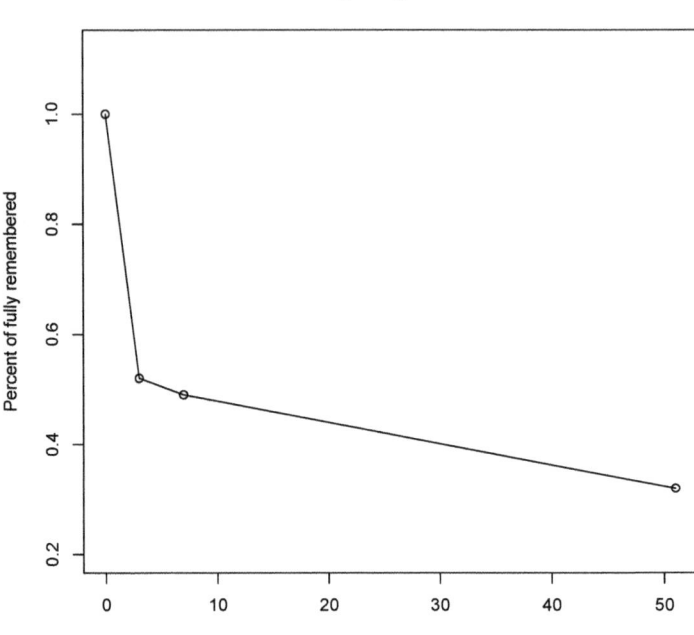

Fig. 3. Forgetting curve for association passwords

Table 7 shows the categories of the recall results, based on the password categories introduced in the suggested guidelines. Looking at the first and second recall sessions from the point of view of this categorization, non-word passwords are the best remembered. Data from the second recall session reveals that the rehearsal of the passwords has an effect on memorability. The primary recall-rate is the percentage of fully remembered, originally designed passwords. The secondary recall-rate gives the percentage of the passwords, which were misspelled exactly the same way in recall sessions one and two.

ANOVA analysis was again used to investigate the memorability of the passwords against strength of the passwords in all three recall sessions. However, in these analyses, only those passwords that were fully remembered (also being primary in the second and third recall sessions) are taken as fully recalled passwords. The analysis shows that in the first recall session, the strength of the password had a very strong positive statistical effect on memorability ($t - value = 5.081$ and $p - value = 5.39 \cdot 10^{-7}$). In the second session (one week after designing

Table 6. First recall percentages among good and weak passwords

Category	Fully remembered	1-2 errors	Not remembered
Good ones	61.7 %	14.9%	23.4%
Weak ones	47.5 %	15.7%	36.8%

Table 7. First and second recall percentages among password categories

	1. Recall session		2. Recall session	
Category	Fully remembered	1-2 errors	Primary	Secondary
Word	38.8%	13.6%	42.5%	44.0%
Mixture	48.6%	16.8%	40.5%	48.0%
Non-word	64.5%	14.8%	66.4%	50.0%

session), the strength of the password still has a statistically strong effect on memorability ($t - value = 3.654$ and $p - value = 2.94 \cdot 10^{-4}$). Finally, in the third session (1.5 months after the designing session), the effect is no longer significant.

At first glance, this result seems to be illogical, but when considering the actual memorizing process, it is not. The students were not asked to recall ten random-string passwords. They were asked to create password structures, which would make their passwords not only strong, but also memorable, by applying a "password formula" with two seeds: the Associative Factor of the password (which could be retrieved on the login site) and the Personal Factor (associated to the site or something very close to the user). Thus, in order to recall their passwords, the participants only needed to recall their own password-designing formula and then apply it with the seeds they would get from the sites. It might also be the case that those participants who designed weak passwords used seeds that did not have enough meaning for them, and therefore the memorization achieved become closer to that of ten random passwords.

5   Conclusions and Further Work

The challenge to users to remember a large number of good passwords has been regarded as the Achilles heel of the use of passwords as an authentication mechanism. One-time password generators, creative design techniques, and challenge-response protocols have been suggested as approaches to meet this challenge. However, each of these introduces new challenges such as portability, scalability, and cognitive overload. Inspired by Grawemeyer and Johnson [6], the current paper provides a set of concrete guidelines for the design of passwords, with mechanisms for creating, encoding, retrieving, and executing multiple passwords. We have suggested an approach in which users for a given service take an element associated to the service and a personal element as input to the process of password creation. This process is guided by a small set of criteria, which inform the user of the elements that constitute a good password.

In order to evaluate the suggested approach, a three-phased experiment including instruction, password-generation and recall sessions was carried out. The recall sessions were distributed over one and a half months and allowed an investigation into whether the participants had understood the guidelines, to what extent they had been applied, the strength of the generated passwords and their memorability. The analysis performed indicates that the guidelines regarding the use of an Association Element and Personal Factor had been well conceived.

However, a minority of the participants actually managed to transform these two elements into passwords that can be considered good.

For the most part, the resulting passwords were too short and lacked special characters. The collected data shows that the concepts of Association Elements and Personal Factors were well understood. We introduced the concepts of primary, secondary, and tertiary associations to describe the nature of the associations. For Personal Factors, we identified service-related, site-related and not related factors. The majority of the factors chosen were not related to the site or the service, and it is also noted that a non-negligible fraction of the participants did not include a Personal Factor. Ten different ways of combining the Association Element and the Personal Factor were identified. The participants' ability to recall the passwords generated was compared to a previous study, in which the concepts of Association Elements and Personal Factors were not used. Using an ANOVA test, we have shown that, at a significance-level of close to 5%, the memorability of the passwords is better with the guidelines presented in the current paper. The memorability of the passwords over time was also traced with a Forgetting Curve, an approach that can be suggested as a reference point for comparing different guidelines and mnemonic techniques.

Finally, we investigated the memorability versus the strength of the passwords. It is commonly believed (discussed in [6]) that passwords with a common word or name have a memorability advantage, and that random, look-alike passwords are difficult to remember. A noteworthy result of the current paper is that after a few days, the strength of the passwords generated had a very positive effect on memorability, but after several weeks, the effect was less significant, and at the final recall session, password-strength had no effect on memorability. However, this indicates that workarounds can be achieved for the well-established assumption that good passwords are difficult to remember. The memorability of the passwords generated according to the suggested guidelines results from the fact that the participant does not need to recall the password itself, but just remember how it was created. He or she will get seeds for the generation of the passwords from the account login site to help his or her memory. We also stress that users do not come to these ideas by themselves. They have to be taught and encouraged to be creative in the process of generating passwords. It should not be taken for granted that all users can design good passwords with the help of a short guideline alone.

Our perception is that by following the recommendations in this paper, the risk of using same password in different accounts could also be reduced. Even if a user uses the same password structure, the variations in secondary or tertiary association prevent this one password from revealing all the others. When users are allowed to use their own associations and their own style of password generation, the burden to memory is smaller than the burden of recalling passwords to which they have no connection. Keeping this in mind, users can remember and use very long passwords, and still perceive them as user friendly. Users should also be cautioned that the generation of passwords should not be undertaken hastily. The best results are achieved, both from a security and memorability point of view, when users invest a bit of time in the creation of their passwords. And as with many other tasks, rehearsal also appears to be beneficial to the process of designing passwords.

Further work will include analysis of the effect the layout of the websites on the selection of the language used, the Association Elements and the Personal Factors. It will also be of interest to evaluate the strength of the passwords produced when different amounts of information are given to an adversary, in order to further assess the security of the password as an authentication mechanism.

Acknowledgements. We are grateful to all the participants who took part in this study.

References

1. Adams, A., Sasse, M.A.: Users are not the enemy. Communications of the ACM 42, 40–46 (1999)
2. Averell, L., Heathcote, A.: The Form of the Forgetting Curve and the fate of Memories. Journal of Mathematical Psychology 55, 25–35 (2010)
3. Bonneau, J., Preibusch, S.: The password thicket: technical and market failures in human authentication on the web. In: WEIS 2010: Proceedings of the Ninth Workshop on the Economics of Information Security, Boston, MA, USA (June 2010)
4. Dhamija, R., Perrig, A.: Déjà Vu: A User Study Using Images for Authentication. In: Proceedings of 9th USENIX Security Symposium (2000)
5. Gehringer, E.F.: Choosing Passwords: Security and Human Factors. In: Proceedings of International Symposium on Technology and Society, pp. 369–373 (2002)
6. Grawemeyer, B., Johnson, H.: Using and Managing Multiple Passwords: A Week to a View. Interacting with Computers 23(3), 256–267 (2011)
7. Halderman, J.A., Waters, B., Felten, E.W.: A Convenient Method for Securely Managing Passwords. In: Proceedings of the 14th International Conference on World Wide Web, pp. 471–479 (2005)
8. Helkala, K.: An Educational Tool for Password Quality Measurements. In: Proceedings of Norwegian Information Security Conference, pp. 69–80. Tapir Akademisk Forlag (2008)
9. Helkala, K.: Password Education Based on Guidelines Tailored to Different Password Categories. Journal of Computers 6(5) (2011)
10. Helkala, K., Snekkenes, E.: Password Generation and Search Space Reduction. Journal of Computers 4(7), 663–669 (2009)
11. Hopper, N.J., Blum, M.: Secure Human Identification Protocols. In: Boyd, C. (ed.) ASIACRYPT 2001. LNCS, vol. 2248, pp. 52–66. Springer, Heidelberg (2001)
12. Ives, B., Walsh, K.R., Schneider, H.: The domino effect of password reuse. Communication of the ACM 47, 75–78 (2004)
13. Jermyn, I., Mayer, A., Monrose, F., Reiter, M.K., Rubin, A.D.: The Design and Analysis of Graphical Passwords. In: Proceedings of the 8th Conference on USENIX Security Symposium, vol. 8, p. 1 (1999)
14. Kuhn, B.T., Garrison, C.: A survey of passwords from 2007 to 2009. In: 2009 Information Security Curriculum Development Conference, InfoSecCD 2009, pp. 91–94. ACM, New York (2009)

15. Kuo, C., Romanosky, S., Cranor, L.F.: Human Selection of Mnemonic Phrase-Based Passwords. In: Proceedings of 2nd Symposium on Usable Privacy and Security, pp. 67–78. ACM Press (2006)
16. Li, X.-Y., Teng, S.-H.: Practical Human-Machine Identification over Insecure Channels. Journal of Combinatorial Optimization 3(4), 347–361 (1999)
17. Matsumoto, T.: Human-Computer Cryptography: An Attempt. In: Proceedings of the 3rd ACM Conference on Computer and Communications Security, pp. 68–75 (1996)
18. Sasse, M.A., Brostoff, S., Weirich, D.: Transforming the "Weakest Link" - Human/Computer Interaction Approach to Usable and Effective Security. BT Technol. 19, 122–131 (2001)
19. Stubblefield, A., Simon, D.: Inkblot Authentication. Technical report, Microsoft Research, Microsoft Corporation (2004)
20. Villarrubia, C., Fernandez-Medina, E., Piattini, M.: Quality of Password Management Policy. In: The First International Conference on Availability, Reliability and Security, ARES 2006, p. 7 (April 2006)
21. Vu, K.-P.L., Proctor, R.W., Bhargav-Spantzel, A., Tai, B.-L.(Belin), Cook, J., Schultz, E.: Improving Password Security and Memorability to Protect Personal and Organizational Information. International Journal of Human-Computer Studies 65, 744–757 (2007)
22. Weinshall, D.: Cognitive Authentication Schemes Safe Against Spyware (Short Paper). In: Proceedings of the 2006 IEEE Symposium on Security and Privacy (S&P 2006), pp. 295–300 (2006)
23. Yan, J., Blackwell, A., Anderson, R., Grant, A.: Password Memorability and Security: Empirical Results. IEEE Security & Privacy 2(5), 25–31 (2004)
24. Zviran, M., Haga, W.J.: User authentication by cognitive passwords: an empirical assessment. In: Proceedings of the 5th Jerusalem Conference on Information Technology, pp. 137–144 (1990)
25. Zviran, M., Haga, W.J.: A Comparison of Password Techniques for Multilevel Authentication Mechanisms. Computer Journal 36(3), 227–237 (1993)

Increasing Service Users' Privacy Awareness by Introducing On-Line Interactive Privacy Features

Elahe Kani-Zabihi and Martin Helmhout

Information Security Group, Royal Holloway University of London,
Egham, Surrey, TW20 0EX
{Elahe.Kani,Martin.Helmhout}@rhul.ac.uk

Abstract. The work presented in this paper introduces the concept of *On-line Interactive (OI) privacy feature* which is defined as any on-line interactive tool, component or user-interface that creates privacy awareness and supports users in understanding their on-line privacy risks. These features have been developed as an *interactive social translucence map* that discloses the flow of personal information, a *privacy enquiry* for a direct chat about users' privacy concerns and a *discussion forum* presenting users' privacy concerns using their language in an interactive FAQ format. The paper presents an evaluation of a prototype of this set of embedded OI privacy features. The field study presented evaluates the prototype's usability and its effect on users' privacy awareness, understanding and attitude. 100 participants took part in the study and were drawn from groups of *experienced* and *less experienced* users. Both quantitative and qualitative data collection methods were used. Findings suggest that OI privacy features increase users' privacy awareness and encourage users to find out more about the uses of their personal data. However, users' ICT skills and Internet experience significantly influence whether a feature is favoured or otherwise. In general, it is concluded that privacy features are very much welcomed and necessary to empower users to manage their privacy concerns but some groups need to be further supported by social and institutional privacy management processes.

Keywords: On-line privacy, interactive privacy feature, privacy awareness, privacy concern, usability study, mixed-method research method, privacy transparency, user study, social translucence, HCI.

1   Introduction

This paper continues previous research [13] and is part of a project entitled **Visualisation and Other Methods of Expression (VOME)**. VOME's main objective is to develop methods of expressing privacy that enable a wider range of privacy concerns to be articulated. An increasing number of organisations deliver their products and services on the Internet, which attracts people (on-line service users) from all walks of life to use these services. For the past two years we have studied and participated in privacy and security related workshops and nevertheless, it is clear that there

P. Laud (Ed.): NordSec 2011, LNCS 7161, pp. 131–148, 2012.

Table 1. Service Users' Requirements

The on-line service platform should consider the following:
1. Display information about the service provider on screen before the registration process.
2. Display feedback from other organisations and service users about the service provider.
3. Inform service users of their personal information requirements before the registration process.
4. Display the service provider's privacy policy on screen.
5. The information provided on privacy policy should be readable, concise, noticeable and in a language understandable by all types of users.
6. Display the service agreement between service user and service provider on screen.
7. Provide a printable and saveable service agreement between the service user and the service provider.
8. Inform the service user about what is going on by providing appropriate feedback within reasonable time.
9. Allow the service user to frequently engage in an interaction practice at each stage of the registration process enabling the user to raise concerns through a communication channel with the service provider.
10. Provide information on the security technology implemented by the service provider.
11. Provide a secure channel only available to a valid service user.
12. Request only personal information that is necessary for delivering the service.
13. Immediately inform users of any changes made to an online service by the service provider.
14. Give service users a reasonable amount of freedom to decide on how they will maintain their relationship with the service provider.
15. Adapt to the service users' characteristics.
16. The service users should have control over personal information collected by the service provider.
17. Inform the service user of the purpose for collecting each personal detail.

is still a gap between the current privacy related studies and the real need of users with respect to their on-line privacy concerns.

On-line service users have privacy concerns when they are forced to disclose their personal information [11, 13]. On the one hand, service users want to know what happens to their data [15]. On the other hand, system developers have ignored the importance of privacy in technology design [16, 24]. A study in Belgium [15] reported that young adults are more vulnerable to privacy threats and at risk when revealing personal information has become easier. Moreover, it is stated that service users disclose personal information more frequently without any indication of the possible consequences. Therefore, one of the aims of VOME is to address this issue by introducing new On-line Interactive (OI) privacy features, which enable users to make clearer on-line disclosure choices. The term 'on-line interactive privacy feature' is defined as any on-line interactive tool, component or user-interface that creates privacy awareness and support users in understanding their on-line privacy risks. OI privacy features can increase users' privacy awareness by informing them on how their personal information is used by the service provider(s). The study presented in this paper introduces the first version of a user-centric web service prototype with embedded OI privacy features. The central component of the prototype is a 'translucence[1] map' presenting service users' data flow between user and service-provider(s).

---

[1] Translucence in this paper is defined as semi or partly transparency. For example in the context of information: anonymised information or aggregated information.

Other OI privacy features were selected from current on-line interaction tools such as an on-line chat system and a forum. In this paper we also present the results obtained from a user study. We evaluated the privacy features and tested them concerning usability and change of privacy awareness. Consequently, in this paper, the importance of embedding OI privacy features during on-line registration process has been argued. In the attempt to design a user-centred prototype [14] of an on-line service, we elicited users' requirements with respect to on-line privacy. Based on the result which has been reported in [13] and [9], a list of user requirements for on-line services was gathered (Table 1). Hence the first version of an on-line service platform with embedded OI privacy features prototype was designed. The description of the design and design principles are provided in section 3. In order to test and evaluate the usability of OI privacy features, a user-centred study approach was conducted. Hence users were asked to interact with the prototype. The outcome of this study is reported in section 4. Finally, in section 5 we conclude our study and discuss our future work.

2   Related Work

The world is moving towards a virtual environment where users benefit from the convenience of using services on-line but are also expected to be digitally enabled and confident in all aspects regarding the use of on-line services. Considering that there are few system developers who think about privacy in their technology design [24], our research explores how recent privacy research has contributed to a better communication and interaction between both service users and service providers. We conducted a literature review and gathered a list of the relevant long term privacy projects running worldwide:

Ensuring Consent & Revocation (EnCoRe) project is working on a prototype system to allow users to have more control over their data[2]. Our research is similar to EnCoRe by looking at users' requirements with regards to privacy and more meaningful consent. However, our study takes a step further by eliciting these requirements from service users implicitly as well as explicitly (more details given in next section). Moreover, we are designing an interactive system where both users and service providers can exchange information about on-line privacy.

Privacy Value Networks (PVNets) project is developing and applying new methodologies for the study of privacy[3]. Our study (with a different focus) is in line with PVNets by looking at an appropriate research methodology to study privacy. However, while PVNets explores privacy value chains, our research is focused specifically on the privacy features and the relationship between service users and service providers.

According to **Privacy-aware Secure Monitoring** (PRISM), network monitoring could become a threat to users' privacy by keeping individual communications under surveillance[4]. Therefore, to enhance the level of data protection, the aim of PRISM is to develop a traffic monitoring architecture which guarantees privacy preservation by

---

[2] http://www.encore-project.info/press.html
[3] www.pvnets.org
[4] www.fp7-prism.eu

avoiding disclosure of raw data even inside the controller domain itself. Despite the fact that PRISM identifies a technology solution to preserve the service users' privacy by avoiding disclosure of data, this is still not helping the fact that users themselves are not informed why their personal data should be given in the first place.

Privacy and Identity Management for Community Services (PICOS) project is testing and evaluating a mobile communication service prototype which uses a location identifier system[5]. A "privacy advisor" technology has been implemented in this system where users are informed about the privacy risk at each stage when users reveal their location to other service users. Our work in a different context is similar to the PICOS project by informing users about their on-line privacy risk in advance of personal data revelation.

PrimeLife[6] is based on the FP6 project **PRIME** (Privacy Identity Management) has demonstrated that privacy technologies can enable citizens execute their legal rights and control personal information in on-line transactions. PRIME was also a continuation project after the **PISA** (Privacy Incorporated Software Agent) project. PISA built a prototype and created a list of requirements necessary to develop software agents that safeguard users' privacy.

EU FP7 PrimeLife project launched (February 2010) Clique as a privacy enhanced social networking site. The privacy control functionality in Clique enables users to modify privacy settings in a way that users can choose who can see their new information before it is published on the site. PrimeLife also produced a privacy awareness tool called Privacy Dashboard[7]. The tool informs users of possible embedded browser-cookies. Service providers use those cookies to collect data about users' online behaviour. Our study focuses on the service provider explicitly informing the user about the use of their personal information. Hence, in our study, we implement online interactive tools that inform users beforehand of what will happen with their disclosed personal information after a registration process. Besides that, our work aims to include less-experienced users whereas Privacy Dashboard requires users to have a certain level of ICT skills.

In PICOS and PrimeLife (including finished projects: PISA and PRIME), the focus is on privacy protection, communication of privacy stances by either party, or the reporting of privacy status and risks. However, tools are not being developed to encourage interaction and create dialogues enabling both parties to respond to each other's concerns.

Many researchers [6, 7, 8, 15, 16, 17, 18 and 22] highlighted the 'relationship between privacy and technology' [18] and the importance of knowing what data is collected and stored by whom [6]. However, few studies have focused on a pioneer in privacy awareness using technology. A summary of related studies is reported in this section. In an article by [22], Web 2.0 users' privacy issues are discussed and classified into four categories: users' personal information; users' seeking behaviour privacy; threat from a third party and leaking of users' privacy documents. We are

---

[5] http://www.picos-project.eu

[6] www.primelife.eu

[7] http://www.primelife.eu/results/opensource/76-dashboard

inclined with their opinion of: "privacy protection should not only be approached as a technical concern but also as social consideration". Moreover, the authors introduced a list of privacy-enhancing measures. Relevant to our study is their Privacy Policy Statements measure, in which the authors state: users should be informed of the privacy of their sensitive data; how and when the data will be collected and processed; for which purposes it will be used and by whom. Interestingly, in compromising between privacy and trust, the author suggests: an effective collaboration between service providers and users is important in promoting privacy awareness (educating users on privacy and the risk of identity disclosure). Similarly, as the authors suggested, in our prototype a "synchronous interactive behaviour (chat)" [22] is provided as an option to increase users' privacy awareness. Therefore, the on-line chat option enables users to communicate with the service provider about their privacy concerns. With relation to privacy awareness, research indicates that privacy salience [1] or increase in awareness can increase people's worries about their privacy. With taking context into consideration and adopting customer relationship management principles (see next section), the provider is able to create a trustworthy (and trust building) environment. Hence, managing the relationship between the user and provider can create confidence and turn the negative effects of salience into a positive attitude towards the provider. Another study (in Web 2.0 users' privacy issues) by [15] conducted three user studies looking into three ethical issues: trust, privacy and etiquette in developing Web 2.0 applications. Hence the authors revealed a set of important user requirements of Web 2.0 applications of which one is in line with our study: privacy. The first study conducted in Norway with 200 participants (from various age groups) used a survey to collect the data. The study investigated the problem users experienced using social network sites (SNSs) and reported: users require control of their personal information. This relates to the control privacy mechanisms in different forms of intervened interaction designed to protect access to and publication of personal information. These privacy mechanisms should be user friendly. Otherwise the complexity of such settings will be ignored and avoided by users, despite the importance of privacy. Moreover, it was reported that students were careless in the revelation of personal information in SNSs; and finally, users have privacy concerns and want to know what happens to their data. Likewise, in designing our first version of the prototype (section 3), we considered that the OI privacy features should be accessible to different kinds of users and therefore complexity in the functionality needs to be reduced to a minimum. Furthermore, translucence maps (described in section 3.2) were used to explain users what will happen to their data when they submit their data to the service provider. The second study by [15] consists of 30 members of two on-line communities. The first group was a community of 50+ years old who had no ICT skills. The second group was a community of young men with good ICT skills and interested in photography. Participants from the first community were asked to answer questions on a blog on the on-line community site. The second community was asked to use provided diaries to report on a daily basis. Both groups were questioned on their on-line activities and the type of communication channels they used. The study revealed that the most important issue for all participants was privacy. When sharing information on-line, the younger adults used privacy options whereas the seniors used the more traditional way of privacy practice by avoiding disclosure of personal information. Similar to [15], in choosing our participants for the user study, both ICT skilled users and inexperienced users were recruited. However, as opposed to [15], the same research methodology was used for both groups. This is described in section 4. Finally, [15] conducted another study in Belgium with two communities: the first an unstructured group of 85 families with children and the second a structured group of 50 gay males (40 to 50 years old). The participants were given access to an on-line community platform and provided with a digital camera to generate and share contents. Their activities were observed, monitored and logged. The participants were interviewed and various focus groups were organised to collect data. On the subject of privacy, the authors reported that the website's restricted access gained users confidence to share more personal information. Furthermore, users found it important to have control of how and with whom they shared their personal information. On the subject of transparency, the authors concluded that the on-line community site should be transparent implying that messages or comments on the website should be presented clearly. Moreover, messages should indicate whether they are viewable for everyone or only to specific persons. Likewise, in our prototype (section 3.2), the inspiration of transparency (translucence maps) is considered to be one of the more important OI privacy features in the design.

Correspondingly, on the same subject of transparency, the work presented by [10] introduces a privacy policy visualization model where users are able to better capture the designed privacy policies. The proposed theoretical visualization model facilitates understanding the privacy policy in place and avoids users reading the entire statement. Hence both service users and providers will be able to understand the policies without the need of reading the entire privacy policy statement. In designing our prototype, we have taken an approach contrary to [10]. Rather than just focusing on privacy policy statements, the focal point was more on presenting what happens to service users' data and providing a communication channel where users can raise their privacy concerns.

Finally, [19] introduces a user-centric privacy architecture that enables the provider-independent protection of personal data. The prototype designed for an on-line privacy community, facilitates the open exchange among users of privacy-related information about service providers. As opposed to the 'provider-independent' approach taken by [19], we believe that it is beneficial to users when service providers are involved in both privacy protection and privacy awareness processes.

3   Design Principles

In designing an on-line service with embedded OI privacy features, we adopted HCI usability design guidelines and principles by Nielsen [25] and Raymond [21]. These are important principles that designers should consider when developing usable and accessible systems. Table 2 shows a list of system requirements for an on-line service with embedded OI privacy features using the HCI usability design principles.

Table 2. System requirements using HCI principles

No.	HCI design principles	System requirements for an on-line service with embedded OI privacy features
SR1	Match between system and the real world	The communication channel provided, should feel similar to off-line dialogue when users freely discuss their privacy concerns.
SR2	Recognition rather than recall	Links to privacy policy statements and service's term and conditions should be clearly visible and familiar to all users.
SR3	Aesthetic and minimalist design	The system should avoid using information that is irrelevant or rarely needed.
SR4	Visibility of system status	The system should inform the user about what is going on by providing appropriate feedback within reasonable time.
SR5	Rule of confirmation	The system should provide a contract (an agreement between the user and the provider) stating that the user's personal information will be safe and confidential.

Table 3. System requirements using CRM principles

No.	CRM principles	System requirements for online service with embedded OI privacy features
SR6	*Initiating behaviour:* Service provider pro-actively initiates efforts to better understand a user's needs and requirements	Informing a user about services and particularly making users more aware (in advance) about privacy.
SR7	*Signalling behaviour:* Service provider provides advance information about intended changes in its marketing programs	HCI components that allow interaction between user and provider about intended changes.
SR8	*Disclosing behaviour:* Service provider is perceived to provide *sensitive* information about itself.	The service provider is disclosing sensitive information (working practises, relationships with third parties).
SR9	*Interaction frequency:* The inverse of the average time elapsed between consecutive user and service provider interactions.	When interactions take place more often, mutual trust in a relationship gets a chance to increase.
SR10	*Richness:* The richer the channel, the more complex messages can be transferred.	Richness can vary on a scale from high to low: video conference, voice chat, text chat, and email.

In order to understand the user better, the service provider needs to invest in building relationships with its users or customers. Customer Relation Management (CRM) theory [3] is a strategy that can be adopted for managing service provider's interactions. Hence, when applied properly, CRM can have a significant impact on customer satisfaction and create a closer relationship between service provider and user. Therefore, in designing the prototype, we considered CRM design principles to be as important as HCI design principles. Table 3 shows the list of possible CRM principles and the requirements for an on-line service.

3.1   The Prototype

The disclosure of users' personal information often happens at the point of registration for an online service. Registration processes are often used when a relationship is needed for the longer term in order to deliver a service. In the following sections we exemplify our proposal with screenshots taken from the prototype. Consequently, we embedded OI privacy features during an on-line service registration. The prototype represents a mock-up council, Your Local Council (YLC), which offers an on-line smartcard registration service. The smartcard is used by the council to combine several services: a Library service, a Local Shops discount scheme and Local Transport, as part of one card. Figure 1 shows the first web page (Services) displayed after users selected the "Register me" link on the Home page.

For the purpose of this user study, all participants were asked to select 'Smartcard Services' from the list and move to the next page by clicking on the 'Next' button. All users are first directed to four pages before the registration page:

1. Introduction to smartcard services and selection of services

This page is shown in Figure 1. The user will start the registration process by selecting their services. This is an opportunity for the user to be in control of the type of services they register for. This procedure meets the following requirements: CRM principle: Initiating behaviour (SR6, Table 3) and User Requirements: 8 and 16 (Table 1);

2. About us

The service provider will display information about the nature of the organisation and other useful information for the user: description; contact details; and information about their partners (CRM principles: SR6 and SR8 (Table 3) and Users' requirements: 1 (Table 1));

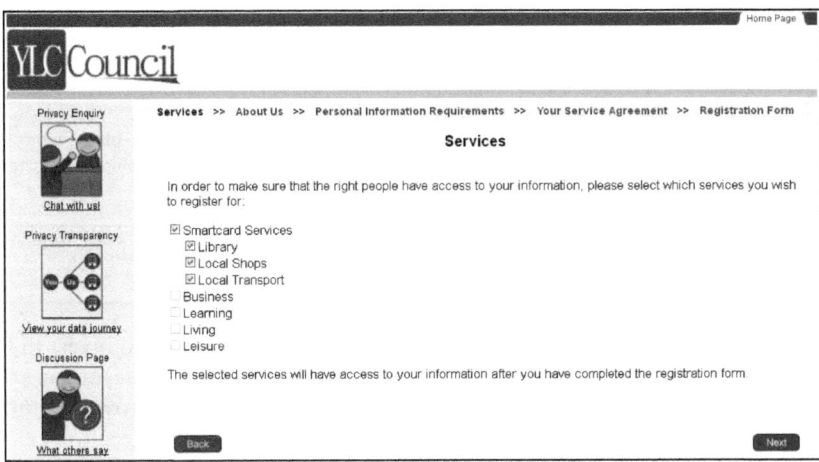

Fig. 1. Smartcard services offered by YLC Council

3. Personal Information Requirements

Displayed in Figure 6 (Appendix). The service provider informs the user that certain personal information is required to use the service, what will happen to the data as well as the reason for collecting it. This information will be communicated to the user with help of an interactive dataflow map that displays who has access to what type of personal information (CRM principle: SR8 (Table 3) and User Requirements: 3 and 17 (Table 1));

4. Service Agreement

The service provider gives a contract of their agreement for the user to keep as a reference. An overview of selected services, privacy policy and terms & conditions (User Requirement: 6 (Table 1));

5. Registration form

Displayed in Figure 7 (Appendix). The final step of the process displays a registration form where the user discloses the necessary personal information for getting the selected service(s). During the registration process, the user is able to get help and access the three OI privacy features (left panel in Figure 1). The next section elaborates this further.

3.2   On-Line Interactive Privacy Features

The OI privacy features are designed with usability and (social) interaction / sociability in mind. Usability and sociability in design are important when interaction between user(s) and provider takes place, especially when interaction needs to be (partly) controlled by bringing in social policies [20].

1. Privacy Enquiry: Fulfilling CRM principles (SR9 and SR10, Table 3) and also meeting the needs of users for a private and synchronous communication channel calls for an on-line chat tool. Users can instantly communicate with a service provider regarding their privacy concerns. In order to meet CRM *signaling* principle (SR7, Table 3) and Users Requirements 10 and 11 (Table 1), the chat tool informs users of a secure private channel of communication by displaying three icons: a 'live' icon assuring the user that there is a person on the other side ready to listen, a 'padlock' icon indicating the communication channel is secure, and a '1:1': icon showing the user that the communication is a one-to-one conversation. This is shown in Figure 2. The disadvantages of chats, besides not seeing the other person, are that they do not give much time to reflect or correct faults which can lead to chaotic interaction. However, people who are regular users are enthusiastic and do not have such complaints [20]. A final aspect to consider is whether the privacy enquiry gives the user enough comfort to discuss concerns that are sensitive and personal.

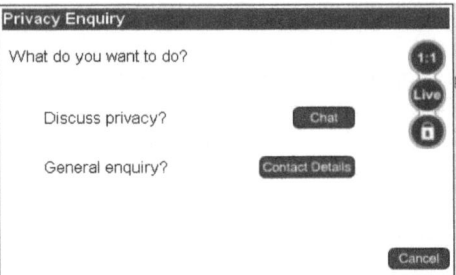

Fig. 2. Initiating on-line privacy communication

2. Privacy Transparency[8]: One of the aspects of privacy is personal information and the need for more transparency. Whereas privacy is difficult to describe and is perceived differently depending upon cultural background, personal information is an easier way to address many common problems concerning privacy. Besides that, because of interaction and location, personal information (or its perceived meaning) is situated and part of the perceived inner context as well as the perceived outer context. Concerning context and interaction, we adopt the notion of context as an interactional problem [4], which states that context is a relational, dynamic and occasioned property and arises from activity and is produced and maintained by that activity. Concerning (semi) transparency, we adopt *social translucence* [5] which makes users aware of the presence of other groups or activities, but does not (necessarily) reveal their identity. Figures 3 and 4 both depict a user interacting with the translucence map and shows what data is needed when eventually the user registers for a particular service. Figure 3 shows that *gender* information is only given to the Council, consultancy company 'CardSmart' and 'Local Shops', and not to parties whose access is blocked by a cross. Figure 4 shows which information is accessed by 'Local Shops'.

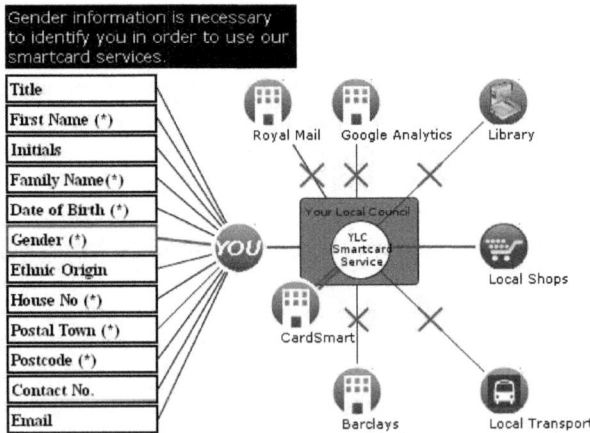

Fig. 3. Translucence Map (1)—User moves mouse over Gender field

---

[8] In the prototype we use the term Privacy Transparency because transparency is understandable language (User Requirement 5 (Table 1)) whereas 'Translucence' could puzzle the user.

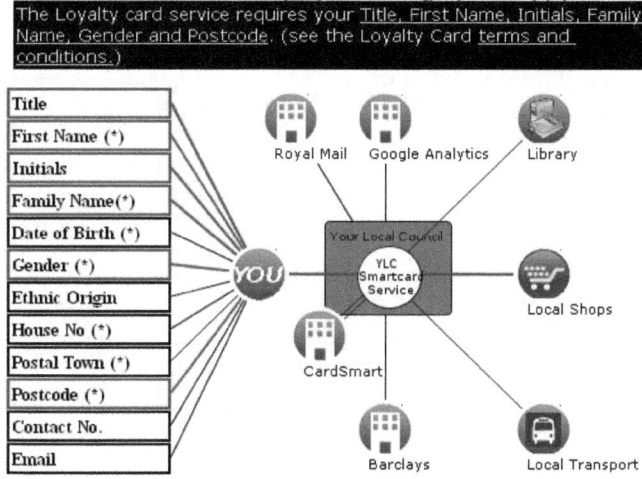

Fig. 4. Translucence Map (2)—User moves mouse over Local Shops icon

3. Discussion Page: The discussion forum (Figure 5) is designed as a knowledgebase for users to find answers to the concerns they have. The knowledge base contains previous users' privacy enquiries and answers from the service provider. The policy of the discussion forum is to allow users to submit comments and let the provider moderate those comments. Hence, the user sends a comment and receives feedback that response will follow the next working day. Registration is not needed and therefore the forum is open to comments from everyone. However, moderating the comments assures the knowledge base to present reliable answers of the provider but also represent the questions and views of the users.

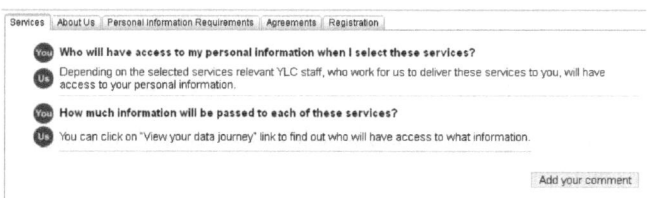

Fig. 5. Discussion forum

4   User Study

In order to evaluate the usability of the OI privacy features, there is a need to elicit on-line service users' opinions and observe their behaviour during interaction with the prototype. We were interested in a wide range of Internet users. In addition to Internet users with more than five years experience we recruited 'non-users' as well. In HCI non-users are regarded as potential users who might in the future engage with the system but are currently inactive users. The current state of technology has not the right answer to gain their confidence and reduce their privacy concerns. We suggest that designers should consider non-users' opinions in cases where OI privacy features are adopted for the development of on-line services. When non-users feel comfortable and have their needs fulfilled, they possibly return and eventually can become future on-line service users [23].

4.1   Participants

We recruited participants from nine UK online centres[9]. All participants were recruited by the Centre Manager and were offered a shopping voucher as a reward for their contribution to the research. Following the result reported by [15] (students have less privacy concerns), we recruited 10 students from Royal Holloway University of London (undergraduate and postgraduate levels) to study their behaviours towards and opinions of OI privacy features. Correspondingly, 100 users (65 Female and 35 Male) between 16 to 60 years old participated in our user study. Participants were questioned about their Internet experience. Hence, it is reported that 64 of them had more than five years; 21 between one to five years; and 15 less than one year experience with Internet as source of information. Participants were also questioned about their IT literacy. Using the IT literacy questionnaire [12], 41 were categorized as novice, 36 as intermediate and 23 as advanced users. Categorising participants based on their IT literacy helped us in usability evaluation of the OI privacy features and also to better understand different types of users' attitudes towards these features. We also were interested into two groups of *Experienced* and *Less-experienced* users. Therefore, participants were questioned with respect to their experience with on-line services as "have you registered with any on-line services in the past?". Accordingly, based on their Internet usage, IT literacy and also their experience with on-line services, 100 users were equally distributed between the Experienced and Less-experienced groups.

4.2   Research Methodology

The research methodology conducted was a mixed-method research [14] which is a combination of qualitative and quantitative methods with flexible and fixed questions. Therefore, data were collected using interview, observation, think-out-loud and questionnaire techniques. The study started with a questionnaire about general demographics including the computer expertise and the privacy attitudes about websites mostly focused on personal information. Following the questionnaire, users were introduced to the prototype as: "a website that projects the portal of a council, *Your Local Council (YLC)*". Each user was asked to take the role of a citizen and imagine the council to be his/her 'real' council. Then, the user was introduced to a *smartcard* service provided by the council. After the introduction, the user was asked to interact with the website and try to register with the council. Users were given approximately five

---

[9] The UK online centres network was set up by UK government to provide public access to computers in year 2000. http://www.ukonlinecentres.com

minutes to register. In an unsuccessful attempt to register, users were then given support by one of the researchers present in the field. Users who had successfully registered with the website were asked to interact further with the prototype to accomplish their tasks. The aim of these tasks was to make sure users interact with OI privacy features. While giving support, users were questioned to comment on what they would have expected to see in order to achieve the task. We applied think aloud protocol [9, 2] that helped us analyzing the interaction of the user with the website while thinking out loud. Simultaneously, we asked users to rank the usability of each task using an on-line questionnaire. Upon completion of all the tasks, users were asked to reply to a list of questions eliciting their privacy concerns with regards to the YLC council. The complete analysis of the data will be presented in a separate paper. Finally, we conducted a fifteen minutes interview to explore users' views and obtain a deeper understanding of users' requirements with respect to the embedded OI privacy features. Moreover, this was an opportunity to discuss users' behaviours during the interaction and their opinions about the features.

4.3   Results

In this section, we report the outcome of the prototype as a whole concerning privacy attitude and awareness and the results regarding the usability of the OI privacy features. Although the experiment was not conducted in a laboratory setting, we can conclude that in general many users mentioned that the prototype helped them understand what happened to their information. Users were asked about their general attitude in advance of the experiment and asked similar questions concerning their attitude concerning the prototype. Regarding users' privacy concern, we saw a reduction of 34% in users stating that they have concerns and a 33% increase in users that have no concern when comparing the YLC prototype with their general privacy attitude. Concerning disclosure and the way YLC collects processes and uses data, users were less concerned (35%). Finally, users commented that the YLC website helped them to be aware of how their personal information will be used in comparison to other websites they used in the past. The result shows an increase of 40% and only 14% disagree that YLC makes them aware. In general, the prototype with embedded OI privacy features seems to be very promising, but for a better understanding, we need to look at the usability of the OI privacy features. The usability study involved participants with different age and varying Internet experiences. Almost all users (93%) felt the registration process was easy to do. However 43% of users indicated they needed help in order to complete the task. The data gathered from think-out-loud and observation methods explain that less-experienced users had difficulties with finding the relevant links to proceed to 'Registration Form'. Therefore, non-users who had no experience with on-line services represent a further design challenge. Even though this type was concerned about their privacy, the OI privacy features were still insufficient to facilitate them in understanding the privacy information. Some of these users stopped interacting at the "Personal Information Requirements" page believing that they reached the registration page and hence completed the registration task without studying the 'translucence map'. During the interview session we learned that once users were directed to the right direction, they were able to interact with the interface. One user commented that his lack of IT experience was the only barrier for him but once he was given guidance, he found the prototype very easy to use. Surprisingly, we noted that most users failed to notice the OI privacy features on the left hand side of the screen. One user commented: "I usually ignore this section as it belongs to advertisement". We will consider in the next development stage whether using the left hand side panel as part of the design needs to be avoided. The feedback from all participants was optimistic with regards to the translucence maps (Figure 4 & 5). Users were more in favour of receiving information given in figures and diagrams rather than reading them in text i.e. privacy statements. 89% of users said it was easy to use the map and 52% of them said no help was required. However, we learned in the interview that the 'red cross sign' on the map indicating that there is no flow of data, confused users. Moreover, the guiding text box on the top of the diagram was invisible to most users. The black background colour with white texts was not readable. As opposed to experienced users who found the diagram very easy to understand, the less-experienced users commented they were unsure about the functionality of the maps as there was too much information on the screen. This made them confused about what the purpose of the map was. 68% of users felt the service provider is trustworthy at this stage whereas only 17% said otherwise and 18% stayed neutral. The 'Privacy Enquiry' option was the least favourable OI privacy feature. The idea of chatting on-line only via text raised a privacy concern by itself. Users prefer to see or hear the other person when they have a dialogue with the service provider discussing their privacy concerns. Nevertheless, this option was necessary according to some experienced users who have prior experience with on-line chat channels. One user said that the availability of this option gives him a feeling of security and more confidence as there will be always someone to help. Therefore in the next version of the prototype, this communication channel should be developed further to not only a text chat but possibly include voice as well. Furthermore, by using this option, 70% of users felt they can rely on the service provider at this stage. Similarly, the 'Privacy Discussion' was mainly favourable by those who previously had experience with Frequently Asked Questions (FAQ). The importance of having this option available was highlighted by users. In the interview, users suggested that it was beneficial to read this information. However, it was unclear to them who raised these privacy concerns. Therefore, the next version of the prototype should be designed to make this information more transparent to users by clearly indicating who the users are that actually raise those privacy concerns.

5   Conclusion and Future Work

Previous researches [7, 9 &13] as well as our current study have shown that in general users are concerned when they are asked to disclose personal information. Whether this is caused by a lack of information received or inexperience, there is clearly a need to reduce uncertainty and increase the interaction between service user and provider. The user study and the prototype with embedded OI privacy features, in particular the social translucence maps, demonstrate that users by interacting with the user interface are encouraged to explore and gather information. Moreover, users are also more aware about what to expect and what the consequences are regarding privacy when they register for a certain service. The prototype was designed according to a combination of user requirements, HCI and CRM principles. Together, they act as a guideline to design an interface that makes user and provider as well as the designer more aware of privacy issues. The HCI principle encourages the design of a usable and accessible system. The CRM principles put the emphasis on sociability and building a relationship between the user and service provider. The combination of requirements and principles led to the three components we implemented in our prototype: Privacy Enquiry, Privacy Transparency and Discussion Page. Although the participants in the study were aware of our research and the mock-up council website, the application of mixed-methodology allowed us to get a deeper understanding about how the user perceives and understands the interface. The 'think aloud protocol' gave us a better understanding about what needs to be improved about the prototype and specifically the features. The qualitative interview gave us more insight about how comfortable or confident a user feels. From the gathered results, we can conclude that our first prototype is a good step in the right direction. The feedback received from the participants makes clear that more research is necessary. The result from the user study also indicates that users are in favour of the interactive data flow map (translucence) and prefer to be informed of their personal information privacy. However, further work needs to be done on privacy communication channels and in this case the on-line chat tool was the least favourable privacy feature. Another part of further research is to involve the service provider in the design process and to investigate how much a service provider is willing to disclose sensitive information. Considering the needs and limits of a service provider can influence a design as well as contribute to the implementation of new features. Gathering information about the dialogue between a service provider and its users is crucial for a successful implementation of privacy features. In our future research, we will embed our privacy features in an existing website and gather feedback from 'real' online-service providers and users. Finally, as part of further research is a controlled HCI lab-experiment to measure differences in the relationship between privacy awareness, attitudes and how different groups respond to privacy features. The outcome of the experiment can help adjusting the privacy features towards groups with different needs.

Acknowledgements. We are grateful to all 100 participants who took part in this study. We also like to thank Consult Hyperion (www.chyp.com) for their contribution in implementing the web interface. This work was supported by the Technology Strategy Board; the Engineering and Physical Sciences Research Council and the Economic and Social Research Council [grant number EP/G00255/X].

References

[1] John, L.K., Acquisti, A., Loewenstein, G.: The Best of Strangers: Context Dependent Willingness to Divulge Personal Information (2009), SSRN
     `http://ssrn.com/abstract=1430482`

[2] Constantine, L.L., Lockwood, L.A.D.: Software for Use: A practical guide to the models and methods of usage-centred design. Addison Wesley (2000)

[3] Leuthesser, L., Kohli, A.K.: Relational Behavior in Business Markets: Implications for Relationship Management. Journal of Business Research 34, 221–223 (1995)

[4] Dourish, P.: What we talk about when we talk about the context. Personal and Ubiquitous Computing 8(1), 19–30 (2004)

[5] Erickson, T., Kellogg, W.A.: Social translucence: an approach to designing systems that support social processes. ACM Transactions on Computer-Human Interaction 7(1), 59–83 (2000)

[6] Breznitz, D., Murphree, M., Goodman, S.: Ubiquitous Data Collection: Rethinking Privacy Debates. Computer 44, 100–102 (2011)

[7] Coles-Kemp, L., Kani-Zabihi, E.: On-line privacy and consent: A dialogue not a monologue, September 21-23, pp. 1–15. ACM Press (2010)

[8] Hiok, C.Y., Khoo, V.K.T.: Education Services Mashup: Examining the Impact of Web Design Features on User Trust. In Second International Conference on Computer Research and Development, pp. 349–353. IEEE (2010)

[9] Coles-Kemp, L., Kani-Zabihi, E.: Practice Makes Perfect- Motivating confident on-line privacy protection practices. In: IEEE International Conference on Social Computing (forthcoming, 2011)

[10] Ghazinour, K., Majedi, M., Barker, K.: A model for privacy policy visualization. In: 33rd Annual IEEE International Computer Software and Applications Conference, pp. 335–340 (2009)

[11] Jensen, C., Potts, C., Jensen, C.: Privacy practices of Internet users: self-reports versus observed behaviour. International Journal of Human-Computer Studies 63, 203–227 (2005)

[12] Kani-Zabihi, E., Ghinea, G., Chen, S.Y.: Digital libraries: what do users want? Online Information Review 30, 395–412 (2006)

[13] Kani-Zabihi, E., Coles-Kemp, L.: Service users' requirements for tools to support effective on-line privacy and consent practices. In: The 15th Nordic Conference in Secure IT Systems (NordSec 2010), October 24-30. LNCS, pp. 106–120. ACM Press (2010)

[14] Kani-Zabihi, E., Ghinea, G., Chen, S.Y.: Experiences with Developing a User-Centered Digital Library. International Journal of Digital Library Systems 1, 1–23 (2010)

[15] Karahasanovic, A., Brandtzæg, P.B., Vanattenhoven, J., Lievens, B., Nielsen, K.T., Pierson, J.: Ensuring Trust, Privacy, and Etiquette in Web 2.0 Applications. Computer 42, 42–49 (2009)

[16] Karat, C.M., Brodie, C., Karat, J.: Usable privacy and security for personal information management. Communications of the ACM 49, 56–57 (2006)

[17] Information Commissioner's Office "Privacy by Design",
     `http://www.ico.gov.uk/upload/documents/pdb_report_html/`
     `index.html` (last accessed August 5, 2010)

[18] Palen, L., Dourish, P.: Unpacking privacy for a networke d world. In: Proceedings of the SIGCHI Conference on Human Factors in Computing Systems, pp. 129–136. ACM (2003)

[19] Pernul, G., Kolter, J., Kernchen, T.: Collaborative Privacy Management. Computers & Security 29, 580–591 (2010)

[20] Preece, J.: Online Communities; Usability, Sociability, Theory and Methods. In: Earnshaw, R., Guedj, R., van Dam, A., Vince, T. (eds.) Frontiers of Human-Centred Computing, Online Communities and Virtual Environments, pp. 263–277. Springer, Amsterdam (2001)

[21] Preece, J., Rogers, Y., Sharp, H.: Interaction design: beyond human-computer interaction. John Wiley (2009)

[22] Xiaozhao, D., Jianhai, R.: Users' Privacy Issues with E-learning in Library 2.0. In: International Conference on Multimedia Information Networking and Security, pp. 90–92. IEEE (2009)

[23] Satchell, C., Dourish, P.: Beyond the user: use and non-use in HCI. In: Proceedings of the 21st Annual Conference of the Australian Computer-Human Interaction Special Interest Group: Design: Open 24/7, pp. 9–16. ACM (2009)

[24] Spiekermann, S., Cranor, L.F.: Engineering privacy. IEEE Transactions on Software Engineering 35, 67–82 (2009)

[25] Nielsen, J.: Usability Engineering. Academic Press, Boston (1993)

Appendix

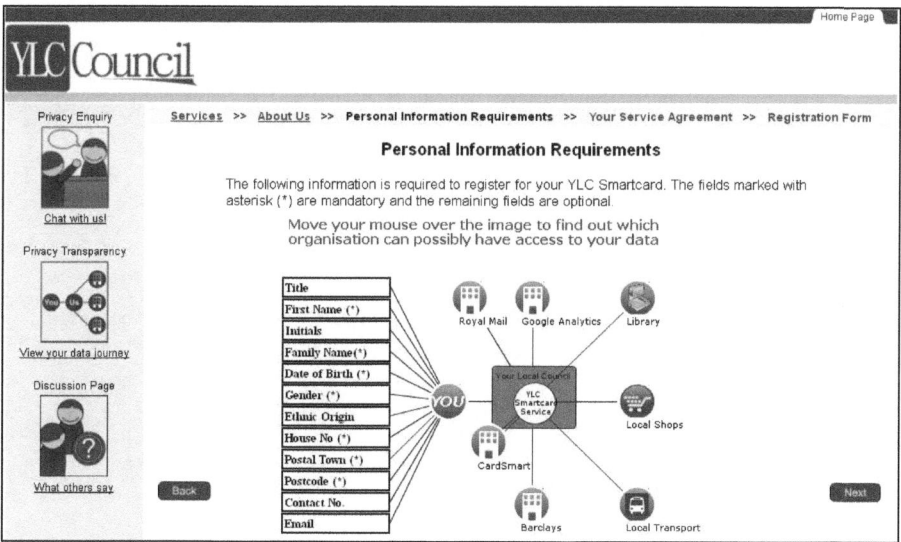

Fig. 6. Personal Information Requirements page

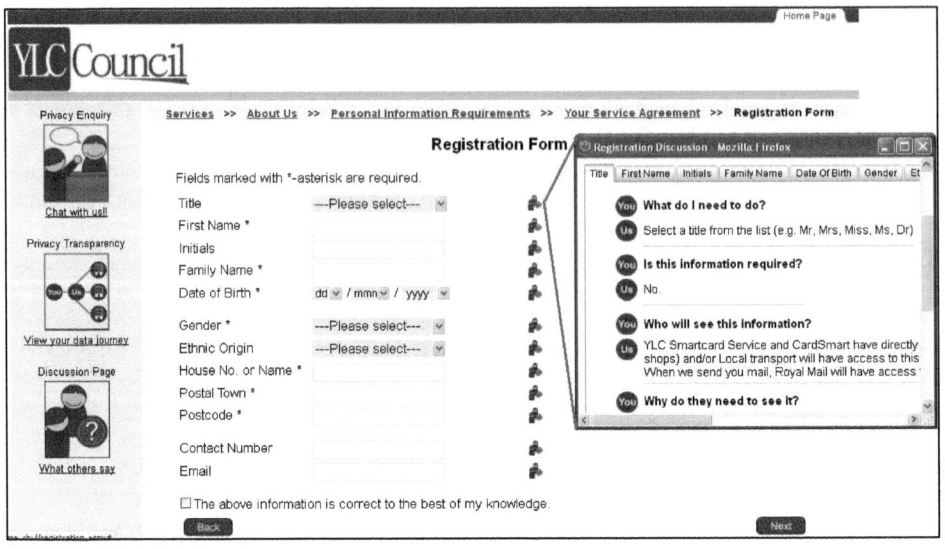

Fig. 7. Registration Form page

Optimized Inlining of Runtime Monitors

Frédérick Lemay[1], Raphaël Khoury[1,2], and Nadia Tawbi[1]

[1] Laval University, Department of Computer Science and Software Engineering,
Pavillon Adrien-Pouliot, 1065, avenue de la Medecine Quebec, Qc, Canada G1V 0A6, Canada
[2] Defence Research and Development Canada, Canadian Department of National Defence,
2459 Pie-XI Blvd North Quebec, QC, Canada G3J 1X5
{frederick.lemay.1,raphael.khoury.1}@ulaval.ca,
nadia.tawbi@ift.ulaval.ca

Abstract. A previous study showed how a monitor can be inlined into a potentially untrusted program, producing an instrumented version of this program which provably respects the desired security policy. That study extended previous approaches to the same problem in that it allowed non-safety properties to be monitored, and did not incur any runtime overhead. However, the algorithm itself runs in time $\mathcal{O}(2^{m \cdot n})$, where n is the size of the original program and m that of the property being monitored, and the resulting instrumented program is increased in the order of $\mathcal{O}(m \cdot n)$. These algorithmic factors limit the usefulness of the approach in practice. In this paper, we suggest several optimizations which reduce the algorithm's run time and the size of the resulting instrumented code. Using these optimizations, the monitor inlining can run in time $\mathcal{O}(v + e)$ where v and e are respectively the size and number of transitions present in the synchronous product of the original program and the property. Furthermore, we show how the size of the instrumented program can be minimized.

Keywords: security policies, security properties, omega-automata, runtime monitors.

1 Introduction

An increasingly popular solution to the problem of securing mobile code is monitor inlining, a process by which a monitor, representing a security property, is injected into an untrusted program. This results in a new instrumented version of the program which provably respects the desired property.

Much research has gone into determining precisely which properties are enforceable using this approach, and which are not. Initial research showed that this method was limited to the enforcement of safety properties, and implementations of formal monitors naturally focused on this class of security properties. Yet, further studies on security policy enforcement mechanisms showed that an a priori knowledge of the target program's behavior increases the power of these mechanisms [21,6].

Nonetheless, most practical implementations of monitors do not take advantage of this possibility and are thus restricted to enforcing safety properties. Furthermore the needed abstraction is often already available, and is used to minimize the runtime overhead incurred by the property monitoring process.

P. Laud (Ed.): NordSec 2011, LNCS 7161, pp. 149–161, 2012.

In [11,10] Chabot et al. present a monitor inlining algorithm in which the monitor relies on a model of the program's possible behavior to enforce non-safety properties. While their method is strictly more expressive than previous similar monitor inlining algorithms and the instrumentation induces no added runtime overhead, the very high computational complexity of the algorithm limits the applicability of the method.

In this paper, we propose several optimizations to the original monitor inlining algorithm from [11]. These allow the algorithmic complexity to pass from $\mathcal{O}(2^{n \cdot m})$ for a program of size n and a property of size m to a much more tractable $\mathcal{O}(v + e)$, where v and e are respectively the number of states and transitions present in the synchronous product of the original program and the desired property. We also show how to minimize the size of the resulting instrumented code, which stood at $\mathcal{O}(n \cdot m)$ in the original approach.

These optimizations derive from two insights: first, using an alternative formalism to express the desired security policy can speedup certain computations, specifically cycle detection, which is the most time consuming aspect of the algorithm. Second, the target program, when abstracted into a graph, exhibits specific properties that can be used to our advantage throughout the transformation process. Empirical results show that we can successfully reduce the time needed to perform the program transformation.

The remainder of this paper is organized as follows: Section 2 presents a review of related work, Section 3 introduces some preliminary notions and Section 4 presents the monitor inlining algorithm from [11]. Section 5 gives the proposed optimizations. Empirical results are given in Section 6. Concluding remarks are given in Section 7.

2   Related Works

In [38], Schneider delineates the set of properties enforceable by monitors. He focuses on a class of monitors that enforce the property by aborting the execution when faced with a violation of the security policy, and operate without any prior knowledge of their target's possible behavior. In these conditions, he determined that the set of security properties enforceable by this mechanism is the set of safety properties [25], a class of properties which proscribe that a certain unwanted behavior will not occur during a given execution of the target program. However, he also suggests that non-safety properties can be monitored in several situations, for example if the monitor had access to a model of its target possible behavior, which can be constructed from data collected by static analysis. In this case, the monitor can tolerate a potentially invalid behavior on the part of the target program, with the confidence that it will eventually be corrected. Subsequent research by Ligatti et al. [6] confirmed the feasibility of extending the set of monitorable properties using such an enforcement paradigm.

Several subsequent studies show how monitors can be inlined into their target, thus producing a new version of an untrusted program that provably respects the desired security policy. For instance, in [16], Schneider et al. proposed a method to inline a security property in object code, while Colcombet et al. [13] propose a similar approach which seeks to secure source code. In both cases, the method is limited to the enforcement of safety properties. The inlining process involves synchronizing the program with the security property by way of runtime checks that simulate the behavior of the security automaton into the target program. These checks detect any violation of the security property at runtime, and abort the execution. Both Schneider et al. and Colcombet et al. propose a number of optimizations which minimize the number of runtime checks needed to enforce the property.

In [10,11], Chabot et al. extend these approaches by allowing the monitoring of non-safety properties. Drawing upon the insight of [38] and [6], they propose a monitor which relies upon a statically constructed model of the target to enforce non-safety properties in some cases. While their approach is strictly more expressive than previous the ones, its algorithmic complexity, which stands in the order of $\mathcal{O}(2^{n \cdot m})$ for a program of size n and a property of size m, is a major hindrance to its wider usage.

Numerous other implementations of inlined monitors exist. For instance, in [34,33] and [35], Ould-Slimane et al. give an automata based inlining procedure which relies on a new operator that embeds a property automata into a target program. The monitoring of security protocols is discussed in [4] and [5]. That of information flow policies is discussed in numerous papers including [12] and [17]. In [39] Sen at al. propose a decentralized monitor which monitors safety properties in distributed programs. The optimization of monitors is further discussed in [44]. The inlining of monitors in concurrent programs is discussed in [27]. An algebraic method to inline a safety property into a program is given in [26] and [28]. In this approach, both the property and the program are stated using process algebra. The instrumented program is shown to be equivalent to the original one using a notion of equivalence based on bisimulation. The monitoring of networks is discussed in [31].

The monitoring of nonsafety properties is also discussed in [29], which shows that such properties can be monitored by an enforcement mechanism capable of transforming the execution sequence.

3   Preliminaries

We begin by introducing in more detail the notation and the various types of ω-automata which we will manipulate in this paper, and explain how such automata accept or reject their input.

An alphabet is a finite non-empty set of symbols. A word over alphabet Σ is a sequence of symbols from Σ. In what follows Σ^* denotes the set of all finite words from Σ while Σ^ω denotes that of all infinite words. A language $\mathcal{L}$ is a subset of Σ^ω and/or Σ^*. Security properties are also modeled as subsets of Σ^ω and automata are a convenient formalism to represent them [2].

An ω-automaton $\mathcal{A}$, over alphabet Σ is a tuple $(Q, \mathcal{I}, \delta, C)$ such that

- Σ is a finite or countably infinite set of symbols;
- Q is a finite or countably infinite set of states;
- $\mathcal{I} \subseteq Q$ is the set of initial states;
- $\delta \subseteq Q \times \Sigma \times Q$ is a (possibly partial) transition function;
- C is an acceptance condition which specifies whether or not an infinite sequence ρ is accepted by the automaton as depending on the states which occur or do not occur infinitely often in ρ. This condition is stated differently in the various types of ω-automata which we will study, sometimes leading to variations in expressive power. Accepted sequences are said to be valid, while rejected sequences are said to be invalid.

The set of all accepted sequences of $\mathcal{A}$ is the language recognized by $\mathcal{A}$, noted $\mathcal{L}_\mathcal{A}$.

A *path* ρ, is a finite (respectively infinite) sequence of states $\langle q_1, q_2, ..., q_n \rangle$ (respectively $\langle q_1, q_2, ... \rangle$) such that there exists a finite (respectively infinite) sequence of symbols $a_1, a_2, ..., a_n$ (respectively $a_1, a_2, ...$) called the label of ρ such that $\delta(q_i, a_i) = q_{i+1}$ for all $i \in \{0, ..., n - 1\}$ (respectively $i \geq 0$). In fact, a path is a sequence of states that form a possible run of the automaton, and the label of this path is the input sequence that generates this run. The empty path is noted ϵ.

Let ρ be a path in some automaton, we write $inf(\rho)$ for the set of states that are visited infinitely often in ρ. The study of ω-automata was pioneered by Büchi in [7], where he introduced the Büchi automaton. The acceptance condition of such an automaton is given as a set of states, at least one of which must be visited infinitely often by a sequence for it to be accepted by the automaton. Formally:

Definition 1. *A Büchi automaton $\mathcal{B}$ is an ω-automaton $(Q, \mathcal{I}, \delta, F)$ whose acceptance condition is a set $F \subseteq Q$. A path ρ is valid iff $inf(\rho) \cap F \neq \emptyset$.*

A cycle of states from an automaton $\mathcal{A}$ is said to be a *valid cycle* iff the states composing it would respect the acceptance condition were they are the only states visited infinitely often in a path over this automaton. A cycle is said to be invalid otherwise.

Observe that in a non-deterministic Büchi automaton $\mathcal{B}$, only a single run of the automaton needs to be valid for its label to be a word accepted by $\mathcal{L}_\mathcal{B}$. The class of languages recognizable by Büchi automata is termed ω-regular languages [36]. A language $\mathcal{L} \subseteq \Sigma^\omega$ is said to be ω-regular iff it is of the form UV^ω where $U, V \subseteq \Sigma^*$ are regular languages. The use of nondeterministic automata sometimes adds a layer of complexity to proofs and automata manipulations. A deterministic automaton is thus sometimes preferable. Unfortunately, deterministic Büchi automata are strictly less expressive than their nondeterministic counterparts [36].

Yet, with altered acceptance conditions, an automaton class can be defined which is deterministic but still recognizes all ω-regular languages. Several such automata exist. In this paper, we focus on the Rabin automaton [37].

Definition 2. *A Rabin automaton $\mathcal{R}$ is an ω-automaton $(Q, \mathcal{I}, \delta, C)$ whose acceptance condition C is given as a set of pairs of sets of states (G_i, R_i) with $G_i, R_i \subseteq Q$. A run ρ is accepted iff there exists a pair $(G_i, R_i) \in C$ for which $inf(\rho) \cap G_i \neq \emptyset \wedge inf(\rho) \cap R_i = \emptyset$.*

4   Monitor Inlining Algorithm

In [11], Chabot et al. show how a safety or non-safety property can be inlined into an untrusted or possibly malicious program to produce an instrumented version of this program that provably respects the security policy, while maintaining the original program's transparency, (i.e. leaving valid executions present in the original program unaltered [38]).

The method consists of 7 steps.

Property Encoding

The desired security policy is abstracted by a Rabin automaton. This allows much wider expressivity than previous approaches which relied upon the security automaton [2], a subclass of the Büchi automaton limited to express safety properties, while retaining determinism. Any ω-regular property can be stated in this formalism [36].

Program Abstraction

The program is abstracted into a Labeled Transition System (LTS), a widely used formalism for representing programs. Transformations can also ensure that this representation is deterministic, without loss of expressivity.

Automata Product

The next step is to construct the automata product of the property and the program. This results in a new Rabin automaton ($\mathcal{R}^T$), with its own acceptance condition. Since this new automaton accepts the intersection of the language accepted by the original product and that accepted by the property automaton, it would form a natural basis from which to build the instrumented program. However, because the acceptance condition of the Rabin automaton is stated in terms of which states an execution can or cannot visit infinitely often, it is impossible for the monitor to detect at runtime if the current execution is valid or not. The remainder of the method consists of transformations aimed at removing invalid behaviors from the product automaton, while preserving valid ones.

Marking the Halt States

Since the property is enforced by halting the execution, it is necessary to identify all program points where the execution can safely be aborted without violating the security policy. These are indicated by adding a transition to a halt state from any state where the monitor can abort the execution.

Detecting Valid and Invalid Behaviors

The next phase consists in extracting, if possible, a labeled transition system from the product automaton, by pruning it of states and transitions containing invalid cycles w.r.t. its acceptance condition. This process first involves parsing the product automaton into its strongly connected components (scc) and listing the cycles present in each of them. It's at the step of cycle detection that the algorithm's complexity grows to $\mathcal{O}(2^n)$, for an automaton containing n states. Each cycle is then checked against the acceptance condition, and each scc is labeled according to whether it contains either only valid cycles, only invalid cycles, both types of cycles, or no cycles (the trivial scc).

Program transformations

The next step is to construct the quotient graph of the product automaton, in which each node represents a scc. The nodes of this graph are then visited in reverse topological ordering in order to determine, for each one, whether it should be kept intact, altered or removed. Every scc containing invalid cycles must be deleted, to ensure correction w.r.t. the desired security policy, but every scc containing valid cycles must be preserved, to ensure transparency. This approach thus fails in 3 cases: first, if the product automaton contains an scc which exhibits both valid and invalid cycles, second, if an *scc* containing valid cycles is reachable from an *scc* containing invalid cycles, and third, if an *scc* containing invalid cycles does not possess any valid prefixes where the execution could be aborted without ruling out some valid executions.

Concretization

Whenever the previous step is successful, the resulting automaton is a Rabin automaton exhibiting only valid executions, and can thus be treated as an LTS and concretized into an executable program. The resulting program still exhibits all valid behaviors present in the original program, but it possesses no invalid behaviors. Since this program is built from the product automaton of a program of size n and a property of size m it's size is in the order of $\mathcal{O}(m \cdot n)$.

While the method sometimes fail to produce a suitable instrumented code, this never occurs if the desired property is a safety property which can be enforced using existing approaches. This approach is thus strictly more expressive, and the main limitations to its wider use is the algorithmic complexity discussed above. In the following section, we propose three strategies that make the problem more tractable, and reduces the size of the final instrumented program.

5   Proposed Optimizations

In this section, we propose three possible optimizations to the algorithm introduced above.

5.1   Optimization 1: Avoiding Cycle Enumeration Using Büchi Automata

Since the most time-consuming part of the algorithm is the enumeration and evaluation of each cycle, a natural way to reduce the algorithmic complexity of the method is to avoid this task. One option is to state the property in the form of a Büchi automaton, rather than Rabin automaton, as the acceptance condition of the former is stated only in terms of reaching certain states infinitely often. For an algorithm based on Büchi automaton to be equally expressive as one based on the Rabin automaton, we are forced to consider non-deterministic Büchi automata.

The phases of program abstraction, automata product and marking of the halt states proceed in the exact same manner as was the case using the original method.

The detection of the valid and invalid behaviors present in the product automaton proceeds as follows. First, we must once again detect the strongly connected components in the product automaton $\mathcal{R}^T$. This can be performed in linear time using Tarjan's algorithm [40]. We then check each *scc* for the presence of valid and invalid cycles separately.

Since a run of the Büchi automaton is accepting iff it visits an accepting state infinitely often, the presence of a valid cycle in an *scc* can be determined in linear time, namely in $\mathcal{O}(n + e)$ for an automaton with n states and e edges, simply by checking for the presence of an accepting state in the *scc*.

To detect whether or not an *scc* contains any invalid cycles, we have to verify that this *scc* would still contain a cycle after deletion of all its valid states with their incident edges. This task is accomplished using a modified version of Tarjan's *scc* detection algorithm [40], altered to ignore any edge incident to a valid state. An invalid cycle is present if a run of this algorithm detects a non-trivial *scc*. It is not necessary to enumerate all cycles, which is what lead to exponential algorithmic complexity of the algorithm based on the Rabin automaton. Instead, the simple detection of the presence of a cycle can be performed in linear time, since Tarjan's algorithm has a complexity in the order of $\mathcal{O}(n + e)$ for an automaton with n states and e edges.

The remainder of the algorithm, namely deleting the *scc*s containing invalid cycles, if doing so is allowed, and concretization, are performed in the same manner whether a Rabin or Büchi automaton is used. The complexity of the overall monitor inlining algorithm thus passes from $\mathcal{O}(2^n)$ to a much more tractable $\mathcal{O}(n + e)$, where n is the size of the product automaton and e is the number of transitions it contains. This optimization does however come at a cost. Since the Büchi automaton is non-deterministic, and a sequence is accepted if *any* of its possible runs over the automaton visits an accepting state infinitely often, any run containing invalid cycles may reflect a label that also generates valid runs over the same automaton. Whenever the product automaton contains some behavior that prevent the algorithm from pruning it of all invalid behaviors, such as, for instance, an *scc* containing both valid and invalid sequences, it may be possible that any run of the automaton reaching these problematic *scc*s corresponds to a sequence which also reaches both valid and invalid *scc*s for which the property is monitorable. The algorithm thus unnecessarily fails to output an instrumented program.

It follows that stating the desired property using a Büchi automaton results in a somewhat more conservative approximation than was the case with a Rabin automaton. However, in practice, we found it very difficult to construct examples of real properties and real programs that were monitorable using the original algorithm based upon the Rabin automaton, but not using the optimization described above. Furthermore, a relatively simple reachability analysis of the automaton, may allow us to enforce the same set of properties (for any given program) in both cases.

It is also important to note that the main contribution of [11] is to extend previous work by proposing a method capable of enforcing some non-safety properties, something that was not possible with previous techniques. Although the approach proposed in [11] is strictly more expressive than the optimization presented in this section, whenever the security policy is a safety property it can be stated as a deterministic automaton [23], and can thus be enforced using either methods. Both the method from [11] and the one presented in this section are therefore strictly more expressive than those proposed in previous works.

5.2 Optimization 2: Optimizing Cycle Detection Using Reducibility

If we wish to keep the Rabin automaton as the basis for stating the desired security policy, but still wish to avoid the exponential overhead incurred when enumerating the set of cycles, another interesting option is to draw upon the particular shape of the automaton being transformed to optimize the cycle detection phase.

Automata representing programs or properties often have a particular shape, termed reducibility. Reducible graphs were first described in [18]. Intuitively, a graph is reducible iff the graph can be reduced to a singleton by iteratively applying two graph transformations, T1 and T2. T1 removes self loops while T2 collapses a node with a single predecessor into that predecessor.

Such graphs exhibit several properties that make them attractive to static analysis. Amongst them is the fact that they contain no loop with multiple entry points, and no adjacent loops. Each strongly connected component has a single entry point. Several static analyzes and optimizations can be performed more efficiently when manipulating reducible graphs. Amongst them is cycle detection, which can be performed in time linear to the number of backedges present in the graph.

Reducible graphs arise naturally in graphs that model the control flow of programs written in many commonly used programming languages. Nonetheless, several widely used programming languages, such as C, C++ Lisp or Pascal can produce irreducible control flow. When this occurs, several algorithms exist to transform an irreducible graph to an equivalent (in the sense that it accepts the same sequences) reducible graph. The most common algorithms are based on node splitting. This technique consist in duplicating certain states, and modifying the control frow, until the graph becomes reducible. Various heuristics have been proposed to minimize the amount of duplication. While in the worst case, an exponential blowup in the size of the model is unavoidable, in general the size of the equivalent reducible graph is quite reasonable (in the order of a 2.9% increase for some heuristics [20]). Furthermore, in [3], an algorithm is given which can produce an equivalent reducible graph with the minimal amount of duplication.

In our case, even though both the program abstraction and security property are stated by reducible automaton, the product automaton itself may not be reducible since the automaton product transformation does not preserve reducibility. However, our experience shows that in most cases, the product automaton can be seen as "quasi-reducible" in the sense that it can be made reducible with minimal overhead. This is because the property is generally much smaller than the target program, and involves only a small subset of security relevant instructions. We have found that transforming the product automaton to reducible form before proceeding with the cycle detection is an efficient way to reduce the runtime of transformation procedure. In our tests, we have used Janssen et al.'s [20] algorithm to transform the automaton to reducible form and Hetch's algorithm described in [1] to compute the set of cycles.

5.3 Other Optimizations

The size of the final instrumented code is in the order of $\mathcal{O}(n \cdot m)$ for an original program of size n and a property of size m. This increase in the size of the final program resulted from our objective that the runtime tests themselves incur no overhead. Still, reducing the size of the state space of the product automaton would further speedup the program transformation, and optimize the final code.

Unfortunately, producing a minimal ω-automaton is a complex problem [14]. In the case of the Büchi automata, for instance, it is PSPACE-hard. This makes it difficult to reduce the product automaton after it is created, and benefit from the smaller space state during the cycle detection and program transformation phases. However, if the program transformation is successful, the final automaton takes a particular form, called a weak automaton, which allows efficient minimization to be performed. In [30] Löding shows that the acceptance condition for this class of ω-automata can be restated into an equivalent normal form, a procedure that can be done in time $\mathcal{O}(n)$ for an automaton with n states, and that once in normal form the state space minimization algorithms devised for deterministic finite automata can be applied to this automaton to produce an equivalent minimal automaton. The problem of minimizing a Deterministic Finite Automata is well studied and the most efficient algorithms run in time $\mathcal{O}(n \cdot \log n)$, to minimize an automaton with n states [19,42,43].

A final optimization we can consider is to minimize the number of pairs present in the acceptance condition of the Rabin automaton. Any improvement in this respect greatly speeds up the runtime of the algorithm since every cycle must be checked against each pair.

The minimal number of pairs needed in any deterministic Rabin automaton that accepts a given language is called the Rabin Index of that language [41,22], and various algorithms exist that can perform this minimization. While there can be a substantial blowup in the size of the state-space when these transformations are performed (given as $\mathcal{O}(n^p \cdot 4^{2p^2})$ in [9], $\mathcal{O}(n \cdot 2^{p \log p})$ in [15] and $\mathcal{O}(n \cdot p^k)$ in [24], for an automaton with n states, p pairs and a Rabin Index of k)[1] the fact that a Rabin automaton representing a real property typically has only a few states at most may make this transformations worthwhile.

6   Empirical Results

Our preliminary empirical results are very encouraging. Representative results are shown in Figures 2 and 3. To generate these results, we ran two test sets, each of which consisted of applying both algorithms using two versions (Rabin and a Büchi) of the same property on the same program. This property accepts all executions containing only a finite non-empty number of a actions and such that finite executions end with a b action. The program was then extended by arbitrarily selecting any one of it's nodes, transitions or subgraphs, and replicating it using a multiplicative constant ranging from 1 to 200. We are then able to compare the performance of both algorithms when applying the same property to LTSs that grow in size, but still maintain some similarity.

Figure 2 highlights the potential gains of the Büchi automaton-based algorithm, as it shows the results of the enforcement of the same property as was used in the running example in [11] on an LTS built from a clique, with multiplicative constants 1-9. The Rabin automaton capturing this property is reproduced in Figure 1

We obtained similar results when enforcing a real security property on a real program. We tested the approach using an interesting real-life property with both a safety and a liveness component. The safety component is a mutual exclusion property stating that two processes are never enabled simultaneously. This is combined with a liveness requirement that both processes always be eventually enabled. This property was stated as a Müller automaton [32] and was subsequently translated into both a Rabin and a

---

[1] Strictly speaking, this refer to the transformation of a Rabin automaton into a special form called the Chain automaton, which is the critical step in reducing the Rabin automaton's acceptance condition. Once a Rabin automaton is stated in this form, the algorithm to reduce its acceptance condition is given in [9,8].

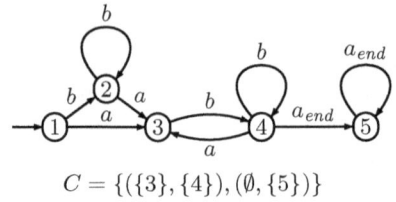

$$C = \{(\{3\}, \{4\}), (\emptyset, \{5\})\}$$

Fig. 1. The property from [11]

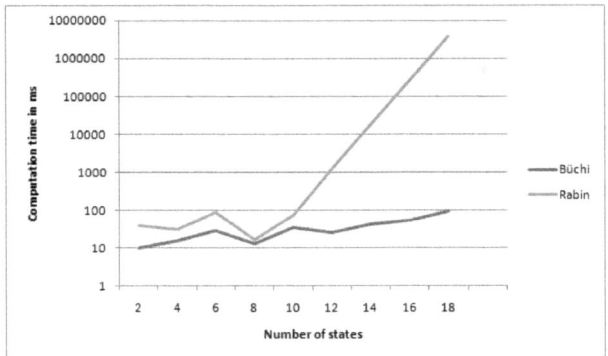

Fig. 2. Results of algorithms using the property from [11], with Rabin and Büchi

Büchi automaton. We used a program whose control flow always respect the property. The program consists in multiple "transactions", each of which represents a process that requests a resource, uses it, and then releases it. The program is extended by nesting multiple such transactions. The results, with multiplicative constants 1-200, can be seen in Figure 3.

Empirical results obtained while running the reducibility-based optimization proposed in section 5.2 are less striking, but still indicate that the optimization is

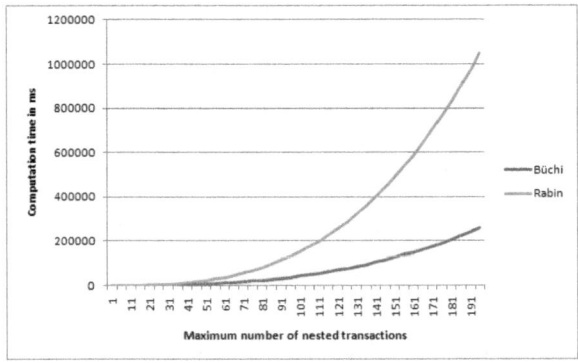

Fig. 3. Results of algorithms using the mutual exclusion property, with Rabin and Büchi

worthwhile. However, because of the costs associated with the node-splitting transformation, this optimization is advantageous only if the synchronous product of the LTS and the property is both quasi-reducible and has a substantial size.

7 Conclusion and Future Work

In this paper, we propose several optimizations to an inline monitoring algorithm previously presented in the literature. These optimizations allow the inlining process to decrease the complexity from exponential to linear time in the size of the space-state of the product of the property being monitored and of the target program. We also show how the size of the resulting instrumented code can be minimized. These optimizations highlight a tradeoff between efficiency and the range of enforceable properties.

In future work, we hope to extend the algorithm so that it becomes possible to enforce the property in all cases. This may involve relying on monitors capable of more varied responses to potential violation of the security policy than simply aborting the execution.

References

1. Aho, A.V., Sethi, R., Ullman, J.D.: Compilers: principles, techniques, and tools. Addison-Wesley Longman Publishing Co., Inc., Boston (1986)
2. Alpern, B., Schneider, F.B.: Recognizing safety and liveness. Distributed Computing 2, 117–126 (1987)
3. Ammarguellat, Z.: A control-flow normalization algorithm and its complexity. IEEE Trans. Softw. Eng. 18, 237–251 (1992)
4. Bauer, A., Jürjens, J.: Security protocols, properties, and their monitoring. In: Proceedings of the Fourth International Workshop on Software Engineering for Secure Systems (SESS)
5. Bauer, A., Jürjens, J.: Runtime verification of cryptographic protocols. Computers & Security 29(3), 315–330 (2010)
6. Bauer, L., Ligatti, J., Walker, D.: More enforceable security policies. In: Foundations of Computer Security, Copenhagen, Denmark (July 2002)
7. Büchi, J.: On a decision method in restricted second order arithmetic. In: Proceedings of the International Congress on Logic, Method, and Philosophy of Science, pp. 1–12. Stanford University Press, Stanford (1962)
8. Carton, O.: Mots infinis, ω-semigroupes et topologie. PhD thesis, Universite de Paris 07 (1993)
9. Carton, O.: Chain automata. In: IFIP World Computer Congress 1994, Hamburg, pp. 451–458. Elsevier (North-Holland) (1994)
10. Chabot, H., Khoury, R., Tawbi, N.: Generating In-Line Monitors for Rabin Automata. In: Jøsang, A., Maseng, T., Knapskog, S.J. (eds.) NordSec 2009. LNCS, vol. 5838, pp. 287–301. Springer, Heidelberg (2009)
11. Chabot, H., Khoury, R., Tawbi, N.: Extending the enforcement power of truncation monitors using static analysis. In: Computers & Security (forthcoming)
12. Chudnov, A., Naumann, D.A.: Information flow monitor inlining. In: Proceedings of the 23rd IEEE Computer Security Foundations Symposium, CSF 2010, Edinburgh, United Kingdom, July 17-19, pp. 200–214 (2010)

13. Colcombet, T., Fradet, P.: Enforcing trace properties by program transformation. In: Conference record of the 27th ACM SIGPLAN-SIGACT Symposium on Principles of Programming Languages (January 2000)
14. Ehlers, R.: Minimising Deterministic Büchi Automata Precisely Using SAT Solving. In: Strichman, O., Szeider, S. (eds.) SAT 2010. LNCS, vol. 6175, pp. 326–332. Springer, Heidelberg (2010)
15. Emerson, E.A., Jutla, C.S.: Tree automata, mu-calculus and determinacy. In: SFCS 1991: Proceedings of the 32nd Annual Symposium on Foundations of Computer Science, pp. 368–377. IEEE Computer Society, Washington, DC, USA (1991)
16. Erlingsson, U., Schneider, F.B.: Sasi enforcement of security policies: A retrospective. In: WNSP: New Security Paradigms Workshop. ACM Press (2000)
17. Le Guernic, G.: Automaton-based Confidentiality Monitoring of Concurrent Programs. In: Proceedings of the 20th IEEE Computer Security Foundations Symposium (CSFS20), July 6-8, pp. 218–232. IEEE Computer Society (2007)
18. Hecht, M.S., Ullman, J.D.: Characterizations of reducible flow graphs. J. ACM 21, 367–375 (1974)
19. Hopcroft, J.E.: An n log n algorithm for minimizing states in a finite automaton. Technical report, Stanford, CA, USA (1971)
20. Janssen, J., Corporaal, H.: Making graphs reducible with controlled node splitting. ACM Trans. Programming Languages and Systems 19, 1031–1052 (1997)
21. Morrisett, G., Hamlen, K.W., Schneider, F.B.: Computability classes for enforcement mechanisms. Technical Report TR2003-1908, Cornell University (2003)
22. Kaminski, M.: A classification of omega-regular languages. Theoretical Computer Science 36, 217–229 (1985)
23. Klein, J.: Linear Time Logic and Deterministic omega-Automata. PhD thesis, The University of Bonn, Bonn, Germany (January 2005)
24. Krishnan, S.C., Puri, A., Brayton, R.K., Varaiya, P.P.: The Rabin Index and Chain Automata, with Applications to Automata and Games. In: Wolper, P. (ed.) CAV 1995. LNCS, vol. 939, pp. 253–266. Springer, Heidelberg (1995)
25. Lamport, L.: Proving the correctness of multiprocess programs. IEEE Transactions on Software Engineering 3(2), 125–143 (1977)
26. Langar, M., Mejri, M.: Formal and efficient enforcement of security policies. In: Proceedings of The 2005 International Conference on Foundations of Computer Science (FCS 2005), pp. 143–149 (2005)
27. Langar, M., Mejri, M., Adi, K.: Formal monitor for concurrent programs. In: Workshop on Practice and Theory of IT Security (2006)
28. Langar, M., Mejri, M., Adi, K.: A formal approach for security policy enforcement in concurrent programs. In: Proceedings of the 2007 International Conference on Security & Management, pp. 165–171 (2007)
29. Ligatti, J., Bauer, L., Walker, D.: Run-time enforcement of nonsafety policies. ACM Transactions on Information and System Security 12(3), 1–41 (2009)
30. Löding, C.: Efficient minimization of deterministic weak omega-automata. Information Processing Letters 79(3), 105–109 (2001)
31. Mechri, T., Langar, M., Mejri, M., Fujita, H., Funyu, Y.: Automatic enforcement of security in computer networks. In: New Trends in Software Methodologies, Tools and Techniques - Proceedings of the Sixth SoMeT 2007, pp. 200–222 (2007)
32. Muller, D.E.: Infinite sequences and finite machines. In: Switching Circuit Theory and Logical Design, pp. 3–16 (1963)
33. Ould-Slimane, H., Mejri, M.: Enforcing security policies by rewriting programs using automata. In: Proceedings of the Workshop on Practice and Theory of IT Security (PTITS), pp. 195–207 (2006)

34. Ould-Slimane, H., Mejri, M., Adi, K.: Enforcing security policies on programs. In: New Trends in Software Methodologies, Tools and Techniques - Proceedings of the Fifth SoMeT 2006, Quebec, Canada, October 25-27, pp. 195–207 (2006)
35. Ould-Slimane, H., Mejri, M., Adi, K.: Using Edit Automata for Rewriting-Based Security Enforcement. In: Gudes, E., Vaidya, J. (eds.) Data and Applications Security XXIII. LNCS, vol. 5645, pp. 175–190. Springer, Heidelberg (2009)
36. Perrin, D., Pin, J.E.: Infinite Words. Pure and Applied Mathematics, vol. 141. Elsevier (2004)
37. Rabin, M.O.: Decidability of second-order theories and automata on infinite trees. Transactions of the American Mathematical Society 141, 1–37 (1969)
38. Schneider, F.B.: Enforceable security policies. Information and System Security 3(1), 30–50 (2000)
39. Sen, K., Vardhan, A., Agha, G., Roşu, G.: Efficient decentralized monitoring of safety in distributed systems. In: ICSE 2004: Proceedings of the 26th International Conference on Software Engineering, pp. 418–427. IEEE Computer Society, Washington, DC, USA (2004)
40. Tarjan, R.E.: Depth-first search and linear graph algorithms. SIAM J. Comput. 1(2), 146–160 (1972)
41. Wagner, K.: On omega-regular sets. Information and Control 43(2), 123–177 (1979)
42. Watson, B.W.: A taxonomy of finite automata construction and minimization algorithms. Technical report, Computing Science (1993)
43. Watson, B.W., Daciuk, J.: An efficient incremental dfa minimization algorithm. Nat. Lang. Eng. 9(1), 49–64 (2003)
44. Yan, F., Fong, P.W.L.: Efficient irm enforcement of history-based access control policies. In: Proceedings of the 2009 ACM Symposium on Information, Computer and Communications Security, ASIACCS 2009, Sydney, Australia, pp. 35–46 (2009)

Identity-Based Key Derivation Method for Low Delay Inter-domain Handover Re-authentication Service

Radu Lupu[1], Eugen Borcoci[1], and Tinku Rasheed[2]

[1] University Politehnica of Bucharest, Bucharest, Romania
{rlupu,eugen.borcoci}@elcom.pub.ro
[2] CREATE-NET, Povo, Italy
tinku.rasheed@create-net.org

Abstract. Several statistics on the factors of attacks' proliferation revealed the scarce deployment of entity authentication mechanisms being one of the most important. Particularly, providing seamless mobile re-authentication service for real-time inter-domain handover procedures is still an open issue. This paper is focused on the re-authentication architecture and mechanisms design, aiming to low latency re-authentication services for roaming WLAN or WiMAX terminals. Authentication architecture is specified to integrate the proposed mechanisms and a novel generic key material concept is defined in addition to the current state-of-the-art. An identity-based key material derivation method is developed, relying on the multiplicative group associativity property and the intractable underlying RSA problem. Then, the required cryptographic properties are evaluated. A simple generic key material pre-distribution mechanism is proposed and the related local re-authentication protocol. Eventually, the validation of the security properties of the re-authentication protocol, as well as the functional correctness validation of the re-authentication service is performed.

Keywords: entity authentication, key derivation, inter-domain handover, real-time.

1 Introduction

The pervasive and secure Internet real-time multimedia communications need enhanced design solutions for the mutual authentication mechanisms, capable to offer low latency operations (i.e. tens of milliseconds). This paper proposes a new solution designed[1] for real-time re-authentication service that could be integrated within the handover procedure of the roaming WLAN [1] and WiMAX [3] mobile devices. Even though considerable research work has been performed with notable results in this field of research [4, 5, 6, 7, 8], providing seamless real-time re-authentication service for inter-domain handover procedures is still an open issue. Both, reactive and proactive techniques have been employed in the design of the fast re-authentication solutions, relying on minimum one transaction crossing the Internet, either with the

---

[1] Within EU funded project Alicante IST 248652-IP.

P. Laud (Ed.): NordSec 2011, LNCS 7161, pp. 162–175, 2012.

previously visited domain, with the home domain, or with a trusted third party. The current reactive solutions have been optimized with respect to the number of transactions per re-authentication phase or per visited domain. In both cases, these solutions expose high latency (hundreds of milliseconds) which directly affects the real-time communications performances. It has been shown empirically [9] that 90% of the re-authentication delay is due to the communication over Internet. On the other side, the proposed proactive solutions have high complexity in terms of communication, processing operations and trust relationships. Moreover, if prediction techniques are employed to guess the mobile next target visiting network, the low latency guarantees are at most only statistic ones and come often with an important overhead. The complexity is mainly inherited from Public Key Infrastructure (PKI) management [10] and the asymmetric cryptographic mechanisms utilization. In addition, due the trust relationships they introduce part of the proactive solutions are sensible to the domino effect [11, 12].

Our solution also belongs to the proactive class due the key material pre-distribution procedure it employs. The key idea (to overcome the current state-of-the-art limitations) consists in re-authentication phase decoupling from key material distribution phase, through the use of a special key material derivation method. Furthermore, the scalable pre-distribution procedure design was possible to be achieved, due the definition of the generic key material concept and the adoption of the identity-based cryptographic techniques. However, the solution proposed in this paper is still compatible with the legacy related protocols (e.g. EAP, Radius, Diameter) and architectures [2].

The paper is organized as follows. In Section I, the motivation of this work is presented. Section II, outlines the main phases of the new re-authentication service; each phase is defined and its role is pointed out. Section III specifies the new local mutual re-authentication protocol offering guarantees for authentication service continuity. In Section IV, it is specified the key hierarchy design needed to implement our cryptographic mechanisms. Section V, introduces the concept of generic key material and defines the methods proposed for derivation of the generic key material, and for the re-authentication key. Also, the main design requirements are specified for our methods. In Section VI we specified the distribution protocol for provisioning of the generic key material to the local re-authentication server. Section VII presents the main activity and the related results, to prove the design correctness. Afterwards, we evaluated the performance of the re-authentication service to prove feasibility of our approach, in Section VIII. The paper ends with Section IX that concludes this work and points out the related directions for further research.

2   The Re-authentication Service Architecture

For the definition of our re-authentication service we focused on satisfaction of the following overall design requirements: compatibility with legacy technologies, mutual authentication, low overall re-authentication delay to the level acceptable by real-time communications, minimization of trust relationships and prevention of the domino effect, low processing and communication complexity, resilience of the related mechanisms.

We chose to design the security architecture for our re-authentication service upon the HOKEY security model [13]. Thus, we will further assume the same type of principals with their roles and the related terminology, as specified by the standard. However, we will define new procedures of interaction between the principals and their related mechanisms. Figure 1, depicts the main phases of the re-authentication service we designed that are run according to HOKEY standard model. As it can be seen, our solution is made up of four distinct phases.

The *"Home Authentication"* relies on complete legacy Extensible Authentication Protocol (EAP) [14] with Master Session Key (MSK) and Extended MSK (EMSK) material establishment support, achieved according to IEEE 802.1x, in between mobile node MN (EAP supplicant role) and home AAA (H-AAA) (EAP authentication server role) via access point (AP) (EAP Authenticator role). In this case, foreign AAA (F-AAA) plays the AAA proxy role. Particularly, for our solution EMSK is assigned Mobile Specific – Root Key (MS-RK) alias and computed by the generic key material derivation function we designed with special properties which is defined in a separate section of the paper. In addition, H-AAA server assigns an index to the current MS-RK and conveys it to MN entity concatenated with MS-RK. In our solution, this phase is initiated by MN entity when it enters the access network for the first time (e.g. after reboot), as well as, whenever MN needs to refresh MS-RK.

For *"Local Re-authentication"* phase we designed a new mutual authentication protocol with support for session key establishment and augmented with mechanisms for checking MS-RK synchronization. It was dedicated a separate section in this paper for detailed specification of this protocol (see Section III). The related messages are exchanged according to HOKEY model in between MN (EAP supplicant), AP (EAP authenticator) and F-AAA (EAP re-authentication server). It is invoked periodically by MN to get its communication sessions reauthorized, whenever the local AAA server notifies support for it.

"Local Authentication" phase relies on legacy "4-way Handshake" protocol to achieve the goals as specified in [1]. It is initiated by AP (EAP Authenticator) subsequently to successful authentication of MN and H-AAA by "Home Authentication" or "Local Re-authentication" phase, respectively.

"DS-RK (Domain Specific – Root Key) distribution" is carried out through periodic secured transfer of the generic key material (DS-RK), from the home domain H-AAA (in key distribution center role) to each access network F-AAA it wants to enable for running "Local Authentication" phase with its mobile subscribers. The DS-RK derivation procedure with special properties and the related pre-distribution protocol we designed are defined in separate sections of the paper. Analogous to MS-RK, H-AAA server, also assigns an index to each DS-RK and conveys them concatenated to F-AAA entity.

The design of the procedures we propose is based on the underlying hybrid cryptographic techniques to facilitate performances and cost trade-off. In this regard, we involved in the design process the asymmetric techniques for less frequent operations, such as generic key material generation (i.e. MS-RK, DS-RK), and symmetric techniques for more frequent operations, such as MN re-authentication, respectively. Due the new generic key material generation procedure with support for scalable pre-distribution, we enabled the overall re-authentication procedure latency for inter-domain handover scenario to be reduced to the values corresponding to the local legacy intra-domain authentication procedures. Moreover, for the certification of the DS-RK generic key material, that is transferred from H-AAA server to each F-AAA server, our solution relies on the pre-established trust relationships and the related SAs defined for the legacy AAA overlay [15]. This way, our solution completely avoids the costs entailed by the PKI management procedures, as well as, maintains the number of the trust relationships required at the same level as for the underlying AAA overlay.

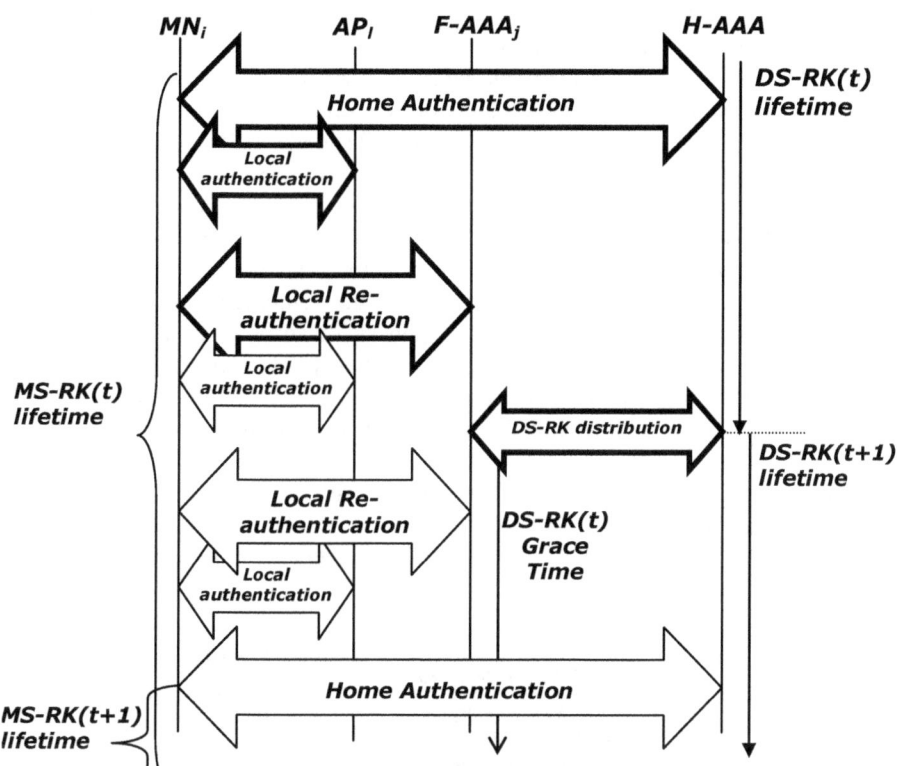

Fig. 1. The Re-authentication Service Workflow Design

The re-authentication key material generation method relies on the identity-based mechanism in order to enable scalable pre-distribution procedure and key usage control function. Moreover, it prevents the domino effect and allows the minimization of communication complexity in terms of the number of the messages exchanged. The robustness of our re-authentication service against interruptions experienced over the communication path with the home domain is enabled through the distribution of the generic key material required prior to the re-authentication moment in conjunction with the delegation (according to HOKEY architecture) of the re-authentication server role from home to the homologous server from the potential visiting domains. Therefore, we expect our approach to be appropriate for networks with dynamic topologies where the multi-hop connectivity issues are mundane.

In the following sections we will focus on the specification of the mechanisms we designed for re-authentication service.

3   Enhanced Two-Key Re-authentication Protocol

In this section, we will specify a new entity re-authentication protocol for the low delay "Local Re-authentication" phase, which works in conjunction with the generic key material pre-distribution procedure we designed. This protocol aims to provide the following functionalities: mutual authentication of the principals, re-authentication key material synchronism verification and notification and session key establishment.

It is designed to run in between the mobile node (MN) and the local re-authentication server (F-AAA) on behalf of the visited access network. The specification of the protocol is achieved in the MSC diagram in Figure 2. It can be seen, that this protocol belongs to the class of "challenge-response" protocols with the nonces of type random number. The principals independently generate a nonce and exchange their values with the following goals: to prove the re-authentication messages are fresh, to contribute to the new session key generation in order to avoid session key control by the corresponding principal. Alternatively, a Diffie-Hellman technique could be used to achieve perfect forward secrecy property for the session keys. The yielded session key will be denoted further root MSK (rMSK) to highlight on its usage by the "Local Authentication" phase to produce traffic protection keys (i.e. PTK, GTK [1]). Optionally, the protocol messages should offer support to convey the principal's identifier (i.e. ID_{DS}, ID_{MS}) to the peer to enable the re-authentication key (rAK) derivation. Alternatively, there must be an independent reciprocal mechanism for the identification of the principals.

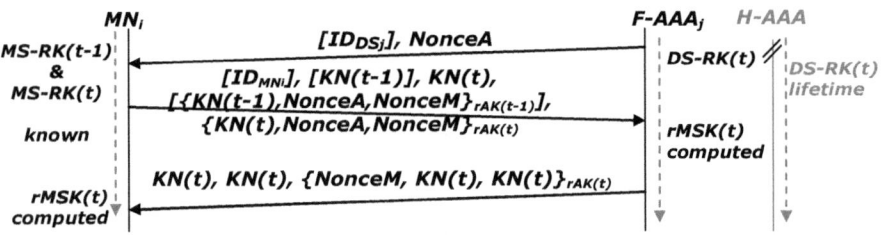

Fig. 2. The Two-Key Re-authentication Protocol with Key Sync Mechanism

To avoid the re-authentication service interruptions due the related system state inconsistence during the generic key material update, we designed the protocol to work simultaneously with two consecutive re-authentication keys, rAK(t-1) and rAK(t), assigned to the time intervals (t-1) and (t), respectively. Note, the F-AAA server shall be able to work with the most recent two key materials DS-RK(t-1) and DS-RK(t) it has received from H-AAA. KN(.) denotes the generic key material index which is associated to rAK(.) for some time interval, to be used for generic key material synchronization in between MN and F-AAA server, as well as to point out which rAK(.) to be used for validation of the authentication token by the peer principal. If either of the authentication tokens in the second message {KN(t), NonceA, NonceM}rAK(t) or {KN(t-1), NonceA, NonceM}rAK(t-1) is valid, then F-AAA declares MN genuine. Where, the authentication tokens are computed through some MAC transform with the keys rAK(t) and rAK(t-1), respectively. On the other side, MN entity relies on the third message validity and the trust relationship shared by H-AAA and F-AAA to declare F-AAA is genuine. Regarding the structure of the last message, the first index KN(.) sent in clear points to the rAK(t) to be used by MN to check the authenticity of the message. The second index KN(.) notifies MN what is the most recent key material known by F-AAA (e.g. in Figure 2, the last message shows the key materials are synchronized. Therefore, the MN's generic key material is up to date). Whenever, MN finds out this way a new key material has been distributed, it enters "Home Authentication" phase in order to refresh its key material (i.e. MS-RK). Also, if none of the two key materials is valid, the re-authentication protocol fails and MN shall enter "Home Authentication" phase. The transmission of the last message in this case is optional, since its integrity cannot be verified, in order to prevent DoS attacks on the protocol.

4   The Key Hierarchy

Figure 3 depicts the key hierarchy we designed to allow the cryptographic-based re-authentication security service with required properties.

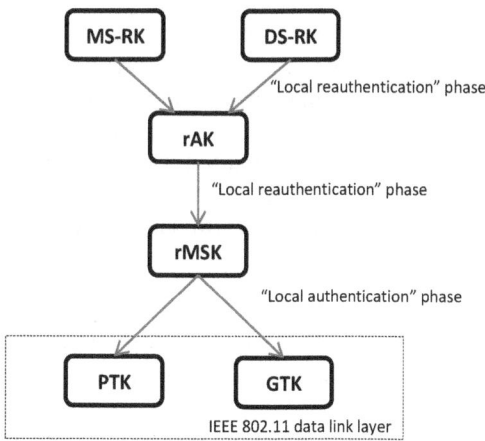

Fig. 3. The Design of the Key Hierarchy

We remark the whole hierarchy is derived starting from the two generic key materials MS-RK and DS-RK. For a given 3-tuple (MNi, F-AAAj, t), each principal shall be able to independently compute the same re-authentication symmetric key rAK(t) based on the key derivation mechanism we designed (specified within a separate section of this paper). Whenever, successful re-authentication of the principals is achieved, the master session key rMSK(t) is derived independently by principals according to the following formula:

$$rMSK(t) = hash(NonceA, NonceM, rAK(t)) \, .$$

Nevertheless, the properties of the hash function guarantee the potential correlations-based attacks mounted on several re-authentication keys are avoided. Thereafter, rMSK(t) is securely transported from F-AAA to authenticator (typically an access point) to enable "Local Authentication" phase. The derivation of the traffic encryption keys from rMSK(t) is out of the scope of our solution. For instance, in the case the MN's communications are run on top of the IEEE 802.11 link layer, the derivation of the (PTK, GTK) keys shall be accomplished according to the standard [1].

5   The Generic Key Material and Re-authentication Key Derivation

In this section we present the method we designed for the computation of the re-authentication symmetric key (rAK) with cryptographic guarantees, which enables scalable rAK pre-distribution procedures from H-AAA to each potential visiting F-AAA. Note, rAK shall be unique for each instance of the pair of principals which share this key (MN, F-AAA).

The key idea was to enable each principal to locally derive rAK "on-the-fly", at the visiting access network, from two components the generic key material uniquely assigned to the principal and the peer principal's identity. While the generic key material provides the authenticity for rAK and supplies the necessary entropy, the peer identity binds rAK to the current instance of the pair of principals. The generic key material is cryptographically bound to the corresponding principal through its construction, as well as totally decoupled from any of its potential peers. Due the last property the scalable generic key material pre-distribution it is feasible, before any tentative of re-authentication of the related principals.

The rAK derivation method was designed to satisfy the following overall cryptographic requirements:

(Req.1) the re-authentication key derived shall have high level of entropy;
(Req.2) the derivation method must have one-way property;
(Req.3) to guarantee both principals shall independently compute the same re-authentication key;
(Req.4) the key material owned by one principal can be used to compute neither the key material of any other principal nor the re-authentication key corresponding to another pair of principals

Besides, the generic key material shall be transported over a secure channel (with confidentiality and authenticity guarantees) from H-AAA principal to each potential F-AAA principal and MN principal.

The problem: For a given pair of principals, MN and F-AAA (on behalf of the visiting domain) we further denote the generic key material assigned with MS-RK and DS-RK, respectively. Also, we will denote with ID_{MN} the MN's identifier and with ID_{DS} the visiting domain identifier. Assuming the parameters RAND (i.e. a random number), ID_{MN}, ID_{DS} defined over Z_n, we had to research two functions f(.) and g(.), such that *(Req.3)* property holds on their composition, as follows:

$$f, g : Z_n \times Z_n \to Z_n .$$

$$f(g(RAND, ID_{DS}), ID_{MN}) = f(g(RAND, ID_{MN}), ID_{DS}) .$$

Furthermore, assigning to g(.) the generic key material computation role, and to f(.) the re-authentication key derivation role, we claim the following definitions:

$$MS\text{-}RK = g(RAND, ID_{MN}) \text{ and } DS\text{-}RK = g(RAND, ID_{DS})$$

$$rAK = f(MS\text{-}RK, ID_{DS}) = f(DS\text{-}RK, ID_{MN}) .$$

Within our work we considered two associative one-way functions f(.) and g(.) with the following definition:

$$g(x, y) = f(x, y) = x^{h(y) + A} \mod n, \ \square \ x \in Z_n\backslash\{0, 1\}, \ \square \ y \in Z_n . \tag{1}$$

Where, n – it is a composite number hard to factor, defined in the same way as for RSA algorithm (n = p*q with p, q – two big prime numbers, $p \neq q$).
The expression of the exponent has been figured out such that *(Req.1)* and *(Req.4)* holds. In this regard, the constant value $A = 2^w$ has the role to shift the interval of values of the exponent, such that there are not factors of $\Phi(n)$ within its interval of values. Also, shall be assured that A is greater than the order of the set of y values that will be leveraged by this crypto scheme. On the other part, h(.) is the hash function with values within interval [0, a], where $a \leq A\text{-}1$ and greater than the order of the set of y values. It may be remarked that it is not necessary to have h(.) with one-way property.

Proof: It can be easily verified that property *(Req.3)* holds on (1):

$$f(g(x, y), z) = (x^{h(y)+A} \mod n)^{h(z)+A} \mod n = (x^{h(z)+A})^{h(y)+A} \mod n = f(g(x, z), y) .$$

The deployment of this crypto scheme for re-authentication service introduced in Section II, requires the following initiation operations from the part of each H-AAA entity in the network. Independently, each H-AAA server has to establish the value of n, which will openly be shared with its mobile subscriber and F-AAA servers. H-AAA chose the value of a to be at least the number of mobile subscribers registered. Greater values of a are recommended to avoid too frequency updates. Afterward, H-AAA entity figures out the appropriate value of w. Eventually, the RAND value is established randomly, then DS-RKs are computed and transferred together with n and A toward each F-AAA entity.

Security analysis of the re-authentication key

The security of the re-authentication key is guaranteed by the cryptographic properties stated previously as *(Req.1) … (Req.4)* and fulfilled through design of f(.) and g(.).

The entropy of the re-authentication keys is assured by the entropy of RAND value and the calculus of the powers of f(.) and g(.). The size of n shall be selected according to the security level required by the authentication service. It is expected at least a value of 1024 bits for n to be used.

The confidentiality is guaranteed by the security channel during the generic key material transfer between H-AAA and F-AAA. Moreover, the small subgroup attack on the confidentiality mounted by internal/external attacker is avoided through the condition on the powers of f(.) and g(.) to be prime with $\Phi(n)$. Also, the condition on the values of h(.) guarantees protection against internal attack in which one principal tries to compute another one keys through exponentiation of his keys. To note, that neither the size of hash value nor w does influence the confidentiality property. The one-way property guarantees the confidentiality of RAND, therefore precludes principals key computation and impersonation attacks launched by internal attackers.

The authenticity guarantee is provided by including of the identity information directly into the calculus of the generic key material and the re-authentication key.

The ID information is cryptographically bounded to the key based on the one-way property of the f(.) and g(.). This warranty together with the high-level of the entropy assures the yielded re-authentication key pair-wise uniqueness. To note, that the size of w does not influence the authenticity property. On the other part, the space of the hash values must be greater than the potential number of entities (mobile subscribers and AAA servers) in order to avoid yielded keys collision.

The strength of the one-way property of f(.) and g(.) is guaranteed by the complexity of solving the RSA underlying problem [16].

6   The DS-RK Generic Key Material Distribution Protocol

The main goal of this protocol is to proactively transport DS-RK together with the assigned index from H-AAA to each potential re-authentication server F-AAA. The operation of this protocol is illustrated in Figure 4. H-AAA is the only entity responsible with DS-RK update. A secured AAA protocol (e.g. secured RADIUS) may be used to push DS-RK encapsulated as AVP (Attribute Value Pair) digital object toward all F-AAAs with confidentiality and integrity guarantees. Note, DS-RK is specific for each F-AAA and is critical for real-time re-authentication of all MNs principals that administratively belongs to the same H-AAA. Besides, it is important to have DS-RK updated periodically. The exact period of time for DS-RK update could be a subject of further research. With respect to the security level needed by some application we foresee the update period and the multiplicative group order tradeoff is achievable. We highlight here the time period to be at least the delay required for updating all F-AAAs (denoted with Δ in Figure 4). Moreover, to ensure re-authentication service continuity the DS-RK lifetime must be twice the update period.

In Figure 4, the moment (A) corresponds to the MN entry in the network, for instance after a reboot. It is now that MN applies "Home Authentication" phase and get MS-RK(t-1) from H-AAA. Afterward, MN is periodically re-authenticated through "Local Re-authentication" phase, based on the MS-RK(.) it knows. See the moment (B) related to such an event run in between MN and L-AAAj. At the moment (B), the MN is locally re-authenticated with MS-RK(t-1) and notified that a new generic key material was released (based on KN(t) index). Thereafter, MN initialize "Home Authentication" phase to get the new MS-RK(t), without interrupting MN's data transfer. Later, MN hands-off to another access network within jurisdiction of L-AAAl. When MN tries to re-authenticate again at the moment (C), it will succeeds to do it locally based on the MS-RK(t). Then MN finds out that a new generic key material was released and proceeds further to get MS-RK(t+1), as previously mentioned without interrupting MN's data transfer.

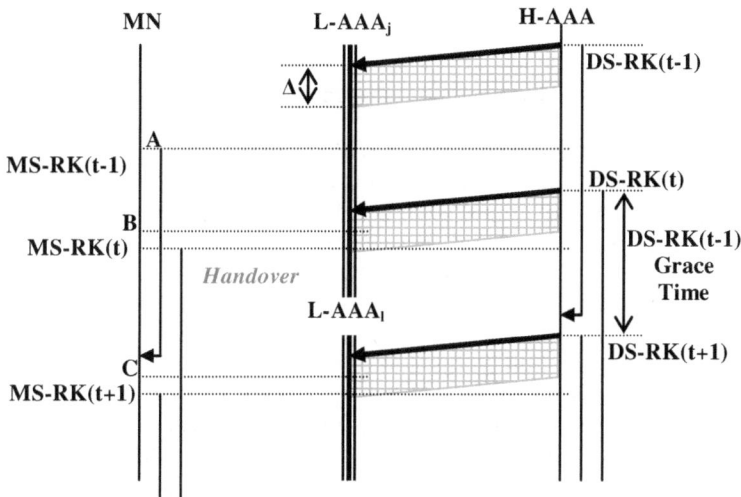

Fig. 4. DS-RK Material Distribution Protocol

We claim this method of update is scalable with communication complexity in O(N), where N represents the number of potential visited domains (i.e. F-AAAs) to update.

7   Validation of the Re-authentication Service Mechanisms

To prove the correctness of the re-authentication service our aim was twofold: to verify the security properties of the re-authentication protocol and to check the complete-
ness and soundness of the whole re-authentication system with respect to the most
representative scenarios. In this regard, we chose a simulation-based approach and
settled intra/inter-domain handover conditions for several scenarios. To accomplish
the first objective, we built-up the formal model of the re-authentication protocol
using High-Level Protocol Specification Language (HLPSL) and used the AVISPA
tool [17] for automated security properties verification against the generic Dolev-Yao
attacker offensive [18]. We formalized the security requirements in terms of HLPSL
authentication and confidentiality goals. The following HLPSL code shows the goals
we specified within HLPSL mobile node module, identified here by M. The first two
goals specify the requirement that rMSK_old and rMSK_new, corresponding to (t-1)
and (t) key intervals respectively, are established with guarantees of confidentiality
for the two principals. The following two goals specify the requirement that rAK_old
and rAK_new, corresponding to the two successive key intervals remain secret after
re-authentication protocol execution. The fifth goal, *witness(.)* together with the cor-
respondent *request(.)* goal specified within the peer HLPSL module denoted here by
A, claim the principal A shall be authenticated by the peer principal M, by means of
NonceM. Analogously, the last goal together with the related *witness(.)* goal from the
peer principal A are provided to assure the principals are mutually authenticated.

> ∧ secret (rMSK_old, ma_rmsk_old, {M, A})
> ∧ secret (rMSK_new, ma_rmsk_new, {M, A})
> ∧ secret (rAK_old, m_rak_old, {M})
> ∧ secret (rAK_new, m_rak_new, {M})
> ∧ witness (M, A, ma_nm, NonceM')
> ∧ request (M, A, ma_na, NonceA)

Thereafter, we achieved four optimized model-checking analyses by means of the
following AVISPA's back-ends: On-the-fly model checker (OFMC), Constrain-
Logic-based Attack Searcher (CL-AtSe), SAT-based Model Checker (SATMC) and
Tree Automata-based analyzer for Security Protocols (TA4SP). All the analyzers'
outcome was "SAFE", proving our re-authentication protocol fulfills the required
security goals. More specifically, our protocol guarantees the secrecy of the session
key and resilience against replay attacks.

On the other hand, we implemented the formal model of the re-authentication service mechanisms using Specification and Description Language (SDL) and specified
the required liveness properties for the whole system. We stated initially the properties using Linear Temporal Logic (LTL) formulas, thereafter we had automatically
translated them into a distinct Büchi automata [19, 20], each of which we eventually
built-up the corresponding SDL model. For instance, a liveness property we verified
was "all events of type new generic key material notification shall be pursued by
'Home authentication' phase", which we formally expressed upon the following LTL
(negated) formula:

$$F((p->X(G \ (!q))) \ \&\& \ p) \ .$$

Where p, q denote here, the two boolean propositions in the sentence above. The verification of the re-authentication model against liveness properties was achieved on several scenarios (as previously mentioned) through the model-checking method implemented by IFx tool [21]. The model-checking process have been run over a three days interval on a computer configured with Debian, CPU Intel Pentium D, 3GHz, 2G RAM and 1.5G swap. At the end of the interval this process had been analyzed over 10 million of transitions and 4 millions of states, without error state being reached by Büchi automata. Based on the model-checking process outcome, we claim the re-authentication system satisfy the critical liveness properties we specified for the most representative scenarios.

8   Performance Evaluation

According to our architecture, the generic key material derivation transformation shall be run periodically by H-AAA server, while the re-authentication key derivation transformation is run by MN and F-AAA entities at the moment of first re-authentication that means when MN enters the new visiting network domain. Both derivation transformations have the same complexity in $O(|n|^2)$ multiplications, where $|n|$ represents the length of the modulus. We remark it has the same complexity as RSA encryption transformation, lesser than the RSA digital signing transformation in $O(|n|^3)$. Furthermore, to assure the derivation of the identity-based distinct key material for all subscribers, as fast as possible, a maximal length of 30 bits for the h(.) we estimate to be sufficient in the real world. To note, that our transformation is applied once per each generic key material or re-authentication key derived.

We remark the frequency the derivation transformation is run by the three architectural entities, follows the heuristic of asymmetry of the computational power distribution between network entities. Since it is expected the MN entity rarely roams the computational resources required by our solution are lesser than for the case of the traditional asymmetric mechanisms, such as the digital signatures based re-authentication protocols.

In order to evaluate how much our derivation transformation overloads the H-AAA and F-AAA servers, we measured its computation elapsed time to be roughly 190μs using sage toolkit [22] on the PC 32 bit architecture with CPU Pentium 4, 2.8 GHz, 1GB RAM.

We can observe that H-AAA server is overloaded periodically at the moment of the generic key material derivation for all the potential visiting domains. It yields that over a one hour period more than 18 billions generic key materials may be derived, which is far more than it is required in the real-world scenarios.

The F-AAA re-authentication server computational capacity is the most critical for the whole performance of our solution. In other words it determines the number of the roaming MN entities that could be handled with better performances than traditional solutions. For performance comparisons we assumed a 100ms time interval as reference, which roughly corresponds to one transaction delay over the Internet. Thus, we figured out that roughly 500 roaming terminals per second could be re-authenticated at the performance claimed by our solution, which is more than required by real-world scenarios.

9   Conclusion and Future Work

This paper proposed several mechanisms designed to support development of the real-time re-authentication service for intra/inter-domain mobile WiFi and/or WiMAX terminals. Even though our solution was designed with the aim to be part of the access control service at the data-link OSI layer, the authors considers it could be easily adopted at the others OSI layers (e.g. network or application layer). Furthermore, our mechanisms are compatible with legacy (re-)authentication mechanisms (e.g. EAP, AAA, HOKEY). Although, several modifications of the EAP state machine work flow are necessary, e.g. to include the logic required to process the events associated to generic key material distribution and synchronization.

Upon the functional validation results we obtained so far, we claim that proposed identity-based key derivation methods, represents the promised paradigm enabling local re-authentication service operation with continuity guarantees even for roaming terminals. The performance evaluation we accomplished on the identity-based key derivation mechanisms shows they will succeeds on real world scenarios. Furthermore, our approach proved to be operational with better performances than other similar solutions, due the elimination of the transaction over the Internet whenever the mobile entity is re-authenticated. The scalable generic key material pre-distribution procedure design relies on the hybrid push-pull model with resilience to DoS attacks. Moreover, the generic key material and re-authentication key derivation transformations prove they fulfill the commonly required cryptographic properties.

Future work will be devoted by authors for implementation of the re-authentication service presented in this paper for further evaluation on the real-life testbed.

Acknowledgments. This work has been supported by the IST Program, Alicante project FP7 IST No. 248652-IP.

References

1. Part 11: Wireless LAN Medium Access Control (MAC) and Physical Layer (PHY) Specifications, IEEE Std. 802.11 (2007)
2. IEEE-SA Standards Board, Port-based Network Access Control, IEEE Std. 802.1x-2001 (2001) ISBN 0-7381-2626-7
3. IEEE-SA Standards Board, Part 16: Air Interface for Fixed and Mobile Broadband Wireless Access Systems. Amendment 2: Physical and Medium Access Control Layers for Combined Fixed and Mobile Operation in Licensed Bands and Corrigendum 1, IEEE Std. 802.16e (2006)

4. Chen, J.J., Tseng, Y.C., Lee, H.W.: A Seamless Handoff Mechanism for IEEE 802.11 WLANs Supporting IEEE 802.11i Security Enhancements,
   http://www.cs.nctu.edu.tw/~yctseng/papers.pub/mobile79-handover-tunnel-apwcs2007.pdf
5. Lin, X., Ling, X., Zhu, H., Ho, P.H., Shen, X.: A novel localized authentication scheme in IEEE 802.11 based wireless mesh network. Intl. Journal Security and Networks 3(2) (2008)
6. Hong, Z., Rui, H., Man, Y.: A novel fast authentication method for mobile network access (2003), http://www.cnnic.net.cn/download/2003/11/27/142157.pdf
7. Calhoun, P., Montemurro, M., Stanley, D.: Control and Provisioning of Wireless Access Points (CAPWAP) Protocol Specification, IETF, RFC 5415 (2009)
8. Clancy, T.: Secure Handover in Enterprise WLANs: CAPWAP, HOKEY and 802.11r. IEEE Wireless Communications Journal 15(5) (2008)
9. Mishra, A., Shin, M., Arbaugh, W.: An Empirical Analysis of the IEEE 802.11 MAC Layer Handoff Process. ACM SIGCOMM Computer Communication 3(2) (2003)
10. Long, M., Wu, C.-H., David Irwin, J.: Localized Authentication for Wireless LAN Internetwork Roaming. IEEE Communications 151(5) (2004)
11. Komarova, M.: Fast authentication and trust based access control in heterogeneous wireless networks, Ph.D. Thesis, Telecom-ParisTech (2008)
12. Huang, P.J., Tseng, Y.C.: A Fast Handoff Mechanism for IEEE 802.11 and IAPP Networks. In: Proc. of Vehicular Technology Conference, VTC 2006-Spring (2006)
13. The HOKEY working group documents homepage,
    http://datatraker.ietf.org/wg/hokey/
14. Aboba, B., Blunk, L., Vollbrecht, J., Carlson, J., Levkowetz, H.: Extensible Authentication Protocol (EAP), IETF, RFC 3748 (2004),
    http://www.ietf.org/rfc/rfc3748.txt
15. Housley, R., Aboba, B.: Guidance for Authentication, Authorization and Accounting (AAA) Key Management, IETF, RFC 4962 (2007)
16. Menezes, A., van Oorschot, P., Vanstone, S.: Handbook of applied cryptography. CRC Press (1996)
17. AVISPA project website, http://www.avispa-project.org
18. Dolev, D., Yao, A.: On the security of Public-Key Protocols. IEEE Transactions on Information Theory 2(29) (1983)
19. Vardi, M.: An automata theoretic approach to LTL,
    http://www.cs.rice.edu/~vardi/papers/banff94rj.ps.gz
20. LTL2BA translator website,
    http://www.lsv.ens-cachan.fr/~gastin/lt2ba/index.php
21. IFx tool website, http://www-if.imag.fr
22. Sage Math, tool website http://www.sagemath.org

Feature Reduction to Speed Up Malware Classification

Veelasha Moonsamy, Ronghua Tian, and Lynn Batten

Deakin University, School of Information Technology,
Melbourne, Australia
{v.moonsamy,rtia,lmbatten}@deakin.edu.au

Abstract. In statistical classification work, one method of speeding up the process is to use only a small percentage of the total parameter set available. In this paper, we apply this technique both to the classification of malware and the identification of malware from a set combined with cleanware. In order to demonstrate the usefulness of our method, we use the same sets of malware and cleanware as in an earlier paper. Using the statistical technique Information Gain (IG), we reduce the set of features used in the experiment from 7,605 to just over 1,000. The best accuracy obtained in the former paper using 7,605 features is 97.3% for malware versus cleanware detection and 97.4% for malware family classification; on the reduced feature set, we obtain a (best) accuracy of 94.6% on the malware versus cleanware test and 94.5% on the malware classification test. An interesting feature of the new tests presented here is the reduction in false negative rates by a factor of about 1/3 when compared with the results of the earlier paper. In addition, the speed with which our tests run is reduced by a factor of approximately 3/5 from the times posted for the original paper. The small loss in accuracy and improved false negative rate along with significant improvement in speed indicate that feature reduction should be further pursued as a tool to prevent algorithms from becoming intractable due to too much data.

Keywords: dynamic analysis, feature reduction, malware classification.

1   Introduction

Malicious software classification supports the products of anti-virus vendors and so is important to the computer industry. In the last several decades, many papers have appeared demonstrating varying approaches to such classification. The papers [12, 17, 5] and the references therein provide the reader with a sample of such work. In all cases, statistical analysis methods are applied and the accuracy of the resulting classification is measured.

In choosing features to use as input to the analysis, the usual approach is to use as many as possible. However, some schools of thought argue that, in general, only a small percentage of available features are needed to provide good classification [1, 6]. The authors of [6] argue as follows: 'In a great variety of fields ... the input data are represented by a very large number of features, but only few of them are relevant for predicting the label. In addition, many algorithms become computationally intractable

P. Laud (Ed.): NordSec 2011, LNCS 7161, pp. 176–188, 2012.

when the dimension is high. On the other hand, once a good small set of features has been chosen, even the most basic classifiers ... can achieve desirable performance. Therefore, feature selection, i.e. the task of choosing a small subset of features which is sufficient to predict the target labels well, is critical to minimize the classification error. At the same time, feature selection also reduces training and inference time and leads to better data visualization, reduction of measurement and storage requirements.'

The aim of our work is to show empirically that a significant reduction in the number of features is possible while at the same time maintaining a good level of accuracy. We use as a benchmark, the work in [12] which classified a set of 1368 executable samples with an accuracy of 97.4% and correctly distinguished clean from malicious files with an accuracy of 97.3%.

Based on the same set of executables, as a means of significantly reducing the speed at which the test executes, in this paper, we identify a significantly smaller feature set which produces close to the same levels of accuracy as those in [12]. In order to choose an appropriate set likely to retain accuracy, we use Information Gain [16] which is a statistical method discriminating between important and less important features across homogeneous data sets. We are able to reduce running time of the tests by a factor of approximately 3/5.

In Section 2, we review the literature in this area. In Section 3, we describe our experimental set-up. In Section 4, we describe the classification model and in Section 5, we analyse the results. In the final section, we draw our conclusions.

2   Literature Review

Although a new malware variant is disguised, its underlying structure still remains the same and retains the target of propagating the infection. Therefore, the features that appear frequently within a known malware can be used to identify and distinguish between cleanware and malware. Below, we present a few examples of the recent work conducted in the area of feature selection and reduction for malware.

Komashinskiy and Kotenko [4] test their feature selection and reduction technique on 5854 malicious files and 1656 cleanware files. They collect 65,536 features through static analysis and apply Information Gain (IG) to differentiate between most and least important features. The authors then form five different size feature sets which contain 50, 100,150, 200, 250 features respectively and use them to train the classifiers in WEKA [15]. The set of 250 features gives the best classification accuracy of 98%. Using a similar feature reduction method, Wang et al. [13] used IG and gain ratio to decrease the number of features from 1656 to 645, a 60% reduction. The authors used a dataset comprising of 1908 clean files and 7863 malicious files, and obtained an average classification accuracy of 95%.

Mehdi et al. [9] develop a framework that can analyze and detect in-execution malware. They experiment on a set of 100 Linux malware files, collected from a publicly available online database, and 180 cleanware files. Their methodology uses dynamic analysis together with the n-grams method. The authors claim that they present a novel idea by introducing a component known as a 'Goodness Evaluator' into their framework to reduce the feature set. After classification, the authors conclude that the dataset from 6-grams outperforms that from 4-grams. They also test their classification method against four other algorithms, and obtain a best accuracy of 77%.

The authors of [3, 7, 8, 14] also apply various feature reduction approaches in their respective work to contribute towards malware detection and classification.

3   Experimental Setup

3.1   Data Preparation

In order to benchmark our work against that of [12], we perform the same experiments on the same dataset with the exception that we apply Information Gain to reduce the feature set. We reduce the feature sets separately for each of the tests, malware versus cleanware and malware family classification. IG analyzes the API calls and their parameters separately and examines their effect on the classification results.

For the purpose of their work, Tian et al. [12] executed the data set, comprising 1368 malware files and 456 clean files, for 30 seconds and obtained 1824 log files. To ensure that we were not missing any important features, using the same data set, we let each executable run for 60 seconds and obtained 12 additional log files. Upon investigating the contents of the additional files, we found no relevant additional information. Hence, it can be deduced that a further 30 seconds does not impact on the experiments in any way and so we used the same 1824 log files as in [12] and stored these in our database.

3.2   Data Pre-processing

We first introduce some terminology that we will refer to as we progress through the explanation of our experiments.

An '*APIString*' is made up of an API call together with its corresponding parameters. Below are two examples of APIStrings from our database.

- *RegSetValueExW, 0x18c, IntranetName, 0100000*
- *CreateFileW, \\.\MountPointManager*

The components *RegSetValueExW* and *CreateFileW* are API calls while the remaining segments are parameters.

We use the term '*String*' to refer either to an API call or to a parameter. Thus, using the above excerpt of the log file presented in bullet points, we consider the following items: '*RegSetValueExW*', '*0x18c*', '*IntranetName*', '*0100000*', '*CreateFileW*' and '*\\.\MountPointManager*' to be Strings.

To have a consistent comparison, we conduct the same two experiments as in [12], malware versus cleanware detection and malware versus malware family classification.

3.3   Feature Extraction and Selection

We make use of a database management system program because of its usability and integrated management interface. We store the features to be used in the test as shown in Table 1 along with a description of the purpose of each field.

Table 1. Strings Database Scheme

Column Name	Description
FileID	Unique file identification number which is generated during execution.
Family	File's family name.
String	Stores the content of String extracted from the file.
Type	Identifies whether the String is an API call or parameter
FreqofStringInFile	Total number of times a String appears within a file.

The number of times a String occurs in the feature set is indicative of its importance in the classification process because the more often it appears in a given malware or cleanware family, the higher the probability that it differentiates itself from the features belonging to other families.

Thus, our next step is to derive a feature selection method and apply it to the String data to select the most significant features. There are two standard approaches to this task, one known as the filter method and the other as the wrapper method ([2], p. 141). The filter method is more appropriate to our data set because it uses an evaluation function which relies on the distance metric. In other words, the most desirable attributes have a greater difference among the entire feature set. While there are several sophisticated feature selection methods available, such as Information Gain, Chi-Square, Fisher's Score, n-grams [8], we choose IG as it has a high adoption rate and is well understood. Some preliminary tests using three feature selection algorithms indicated that IG selected a more comprehensive set of highly weighted features. Moreover, the IG selection method is available to us in the WEKA set of algorithms from which we draw the classifiers for later use in the test.

IG was chosen as it is regarded as a powerful technique for discriminating between important and less important features across homogeneous data such as ours.

Information Gain evaluates the importance of an attribute by measuring the IG value with respect to the class. An example of calculating IG values is provided by [1]: "For a given attribute X and a class attribute $Y \in \{Cleanware, Malware\}$, the uncertainty is given by their respective entropies H(X) and H(Y)". Then the IG of X with respect to Y is given by IG(Y;X):

$$IG(Y; X) = H(Y) - H(Y/X).$$

We begin by selecting the distinct Strings in each family, as shown in Table 2 and use the numbers in the third column of the table to apply feature selection for two tests.

Table 2. Number of Distinct Strings per Family

Type	Family	Number of Files per Family	Number of distinct Strings
Malware	Agobot	340	1280
	Alureon	58	1375
	Bambo	70	884
	Beovens	144	1022
	Boxed	366	1268
	Clagger	47	1095
	Emerleox	78	1051
	Looked	67	774
	Robknot	119	1145
	Robzips	82	905
	SUB TOTAL	*1371*	
Cleanware	Clean	465	998
	TOTAL	1,836	11797 Strings (with repeats)

3.3.1 Malware Versus Cleanware (M/C)

In this test, we ignore the malware families and treat the set of malware files as a single set. It can be noted from Table 2 that the numbers of malware and cleanware executable files are not proportionate. To deal with this imbalance, we follow the recommendations of [10] and split the total malware executable files into groups of same size as that of the cleanware.

After merging all the malware executables, we obtain a total of 1371 files. We then proceed to build groups of 465 malware files, which is the number of files present in the cleanware group. After generating the first 2 groups, *mGroup₁* and *mGroup₂*, we are left with 441 malware executable files. To build the third group, *mGroup₃*, we then randomly select an additional 24 (465-441) files from the first two groups, as shown in Figure 1.

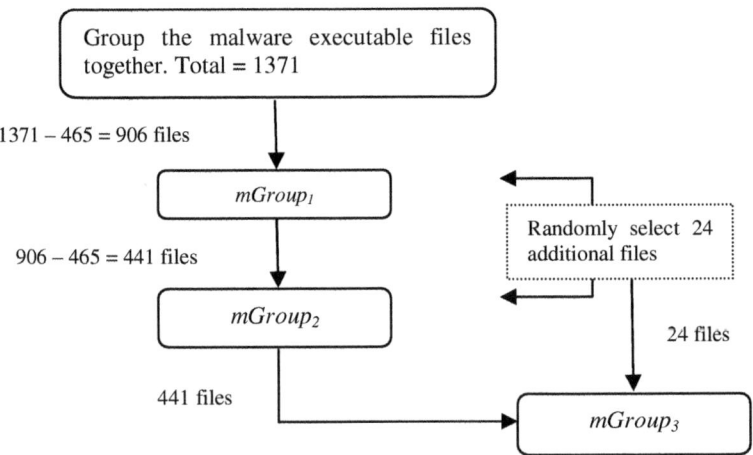

Fig. 1. Generate Malware Groups

We then take each *mGroup_i* and select the distinct Strings in that particular group. Next, we use the list of distinct Strings to generate a vector for each file within the current *mGroup_i*, where an element within a vector represents the presence or absence of a particular String from the distinct String list. Below is an example on how to generate the vectors.

Suppose distinct String list includes 10 Strings, as shown below:

distinctStringList =
{GetProcAddress,
0x77e60000,
LoadLibraryA,
ExitProcess,
LoadLibraryExW,
ADVAPI32.dll,
0x77dd0000,
RegCloseKey,
WININET.dll,
InitializeCriticalSectionAndSpinCount}

Assuming that file *F* is made up of 3 Strings (shown as italicized) from the above list, therefore:

File *F* =
{LoadLibraryA,
ExitProcess,
LoadLibraryExW}

Since the feature vector for *F* is made up of the frequency of each String within the file, then the vector for file *F* might look as follows:

Vector_F = (0,0,6,3,16,0,0,0,0,0),
where 0 represents the absence of a String and any other number denotes the frequency of that particular String in the file.

We repeat this process for *mGroup1*, *mGroup2* and *mGroup3* to generate the ARFF files and input them into WEKA for feature selection by IG.

3.3.2 Family by Family (F/F)

In the second test, we apply a feature reduction family by family in order to differentiate between the Strings which are representative of a malware family.

We start by selecting the distinct Strings from each family in our dataset to build the vectors. For example, in Table 2, the malware family Agobot includes 340 files and has 1280 distinct Strings. For each file, we then generate a vector to indicate the presence of any of the 1280 distinct Strings.

We repeat the above for all the 11 families and use the vectors to generate the ARFF files to input in WEKA.

3.4   Feature Reduction

In this subsection, we proceed with the feature reduction phase of our experiment. We select the most important Strings which are rated based on their corresponding Information Gain values and retain a portion of the highest ranked Strings for the classification stage, as discussed in Section 4.

In WEKA, IG is a single attribute evaluator ([16], p.489) where IG evaluates an attribute based on its information gain. We use the ranker search method [11] for attribute selection, as it allows WEKA to rank attributes based on their individual IG evaluation.

At the end of the attribute selection process, we obtain a file for each family (and mGroup$_i$) with IG values for each of the Strings. The files are then ranked in terms of highest to lowest values. The next step is to determine the 'n' most important IG values with which to build the reduced feature set.

Since the families in our dataset have varying sizes, we had to ensure that we do not discriminate between families with large number of files against those with lesser files. Hence, we did some preliminary tests to determine the cut-off values. We start by finding the average number of Strings per family and use that number as a threshold. Finally, depending on the threshold value, we selected the Strings from the IG results. The final number of Strings selected from each family is shown in Table 3.

Table 3. Number of Strings Selected

Family	Number of Files in Family	Number Strings selected from IG results
Agobot	340	1067
Alureon	58	34
Bambo	70	45
Beovens	144	303
Boxed	366	534
Clagger	47	14
Emerleox	78	79
Looked	67	11
Robknot	119	140
Robzips	82	101
Clean	465	107

In order to obtain a reduced set of Strings for the M/C test, we compute the sum of the numbers for all the malware families (column three in Table 3) and divide the total by 3 (i.e. by the number of *mGroups*). We then use the resulting number to select the Strings ranked by IG. We refer to the reduced feature set for M/C as 'Information Gain Feature Reduction (IGFR – M/C)' and it consists of 1078 Strings.

The reduced set for the F/F test includes all the distinct Strings after the threshold value is applied. The final reduced list, referred to as IGFR-F/F includes 1266 Strings.

4   Experimental Work

4.1   The Classification Model

We summarize the steps in the classification model: the experimental data (both malware and cleanware files) are executed in a virtual machine; the execution behaviors are recorded in log files, which are collected at the end of the executable file run-time; the features are extracted from the log files and stored in the database table; 2 separate reduced feature sets are generated (IGFR-M/C and IGFR-F/F), which are then converted into vector form, representing the features' frequencies, to generate the input files to WEKA.

For the classification process, for the purpose of comparison, we use the same four WEKA classifiers as in [12] and apply 10-fold cross validation [8]. The classification model selects the malware executables for a particular family, M, and chooses the same number of files in the selected one at random from other families- referred to as *Other*, using a random function. The classifier then divides M into 10 groups of equal size as follows:

- If $10 \mid |M|$, then each group has size $\frac{|M|}{10}$.
- If $10 \nmid |M|$, write

$$|M| = 9 * B + r, \text{ where } 0 \leq r < 9,$$

and generate 9 groups of size B and place the remaining r executables in a 10th group along with $(B\text{-}r)$ randomly chosen executables from M. Once the 10 groups are formed, the classifier then generates their corresponding arff files to be used as input to WEKA. The same steps are repeated to divide the set, *Other*, into 10 groups and generate the arff files.

The classifier then takes 9 groups from M and *Other* to set up the training set and the remaining one group from M and *Other* is used as the testing set. The process is repeated for each of the 11 families. Moreover, the authors of [12] noted that when applying the meta-classifier AdaboostM1 on top of the base-classifiers, better accuracy results were obtained (pg. 5). Therefore, we only present classification results where Adaboost is applied.

4.2   Classification Results

In this section, we proceed with the data preparation for the classification stage. We commence by generating the input files in the format that is required by WEKA and then applying the algorithms to obtain the classification accuracies.

We use the IGFR-M/C and IGFR-F/F lists obtained from Table 3 to generate the feature vectors for the two tests: M/C and F/F, where each vector is made up of String frequencies within a file. The vectors are then used to construct the WEKA (.arff) files using our Java procedure 'WriteToArff'.

Table 4 compares the classification results obtained using the reduced feature sets for the IGFR tests with those from [12]. In this table, the weighted accuracies for the four meta-classifiers are indicated. Table 5 lists the false positives and false negatives for these same tests.

Table 4. Classification Accuracy with Adaboost (Weighted Average)

| | Malware 2010 [12] | | Our method (IGFR) | |
	M/C	F/F	M/C	F/F
SMO	96.1	95.2	93.7	94.3
IB1	92.7	93.5	89	90
DT	97.1	93.9	94.5	94.5
RF	97.3	97.4	94.6	94.5
Number of features	7605 strings	7605 strings	1078 strings	1266 strings

Table 5. False Positives and False Negatives

| | Malware 2010 [12] | | | | Our method (IGFR) | | | |
| | M/C | | F/F | | M/C | | F/F | |
	FP	**FN**	**FP**	**FN**	**FP**	**FN**	**FP**	**FN**
SMO	0	0.03	0.017	0.084	0.0878	0.038	0.075	0.039
IB1	0.02	0.06	0.06	0.08	0.197	0.022	0.199	0.022
DT	0.01	0.04	0.02	0.11	0.075	0.035	0.074	0.036
RF	0.01	0.04	0.021	0.04	0.074	0.035	0.071	0.039

5   Analysis of Results

In this section, we analyze our results and compare them with the results from [12]. We also compare the tests on the basis of speed.

Figure 2 summarizes the weighted average accuracies by classifier for the four tests. Random Forest provides the best accuracy overall, while IB1 displays the largest spread (4.5%) across the four tests. For the M/C test, the smallest difference is 2.6% with DT; for the F/F test, the smallest difference is 0.6, also with DT. Note that in all cases but one, the test of [12] has better accuracy than IGFR; however, with DT, the IGFR test shows better results than those of [12] for family by family malware classification.

Turning to the false positives and false negatives identified in the tests, Figures 3 and 4 summarize the results of Table 5. In the false positive case, there are large discrepancies between the IGFR approach and that in [12] with the latter faring much better than the former; Figure 3 presents these discrepancies clearly. On the other hand, in the case of false negatives, Figure 4 indicates that the IGFR approach is superior to that in [12] in both tests. At this time, we are not able to explain why this would be the case.

Overall, then, the ability of the new tests to identify malware is close to that of the tests in [12] based on the identical data set, and in some cases surpasses that of [12]. Thus, a reduction in number of features used, if this is done well, can indeed produce good quality results. Recall that the IGFR-M/C test used 1078 strings and the IGFR-F/F test used 1266 strings. This contrasts with the tests of [12] which used 7605 strings for each test.

Weighted Average Accuracy

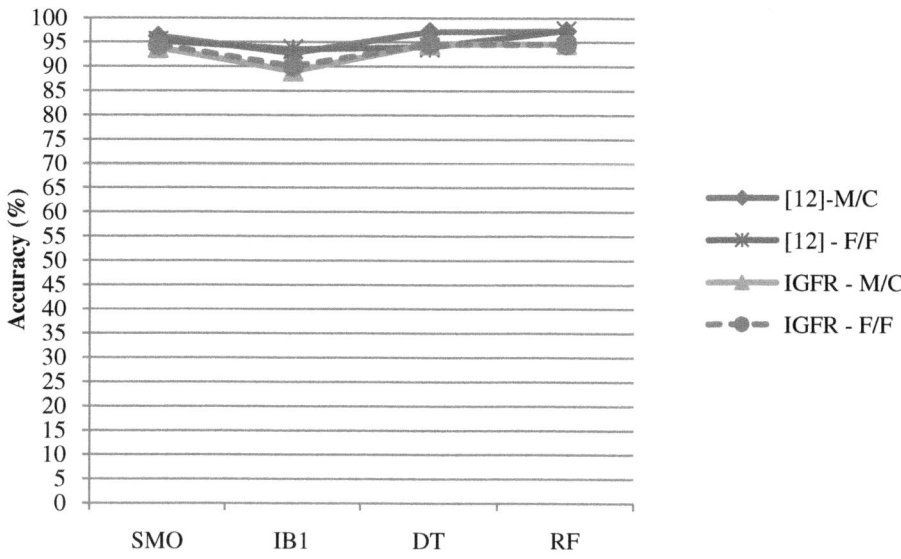

Fig. 2. Classification Accuracy

False Positive

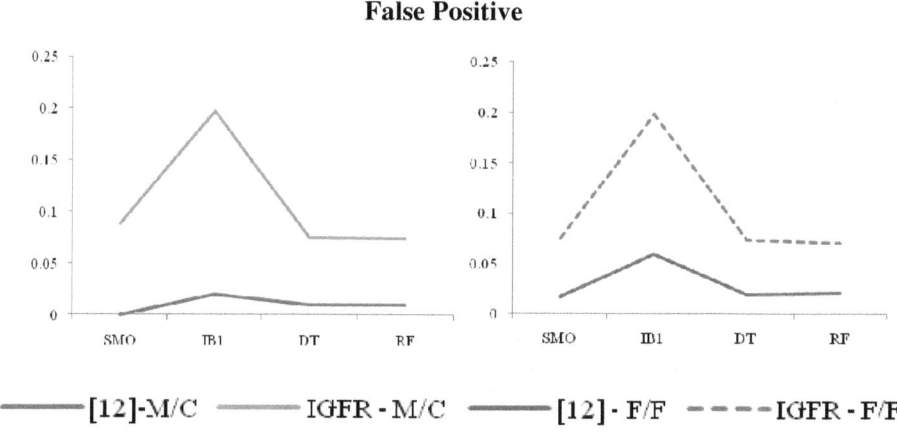

Fig. 3. Comparison of False Positive

We now turn to the question of speed with which the tests ran. Table 6 gives the to-tal time in minutes for each of the four tests in question and Figure 5 presents a bar chart comparison of this data. The M/C test with the IGFR method ran in 65% of the time of the M/C test using the method of [12]. The IGFR-F/F test ran in 52% of the time of the F/F test using the method of [12]. Thus, both IGFR tests show a dramatic reduction in time needed to perform the tests while retaining good accuracy.

False Negative

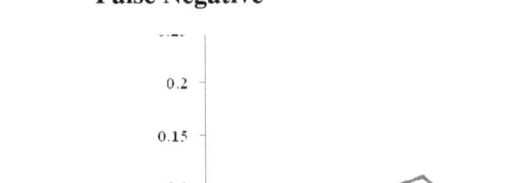

Fig. 4. Comparison of False Negative

Table 6. Total Classification Time (mins)

Experiment	Total Classification Time (mins)
[12] – M/C	402
[12] – F/F	560
IGFR – M/C	260
IGFR – F/F	293

Total Classification Time

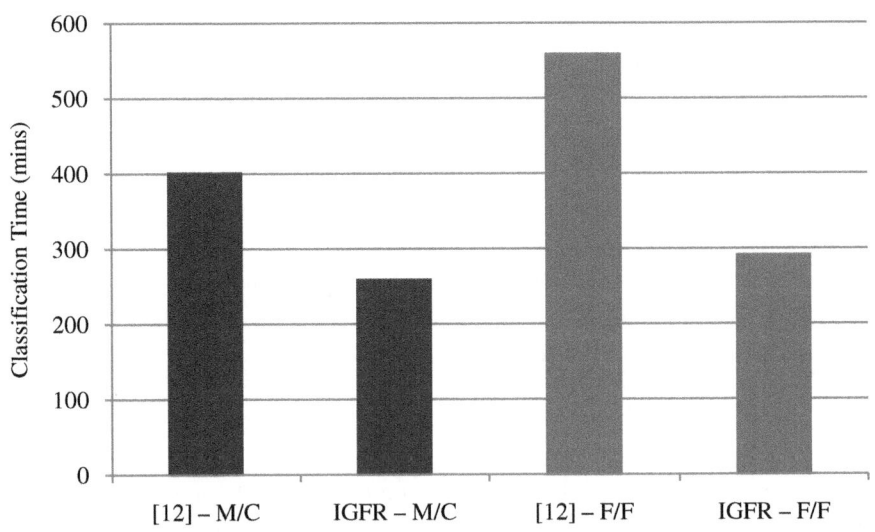

Fig. 5. Classification Time

6   Conclusions

We have taken advantage of a rare opportunity to re-use a data set from previous work ([12]) to compare running time and accuracy of that work against a new method proposed in this paper. Our aim was to significantly reduce the time needed to classify malware and to distinguish malware from cleanware. Table 6 and Figure 5 indicate that we were successful in achieving this as the time needed to perform each test was reduced by a factor of approximately 3/5. In addition, we were able to retain levels of accuracy of the results within 3% of the results of [12] on both tests.

The approach to saving time in our new method was to reduce the feature set by means of the statistical method Information Gain which is used to identify the most relevant features.

A feature of our work is the astonishing improvement we achieved in the false negative detection rate in classifying malware by family as presented in Figure 4. However, our approach did not improve on the false positive rate (Figure 3), and in future work, we shall investigate the possible reasons for this.

The small loss in accuracy and improved false negative rate along with significant improvement in speed of our tests indicate that feature reduction should be further pursued as a tool to prevent algorithms from becoming intractable due to the presence of too much data.

References

[1] Ahmed, F., Hameed, H., Shafiq, M.Z., Farooq, M.: Using spatio-temporal information in API calls with machine learning algorithms for malware detection. In: AISec 2009: Proceedings of the 2nd ACM Workshop on Security and Artificial Intelligence, pp. 55–62 (2009)

[2] Drozdz, K., Kwasnicka, H.: Feature Set Reduction by Evolutionary Selection and Construction. In: Jędrzejowicz, P., Nguyen, N.T., Howlet, R.J., Jain, L.C. (eds.) KES-AMSTA 2010. LNCS, vol. 6071, pp. 140–149. Springer, Heidelberg (2010)

[3] Henchiri, O., Japkowicz, N.: A feature selection and evaluation scheme for computer virus detection. In: Proceedings of the Sixth International Conference on Data Mining, ICDM 2006, pp. 891–895 (2006)

[4] Komashinskiy, D., Kotenko, I.: Malware detection by data mining techniques based on positionally dependent features. In: 2010 18th Euromicro International Conference on Parallel, Distributed and Network-Based Processing (PDP), pp. 617–623 (2010)

[5] Kolter, J.Z., Maloof, M.A.: Learning to detect and classify malicious executables in the wild. Journal of Machine Learning Research 7, 2721–2744 (2006)

[6] Li, Y., Lu, B.: Feature selection based on loss-margin of nearest neighbor classification. Pattern Recognition 42(9), 1914–1921 (2009)

[7] Lu, Y., Din, S., Zheng, C., Gao, B.: Using multi-feature and classifier ensembles to improve malware detection. Journal of CCIT 39(2), 57–72 (2010)

[8] Masud, M.M., Khan, L., Thuraisingham, B.: Feature Based Techniques for Auto-Detection of Novel Email Worms. In: Zhou, Z.-H., Li, H., Yang, Q. (eds.) PAKDD 2007. LNCS (LNAI), vol. 4426, pp. 205–216. Springer, Heidelberg (2007)

[9] Mehdi, S.B., Tanwani, A.K., Farooq, M.: IMAD: in-execution malware analysis and detection. In: Proceedings of the 11th Annual Conference on Genetic and Evolutionary Computation, GECCO 2009, pp. 1553–1560. ACM (2009)

[10] Moskovitch, R., Stopel, D., Feher, C., Nissim, N., Elovici, Y.: Unknown malcode detection via text categorization and the imbalance problem. In: 2008 IEEE International Conference on Intelligence and Security Informatics, pp. 156–161 (2008)

[11] Ranker Search Method, `http://weka.sourceforge.net/doc.stable/weka/attributeSelection/Ranker.html`

[12] Tian, R., Islam, R., Batten, L., Versteeg, S.: Differentiating malware from cleanware using behavioural analysis. In: Proceedings of the 5rd International Conference on Malicious and Unwanted Software: MALWARE 2010 (2010)

[13] Wang, T.-Y., Wu, C.-H., Hsieh, C.-C.: A virus prevention model based on static analysis and data mining methods. In: IEEE 8th International Conference on Computer and Information Technology Workshops, CIT Workshops 2008, pp. 288–293 (2008)

[14] Wang, T., Wu, C., Hsieh, C.: Detecting unknown malicious executables using portable executable headers. In: Fifth International Joint Conference on INC, IMS and IDC, NCM 2009, pp. 278–284. IEEE (2009)

[15] Waikato Environment for Knowledge Acquisition (WEKA): Data Mining Software in Java. University of Waikato, `http://www.cs.waikato.ac.nz/ml/weka`

[16] Witten, I., Frank, E., Hall, M.A.: Data mining: Practical machine learning tools and techniques, 3rd edn. Morgan Kaufmann, Burlington (2011)

[17] Ye, Y., Li, T., Jiang, Q., Wang, Y.: CIMDS: Adapting Postprocessing Techniques of Associative Classification for Malware Detection. IEEE Transactions on Systems, Man, and Cybernetics 40(3), 298–307 (2010)

Rooting Android – Extending the ADB by an Auto-connecting WiFi-Accessible Service

Assem Nazar[1,2], Mark M. Seeger[1,3], and Harald Baier[1]

[1] Center for Advanced Security Research Darmstadt (CASED),
Mornewegstraße 32,
64293 Darmstadt, Germany
{mark.seeger,harald.baier}@cased.de
[2] KTH - The Royal Institute of Technology,
Department of Computer & System Sciences,
Forum 100, SE-164 40 Kista, Sweden
anhus@kth.se
[3] Gjøvik University College,
Department of Computer Science,
N-2818 Gjøvik, Norway

Abstract. The majority of malware seen on Android has a top-down approach often targeting application programming interfaces (API) of the financially rewarding telephony and short message service (SMS). In this paper we present a proof of concept of compromising an Android based smartphone by targeting the underlying Linux kernel.

We adopt an unorthodox bottom-up approach on modifying the operating system to allow an application to re-route the Android debug bridge (ADB) daemon onto a wireless link. We support our research using case scenarios to show how information can be extracted and inserted into the smartphone without the knowledge of the user. We discuss how the Android build environment can be changed to harness functionality from secured operations. We also discuss how an application can be designed to function with minimum resources, be hidden and perform operations without user consent or interaction. We also provide an overview of how a rooted Android operating system can be misused.

Keywords: Android, ADB, Mobile Operating System, Rooting, Bottom-Up.

1 Introduction

Android is developed in an environment where security plays an important role and all features and services are designed around this focal point. The Android operating system (OS) is creating ripples in the mobile operating system world with its open, modular and secure operating system. Market shares for Android have risen considerably within the past 12 months [1], however, research associated with it has not seen a similar rise. Limited and unidirectional academic research in the field of security issues associated with Android has formed the

P. Laud (Ed.): NordSec 2011, LNCS 7161, pp. 189–204, 2012.
© Springer-Verlag Berlin Heidelberg 2012

motivating source for our research and the paper at hand. We develop a simple proof of concept for deployment and implementation of an Android application on an Android based smartphone with negligible user interaction.

The Android operating system is based on a modified Linux kernel that is used as an abstraction layer between the hardware and software stack. Core services like security, memory, process management, network stack and driver models are migrated from a Linux kernel version 2.6 [2]. A simple Android application comprises the following components:

- Activity: Almost all of the functionality of the application is fulfilled in the Activity class `android.app.Activity`. The Activity class has the sole responsibility of interacting with the user.
- Service: A service is an application component that is responsible for communicating with other applications, running in the background and providing threading support.
- Broadcast Receivers: Components built into an application that respond to system-wide broadcast announcements. Applications can also initiate broadcasts depending on the nature of data being handled.
- Content Providers: Android uses the Dalvik Virtual Machine (VM) where each application is run in its own instance of the virtual machine. The virtual machines are equipped with all necessary libraries and APIs required for the application to run normally.

The AndroidManifest.xml[1] file contains all the permissions and access rights. These rights are usually cross-checked by the Linux kernel upon installation and presented to the user if necessary. A visual representation of an Android application can be seen in Fig. 1.

By structure of an Android environment, each application is separated from other running applications by its sandbox. Application-specific data is restricted to access by the corresponding application alone, and sensitive global information (e.g. contacts and calender events) is governed by special containers known as content providers. Fig. 2 shows how a content provider works.

Applications can access sensitive data by including relevant content providers and invoking them during run time. These content providers require permissions that have to be confirmed by the application user, and are only mentioned during installation. These permissions are never revoked during the lifetime of an application and there is no indication of these permissions being used when the process takes place.

The Android Market[2] provides another attack vector where a malware can be disguised as a seemingly novice application [3]. Reverse engineering an Android application is a lengthy process and because the Android Market neither requires a developer authentication (e.g. in contrast to Apple's AppStore) nor does con-

---

[1] The manifest file presents essential information about the application to the Android system.

[2] The Android Market is an online software store developed by Google for Android powered devices. http://market.android.com

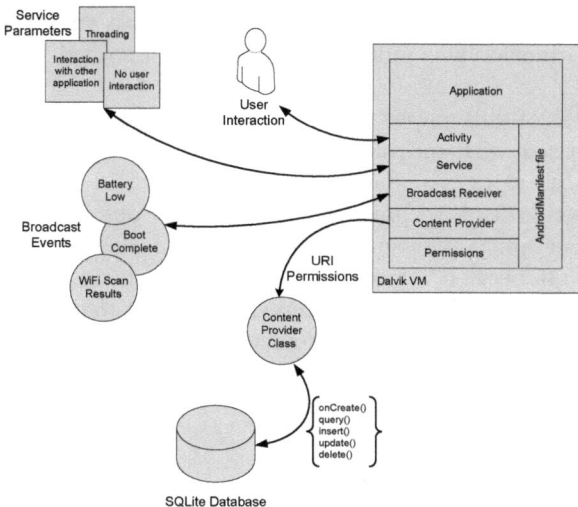

Fig. 1. Android application fundamentals

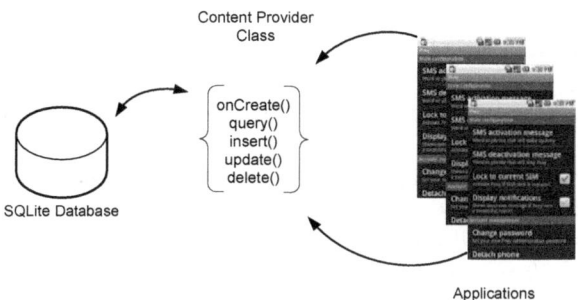

Fig. 2. How a typical content provider works

tain original source codes, determining what an application actually does can be a daunting task.

As the complete Android operating system is developed in Java and open to public view, it can be used to generate an attack vector. The source code can be tinkered with to collect data, share data and even create back doors for malicious purposes. Android operating systems developed by third party vendors such as HTC, Samsung and Acer are usually closed source, however, these are stemmed from the same Android operating system designed by Google and can be replaced easily.

In this paper we present a novel proof of concept to gain unauthorized access to sensitive user information. We perform an attack against the Android system by using its source code and native applications packed alongside the operating system. We show that by tweaking the operating system and adding escalated privileges, a system can be compromised easily. To assess the effectiveness of our approach a modern smartphone[3] was flashed[4] with an optimized operating system, and information was pulled and pushed off the device without any user interaction.

The remainder of this paper is structured as follows. A short terminology is provided to assist with technical terms used in this paper in Section 2. An overview of related work that has been done in the field of Android security is presented in Section 3. A technical groundwork to our approach is defined in Section 4 and Section 5. We outline our approach along with the application design in Section 6. Section 7 contains a detailed technical account of the implementation of the scenario. We define the experiments that we undertook, their results and a brief overview of the outcome in Section 8. An analysis of results is discussed in Section 9. Section 10 concludes this paper.

2   Terminology

Many technical terms are used extensively in this paper and can be taken out of context. The following definitions are provided with regard to the Android system.

Android System: The Android system is the complete environment: It comprises the operating system, the firmware it interacts with, all native applications and developer tools. This in fact comprises of the complete Android source code.

Application: A Java based application that interacts with the Android system.

Operating System: This indicates the operating system deployed on the smartphone. The Android operating system is upgraded at regular time intervals. We make use of the operating system 2.3 also known as Gingerbread. The operating system encompasses all the libraries, framework and APIs required for integration of applications with the hardware.

Firmware: The firmware is a set of hard-coded libraries that are unique to the hardware device. These are required to control the hardware components and interface them to the operating system. These libraries are developed by the organizations that manufacture the device, example HTC, ACER.

Rooting: Rooting is the process by which users/applications can gain access to privileged settings and APIs, allowing the user/appplication to bypass standard security checks in place.

Root Access: Denotes the highest level of access rights an application/user can attain. By having root access, an application/user can traverse through parts of the Android system, that is not possible otherwise.

Application Programming Interface (API): An API is a set of coded rules and specifications that applications can use to communicate with each other or parts of the Android system.

---

[3] The smartphone used was Nexus S co-developed by Google and Samsung.
[4] The process of installing an operating system onto the device.

3   Related Work

Academic research on the Android operating system and its security framework is covered in depth by Shabtai et al. [4]. The team explains the different components that make up the operating system and how security mechanisms are incorporated within each of these components. Possible attack vectors and their mitigation is also addressed. Although the paper gives a detailed account of different mechanisms governing the security and any problems it can pose, the focus point remains the application level and the framework it comes in direct contact with. Our research differs as we follow a bottom-up approach targeting the Linux kernel and moving up towards the application layer.

Other research appearing simultaneously in the IEEE Security and Privacy issue of Jan-Feb 2009 by Enck et al. [5] gives a thorough security architecture of applications running on the Android platform. The authors discuss how applications network, exchange data and interact through components. The paper also gives an account of protected APIs, permissions used by content providers, broadcast and intent providers. The process of sharing data, permissions and security mechanisms governing this process is also defined in great depth here. This paper provides a base in understanding the basic functionality of applications, their interaction with the environment and applications. A basic working of permissions for applications, how they are invoked and implemented is also given in the paper presented by Shin et al. [6].

Coupled with information about the internals of the Dalvik VM obtained from the intricate blog by Ehringer [7], helped gain insight into the internals of the life cycle of an Android application. Major technical breakthroughs have been conducted by individuals that have contributed to the success of our experiments and these include Thomas Cannon, who has implemented attacks related to Android using the Android Market [8][9], reverse engineering [10] to obtain important information and bypassing security locks on an Android based smartphone [11]. However, the methods and tools employed during any research on an Android based smartphone assume a clean off-the-shelf operating system, which can be dreadful if the firmware has been modified or has security holes.

The Internet is flooded with modified Android operating systems and each of them differs in something from the further ones. Unlike the Android OS provided by Google most of its vendors do not reveal their source code and are thus distinguishable from the original Android OS. We took this idea a step further by retaining the original design and functionality of the original operating system, but extracting more privileges, so that a formal comparison shows no difference. In the following sections we provide a detailed description and analysis of how we achieved this.

4   Technical Aspects

The Android operating system is a software stack for mobile operating systems developed in the Java programming language. Android also ships with a set of core developer tools written in native C/C++. The notable element is that this entire source from core Google-developed applications to specialized developer tools are open to general public.

The complete Android source is divided into multitudes of layers, and we make use of the following ones:

- Core applications that the system is shipped with, for example Google Maps, e-mail, calender.
- Developer tools to assist developers, for example monkeyrunner[5], ADB, Logcat[6], sqlite3 among others. [12]
- Libraries needed for interaction between hardware layer and software layer example media libraries for audio-video support, 3D libraries for graphics, among others.

We use these sections of the source code to inject our application, alongside the core applications and extract vital information from the user using the tools and system libraries.

4.1   PIDs and UIDs

The Android environment abstracts application permissions from the Linux kernel it is running on and divides applications depending on permissions assigned. Android applications are primarily written in Java and compiled into a custom byte-code (DEX)[7]. Each application is run in a separate virtual machine and having a unique userID (UID) [13].

Inherited from the Linux kernel underneath, files are divided into either application files or system files. System files are usually owned by the root user or the system user whereas application files are owned by application-specific users [14]. Unlike the Linux desktop environment, every application is run by a different user, if not explicitly defined differently, and this provides an extra level of security where applications cannot interact with each other. The possibility of gaining access to components or public information of other applications is only possible through specialized containers called content providers. Permissions to these content providers should also be defined during development process of the application. Fig. 3 shows how content providers and applications interact to handle data.

In a typical Android environment the number of users usually equals the number of applications. Other than these, system daemons, processes and privileged applications are divided among root user, system user and radio user.

Android daemons running as root include `init`, `mountd`, `debuggerd`, `zygote`, and `installd` [14]. System and radio level user IDs are hardcoded into the kernel to provide additional privileges. Radios are usually used to connect applications

---

[5] Provides an API for writing program to control emulators.

[6] The Android logging system collects and views system debug output.

[7] The Dalvik VM executes `.DEX` files, which are converted from compiled Java-byte-code.

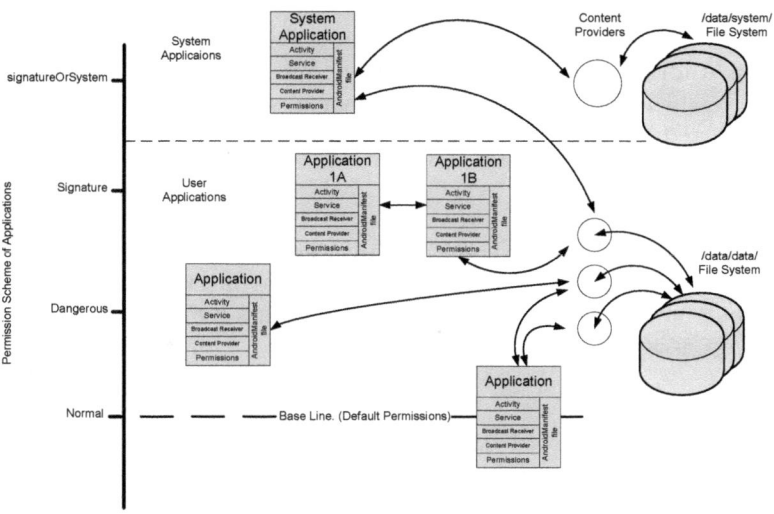

Fig. 3. Distribution of permissions among applications

to specialized hardware like bluetooth, wireless, broadcast receivers, GSM among others.

4.2 File Level Permissions

As described in ample detail by Enck et al. [5], system files and application files are stored separately and are accessible by their respective applications. System applications along with their data are stored under the path /data/system, whereas default applications would go under /data/data [5]. This can also be seen from Fig. 3.

4.3 Application Permissions

Inheriting from the Linux environment, permissions are assigned to files in tuples. Another permission scheme followed by Android is for applications where applications are assigned degrees of security ranging from normal to system level permissions [15] as depicted in Fig. 3. Also built into the Android development environment are system level APIs which are used to change system and security settings. These APIs are only accessible to applications that have required permissions of signatureOrSystem.

Android also protects sensitive information like call logs, contacts through specialized containers known as content providers. A content provider may want to protect itself with read and write permissions, and permissions to use these content providers are declared in the manifest file during application development [15]. All the permissions and providers the application will use are provided to the user at install time.

4.4   Initiating Permission

When the Android system boots, it sets permissions for files, critical settings and defines which core applications and daemons are running at which security level. Of particular importance are the following two files that are used during compilation of the source code:

1. File: *main.mk*
   File path: `android/build/core/main.mk`
   The main make file contains all the different properties that are assigned to different builds of the Android system, which subdirectories to create and any tags assigned to modules.

2. File: *init.rc*
   File path: `android/system/core/rootdir/init.rc`
   This is the top level initialization file that ends up being executed by the init process at boot time. The file sets up the environment, creates mount-points, directories, assigns read and write permissions and composes the basic file structure. Alongside it also tells the system, which properties to set at boot time, which ports to open or block, and lists the daemon processes that should be running.

We make use of both files to create a user build that runs on a standard smartphone with escalated privileges for the ADB daemon. The `init.rc` file builds on the output of the make file and so it is necessary to change properties to suit to our needs. The following properties are of great importance:

1. `persist.service.adb.enable`: This property determines whether the ADB daemon is persistently enabled to listen for open connections or not.
2. `ro.debuggable`: This property determines whether the device is debuggable or not. If the device is not debuggable, dissecting applications will not be possible. It also helps in acquiring the status of executing applications at runtime.
3. `ro.secure`: This property determines whether the smartphone can run root commands or not. By default all builds have shell access. Privileges can be escalated by issuing the `su` command.

All these properties are represented by a single bit: `0` or `1`.

5   Android Debug Bridge

The Android software development kit (SDK) is used for developing applications in conjunction with Java. Google also provides a set of tools to aid development and debugging of applications. One such tool is the Android Debug Bridge (ADB). ADB forms the basis of our attack vector as it suitably covers all aspects of deploying and extracting information from the smartphone. It comprises three blocks:

- ADB Daemon: The ADB daemon is part of the Android system on every smartphone and runs as a background process.
- ADB Server: Running on the development machine, the ADB server handles communication between the daemon and the client.
- ADB Client: The client runs on the development machine as well and is invoked by shell commands. It connects to the ADB daemon through standard communication ports of the Universal Serial Bus (USB) and the Transmission Control Protocol (TCP)[8].

The Android debug bridge was designed to aid developers in debugging applications directly on the device. It has all the advanced functions that a developer would require allowing the user to push and pull data, install and run applications, and execute scripts. We make use of these functions to carry out our attacks. The subsequent sections describe in detail the scenario and phases of our compromise.

6   Rooting and Application Design

For gaining root access on the operating system the following lines were added to the `main.mk` file mentioned in Section 4.4:

Listing 1.1. Code extract for gaining root access

```
ADDITIONAL_DEFAULT_PROPERTIES += ro.secure=0
ADDITIONAL_DEFAULT_PROPERTIES += ro.debuggable=1
ADDITIONAL_DEFAULT_PROPERTIES += persist.service.adb.enable=1
...
tags_to_install += user
tags_to_install += debug
```

The first three lines add properties to the system allowing it to run root commands, the device to be debuggable and the ADB service to be started on boot. In addition to modifications of these parameters, an Android application is developed and included into the source by installing it when the operating system is pushed onto the device. This is done by including the application contents under the install path parallel to the other generic applications.

6.1   Application Design

The application was designed, keeping in mind the requirements of a typical malicious application, where there is no interaction with the user, is stealthy in nature, does not have a fingerprint and has minimum processing load (memory and battery).

---

[8] Android explicitly uses the USB port for connecting to devices. The protocol can also be routed over the TCP but only through privileged commands.

The application implements two broadcast receivers, one for receiving notification of a completed reboot process and another for delivering notification of wireless access point availability. This can be seen from Fig. 4, depicting our application. The application is also designed to extensively make use of the wireless API, included as part of the Android SDK, to scan for wireless networks, connect and bind to them.

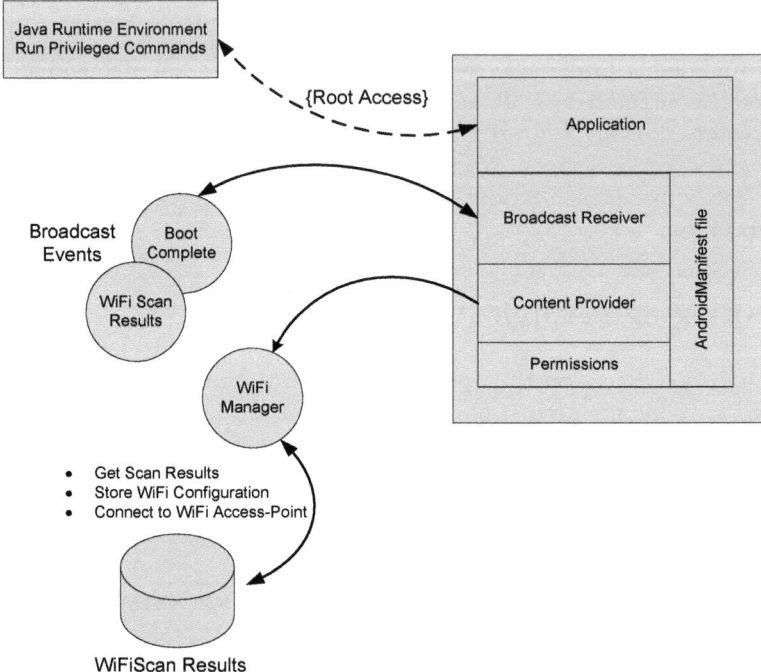

Fig. 4. Design of an application to extract information from an Android smartphone

Our application is designed to not have a user interface and therefore no notifications are generated. This also ensures that there is no other direct communication with the user.

The application uses the Java Runtime Environment to pass commands to the Linux kernel. Using the Linux kernel underneath the application reroutes the ADB daemon to communicate over the TCP link. In normal cases, an application would not be allowed to do so because of the added restrictions from the operating system. The complete application and all its modules are run as threads and therefore they consume considerably less processing power and have minimal footprint.

7 Software Distribution and Attack Scenario

The exploit begins by distribution of the rooted operating system. This distribution can be done through the Internet, spoofing a person to download an updated version of the operating system. Another method of distribution can be through a dedicated software used for flashing ROMs. The scenario developed for carrying out the attack was a simple one as shown in Fig. 5. Since there is no visual difference between the original operating system and the rooted one provided by us, we assume that a typical non-technical user cannot notice any discrepancies. If the ROM is distributed through traditional clients this assumption holds even stronger. The following steps highlight the attack process:

1. The user updates the smartphone with custom ROM off the internet or through a dedicated application like Samsung Kies[9].
2. The device boots up with the rooted ROM under normal procedures.
3. The rogue application runs in the background, waiting for a broadcast signaling successful boot operation.
4. The application starts scanning for wireless access points.
5. It sorts the retrieved access points into non-authenticated networks and authenticated ones.
6. The application traverses through open networks trying to connect to them.
7. To mitigate use of web authentication, we use the application to poll for a random public address.
8. On confirmation of successful connection to the network, the application runs root commands to forward the ADB daemon onto TCP port 5555.
9. The attacker present on the same network scans the network for an Android device using for example Nmap[10].
10. The attacker connects to the device using the ADB client (Command: adb connect <ipaddress>)
11. The attacker carries out attacks to compromise confidentiality, availability or integrity of the system.

7.1   Internals of the Scenario

Internally there is a lot happening on the application and middle layers once an Android system starts up. Fig. 6 shows the typical behavior of an application if it does not have escalated privileges. All access to public and private information is controlled through permissions. The AndroidManifest file contains permissions to content providers and broadcast receivers, the application requires to get access to. Accordingly, it also contains permission levels from either normal level application to system level application.

The Android system assigns all due resources to the application only after confirmation from the user at install time. These resources are never verified again during the run time of the application. Fig. 6 visualizes the application functions in a sand-boxed environment controlled by the Dalvik VM. The virtual machine coordinates between the application and the kernel.

---

[9] Client-side software from Samsung for connecting to smartphones. http://www.samsung.com/ca/kies
[10] A widely used network scanning tool. http://www.nmap.org

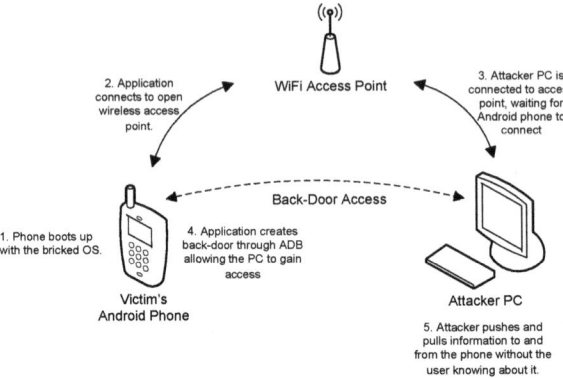

Fig. 5. A visual representation of the attack scenario

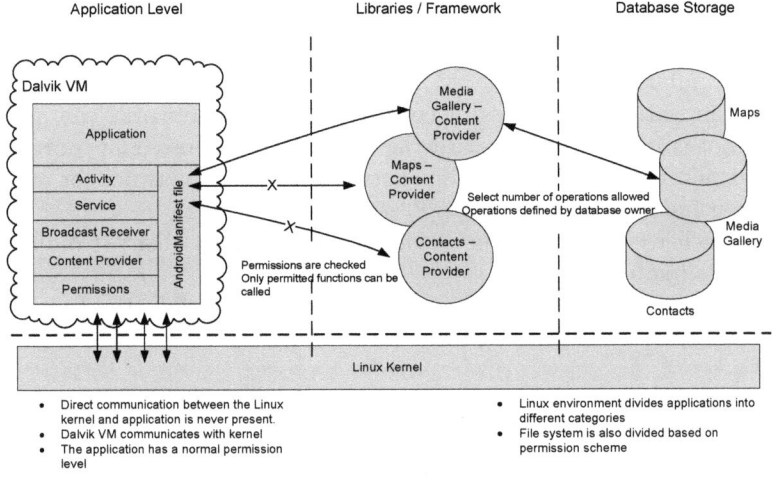

Fig. 6. Normal communication flow of an Android application

Once we have injected our modified operating system, the Android system overlooks certain permission schemes in the AndroidManifest file and assigns escalated privileges to the applandroidsecassessmentication. Once the application has gained these privileges it uses the Java Runtime Environment to issue commands at the kernel level. This is depicted in Fig. 7.

The application is therefore allowed to create a tunnel to the data storage and gets unhindered access to public and private data. Commands issued at the kernel level change parameters of the file system. As discussed in Section 4.2, system files and data files are stored separately. By escalating privileges of the application from a lowly 'normal' to the highest 'system', the application can access files with no restrictions.

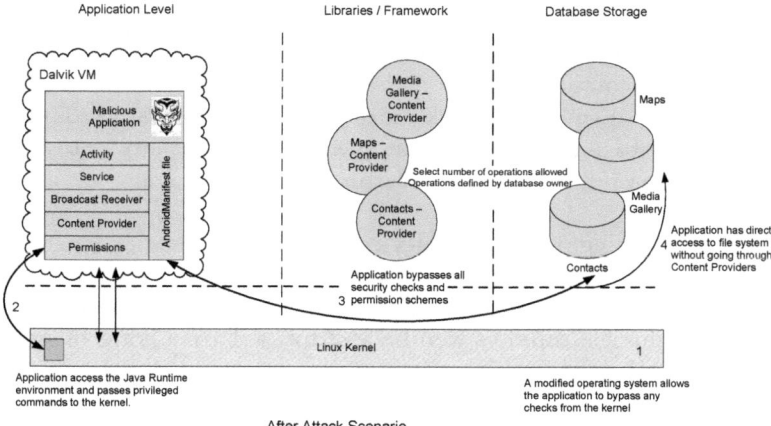

Fig. 7. Communication flow after privilege escalation took place

The application allows a wireless access to consequently make use of the Android system tool ADB to pull and push data, install applications and run scripts at will.

8   Results

As a result of connections to the Android device, we were able to perform operations that are not usually possible over a normal off-the-shelf Android based smartphone. We conducted a number of experiments to determine an effective security breach:

Use-Case 1. Pulling data from the device
   We were able to successfully pull data from the device without notifications to the smartphone user. In order to succeed we used the traditional ADB pull command. We extracted important information with respect to call records made from the phone. The information is stored in an SQLite Database[11] and a simple open source SQLite GUI Browser[12] was used to read the information.
   File extracted: contacts2.db
   Directory: /data/data/com.android.providers.contacts/databases
   Command: adb pull /data/data/com.android.providers.contacts/databases/contacts2.db /hdd08/Desktop/Extracted/

Use-Case 2. Modification of information
   Extracted databases can be easily changed and used to replace originals on the device. We were able to add records to the call logs, modify existing

---

[11] SQLite is a software library that implements an SQL database engine.
   http://www.sqlite.org/
[12] http://sqlitebrowser.sourceforge.net/

ones and delete records at will. This modified database was pushed onto the
device replacing the original one.

File modified: contacts2.db

Directory: `/data/data/com.android.providers.contacts/databases`

Command: adb push `/hdd08/Desktop/Extracted/contacts2.db /data/data/`
`com.android.providers.contacts/databases/contacts2.db`

Use-Case 3. Pushing data to the device

As an example for pushing information onto the device, we were able to push
a picture to the memory card and view it later on the device. It should be
noted that this file could as well be a script, a Trojan horse or a reconnais-
sance application.

File: cased-logo.png

Directory: `/sdcard`

Command: adb push `/hdd08/Desktop/cased-logo.png /sdard/`

Use-Case 4. Installation of an application on the device

The ADB is a rich tool and allows most of the operations that a debugging
tool would also allow. Using native commands of ADB we were able to
successfully install Android applications onto the device. The troubling part
of this exercise is that there is no notification to the user if such a process
has occurred. Any application installed using ADB also circumvents any
permission rules, and can therefore have high level privileges to monetary
applications like SMS and phone dialer without the user knowing about it.

Application: Angry-Birds.apk

Command: adb install Angry-Birds.apk

A thorough study of the ADB tool gave an insight of other manipulations that
can be achieved using the ADB on an Android based smartphone:

- Logcat: We were able to monitor behavior of applications using the debugger.
  A complete device log can be seen with all protocol initiations, all clear text
  communications that take place between modules and lower level hardware
  interaction of applications.
- Reboot: We were able to successfully reboot the device without knowledge
  or confirmation of the user.
- Uninstall Applications: We were also able to uninstall applications once the
  required task is achieved. This process does not show any indication to the
  user of any operation being carried out.
- Device details: We were able to pull information about the device like serial
  number and product name.
- Wiping off complete data partitions from a remote desktop while the device
  is connected over a wireless link is also possible by running a single command
  (`adb -w` or `adb -d`).

9 Analysis

From our analysis we find that critical user information stored on the device is not encrypted, for example call logs and contact details. Application developers can, however, encrypt any data that is stored in databases. Depending on the hash algorithms used, data loss could be prevented.

No notifications are generated once the device is polled for files, or in the case an application is installed on the device. Indicators about anything malicious happening on the device are not given, unless a strong malware detection system is in place as shown by Shabtai et al. in [14] and [16]. Highly privileged commands such as wiping data, installing and executing scripts is also allowed once connected to the device through the ADB protocol.

Since the attacks are carried out over a wireless link, the time required to carry out the attacks are only subject to how close the device is to the access point and the data rate achieved over the wireless link.

10 Conclusion

In this paper we presented a bottom-up approach in compromising an Android system by changing build parameters of the original Android operating system. We devised an Android application to harness resources from the system that a normal application would not have access to. These extra privileges allowed us to create a back-door into the operating system which can be accessed over a wireless link. Piggy-backing on a root access provided by the back-door, we were able to extract, modify and use sensitive information pertaining to the user and the environment. This clearly shows how dangerous a back-door can be, where access to the file system is authenticated only during install time.

Countering such an attack can be difficult since there is no indication to the user that an operation has taken place. Once integrity and confidentiality of information on the device has been compromised, it is imperative that stricter rules for modifying system parameters have to be in place.

References

1. Elmer-DeWitt, P.: Needham: Android's Market Share Peaked in March (June 2011), http://tech.fortune.cnn.com/2011/06/21/needham-androids-market-share-peaked-in-march/ (cited: July 01, 2011)
2. Google Android: What is Android? (2011), http://developer.android.com/index.html (cited: June 22, 2011)
3. BBC News: Android Hit By Rogue App Malware (March 2011), http://www.bbc.co.uk/news/technology-12633923 (cited: May 18, 2011)
4. Shabtai, A., Fledel, Y., Kanonov, U., Elovici, Y., Dolev, S., Glezer, C.: Google Android: A Comprehensive Security Assessment. IEEE Security & Privacy 8, 35–44 (2010)
5. Enck, W., Ongtang, M., McDaniel, P.: Understanding Android Security. IEEE Security & Privacy 7, 50–57 (2009)

6. Shin, W., Kwak, S., Kiyomoto, S., Fukushima, K., Tanaka, T.: A Small but Non-negligible Flaw in the Android Permission Scheme. In: Proceedings of the IEEE International Symposium on Policies for Distributed Systems and Networks (POLICY 2010), Fairfax, VA, USA, pp. 107–110. IEEE Computer Society (July 2010)

7. Erhinger, D.: The Dalvik Virtual Machine Architecture. Technical report (March 2010) (cited: July 02, 2011)

8. Cannon, T.: Android Market Security (February 2011),
http://thomascannon.net/blog/2011/02/android-market-security/
(cited: June 01, 2011)

9. Cannon, T.: Android Data Stealing Vulnerability (November 2010),
http://thomascannon.net/blog/2010/11/android-data-stealing
-vulnerability/(cited: June 01, 2011)

10. Cannon, T.: Android Reverse Engineering (November 2010),
http://thomascannon.net/projects/android-reversing/ (cited: June 01, 2011)

11. Cannon, T.: Android Lock Screen Bypass (February 2011),
http://thomascannon.net/blog/2011/02/android-lock-screen-bypass/
(cited: June 01, 2011)

12. Google Android: Tools (2011),
http://developer.android.com/guide/developing/tools/index.html
(cited: June 22, 2011)

13. Ongtang, M., McLaughlin, S., Enck, W., McDaniel, P.: Semantically Rich Application-centric Security in Android. In: Proceedings of the 25th Annual Computer Security Applications Conference (ACSAC 2009), Honolulu, HI, USA, pp. 340–349. IEEE Computer Society (December 2009)

14. Shabtai, A., Fledel, Y., Elovici, Y.: Securing Android-Powered Mobile Devices Using SELinux. IEEE Security & Privacy 8, 36–44 (2010)

15. Google Android: Security and Permissions (2011),
http://developer.android.com/guide/topics/security/security.html
(cited: June 22, 2011)

16. Shabtai, A.: Malware Detection on Mobile Devices. In: Proceedings of the 11th International Conference on Mobile Data Management (MDM 2010), Kanas City, MO, USA, pp. 289–290. IEEE Computer Society (May 2010)

An Attack on Privacy Preserving Data Aggregation Protocol for Wireless Sensor Networks

Jaydip Sen[1] and Subhamoy Maitra[2]

[1] Innovation Labs, Tata Consultancy Services Ltd.,
Bengal Intelligent Park, Salt Lake Electronic Complex, Kolkata 700 091, India
jaydip.sen@acm.org
[2] Applied Statistics Unit, Indian Statistical Institute,
203 B T Road, Kolkata 700 108, India
subho@isical.ac.in

Abstract. In-network data aggregation in Wireless Sensor Networks (WSNs) provides efficient bandwidth utilization and energy-efficient computing. Supporting efficient in-network data aggregation while preserving the privacy of the data of individual sensor nodes has emerged as an important requirement in numerous WSN applications. For privacy-preserving data aggregation in WSNs, He et al. (INFOCOM 2007) have proposed a Cluster-based Private Data Aggregation (CPDA) that uses a clustering protocol and a well-known key distribution scheme for computing an additive aggregation function in a privacy-preserving manner. In spite of the wide popularity of CPDA, it has been observed that the protocol is not secure and it is also possible to enhance its efficiency. In this paper, we first identify a security vulnerability in the existing CPDA scheme, wherein we show how a malicious participant node can launch an attack on the privacy protocol so as to get access to the private data of its neighboring sensor nodes. Next it is shown how the existing CPDA scheme can be made more efficient by suitable modification of the protocol. Further, suitable modifications in the existing protocol have been proposed so as to plug the vulnerability of the protocol.

Keywords: Wireless sensor network, privacy, data aggregation, cluster-based private data aggregation (CPDA), key distribution, colluding attack, malicious node.

1 Introduction

In recent years, wireless sensor networks (WSNs) have drawn considerable attention from the research community on issues ranging from theoretical research to practical applications. Special characteristics of WSNs, such as resource constraints on energy and computational power and security have been well-defined and widely studied [2][12]. What has received less attention, however, is the critical privacy concern on information being collected, transmitted, and analyzed in a WSN. Such private and sensitive information may include payload

P. Laud (Ed.): NordSec 2011, LNCS 7161, pp. 205–222, 2012.

data collected by sensors and transmitted through the network to a centralized data processing server. For example, a patient's blood pressure, sugar level and other vital signs are usually of critical privacy concern when monitored by a medical WSN which transmits the data to a remote hospital or doctor's office. Privacy concerns may also arise beyond data content and may focus on context information such as the location of a sensor initiating data communication. Effective countermeasure against the disclosure of both data and context-oriented private information is an indispensable prerequisite for deployment of WSNs in real-world applications.

Privacy protection has been extensively studied in various fields related to WSNs such as wired and wireless networking, databases and data mining. Nonetheless, the following inherent features of WSNs introduce unique challenges for privacy preservation in WSNs, and prevent the existing techniques from being directly transplanted: (i) *Uncontrollable environment*: Sensors may have to be deployed to an environment uncontrollable by the defender, such as a battlefield, enabling an adversary to launch physical attacks to capture sensor nodes or deploy counterfeit ones. As a result, an adversary may retrieve private keys used for secure communication and decrypt any communication eavesdropped by the adversary. (ii) *Sensor-node resource constraints*: battery-powered sensor nodes generally have severe constraints on their ability to store, process, and transmit the sensed data. As a result, the computational complexity and resource consumption of public-key ciphers is usually considered unsuitable for WSNs. (iii) *Topological constraints*: the limited communication range of sensor nodes in a WSN requires multiple hops in order to transmit data from the source to the base station. Such a multi-hop scheme demands different nodes to take diverse traffic loads. In particular, a node closer to the base station (i.e., data collecting and processing server) has to relay data from nodes further away from base station in addition to transmitting its own generated data, leading to higher transmission rate. Such an unbalanced network traffic pattern brings significant challenges to the protection of context-oriented privacy information. Particularly, if an adversary holds the ability of global traffic analysis, observing the traffic patterns of different nodes over the whole network, it can easily identify the sink and compromise context privacy, or even manipulate the sink node to impede the proper functioning of the WSN.

The unique challenges for privacy preservation in WSNs call for the development of effective privacy-preserving techniques. Supporting efficient in-network data aggregation while preserving data privacy has emerged as an important requirement in numerous wireless sensor network applications [1][4][8][9][13]. As a key approach to fulfilling this requirement of private data aggregation, *concealed data aggregation* (CDA) schemes have been proposed in which multiple source nodes send encrypted data to a sink along a *converge-cast tree* with aggregation of cipher-text being performed over the route [1][3][4][8][11][13].

He et al. have proposed a *cluster-based private data aggregation* (CPDA) scheme in which the sensor nodes are randomly distributed into clusters [9]. The cluster leaders carry out aggregation of data received from the cluster member nodes. The data communication is secured by using a shared key between each pair of communicating nodes for the purpose of encryption. The aggregate function leverages algebraic properties of the polynomials to compute the desired aggregate value in a cluster. While the aggregation is carried out at the aggregator node in each cluster, it is guaranteed that no individual node gets to know the sensitive private values of other nodes in the cluster. The intermediate aggregate value in each cluster is further aggregated along the routing tree as the data packets move to the sink node. The privacy goal of the scheme is two-fold. First, the privacy of data has to be guaranteed end-to-end. While only the sink could learn about the final aggregation result, each node will have information of its own data and does not have any information about the data of other nodes. Second, to reduce the communication overhead, the data from different source nodes have to be efficiently combined at the intermediate nodes (i.e. aggregation) along the path. Nevertheless, these intermediate nodes should not learn any information about the individual nodes' data. The authors of the CPDA scheme have presented performance results of the protocol to demonstrate the efficiency and security of the protocol. The CPDA protocol has become quite popular, and to the best of our knowledge, there has been no identified vulnerability of the protocol published in the literature so far.

In this paper, we first demonstrate a security vulnerability in the CPDA protocol and then proceed to show how the protocol may be made more efficient and secure. We also propose necessary modifications in the CPDA protocol to defend against the identified vulnerability.

The rest of this paper is organized as follows. Section 2 provides a brief background discussion on the CPDA scheme. In Section 3, we present a cryptanalysis on CPDA and demonstrate a security vulnerability of the scheme. In Section 4, we present some design modifications of the CPDA scheme. Section 4.1 presents an efficient way to compute the aggregation operation so as to make CPDA more efficient. Section 4.2 briefly discusses how the identified security vulnerability can be addressed. Section 5 presents a comparative analysis of the overhead of the original CPDA protocol and its proposed modified version. Section 5.1 provides a comparison of the communication overheads in the network, and Section 5.2 provides an analysis of the computational overheads in the sensor nodes. Section 6 concludes the paper while highlighting some future scope of work.

2   The CPDA Scheme [9] for Data Aggregation in WSN

The basic idea of CPDA is to introduce noise into the raw data sensed by the sensor nodes in a WSN, such that an aggregator can obtain accurate aggregated information but not individual sensor data [9]. This is similar to the data perturbation approach extensively used in privacy-preserving data mining. However, unlike in privacy-preserving data mining, where noises are independently generated (at random) leading to imprecise aggregated results, the noises in CPDA are carefully designed to leverage the cooperation between different sensor nodes, such that the precise aggregated values can be obtained by the aggregator.

The CPDA protocol classifies sensor nodes into two types: cluster leaders and cluster members. There is a one-to-many mapping between the cluster leaders and cluster members. The cluster leaders are responsible for aggregating data received from the cluster members. For security, the messages communicated between the cluster leaders and the cluster members are encrypted using different symmetric keys for each pair of nodes.

The details of the CPDA scheme are provided briefly in the following sub-sections.

2.1   The Network Model

The sensor network is modeled as a connected graph $G(V, E)$, where V represents the set of senor nodes and E represents the set of wireless links connecting the sensor nodes. The number of sensor nodes is taken as $|V| = N$.

A data aggregation function is taken that aggregates the individual sensor readings. CPDA scheme has focused on additive aggregation function, $f(t) = \sum_{i=1}^{N} d_i(t)$ where $d_i(t)$ is the individual sensor reading at time instant t for node i. For computation of the aggregate functions, the following requirements are to be satisfied: (i) privacy of the individual sensor data is to be protected, i.e., each node's data should be known to no other nodes except the node itself, (ii) the number of messages transmitted within the WSN for the purpose of data aggregation should be kept at a minimum, and (iii) the aggregation result should be as accurate as possible.

2.2   Key Distribution and Management

CPDA uses a random key distribution mechanism proposed in [6] for encrypting messages to prevent message eavesdropping attacks. The key distribution scheme has three phases: (i) key pre-distribution, (ii) shared-key discovery, and (iii) path-key establishment. These phases are described briefly as follows.

A large key-pool of K keys and their identities are first generated in the key pre-distribution phase. For each sensor nodes, k keys out of the total K keys are chosen. These k keys form a *key ring* for the sensor node.

During the key-discovery phase, each sensor node identifies which of its neighbors share a common key with itself by invoking and exchanging discovery messages. If a pair of neighbor nodes share a common key, then it is possible to establish a secure link between them.

In the path-key establishment phase, an end-to-end path-key is assigned to the pairs of neighboring nodes who do not share a common key but can be connected by two or more multi-hop secure links at the end of the shared-key discovery phase.

At the end of the key distribution phase, the probability that any pair of nodes possess at least one common key is given by (1).

$$p_{connect} = 1 - \frac{((K - k)!)^2}{(K - 2k)!K!} \tag{1}$$

If the probability that any other node can overhear the encrypted message by a given key is denoted as $p_{overhear}$, then $p_{overhear}$ is given by (2).

$$p_{overhear} = \frac{k}{K} \qquad (2)$$

It has been shown in [9] that the above key distribution algorithm is efficient for communication in a large-scale sensor networks, and when a limited number of keys are available for encryption of the messages to prevent eavesdropping attacks.

2.3 Cluster-Based Private Data Aggregation (CPDA) Protocol

The CPDA scheme works in three phases: (i) cluster formation, (ii) computation of aggregate results in clusters, and (ii) cluster data aggregation. These phases are described below.

Cluster formation: Fig. 1 depicts the cluster formation process. A query server Q triggers a query by sending a *HELLO* message. When the *HELLO* message reaches a sensor node, it elects itself as a cluster leader with a pre-defined probability p_c. If the value of p_c is large, there will be more number of nodes which will elect themselves as cluster leaders. This will result in higher number of clusters in the network. On the other hand, smaller values of p_c will lead to less number of clusters due to fewer number of cluster leader nodes. Hence, the value of the parameter p_c can be suitably chosen to control the number of clusters in the network. If a node becomes a cluster leader, it forwards the *HELLO* message to its neighbors; otherwise, it waits for a threshold period of time to check whether any *HELLO* message arrives at it from any of its neighbors. If any *HELLO* message arrives at the node, it decides to join the cluster formed by its neighbor by

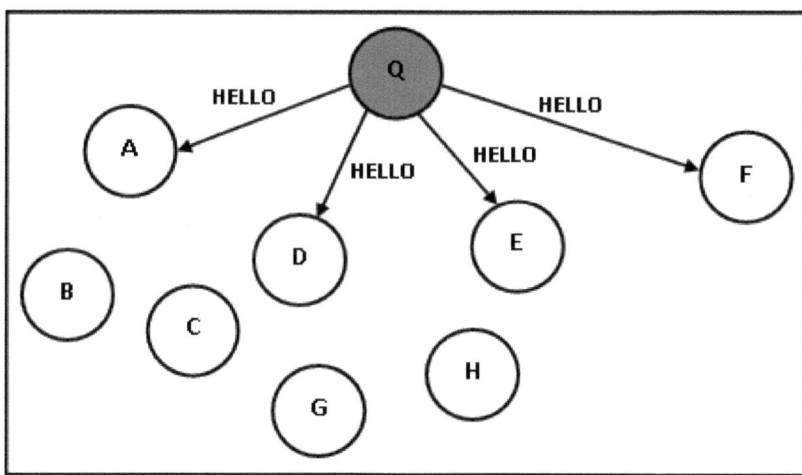

Fig. 1. Query server Q sends HELLO messages for initiating the cluster formation procedure to its neighbors A, D, E and F. The query server is shaded in the figure.

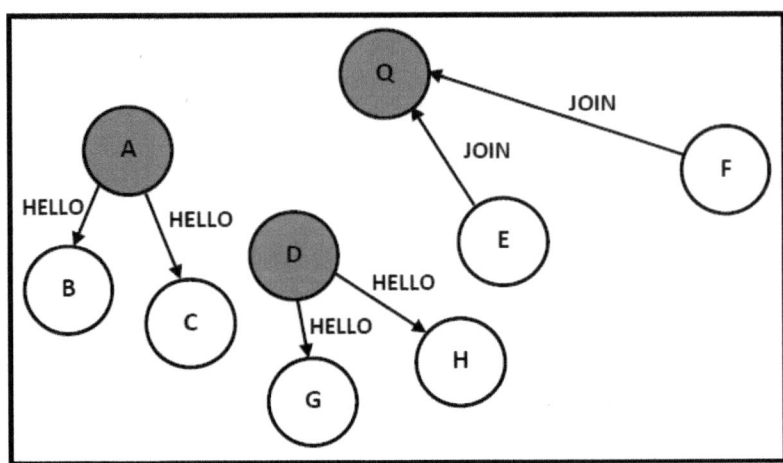

Fig. 2. *A* and *D* elect themselves as the cluster leaders randomly and in turn send *HELLO* messages to their neighbors. *E* and *F* join the cluster formed by *Q*. *B* and *C* join the cluster formed with *A* as the cluster leader, while *G* and *H* join the cluster with *D* as the cluster leader. All the cluster leaders and the query server are shaded.

broadcasting a *JOIN* message as shown in Fig 2. This process is repeated and multiple clusters are formed so that the entire WSN becomes a collection of a set of clusters.

Computation within clusters: In this phase, aggregation is done in each cluster. The computation is illustrated with the example of a simple case where a cluster contains three members: A, B, and C, where A is the assumed to be the cluster leader and the aggregator node, whereas B and C are the cluster member nodes. Let a, b, c represent the private data held by the nodes A, B, and C respectively. The goal of the aggregation scheme is to compute the sum of a, b and c without revealing the private values of the nodes.

As shown in Fig. 3, for the privacy-preserving additive aggregation function, the nodes A, B, and C are assumed to share three public non-zero distinct numbers, which are denoted as x, y, and z respectively. In addition, node A generates two random numbers r_1^A and r_2^A, which are known only to node A. Similarly, nodes B and C generate r_1^B, r_2^B and r_1^C, r_2^C respectively, which are private values of the nodes which have generated them.

Node A computes v_A^A, v_B^A, and v_C^A as shown in (3).

$$v_A^A = a + r_1^A x + r_2^A x^2$$
$$v_B^A = a + r_1^A y + r_2^A y^2$$
$$v_C^A = a + r_1^A z + r_2^A z^2 \tag{3}$$

Similarly, node B computes v_A^B, v_B^B, and v_C^B as in (4).

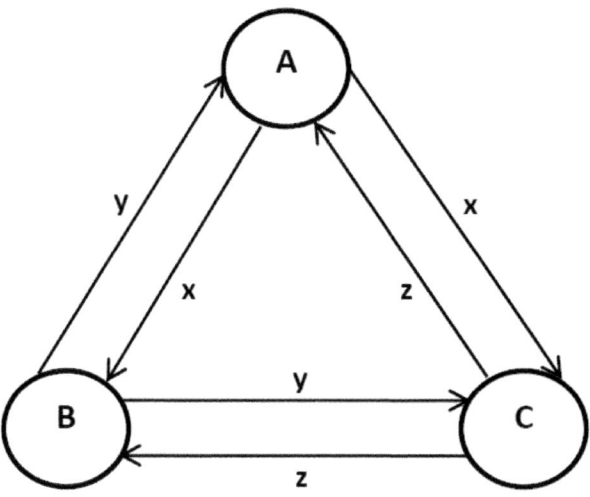

Fig. 3. Nodes A, B and C broadcast their distinct and non-zero public seeds x, y and z respectively

$$v_A^B = b + r_1^B x + r_2^B x^2$$
$$v_B^B = b + r_1^B y + r_2^B y^2$$
$$v_C^B = b + r_1^B z + r_2^B z^2 \tag{4}$$

Likewise, node C computes v_A^C, v_B^C, and v_C^C as in (5).

$$v_A^C = c + r_1^C x + r_2^C x^2$$
$$v_B^C = c + r_1^C y + r_2^C y^2$$
$$v_C^C = c + r_1^C z + r_2^C z^2 \tag{5}$$

Node A encrypts v_B^A and sends it to node B using the shared key between node A and node B. Node A also encrypts v_C^A and sends it to node C using the shared key between node A and node C. In the same manner, node B sends encrypted v_A^B to node A and v_C^B to node node C; node C sends encrypted v_A^C and v_B^C to node A and node B respectively. The exchanges of these encrypted messages is depicted in Fig. 4. On receiving v_A^B and v_A^C, node A computes the sum of v_A^A (already computed by node A), v_A^B and v_A^C. Now, node A computes F_A using (6).

$$F_A = v_A^A + v_A^B + v_A^C = (a + b + c) + r_1 x + r_2 x^2 \tag{6}$$

In (6), $r_1 = r_1^A + r_1^B + r_1^C$ and $r_2 = r_2^A + r_2^B + r_2^C$. Similarly, node B and node C compute F_B and F_C respectively, where F_B and F_C are given by (7) and (8) respectively.

$$F_B = v_B^A + v_B^B + v_B^C = (a + b + c) + r_1 y + r_2 y^2 \tag{7}$$

$$F_C = v_C^A + v_C^B + v_C^C = (a + b + c) + r_1 z + r_2 z^2 \tag{8}$$

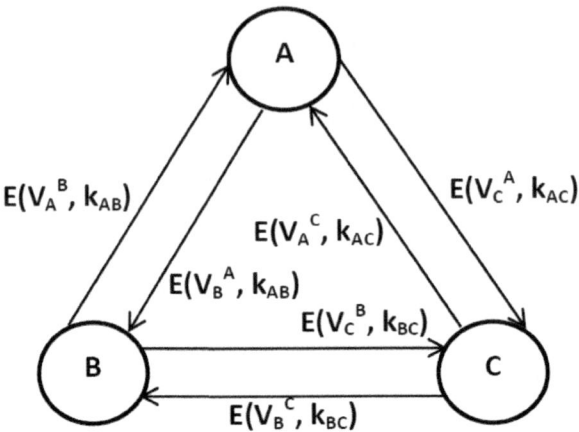

Fig. 4. Exchange of encrypted messages among nodes A, B and C using shared keys of the nodes

Node B and node C broadcast F_B and F_C to the cluster leader node A, so that node A has the knowledge of the values of F_A, F_B and F_C. From these values the cluster leader node A can compute the aggregated value $(a + b + c)$ as explained below.

The equations (6), (7), and (8) can be rewritten as in (9).

$$\mathbf{U} = \mathbf{G}^{-1}\mathbf{F} \tag{9}$$

where, $\mathbf{G} = \begin{bmatrix} 1 & x & x^2 \\ 1 & y & y^2 \\ 1 & z & z^2 \end{bmatrix}$, $\mathbf{U} = \begin{bmatrix} a+b+c \\ r_1 \\ r_2 \end{bmatrix}$, and $\mathbf{F} = \begin{bmatrix} F_A & F_B & F_C \end{bmatrix}^T$.

Since x, y, z, F_A, F_B, and F_C are known to the cluster leader node A, it can compute the value of $(a + b + c)$ without having any knowledge of b and c.

In order to avoid eavesdropping attack by neighbor nodes, it is necessary to encrypt the values of v_B^A, v_C^A, v_A^B, v_C^B, v_A^C, and v_B^C. If node B overhears the value of v_C^A, then node B gets access to the values of v_C^A, v_B^A and F_A. Then node B can deduce $v_A^A = F_A - v_A^B - v_C^A$. Having the knowledge of v_A^A, node B can further obtain the value of a if x, v_A^A, v_A^B and v_A^C are known. However, if node A encrypts v_C^A and sends it to node C, then node B cannot get v_C^A. With the knowledge of v_B^A, F_A and x from node A, node B cannot deduce the value of a. If node B and node C collude and reveal node A's information (i.e., v_B^A and v_C^A), to each other, then node A's privacy will be compromised and its private value a will be revealed. In order to reduce the probability of such collusion attacks, the cluster size should be as large as possible, since in a cluster of size m, at least $(m - 1)$ nodes should collude in order to successfully launch the attack. Higher values of m will require larger number of colluding nodes thereby making the attack more difficult.

2.4   Cluster Data Aggregation

The CPDA scheme has been implemented on top of a protocol known as *Tiny Aggregation* (TAG) protocol [10]. Using the TAG protocol, each cluster leader node routes the sum of the values in the nodes in its cluster to the query server through a TAG routing tree whose root is situated at the server.

3   An Attack on the CPDA Scheme

In this section, we present an efficient attack on the CPDA aggregation scheme. The objective of the attack is to show the vulnerability of the CPDA scheme which can be suitably exploited by a malicious participating sensor node. The intention of the malicious node is to participate in the scheme in such a way that it can get access to the private values (i.e., a, b and c) of the participating sensor nodes. For describing the attack scenario, we use the same example cluster consisting of three sensor nodes A, B and C. Node A is the cluster leader whereas node B and node C are the cluster members. We distinguish two types of attacks: (i) attack by a malicious cluster leader (e.g., node A) and (ii) attack by a malicious cluster member (e.g., either node B or node C). These two cases are described in detail in the following sub-sections.

3.1   Privacy Attack by a Malicious Cluster Leader

Let us assume that the cluster leader node A is malicious. Node A chooses a very large value of x such that $x \gg y, z$. Since y and z are public values chosen by node B and node C which are broadcast in the network by node B and node C respectively, it is easy for node A to choose a suitable value for x.

Nodes A, B and C compute the values of v_A^A, v_B^A, v_C^A, v_A^B, v_B^B, v_C^B, v_A^C, v_B^C, and v_C^C using (3), (4) and (5) as described in Section 2.3. As per the CPDA scheme, node A receives $v_A^B = b + r_1^B x + r_2^B x^2$ from node B. Since x is very large compared to b and r_1^B, node A can derive the value of r_2^B using (10) where we consider integer division.

$$\frac{v_A^B}{x^2} = \frac{b}{x^2} + \frac{r_1^B}{x} + r_2^B = 0 + 0 + r_2^B = r_2^B \tag{10}$$

Using the value of r_2^B as derived in (10), and using $v_A^B = b + r_1^B x + r_2^B x^2$, node A can now compute the value of r_1^B by solving (11).

$$\frac{v_A^B - r_2^B x^2}{x} = \frac{b}{x} + r_1^B = 0 + r_1^B = r_1^B \tag{11}$$

In the same manner, node A derives the values of r_1^C and r_2^C from v_A^C received from node C. Since $r_1 = r_1^A + r_1^B + r_1^C$, and $r_2 = r_2^A + r_2^B + r_2^C$, as shown in (6), (7) and (8), node A can compute the values of r_1 and r_2 (r_1^B, r_2^B, r_1^C, and r_2^C are derived as shown above, and r_1^A and r_2^A were generated by node A).

At this stage, node A uses the values of F_B and F_C received from node B and node C respectively as shown in (7) and (8). Node A has now two linear simultaneous equations with two unknowns: b and c, the values of y and z being public. Solving (7) and (8) for b and c, the malicious cluster leader node A can get the access to the private information of nodes B and C, thereby launching a privacy attack on the CPDA scheme.

3.2   Privacy Attack by a Malicious Cluster Member

In this scenario, let us assume that the cluster member node B is malicious and it tries to access the private values of the cluster leader node A and the cluster member node C. Node B chooses a very large value of y so that $y \gg x,\, z$. Once the value of F_B is computed in (7), node B derives the value of r_2 and r_1 using (12) and (13).

$$\frac{F_B}{y^2} = \frac{(a+b+c)}{y^2} + \frac{r_1}{y} + r_2 = 0 + 0 + r_2 = r_2 \tag{12}$$

$$\frac{F_B - r_2 y^2}{y} = \frac{(a+b+c)}{y} + r_1 = 0 + r_1 = r_1 \tag{13}$$

As per the CPDA scheme, node B receives $v_B^C = c + r_1^C y + r_2^C y^2$ from node C. Since the magnitude of y is very large compared to c, r_1^C and r_2^C, it is easy for node B to derive the values of r_2^C and r_1^C using (14) and (15).

$$\frac{v_B^C}{y^2} = \frac{c}{y^2} + \frac{r_1^C}{y} + r_2^C = 0 + 0 + r_2^C = r_2^C \tag{14}$$

$$\frac{v_B^C - r_2^C y^2}{y} = \frac{c}{y} + r_1^C = 0 + r_1^C = r_1^C \tag{15}$$

Using (12), (13), (14) and (15) node B can compute $r_1^A = r_1 - r_1^B - r_1^C$, and $r_2^A = r_2 - r_2^B - r_2^C$. Now, node B can compute the value of a using $v_A^B = a + r_1^A y + r_2^A y^2$ (received from node A), in which the values of all the variables are known except that of a. In a similar fashion, node B derives the value of c using $v_B^C = c + r_1^C y + r_2^C y^2$ (received from C).

Since the private values of the nodes A and C are now known to node B, the privacy attack launched by participating cluster member node B is successful on the CPDA aggregation scheme.

4   Modifications of CPDA

In this section, we present two modifications of CPDA scheme: one towards making the protocol more efficient and the other for making it more secure.

4.1   Modification of CPDA for Enhanced Efficiency

In this section, a modification is proposed for the CPDA protocol for achieving enhanced efficiency in its operation. The modification is based on suitable choice for the value of x (the public seed) done by the aggregator node A.

Let us assume that the node A chooses a large value of x such that the following conditions in (16) and (17) are satisfied.

$$r_2 x^2 \gg r_1 x \tag{16}$$

$$r_1 x \gg (a + b + c) \tag{17}$$

where, $r_1 = r_1^A + r_1^B + r_1^C$ and $r_2 = r_2^A + r_2^B + r_2^C$. Now, node A has computed the value of F_A as shown in (6). In order to efficiently compute the value of $(a + b + c)$, node A divides the value of F_A by x^2 as shown in (18).

$$\frac{F_A}{x^2} = \frac{(a + b + c)}{x^2} + \frac{r_1 x}{x^2} + r_2 = 0 + 0 + r_2 = r_2 \tag{18}$$

Using (18), node A derives the value of r_2. Once the value of r_2 is deduced, node A attempts to compute the value of r_1 using (19) and (20).

$$F_A - r_2 x^2 = (a + b + c) + r_1 x \tag{19}$$

$$r_1 = \frac{(F_A - r_2 x^2)}{x} - \frac{(a + b + c)}{x} = \frac{(F_A - r_2 x^2)}{x} - 0 = \frac{(F_A - r_2 x^2)}{x} \tag{20}$$

Since, the values of F_A, r_2 and x are all known to node A, it can compute the value of r_1 using (20). Once the values of r_1 and r_2 are computed by node A, it can compute the value of $(a + b + c)$ using (6). Since the computation of the sum $(a + b + c)$ by node A involves two division operations (involving integers) only (as done in (18) and (20)), the modified CPDA scheme will be light-weight and hence much more energy- and time-efficient as compared to the original CPDA scheme. The original CPDA scheme involved additional computations of the values of F_B and F_C, as well as an expensive matrix inversion operation as described in Section 2.3.

4.2   Modification of CPDA for Resisting the Attack

In this section, we discuss the modifications required on the existing CPDA scheme so that a malicious participant node cannot launch the attack described in Section 3.

It may be noted that, the vulnerability of the CPDA scheme lies essentially in the unrestricted freedom delegated on the participating nodes for generating their public seed values. For example, nodes A, B and C have no restrictions on their choice for values of x, y and z respectively while they generate these values. A malicious attacker can exploit this freedom to generate an arbitrarily large public seed value, and can thereby launch an attack as discussed in Section 3.

In order to prevent such an attack, the CPDA protocol needs to be modified. In this modified version, the nodes in a cluster make a check on the generated public seed values so that it is not possible for a malicious participant to generate any arbitrarily large seed value. For a cluster with three nodes, such a constraint may be imposed by the requirement that the sum of any two public seeds must be greater than the third seed. In other words: $x + y > z$, $z + x > y$, and $y + z > x$. If these constraints are satisfied by the generated values of x, y and z, it will be impossible for any node to launch the attack and get access to the private values of the other participating nodes.

However, even if the above restrictions on the values of x, y and z are imposed, the nodes should also be careful in choosing the values for their secret random number pairs. If two nodes happen to choose very large values for their random numbers compared to those chosen by the third node, then it will be possible for the third node to get access to the private values of the other two nodes. For example, let us assume that nodes A and C have chosen the values of r_1^A, r_2^A and r_1^C, r_2^C such that they are all much larger than r_1^B and r_2^B - the private random number pair chosen by node B. It will be possible for node B to derive the values of a and c : the private values of nodes A and C respectively. This is explained in the following.

Node B receives $v_B^A = a + r_1^A y + r_2^A y^2$ from node A and computes the values of r_1^A and r_2^A using (21) and (22).

$$\frac{v_B^A}{y^2} = \frac{a}{y^2} + \frac{r_1^A}{y} + r_2^A = 0 + 0 + r_2^A = r_2^A \tag{21}$$

$$\frac{v_B^A - r_2^A y^2}{y} = \frac{a}{y} + r_1^A = 0 + r_1^A = r_1^A \tag{22}$$

In a similar fashion, node B derives the values of r_1^C and r_2^C from v_B^C received from node C. Now, node B computes $r_1 = r_1^A + r_1^B + r_1^C$ and $r_2 = r_2^A + r_2^B + r_2^C$ since it has access to the values of all these variables. In the original CPDA scheme in [9], the values of F_B and F_C are broadcast by nodes B and C in unencrypted from. Hence, node B has access to both these values. Using (7) and (8), node B can compute the values of a and c, since these are the only unknown variables in the two linear simultaneously equations.

In order to defend against the above vulnerability, the CPDA protocol needs further modification. In this modified version, after the values v_A^A, v_A^B, and v_A^C are generated and shared by nodes A, B and C respectively, the nodes check whether the following constraints are satisfied: $v_A^A + v_A^B > v_A^C$, $v_A^B + v_A^C > v_A^A$, and $v_A^C + v_A^A > v_A^B$. The nodes proceed for further execution of the algorithm only if the above three inequalities are satisfied. If all three inequalities are not satisfied, there will be a possibility that the random numbers generated by one node is much larger than those generated by other nodes - a scenario which indicates a possible attack by a malicious node.

5   Performance Analysis

In this section, we will briefly present a comparative analysis of the overheads of the CPDA protocol and its proposed modified versions presented in Section 4.1 and Section 4.2. Our analysis is based on two categories of overheads: (i) overhead due to message communication in the network and (ii) computational overhead at the sensor nodes.

5.1   Communication Overhead

We compare communication overheads of three protocols - the *tiny aggregation protocol* (TAG), the original CPDA protocol and the proposed modified CPDA protocols. In TAG, each sensor node needs to send 2 messages for the data aggregation protocol to work. One *Hello* message communication from each sensor node is required for forming the aggregation tree, and one message is needed for data aggregation. However, this protocol only performs data aggregation and does not ensure any privacy for the sensor data. In the original CPDA protocol, each cluster leader node sends 4 messages and each cluster member node sends 3 messages for ensuring that the aggregation protocol works in a privacy-preserving manner. In the example cluster shown in Fig. 3, the 4 messages sent by the cluster leader node A are: one *Hello* message for forming the cluster, one message for communicating the public seed x, one message for communicating v_B^A and v_C^A to cluster member nodes B and C respectively, and one message for sending the aggregate result from the cluster. Similarly, the 3 messages sent by the cluster member node B are: one message for communicating its public seed y, one message for communicating v_A^B and v_C^B to cluster leader node A and cluster member node C respectively, and one message for communicating the intermediate result F_B to the cluster leader node A.

In contrast to the original CPDA protocol, the modified CPDA protocol in Section 4.1 involves 3 message communications from the cluster leader node and 2 message communications from each cluster member node. The 3 messages sent by the cluster leader node A are: one *Hello* message for forming the cluster, one message for broadcasting its public seed x, and one message for sending the final aggregate result. It may be noted that in this protocol, the cluster leader node A need not send v_B^A and v_C^A to the cluster member nodes B and C respectively. Each cluster member node needs to send 2 messages. For example, the cluster member node B needs to broadcast its public seed y, and also needs to send v_A^B to the cluster leader node A. Unlike in the original CPDA protocol, the cluster member node B does not send F_B to the cluster leader. Similarly, the cluster member node C does not send F_C to the cluster leader node A. In a cluster consisting of three members, the original CPDA protocol would involve 10 messages (4 messages from the cluster leader and 3 messages from each cluster member). The modified CPDA protocol presented in Section 4.1, on the other hand, would involve 7 messages (3 messages from the cluster leader and 2 messages from each cluster member) in a cluster of three nodes. Therefore, in a cluster of three nodes, the modified CPDA protocol presented in Section 4.1 will involve 3 less message communications. Since in a large-scale WSN the number of clusters will be quite high, there will be an appreciable reduction in the communication overhead in the modified CPDA protocol presented in Section 4.1.

The secure version of the modified CPDA protocol presented in Section 4.2 involves the same communication overhead as the original CPDA protocol. However, if any node chooses abnormally higher values for its public seed or its private random numbers, the secure version of the modified CPDA protocol will involve 2 extra messages from each of the participating sensor nodes. Therefore, in a cluster of three nodes, the secure version of the modified CPDA protocol will involve 6 extra messages in the worst case scenario when compared with the original CPDA protocol.

If p_c is the probability of a sensor node electing itself as a cluster leader, the average number of messages sent by a sensor node in the original CPDA protocol is: $4p_c + 3(1 - p_c) = 3 + p_c$. Thus, the message overhead in the original CPDA is less than twice as that in TAG. However, in the modified CPDA protocol presented in Section 4.1, the average number of messages communicated by a sensor node is: $3p_c + 2(1 - p_c) = 2 + p_c$. As mentioned in Section 2.3, in order to prevent collusion attack by sensor nodes, the cluster size in the CPDA protocol should be as large as possible. This implies that the value of p_c should be small. Since the value of p_c is small, it is clear that the message overhead in the modified CPDA protocol presented in Section 4.1 is almost the same as that in TAG and it is much less (one message less for each sensor node) than that of the original CPDA protocol. In the secure version of the protocol in Section 4.2, the communication overhead, in the average case, will be the same as in the original CPDA protocol. However, in the worst case, the number of messages sent by a sensor node in this protocol will be: $6p_c + 5(1 - p_c) = 5 + p_c$. This is 2.5 times the average communication overhead in the TAG protocol and 1.67 times the average communication overhead in the original CPDA protocol. The secure protocol, therefore, will involve 67% more overhead in the worst case scenario (where a malicious participant sensor node chooses abnormally higher values for its public seed as well as for its private random numbers).

5.2   Computational Overhead

In this section, we present a comparative analysis of the computational overheads incurred by the sensor nodes in the original CPDA protocol and in the proposed efficient version of the protocol.

Computational overhead of the original CPDA protocol: The overhead of the CPDA protocol can be broadly classified into four categories: (i) computation of the parameters, (ii) computation for encrypting messages, (iii) computation of the intermediate results, and (iv) computation of the final aggregate result at the cluster leader node. The details of these computations are presented below:

(i) *Computation of the parameters at the sensor nodes*: Each sensor node in a three member cluster computes three parameters. For example, the cluster leader node A computes v_A^A, v_B^A and v_C^A. Similarly, the cluster member node B computes v_A^B, v_B^B and v_C^B. We first compute the overhead due these computations.

Since $v_A^A = a + r_1^A x + r_2^A x^2$, for computation of v_A^A, node A needs to perform 2 addition, 2 multiplication and 1 exponentiation operations. Hence, for computing v_A^A, v_B^A, v_C^A, node A needs to perform 6 addition, 6 multiplication and 3 exponentiation operations. Therefore, in a cluster consisting of three members, for computation of all parameters, the original CPDA protocol requires 18 addition, 18 multiplication and 9 exponentiation operations.

(ii) *Computations for encrypting messages*: Some of the messages in the CPDA protocol need to be communicated in encrypted form. The encryption operation involves computaional overhead. For example, node A needs to encrypt v_B^A and v_C^A before sending them to nodes B and C respectively. Therefore, 2 encryption operations are required at node A. For a cluster consisting of three members, the CPDA protocol will need 6 encryption operations.

(iii) *Computations of intermediate results*: The nodes A, B, and C need to compute the intermediate values F_A, F_B and F_C respectively. Since $F_A = v_A^A + v_A^B + v_A^C = (a + b + c) + r_1 x + r_2 x^2$ and $r_1 = r_1^A + r_1^B + r_1^C$, and $r_2 = r_2^A + r_2^B + r_2^C$, for computing F_A, node A will need to perform 4 addition operations. Therefore, for a cluster of three members, 12 addition operations will be needed.

(iv) *Aggregate computation at the cluster leader*: For computing the final aggregated result in a privacy-preserving way, the cluster leader node A needs to perform one matrix inversion operation and one matrix multiplication operation.

The summary of various operations in the original CPDA protocol are presented in Table 1.

Computational overhead of the modified CPDA protocol: The overhead of the efficient version of the CPDA protocol presented in Section 4.1 are due to: (i) computation of the parameters at the sensor nodes, (ii) computation of the intermediate result at the cluster leader node, and (iii) computation of the aggregated result at the cluster leader node. The details of these computations are presented below.

Table 1. Operations in the CPDA Protocol

Operation Type	No. of Operations
Addition	30
Multiplication	18
Exponentiation	3
Encryption	6
Matrix Multiplication	1
Matrix Inversion	1

(i) *Computation of the parameters at the sensor nodes*: In the modified version of the CPDA protoocl, the nodes A, B and C need to only compute v_A^A, v_A^B, and v_A^C respectively. As shown earlier, each parameter computation involves 2 addition, 2 multiplication and 1 exponentiation operations. Therefore, in total, 6 addition, 6 multiplication, and 3 exponentiation operations will be needed.

(ii) *Computations for encrypting messages*: The nodes B and C will need to encrypt the messages v_A^B and v_A^C respectively before sending them to the cluster leader node A. Therefore, 2 encryption operations will be required.

(iii) *Computation of intermediate result*: The cluster leader node A will only compute F_A in the modified CPDA. The cluster member nodes B and C need not perform any computations here. As discussed earlier, computation of F_A needs 4 addition operations.

(iv) *Aggregate computation at the cluster leader*: For computation of the final result at the cluster leader node, 2 integer division and 2 subtraction operations will be required.

The summary of various operations in the modified CPDA protocol are presented in Table 2.

Table 2. Operations in the Proposed Modified CPDA Protocol

Operation Type	No. of Operations
Addition	10
Subtraction	2
Multiplication	6
Division	2
Exponentiation	3
Encryption	2

It is clearly evident from Table 1 and Table 2 that the modified version of the CPDA protocol involves much less computational overhead than the original version of the protocol.

6   Conclusion

Innetwork data aggregation in WSNs is a technique that combines partial results at the intermediate nodes en route to the base station (i.e. the node issuing the query), thereby reducing the communication overhead and optimizing the bandwidth utilization in the wireless links. However, this technique raises privacy issues of the sensor nodes which need to share their data with the aggregator node. In applications such as health care and military surveillance where the sensitivity of the private data of the sensors is very high, the aggregation has to be carried out in a privacy-preserving way, so that the sensitive data are not revealed to the aggregator. A very popular scheme for this purpose exists in the literature which is known as CPDA. Although CPDA is in literature for quite some time now, no vulnerability of the protocol has been identified so far. In this paper, we have first demonstrated a security vulnerability in the CPDA protocol, wherein a malicious sensor node can exploit the protocol is such a way that it gets access to the private values of its neighbors while participating in data aggregation process. A suitable modification of the CPDA protocol is further proposed so as to plug the identified vulnerability and also to make the protocol computationally more efficient. We have also made an analysis of the communication and computational overhead in the original CPDA protocol and the proposed modified version of the CPDA protocol. It has been found from the analysis that the modified version of the protocol involves appreciably less message communication overhead in the network and computational load on the sensor nodes.

It may be noted that over the past few years, several schemes have been proposed in the literature for privacy preserving data aggregation in WSNs. A very popular and elegant approach in this direction is *homomorphic encryption* [7]. Westhoff et al. have proposed additive privacy homomorphic functions that allow for end-to-end encryption between the sensors and the sink node and simultaneously enable aggregators to apply aggregation functions directly over the ciphertexts [13]. This has the advantage of eliminating the need for intermediate aggregators to carry out decryption and encryption operations on the sensitive data. Armknecht et al. have presented a symmetric encryption scheme for sensor data aggregation that is homomorphic both for data and the keys [3]. This is called *bi-homomorphic encryption*, which is also essentially an additive homomorphic function. Castellucia et al. have proposed an approach that combines inexpensive encryption techniques with simple aggregation methods to achieve efficient aggregation of encrypted data in WSNs [4]. The method relies on end-to-end encryption of data and hop-by-hop authentication of nodes. Privacy is achieved by using additive homomorphic functions. A very simple approach for privacy-preserving multi-party computation has been discussed by Chaum [5]. The protocol is known as *Dining Cryptographers Problem* which describes the way a channel is created so that it is difficult to trace (i.e. identify) the sender of any message through that channel.

The approaches based on privacy homomorphic functions are more elegant than CPDA for the purpose of carrying out sensor data aggregation in a privacy preserving way. However, they involve large computational overhead due to complexities involved in computing the homomorphic encryption functions and the associated key management related issues. The primary objective of our work in this paper is to demonstrate a security vulnerability of the CPDA protocol. We plan to evaluate the performance of our modified CPDA protocol as a future scope of work, and make a comparative analysis of the protocol with the existing privacy homomorphism-based approaches for sensor data aggregation.

References

1. Acharya, M., Girao, J., Westhoff, D.: Secure Comparison of Encrypted Data in Wireless Sensor Networks. In Proc. of the 3rd International Symposium on Modeling and Optimization in Mobile, Ad Hoc, and Wireless Networks (WIOPT), Washington, DC, USA, pp. 47–53 (2005)
2. Akyildiz, I.F., Su, W., Sankarasubramaniam, Y., Cayirci, E.: Wireless Sensor Networks: A Survey. Computer Networks 38(4), 393–422 (2002)
3. Armknecht, F., Westhoff, D., Girao, J., Hessler, A.: A Lifetime-Optimized End-to-End Encryption Scheme for Sensor Networks Allowing In-Network Processing. Computer Communications 31(4), 734–749 (2008)
4. Castelluccia, C., Chan, A.C-F., Mykletun, E., Tsudik, G.: Efficient and Provably Secure Aggregation of Encrypted Data in Wireless Sensor Networks. ACM Transactions on Sensor Networks 5(3) (2009)
5. Chaum, D.: The Dining Cryptographers Problem: Unconditional Sender and Recipient Untraceability. Journal of Cryptology 1(1), 65–75 (1988)
6. Eschenauer, L., Gligor, V.D.: A Key-Management Scheme for Distributed Sensor Networks. In: Proc. of the 9th ACM Conference on Computing and Communications Security, pp. 41–47 (2002)
7. Fontaine, C., Galand, F.: A Survey of Homomorphic Encryption for Nonspecialists. EURASIP Journal on Information Security 2007, Article ID 13801 (2007)
8. Girao, J., Westhoff, D., Schneider, M.: CDA: Concealed Data Aggregation for Reverse Multicast Traffic in Wireless Sensor Networks. In: Proc. of the 40th IEEE Conference on Communications (IEEE ICC), vol. 5, pp. 3044–3049 (2005)
9. He, W., Liu, X., Nguyen, H., Nahrstedt, K., Abdelzaher, T.: PDA: Privacy-Preserving Data Aggregation in Wireless Sensor Networks. In Proc. of the 26th IEEE International Conference on Computer Communications (IEEE INFOCOM), pp. 2045–2053 (2007)
10. Madden, S., Franklin, M.J., Hellerstein, J.M., Hong, W.: TAG: A Tiny Aggregation Service for Ad-Hoc Sensor Networks. In Proc. of the 5th Symposium on Operating Systems Design and Implementation (OSDI), vol. 36 (2002)
11. Peter, S., Westhoff, D., Castelluccia, C.: A Survey on the Encryption of Convergecast Traffic with In-Network Processing. IEEE Transactions on Dependable and Secure Computing 7(1), 20–34 (2010)
12. Sen, J.: A Survey on Wireless Sensor Network Security. International Journal of Communication Networks and Information Security (IJCNIS) 1(2), 59–82 (2009)
13. Westhoff, D., Girao, J., Acharya, M.: Concealed Data Aggregation for Reverse Multicast Traffic in Sensor Networks: Encryption, Key Distribution, and Routing Adaptation. IEEE Transactions on Mobile Computing 5(10), 1417–1431 (2006)

Disjunction Category Labels

Deian Stefan[1], Alejandro Russo[2], David Mazières[1], and John C. Mitchell[1]

[1] Stanford University
[2] Chalmers University of Technology

Abstract. We present disjunction category (DC) labels, a new label format for enforcing information flow in the presence of mutually distrusting parties. DC labels can be ordered to form a lattice, based on propositional logic implication and conjunctive normal form. We introduce and prove soundness of decentralized privileges that are used in declassifying data, in addition to providing a notion of privilege-hierarchy. Our model is simpler than previous decentralized information flow control (DIFC) systems and does not rely on a centralized principal hierarchy. Additionally, DC labels can be used to enforce information flow both statically and dynamically. To demonstrate their use, we describe two Haskell implementations, a library used to perform dynamic label checks, compatible with existing DIFC systems, and a prototype library that enforces information flow statically, by leveraging the Haskell type checker.

Keywords: Security, labels, decentralized information flow control, logic.

1 Introduction

Information flow control (IFC) is a general method that allows components of a system to be passed sensitive information and restricts its use in each component. Information flow control can be used to achieve confidentiality, by preventing unwanted information leakage, and integrity, by preventing unreliable information from flowing into critical operations. Modern IFC systems typically label data and track labels, while allowing users exercising appropriate privileges to explicitly downgrade information themselves. While the IFC system cannot guarantee that downgrading preserves the desired information flow properties, it is possible to identify all the downgrading operations and limit code audit to these portions of the code. Overall, information flow systems make it possible to build applications that enforce end-to-end security policies even in the presence of untrusted code.

We present disjunction category (DC) labels: a new label format for enforcing information flow in systems with mutually distrusting parties. By formulating DC labels using propositional logic, we make it straightforward to verify conventional lattice conditions and other useful properties. We introduce and prove soundness of decentralized privileges that are used in declassifying data, and provide a notion of privilege-hierarchy. Compared to Myers and Liskov's decentralized label model (DLM) [21], for example, our model is simpler and does not

P. Laud (Ed.): NordSec 2011, LNCS 7161, pp. 223–239, 2012.

rely on a centralized principal hierarchy. Additionally, DC labels can be used to enforce information flow both statically and dynamically, as shown in our Haskell implementations.

A DC label, written $\langle S, I \rangle$, consists of two Boolean formulas over principals, the first specifying secrecy requirements and the second specifying integrity requirements. Information flow is restricted according to implication of these formulas in a way that preserves secrecy and integrity. Specifically, secrecy of information labeled $\langle S, I \rangle$ is preserved by requiring that a receiving channel have a stronger secrecy requirement S' that *implies* S, while integrity requires the receiver to have a weaker integrity requirement I' that is *implied by* I. These two requirements are combined to form a can-flow-to relation, which provides a partial order on the set of DC labels that also has the lattice operations meet and join.

Our decentralized privileges can be delegated in a way that we prove preserves confidentiality and integrity properties, resulting in a privilege hierarchy. Unlike [21], this is accomplished without a notion of "can act for" or a central principal hierarchy. Although our model can be extended to support revocation using approaches associated with public key infrastructures, we present a potentially more appealing selective revocation approach that is similar to those used in capability-based systems.

We illustrate the expressiveness of DC labels by showing how to express several common design patterns. These patterns are based in part on security patterns used in capability-based systems. Confinement is achieved by labeling data so that it cannot be read and exfiltrated to the network by arbitrary principals. A more subtle pattern that relies on the notion of clearance is used to show how a process can be restricted from even accessing overly-sensitive information (e.g., private keys); this pattern is especially useful when covert channels are a concern. We also describe privilege separation and user authentication patterns. As described more fully later in the paper, privilege separation may be achieved using delegation to subdivide the privileges of a program and compartmentalize a program into components running with fewer privileges. The user authentication pattern shows how to leverage a login client that users trust with their username and password (since the user supplies them as input), without unnecessarily creating other risks.

We describe two Haskell implementations: a library used to perform dynamic label checks, compatible with existing DIFC systems, and a prototype library that enforces information flow statically by leveraging Haskell's type checker.

The remainder of the paper is structured as follows. In Section 2, we introduce DC labels and present some of their properties. Section 3 presents semantics and soundness proofs for our DC label system. Design patterns are presented and explained in Section 5, with the implementations presented in Section 6. We summarize related work in Section 7 and conclude in Section 8.

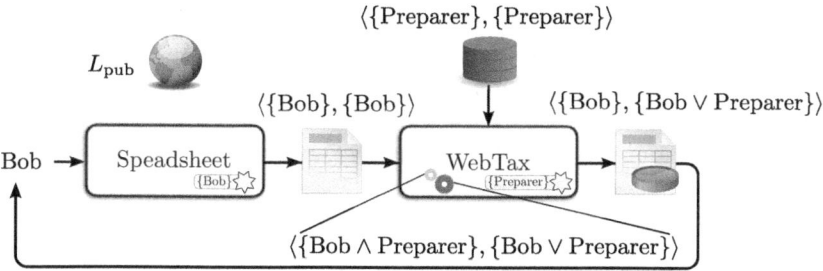

Fig. 1. A tax preparation system with mutually distrusting parties

2   DC Label Model

In a DIFC system, every piece of data is *labeled*, or "tagged." Labels provide a means for tracking, and, more importantly, controlling the propagation of information according to a security policy, such as *non-interference* [10].

DC labels can be used to express a conjunction of restrictions on information flow that represents the interests of multiple stake-holders. As a result, DC labels are especially suitable for systems in which participating parties do not fully trust each other. Fig. 1 presents an example, originally given in [21], that illustrates such a system. Here, user Bob firstly inputs his tax information into the *Spreadsheet* program, which he fully trusts. The data is then exported to another program, called *WebTax*, for final analysis. Though conceptually simple, several challenges arise since Bob does not trust WebTax with his data. Without inspecting WebTax, Bob cannot be sure that his privacy policies are respected and his tax information is not exfiltrated to the network. Analogously, the WebTax author, called Preparer, does not entrust Bob with the source code. Furthermore, the tax preparation program relies on a proprietary database and Preparer wishes to assert that even if the program contains bugs, the proprietary database information cannot be leaked to the public network. It is clear that even for such a simple example the end-to-end guarantees are difficult to satisfy with more-traditional access control mechanisms. Using IFC, however, these security policies can be expressed naturally and with minimal trust. Specifically, the parties only need to trust the system IFC-enforcement mechanism; programs, including WebTax, can be executed with no implicit trust. We now specify DC labels and show their use in enforcing the policies of this example.

As previously mentioned, a DC label consists of two Boolean formulas over principals. We make a few restrictions on the labels' format in order to obtain a unique representation for each label and an efficient and decidable can-flow-to relationship.

Definition 1 (DC Labels). *A DC label, written* $\langle S, I \rangle$, *is a pair of Boolean formulas over principals such that:*

- *Both S and I are minimal formulas in conjunctive normal form (CNF), with terms and clauses sorted to give each formula a unique representation, and*
- *Neither S nor I contains any negated terms.*

In a DC label, S protects secrecy by specifying the principals that are allowed (or whose consent is needed) to observe the data. Dually, I protects integrity by specifying principals who created and may currently modify the data. For example, in the system of Fig. 1, Bob and Preparer respectively label their data $\langle\{Bob\},\{Bob\}\rangle$ and $\langle\{Preparer\},\{Preparer\}\rangle$, specifying that they created the data and they are the only observers.

Data may flow between differently labeled entities, but only in such a way as to accumulate additional secrecy restrictions or be stripped in integrity ones, not vice versa. Specifically there is a partial order, written $\sqsubseteq$ ("can-flow-to"), that specifies when data can flow between labeled entities. We define $\sqsubseteq$ based on logical implication ($\implies$) as follows:

Definition 2 (can-flow-to relation). *Given any two DC labels* $L_1 = \langle S_1, I_1 \rangle$ *and* $L_2 = \langle S_2, I_2 \rangle$, *the can-flow-to relation is defined as:*

$$\frac{S_2 \implies S_1 \qquad I_1 \implies I_2}{\langle S_1, I_1 \rangle \sqsubseteq \langle S_2, I_2 \rangle}$$

In other words, data labeled $\langle S_1, I_1 \rangle$ can flow into an entity labeled $\langle S_2, I_2 \rangle$ as long as the secrecy of the data, and integrity of the entity are preserved. Intuitively, the $\sqsubseteq$ relation imposes the restriction that any set of principals who can observe data afterwards must also have been able to observe it earlier. For instance, it is permissible to have $S_2 = \{Bob \wedge Preparer\}$ and $S_1 = Bob$, because $S_2 \implies S_1$, and Bob's consent is still required to observe data with the new label. Dually, integrity of the entity is preserved by requiring that the source label impose more restrictions than that of the destination.

In our model, public entities (e.g., network interface in Fig. 1) have the default, or *empty* label, $\langle \mathbf{True}, \mathbf{True} \rangle$, written L_{pub}. Although specified by the label $\langle S, I \rangle$, it is intuitive that data labeled as such can be written to a public network with label L_{pub}, only with the permission of a set of principals satisfying the Boolean formula S. Conversely, data read from the network can be labeled $\langle S, I \rangle$ only with the permission of a set of principals satisfying I.

In an IFC system, label checks using the can-flow-to relation are performed at every point of possible information flow. Thus, if the WebTax program of Fig. 1 attempts to write Bob or Preparer's data to the network interface, either by error or malfeasance, both label checks $\langle\{Bob\},\{Bob\}\rangle \sqsubseteq L_{pub}$ and $\langle\{Preparer\},\{Preparer\}\rangle \sqsubseteq L_{pub}$ will fail. However, the system must also label the intermediate results of a WebTax computation (on Bob and Preparer's joint data) such that they can only be observed and written to the network if both principals consent.

The latter labeling requirement is recurring and directly addressed by a core property of many IFC systems: the label lattice property [4]. Specifically, for any two labels L_1, L_2 the lattice property states that there is a well defined, *least upper bound (join)*, written $L_1 \sqcup L_2$, and *greatest lower bound (meet)*, written $L_1 \sqcap L_2$, such that $L_i \sqsubseteq L_1 \sqcup L_2$ and $L_1 \sqcap L_2 \sqsubseteq L_i$ for L_i and $i = 1, 2$. We define the join and meet for DC labels as follows.

Definition 3 (Join and meet for DC labels). *The join and meet of any two DC labels $L_1 = \langle S_1, I_1 \rangle$ and $L_2 = \langle S_2, I_2 \rangle$ are respectively defined as:*

$$L_1 \sqcup L_2 = \langle S_1 \wedge S_2, I_1 \vee I_2 \rangle$$
$$L_1 \sqcap L_2 = \langle S_1 \vee S_2, I_1 \wedge I_2 \rangle$$

where each component of the resulting labels is reduced to CNF.

Intuitively, the secrecy component of the join protects the secrecy of L_1 and L_2 by specifying that both set of principals, those appearing in S_1 and those in S_2, must consent for data labeled $S_1 \wedge S_2$ to be observed. Conversely, the integrity component of the join, $I_1 \vee I_2$, specifies that either principals of I_1 or I_2 could have created and modify the data. Dual properties hold for the meet $L_1 \sqcap L_2$, a label computation necessary when labeling an object that is written to multiple entities. We note that although we use $I_1 \vee I_2$ informally, by definition, a DC label component must be in CNF. Reducing logic formulas, such as $I_1 \vee I_2$, to CNF is standard [23], and we do not discuss it further.

Revisiting the example of Fig. 1, we highlight that the intermediate results generated by the WebTax program from both Bob and Preparer's data are labeled by the join $\langle \{\text{Bob}\}, \{\text{Bob}\} \rangle \sqcup \langle \{\text{Preparer}\}, \{\text{Preparer}\} \rangle$ which is reduced to $\langle \{\text{Bob} \wedge \text{Preparer}\}, \{\text{Bob} \vee \text{Preparer}\} \rangle$. The secrecy component of the label confirms our intuition that the intermediate results are composed of both party's data and thus the consent of both Bob and Preparer is needed to observe it. In parallel, the integrity component agrees with the intuition that the intermediate results could have been created from Bob or Preparer's data.

2.1 Declassification and Endorsement

We model both declassification and endorsement as principals explicitly deciding to exercise *privileges*. When code exercises privileges, it means code acting on behalf of a combination of principals is requesting an action that might violate the can-flow-to relation. For instance, if the secrecy component of a label is $\{\text{Bob} \wedge \text{Preparer}\}$, then by definition code must act on behalf of both Bob and the Preparer to transmit the data over a public network. However, what if the Preparer unilaterally wishes to change the secrecy label on data from $\{\text{Bob} \wedge \text{Preparer}\}$ to $\{\text{Bob}\}$ (as to release the results to Bob)? Intuitively, such a partial declassification should be allowed, because the data still cannot be transmitted over the network without Bob's consent. Hence, if the data is eventually made public, both Bob and the Preparer will have consented, even if not simultaneously.

We formalize such partial declassification by defining a more permissive preorder, $\sqsubseteq_P$ ("can-flow-to given privileges P"). $L_1 \sqsubseteq_P L_2$ means that when exercising privileges P, it is permissible for data to flow from an entity labeled L_1 to one labeled L_2. $L_1 \sqsubseteq L_2$ trivially implies $L_1 \sqsubseteq_P L_2$ for any privileges P, but for non-empty P, there exist labels for which $L_1 \sqsubseteq_P L_2$ even though $L_1 \not\sqsubseteq L_2$.

We represent privileges P as a conjunction of principals for whom code is acting. (Actually, P can be a more general Boolean formula like label components, but the most straight-forward use is as a simple conjunction of principals.) We define $\sqsubseteq_P$ as follows:

Definition 4 (can-flow-to given privileges relation). *Given a Boolean formula P representing privileges and any two DC labels $L_1 = \langle S_1, I_1 \rangle$ and $L_2 = \langle S_2, I_2 \rangle$, the can-flow-to given privileges P relation is defined as:*

$$\frac{P \wedge S_2 \implies S_1 \qquad P \wedge I_1 \implies I_2}{\langle S_1, I_1 \rangle \sqsubseteq_P \langle S_2, I_2 \rangle}$$

Recall that without exercising additional privileges, data labeled $\langle S, I \rangle$ can be written to a public network, labeled L_{pub}, only with the permission of a set of principals satisfying the Boolean formula S, while data read from a public network can be labeled $\langle S, I \rangle$ only with the permission of a set of principals satisfying I. Considering additional privileges, it is easy to see that $\langle S, I \rangle \sqsubseteq_P L_{\text{pub}}$ iff $P \implies S$ and, conversely, $L_{\text{pub}} \sqsubseteq_P \langle S, I \rangle$ iff $P \implies I$. In other words, code exercising privileges P can declassify and write data to the public network if P implies the secrecy label of that data, and can similarly incorporate and endorse data from the public network if P implies the integrity label.

In our WebTax example, the Spreadsheet program runs on behalf of Bob and exercises the {Bob} privilege to endorse data sent to WebTax. Conversely, the WebTax program is executed with the {Preparer} privilege which it exercises when declassifying results from {Bob∧Preparer} to {Bob}; as expected, to allow Bob to observe the results, this declassification step is crucial.

It is a property of our system that exporting data through multiple exercises of privilege cannot reduce the overall privilege required to export data. For instance, if $\langle S, I \rangle \sqsubseteq_{P_1} \langle S', I' \rangle \sqsubseteq_{P_2} L_{\text{pub}}$, it must be that $P_1 \wedge P_2 \implies S$, since $P_2 \implies S'$ and $P_1 \wedge S' \implies S$. A similar, and dual, property holds for multiple endorsements.

The mechanisms provided by $\sqsubseteq_P$ corresponds to the *who* dimension of declassification [25], i.e., whoever has the privileges P can use the relationship $\sqsubseteq_P$ to release (endorse) information. With minimal encoding, it is also possible to address the *what* and *when* dimension using $\sqsubseteq_P$. Specifically, the what dimension can be addressed by carefully designing the data type in such a way that there is an explicit distinction on what part of the data is allowed to be released. The *when* dimension, on the other hand, consists on designing the trusted modules in such a way that certain privileges can only be exercised when some, well-defined, events occurs.

In our model, privileges can be *delegated*. Specifically, a process may delegate privileges to another process according to the following definition:

Definition 5 (Can-delegate relation). *A process with privilege P can delegate any privilege P', such that $P \implies P'$.*

In other words, it is possible to delegate a privilege P' that is at most as strong as the parent privilege P. In Section 5, we give a concrete example of using delegation to implement a privilege separation.

2.2   Ownership and Categories

Our definition of DC label components as conjunctions of clauses, each imposing an information flow restriction, is similar to the DStar [31] label format which uses a set of *categories*, each of which is used to impose a flow restriction. Though the name category may be used interchangeably with clause, our categories differ from those of DStar (or even DLM) in that they are disjunctions of principals— hence the name, *disjunction category* labels.

The principals composing a category are said to *own* the category—every owner is trusted to uphold or bypass the restriction imposed by the category. For instance, the category [Bob ∨ Alice] is owned by both Alice and Bob. We can thus interpret the secrecy component {[Bob ∨ Alice] ∧ Preparer} to specify that data can be observed by the Preparer in collaboration with *either* Bob or Alice. Though implicit in our definition of a DC label, this joint ownership of a category allows for expressing quite complex policies. For example, to file joint taxes with Alice, Bob can simply labels the tax data ⟨{[Bob ∨ Alice]} , {Bob}⟩, and now the WebTax results can be observed by both him and Alice. Expressing such policies in other systems, such as DLM or DStar, can only be done through external means (e.g., by creating a new principal AliceBob and encoding its relationship to Alice and Bob in a centralized principal hierarchy).

In the previous section we represent privileges P as a conjunction of principals for whom code is acting. Analogous to a principal owning a category, we say that a process (or computation) *owns* a principal if it acting or running on its behalf. (More generally, the code is said to own all the categories that compose P.)

3   Soundness

In this section, we show that the can-flow-to relation ($\sqsubseteq$) and the relation ($\sqsubseteq_P$) for can-flow-to given privileges P satisfy various properties. We first show that $\sqsubseteq$, given in Definition 2, is partial order.

Lemma 1 (DC labels form a partially ordered set). *The binary relation $\sqsubseteq$ over the set of all DC labels is a partial order.*

Proof. Reflexivity and transitivity follow directly from the Reflexivity and transitivity of ($\implies$). By Definition 1, the components of a label, and thus the label, have a unique representation. Directly, the antisymmetry property holds.

Recall from Section 2 that for any two labels L_1 and L_2 there exists a join $L_1 \sqcup L_2$ and meet $L_1 \sqcap L_2$. The join must be the least upper bound of L_1 and L_2, with $L_1 \sqsubseteq L_1 \sqcup L_2$, and $L_2 \sqsubseteq L_1 \sqcup L_2$; conversely, the meet must be the greatest lower bound of L_1 and L_2, with $L_1 \sqcap L_2 \sqsubseteq L_1$ and $L_1 \sqcap L_2 \sqsubseteq L_2$. We prove these properties and show that DC labels form a lattice.

Proposition 1 (DC labels form a bounded lattice). *DC labels with the partial order relation $\sqsubseteq$, join $\sqcup$, and meet $\sqcap$ form a bounded lattice with minimum element $\bot = \langle \textbf{True}, \textbf{False} \rangle$ and maximum element $\top = \langle \textbf{False}, \textbf{True} \rangle$.*

Proof. The lattice property follows from Lemma 1, the definition of DC labels, and the definition of the join and meet as given in Definition 3.

It is worth noting that the DC label lattice is actually product lattice, i.e., a lattice where components are elements of a secrecy and (a dual) integrity lattice [29].

In Section 2.1 we detailed declassification and endorsement of data in terms of exercising privileges. Both actions constitute bypassing restrictions of $\sqsubseteq$ by using a more permissive relation $\sqsubseteq_P$. Here, we show that this privilege-exercising relation, as given in Definition 4, is a pre-order and that privilege delegation respects its restrictions.

Proposition 2 (The $\sqsubseteq_P$ relation is a pre-order). *The binary relation $\sqsubseteq_P$ over the set of all DC labels is a pre-order.*

Proof. Reflexivity and transitivity follow directly from the reflexivity and transitivity of ($\implies$). Unlike $\sqsubseteq$, however, $\sqsubseteq_P$ is not necessarily antisymmetric (showing this, for a non-empty P, is trivial).

Informally, exercising privilege P may allow a principal to ignore the distinction between certain pairs of clauses, hence $\sqsubseteq_P$ is generally not a partial order. Moreover, the intuition that $\sqsubseteq_P$, for any non-empty P, is always more permissive than $\sqsubseteq$ follows as a special case of the following proposition.

Proposition 3 (Privileges substitution). *Given privileges P and P', if $P \implies P'$ then P can always be substituted in for P'. Specifically, for all labels L_1 and L_2, if $P \implies P'$ and $L_1 \sqsubseteq_{P'} L_2$ then $L_1 \sqsubseteq_P L_2$.*

Proof. First, we note that if $P \implies P'$, then for any X, X', such that $X \wedge P' \implies X'$, the proposition $X \wedge P \implies X \wedge P' \implies X'$ holds trivially. By Definition 4, $L_1 \sqsubseteq_{P'} L_2$ is equivalent to: $S_2 \wedge P' \implies S_1$ and $I_1 \wedge P' \implies I_2$. However, from $P \implies P'$, we have $S_2 \wedge P \implies S_2 \wedge P' \implies S_1$, and $I_1 \wedge P \implies I_1 \wedge P' \implies I_2$. Correspondingly, we have $L_1 \sqsubseteq_P L_2$.

Informally, if a piece of code exercises privileges P' to read or endorse a piece of data, it can do so with P as well. In other words, $\sqsubseteq_P$ is at least at as permissive as $\sqsubseteq_{P'}$. Letting $P' = \textbf{True}$, it directly follows that for any non-empty P, i.e., for $P \neq \textbf{True}$, the relation $\sqsubseteq_P$ is more permissive than $\sqsubseteq$. Moreover, negating the statement of the proposition (if $L_1 \not\sqsubseteq_P L_2$ then $L_1 \not\sqsubseteq_{P'} L_2$) establishes that if exercising a privilege P does not allow for the flow of information from L_1 to L_2, then exercising a privilege delegated from P will also fail to allow the flow. This property is especially useful in guaranteeing soundness of privilege separation.

4 Model Extensions

The base DC label model, as described in Section 2, can be used to implement complex DIFC systems, despite its simplicity. Furthermore, the model can easily be further extended to support features of existing security (IFC and capability) systems, as we detail below.

4.1   Principal Hierarchy

As previously mentioned, DLM [21] has a notion of a principal hierarchy defined by a reflexive and transitive relation, called *acts for*. Specifically, a principal p can act for another principal p', written $p \succeq p'$, if p is at least as powerful as p': p can read, write, declassify, and endorse all objects that p' can; the principal hierarchy tracks such relationships.

To incorporate this feature, we modify our model by encoding the principal hierarchy as a set of axioms Γ. Specifically, if $p \succeq p'$, then $(p \implies p') \in \Gamma$. Consequently, Γ is used as a hypothesis in every proposition. For example, without the principal hierarchy $\emptyset \vdash p_1 \implies [p_2 \lor p_3]$ does not hold, but if $p_1 \succeq p_2$ then $(p_1 \implies p_2), \Gamma \vdash p_1 \implies [p_2 \lor p_3]$ does hold. We, however, note that our notion of privileges and label component clauses (disjunction categories) can be used to capture such policies, that are expressible in DLM only through the use of the principal hierarchy. Compared to DLM, DC labels can be used to express very flexible policies (e.g., joint ownership) even when $\Gamma = \emptyset$.

4.2   Using DC Labels in a Distributed Setting

For scalability, extending a system to a distributed setting is crucial. Addressing this issue, Zeldovich et al. [31], provide a distributed DIFC system, called DStar. DStar is a framework (and protocol) that extends OS-level DIFC systems to a distributed setting. Core to DStar is the notion of an *exporter* daemon, which, among other things, maps DStar network labels to OS local labels such as DC labels, and conversely. DC labels (and privileges) are a generalization of DStar labels (and privileges)—the core difference being the ability of DC labels to represent joint ownership of a category with disjunctions, a property expressible in DStar only with privileges. Hence, DC labels can directly be used when extending a system to a distributed setting. More interestingly, however, we can extend DStar, while remaining backwards compatible (since every DStar label can be expressed using a DC label), to use disjunction categories and thus, effectively, use DC labels as network labels—this extension is part of our future work.

4.3   Delegation and Pseudo-Principals

As detailed in Section 2.1, our decentralized privileges can be delegated and thus create a privilege hierarchy. Specifically, a process with a set of privileges may delegate a category it owns (in the form of a single-category privilege), which can then be further *granted* or delegated to another process.

In scenarios involving delegated privileges, we introduce the notion of a *pseudo-principal*. Pseudo-principals allows one to express providence on data, which is particularly useful in identifying the contributions of different computations to a task. A pseudo-principal is simply a principal (distinguished by the prefix #) that cannot be owned by any piece of code and can only be created when a privilege is delegated. Specifically, a process that owns principal p may delegate a single-category privilege $\{[p \lor \#c]\}$ to a piece of code c. The disjunction is used to indicate that the piece of code c is responsible for performing a task been delegated by the code owing p, which also does not trust c with the privilege p. Observe that the singleton $\{\#c\}$ cannot appear in any privilege, and as a result, if some data is given to p with the integrity restriction $[p \vee \#c]$, then the piece of code c must have been the originator. In a system with multiple components, using pseudo-principals, one can enforce a pipeline of operations, as shown by the implementation of a mail delivery agent in Section 6.

We note that pseudo-principals are treated as ordinary principals in label operations. Moreover, in our implementation, the distinction is minimal: principals are strings that cannot contain the character '#', while pseudo-principals are strings that always have the prefix '#'.

4.4   Privilege Revocation

In dynamic systems, security policies change throughout the lifetime of the system. It is common for new users to be added and removed, as is for privileges to be granted and revoked [2]. Although our model can be extended to support revocation similar to that of public key infrastructures [11], we describe a selective revocation approach, common to capability-based systems [24].

To allow for the flexibility of selective revocation, it is necessary to keep track of a delegation chain with every category in a delegated privilege. For example, if processes A and C respectively delegate the single-principal privileges $\{a\}$ and $\{c\}$ to process B, B's privilege will be encoded as $\{(\{A \rightarrow B\}, a), (\{C \rightarrow B\}, c)\}$. Similarly, if B delegates $\{[a \vee c]\}$ to D, the latter's privilege set will be $\{(\{A \rightarrow B \rightarrow D, C \rightarrow B \rightarrow D\}, [a \vee c])\}$. Now, to selectively revoke a category, a process updates a system-wide revocation set Ψ with a pair consisting of the chain prefix and a privilege (it delegated) to be revoked. For example, A can revoke B's ownership of $\{a\}$ by adding $(\{A \rightarrow B\}, a)$ to Ψ. Consequently, when B or D perform a label comparison involving privileges, i.e., use $\sqsubseteq_P$, the revocation set Ψ is consulted: since $A \rightarrow B$ is a prefix in both cases, and $a \implies a$ and $a \implies [a \vee c]$, neither B nor D can exercise their delegated privileges. More generally, ownership of single-category privilege $\{c\}$ with chain x is revoked if there is a pair $(y, \psi) \in \Psi$ such that the chain y is a prefix of a chain in x and $\psi \implies c$. We finally note that, although this description of revocation relies on a centralized revocation set Ψ, selective revocation, in practice, can be implemented without a centralized set, using patterns such as Redell's "caretaker pattern" [24,18] with wrapper, or membrane, objects transitively applying the revocation [19,18].

5   Security Labeling Patterns

When building practical IFC systems, there are critical design decisions involving: (1) assigning labels to entities (data, channels, etc.), and (2) delegating privileges to executing code. In this section, we present *patterns* that can be used as a basis for these design decisions, illustrated using simplified examples of practical system applications.

5.1   Confinement and Access Control

A very common security policy is *confinement*: a program is allowed to compute on sensitive data but cannot export it [16,26]. The tax-preparation example of Section 2 is a an examples of a system that enforces confinement.

In general, we may wish to confine a computation and guarantee that it does not release (by declassification) user A's sensitive data to the public network or any other channel. Using the network as an illustrative example, and assuming A's sensitive data is labeled L_A, confinement may be achieved by executing the computation with privileges P chosen such that $L_A \not\sqsubseteq_P L_{\text{pub}}$. A complication is that most existing IFC systems (though not all, see, e.g., [6,14]) are susceptible to covert channel attacks that circumvent the restrictions based on labels and privileges. For example, a computation with no privileges might read sensitive data and leak information by, e.g., not terminating or affecting timing behavior. To address confinement in the presence of covert channels, we use the notion of *clearance* [5], previously introduced and formalized in [30,28] in the context of IFC.

Clearance imposes an upper bound on the sensitivity of the data that the computation can read. To prevent a computation from accessing (reading or writing) data labeled L_A, we set the computation's clearance to some L_C such that $L_A \not\sqsubseteq L_C$. With this restriction, the computation may read data labeled L_D only if $L_D \sqsubseteq L_C$. Observe that in a similar manner, clearance can be used to enforce other forms of discretionary access control.

5.2   Privilege Separation

Using delegation, a computation may be compartmentalized into sub-computations, with the privileges of the computation subdivided so that each sub-computation runs with *least privilege*. Consider, for example, a privilege-separated mail delivery agent (MDA) that performs spam filtering.

As with many real systems, the example MDA of Fig. 2 is composed of different, and possibly untrustworthy, modules. In this example, the components are a network receiver, R, and a spam filter, S. Instead of combining the components into a monolithic MDA, the MDA author can segregate the untrustworthy components and execute then with the principle of least

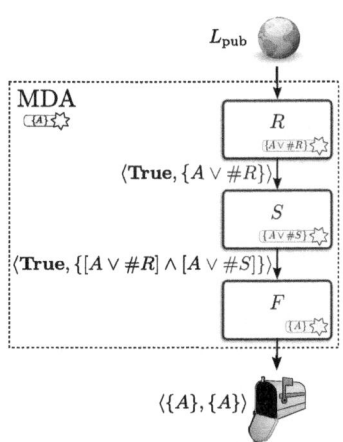

Fig. 2. Simple MDA

privilege. This avoids information leaks and corruption due to negligence or malfeasance on the component authors' part. Specifically, the receiver R is executed with the delegated privilege $\{[A \lor \#R]\}$, and the spam filter S is executed with the privilege $\{[A \lor \#S]\}$. As a consequence, R and S cannot read A's sensitive information and leak it to the network, corrupt A's mailbox, nor forge data on A's behalf.

Additionally, the MDA can enforce the policy that a mail message always passes through both receiver R and spam filter S. To this end, the MDA includes a small, trusted forwarder F, running with the privilege $\{A\}$, which endorses messages on behalf of A and writes them to the mailbox only after checking that they have been endorsed by both R and S. In a similar manner, this example can be further extended to verify that the provenance of a message is the network interface, or that the message took a specific path (e.g., R then S, but not S then R), among other.

5.3   User Authentication

Another common requirement of security systems is user authentication. We consider password-based login as an example, where a successful authentication corresponds to granting the authenticated user the set of privileges associated with their credentials. Furthermore, we consider authentication in the context of (typed) language-level DIFC systems; an influential OS-level approach has been considered in [30]. Shown in Fig. 3 is an example system which consists of a login client L, and an authentication service A_U.

To authenticate user U, the login client *invokes* the user authentication service A_U, which runs with the $\{U\}$ privilege. Conceptually, when invoked with U's correct credentials, A_U grants (by delegating) the caller the $\{U\}$ privilege. However, in actuality, the login client and authentication service are in mutual distrust: L does not trust A_U with U's password, for A_U might be malicious and simply wish to learn the password, while A_U does not trust L to grant it the $\{U\}$ privilege without first verifying credentials. Consequently, the authentication requires several steps.

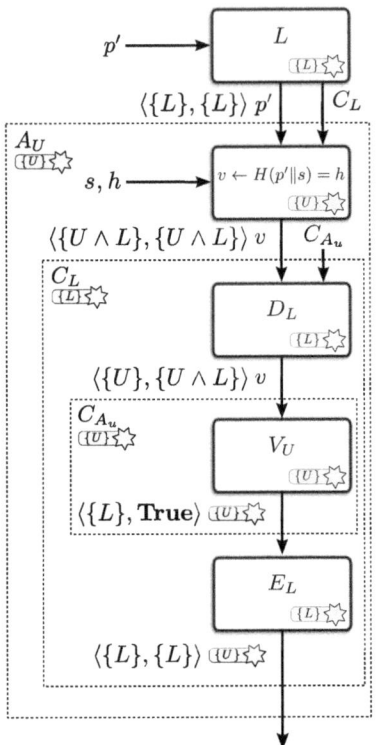

Fig. 3. User Authentication

We note that due to the mutual distrust, the user's stored salt s and password hash $h = H(p\|s)$ is labeled with both, the user and login client's, principals, i.e., h and s have label $\langle\{U \wedge L\},\{U \wedge L\}\rangle$. Solely, labeling them $\langle\{U\},\{U\}\rangle$ would allow A_U to carry out an off-line attack to recover p. The authentication procedure is as follows.

1. The user's input password p' to the login client is labeled $\langle\{L\},\{L\}\rangle$, and along with a closure C_L is passed to the authentication service A_U. As further detailed below, closures are used in this example as a manner to exercise privileges under particular conditions and operations.
2. A_U reads U's stored salt s and password hash h. It then computes the hash $h' = H(p'\|s)$ and compares h' with h. The label of this result is simply the join of h and h': $\langle\{U \wedge L\},\{L\}\rangle$. Since A_U performed the computation, it

endorses the result by adding U to its integrity component; for clarity, we name this result v, as show in Fig 3.

- *Remark:* At this point, neither L nor A_U are able to read and fully declassify the secret password-check result v. Moreover, without eliminating the mutual distrust, neither L nor S can declassify v directly. Consider, for example, if A_U is malicious and had, instead, performed a comparison of $H(p'\|s)$ and $H(p''\|s)$, for some guessed password p''. If L were to declassify the result, A_U would learn that $p = p''$, assuming the user typed in the correct password, i.e., $p = p'$. Hence, we rely on purely functional (and statically-typed) closures to carry out the declassification indirectly.

3. When invoking A_U, L passed a declassification closure C_L, which has the $\{L\}$ privilege locally bound. Now, A_U invokes C_L with v and its own declassification closure C_{A_U}.

4. C_L declassifies v (D_L in Fig. 3) to $\langle\{U\}, \{U \wedge L\}\rangle$, and then invokes C_{A_U} with the new, partially-declassified result.

5. The C_{A_U} closure has the $\{U\}$ privilege bound and upon being invoked, simply verifies the result and its integrity (V_U in Fig. 3). If the password is correct v is true and then C_{A_U} returns the privilege $\{U\}$ labeled with $\langle\{L\}, \textbf{True}\rangle$; otherwise it returns the empty privilege set. It is important that the integrity of v be verified, for a malicious L could provide a closure that forges password-check results, an attempt to wrongfully gain privileges.

6. The privilege returned from invoking C_{A_U} is endorsed by C_L (E_L in Fig. 3), only if its secrecy component is L. This asserts that upon returning the privilege from C_L, A_U cannot check if the privilege is empty or not, and thus infer the comparison result.

7. It only remains for A_U to forward the labeled privilege back to L.

We finally note that the authentication service is expected to keep state that tracks the number of attempts made by a login client, as each result leaks a bit of information; to limit the number of unsuccessful attempts requires the use of a (minimal) code that is trusted by both L and A_U, as shown in [30].

6   Implementing DC Labels

We present two Haskell implementations of DC labels[1]. The first, `dclabel`, is a library that provides a simple embedded domain specific language for constructing and working with dynamic labels and privileges. Principals in the `dclabel` library are represented by strings, while label components are lists of clauses (categories), which, in turn, are lists of principals. We use lists as sets for simplicity and because Haskell supports list comprehension; this allowed for a very simple translation from the formal definitions of this paper to (under 180 lines of) Haskell code. We additionally implemented the instances necessary to use DC labels with the label-polymorphic dynamic DIFC library, LIO [28]. Given the simplicity of the implementation, we believe that porting it to other libraries, such

---

[1] Available at `http://www.scs.stanford.edu/~deian/dclabels`

as [17,13], can be accomplished with minimal effort. Finally, we note that our implementation was thoroughly tested using the QuickCheck[2] library, however formal verification of the implementation using Zeno [27], a Haskell automated proof system, was unsuccessful. This is primarily due to Zeno's infancy and lack of support for analyzing Haskell list comprehension. A future direction includes implementing DC labels in Isabelle or Coq from which a provably-correct Haskell implementation can be extracted.

Although we have primarily focused on dynamic IFC, in cases where covert channels, runtime overhead, or failures are not tolerable, DC labels can also be used to enforce IFC statically. To this end, we implement `dclabel-static`, a prototype IFC system that demonstrates the feasibility of statically enforcing DIFC using secrecy-only DC labels, without modifying the Haskell language or the GHC compiler. Since DC labels are expressed using propositional logic, a programming language that has support for sum, product, and function types can be used, *without modification*, to enforce information flow control according to the Curry-Howard correspondence [12,9]. According to the correspondence, disjunction, conjunction and implication respectively correspond to sum, product, and function types. Hence, for a secrecy-only DC label, to prove $L_1 \sqsubseteq L_2$, i.e., $L_2 \implies L_1$, we need only construct a function that has type $L_2 \to L_1$: successfully type-checking a program directly corresponds to verifying that the code does not violate IFC.

The library exports various type classes and combinators that facilitates the enforcement of static IFC. For example, we provide type constructors to create labels from principals—a principal in this system is a type for which an instance of the `Principal` type class is defined. To label values, we associate labels with types. Specifically, a labeled type is a wrapper for a product type, whose first component is a label, and whose second component, the value, cannot be projected without declassification. The library further provides a function, `relabel`, which, given a labeled value (e.g., $(L_1, 3)$), a new label L_2, and a proof of $L_1 \sqsubseteq L_2$ (a lambda term of type $L_2 \to L_1$), returns the relabeled value (e.g., $(L_2, 3)$). Since providing such proofs is often tedious, we supply a tool called `dcAutoProve`, that automatically inserts proofs of can-flow-to relations for expressions named `auto`, with an explicit type signature. Our automated theorem prover is based a variant of Gentzen's LJ sequent calculus [7].

7 Related Work

DC labels closely resemble DLM labels [21] and their use in Jif [22]. Like DC labels, DLM labels express both secrecy and integrity policies. Core to a DLM label are components that specify an owner (who can declassify the data) and a set of readers (or writers). Compared to our disjunction categories, DLM does not allow for joint ownership of a component—they rely on a centralized principal hierarchy to express partial ownership. However, policies (natural to DLM) which allow for multiple readers, but a single owner, in our model, require a labeling

---

[2] http://hackage.haskell.org/package/QuickCheck

pattern that relies on the notion of clearance, as discussed in Section 5 and used in existing DIFC systems [30,31,28]. Additionally, unlike to DLM labels as formalized in [20], DC labels form a bounded lattice with a join and meet that respectively correspond to the least upper bound and greatest lower bound; the meet for DLM labels is not always the greatest lower bound.

The language Paralocks [3] uses Horn clauses to encode fine-grained IFC policies following the notion of locks: certain flows are allowed when corresponding locks are open. Constraining our model to the case where a privilege set is solely a conjunction of principals, Paralocks be easily used to encode our model. However, it remain an open problem to determine if disjunctive privileges can be expressed in their notion of *state*.

The Asbestos [8] and HiStar [30] operating systems enforce DIFC using Asbestos labels. Asbestos labels use the notion of categories to specify information flow restrictions in a similar manner to our clauses/categories. Unlike DC labels, however, Asbestos labels do not rely on the notion of principals. We can map a subset of DC labels to Asbestos labels by mapping secrecy and integrity categories to Asbestos levels **3** and **0**, respectively. Similarly ownership of a category maps to level $\star$. This mapping is limited to categories with no disjunction, which are equivalent to DStar labels [31], as discussed in Section 4. Mapping disjunction categories can be accomplished by using the system's notion of privileges. Conversely, both Asbestos and DStar labels are subsumed by our model. Moreover, compared to these systems we give precise semantics, prove soundness of the label format, and show its use in enforcing DIFC statically.

Capability-based systems such as KeyKOS [1], and E [19] are often used to restrict access to data. Among other purposes, capabilities can be used to enforce discretionary access control (DAC), and though they can enforce MAC using patterns such as membranes, the capability model is complimentary. For instance, our notion of privilege is a capability, while a delegated privilege loosely corresponds to an attenuated capability. This notion of privileges as capabilities is like that of Flume [15]. However, whereas they consider two types of privilege (essentially one for secrecy and another for integrity), our notion of privilege directly corresponds to ownership and conferring the right to exercise it in any way. Moreover, delegated privileges and the notion of disjunction provides an equal abstraction.

8   Conclusion

Decentralized information flow control can be used to build applications that enforce end-to-end security policies using untrusted code. DIFC systems rely on labels to track and enforce information flow. We present disjunction category labels, a new label format useful in enforcing information flow control in systems with mutually distrusting parties. In this paper, we give precise semantics for DC labels and prove various security properties they satisfy. Furthermore, we introduce and prove soundness of decentralized privileges that are used in declassifying and endorsing data. Compared to Myers and Liskov's DLM, our model is simpler and does not rely on a centralized principal hierarchy, our privilege hierarchy is distributed. We highlight the expressiveness of DC labels by providing several common design and labeling patterns. Specifically, we show how to employ DC labels to express confinement, access control, privilege separation, and authentication. Finally, further illustrating flexibility of the model, we describe two Haskell implementations: a library used to perform dynamic label checks, compatible with existing DIFC systems, and a prototype library that enforces information flow statically by leveraging Haskell's module and type system.

Acknowledgments. This work was supported by DARPA CRASH and PROCEED, Google, the Swedish research agency VR, the NSF, and the AFOSR. D. Stefan is supported by the DoD through the NDEG Fellowship Program.

References

1. Bomberger, A.C., Frantz, A.P., Frantz, W.S., Hardy, A.C., Hardy, N., Landau, C.R., Shapiro, J.S.: The KeyKOS nanokernel architecture. In: Proc. of the USENIX Workshop on Micro-Kernels and Other Kernel Architectures (April 1992)
2. Boneh, D., Ding, X., Tsudik, G., Wong, C.: A method for fast revocation of public key certificates and security capabilities. In: Proceedings of the 10th Conference on USENIX Security Symposium, vol. 10, pages 22. USENIX Association (2001)
3. Broberg, N., Sands, D.: Paralocks: role-based information flow control and beyond. In: SIGPLAN-SIGACT Symposium on Principles of Programming Languages, POPL 2010, pp. 431–444 (2010)
4. Denning, D.E.: A lattice model of secure information flow. Communications of the ACM 19(5), 236–243 (1976)
5. Department of Defense. Trusted Computer System Evaluation Criteria (Orange Book), DoD 5200.28-STD edition (December 1985)
6. Devriese, D., Piessens, F.: Noninterference through secure multi-execution. In: 2010 IEEE Symposium on Security and Privacy, pp. 109–124. IEEE (2010)
7. Dyckhoff, R.: Contraction-free sequent calculi for intuitionistic logic. Journal of Symbolic Logic, 795–807 (1992)
8. Efstathopoulos, P., Krohn, M., VanDeBogart, S., Frey, C., Ziegler, D., Kohler, E., Mazières, D., Kaashoek, F., Morris, R.: Labels and event processes in the Asbestos operating system. In: Proc. of the 20th ACM Symposium on Operating Systems Principles, Brighton, UK, pp. 17–30. ACM (October 2005)
9. Gallier, J.: Constructive logics part i: A tutorial on proof systems and typed λ- calculi. Theoretical Computer Science 110(2), 249–339 (1993)
10. Goguen, J., Meseguer, J.: Security policies and security models. In: I.C.S. Press (ed.) Proc. of IEEE Symp. on Security and Privacy, pp. 11–20 (April 1982)
11. Gunter, C., Jim, T.: Generalized certificate revocation. In: Proceedings of the 27th ACM SIGPLAN-SIGACT Symposium on Principles of Programming Languages, pp. 316–329. ACM (2000)
12. Howard, W.: The formulae-as-types notion of construction. To HB Curry: essays on combinatory logic, lambda calculus and formalism, pp. 479–490 (1980)
13. Jaskelioff, M., Russo, A.: Secure multi-execution in Haskell. In: Proc. Andrei Ershov International Conference on Perspectives of System Informatics. Springer, Heidelberg (June 2011)

14. Kashyap, V., Wiedermann, B., Hardekopf, B.: Timing-and termination-sensitive secure information flow: Exploring a new approach. In: 2011 IEEE Symposium on Security and Privacy (SP), pp. 413–428. IEEE (2011)
15. Krohn, M., Yip, A., Brodsky, M., Cliffer, N., Kaashoek, M.F., Kohler, E., Morris, R.: Information flow control for standard OS abstractions. In: Proc. of the 21st Symp. on Operating Systems Principles (October 2007)
16. Lampson, B.W.: A note on the confinement problem. Communications of the ACM 16(10), 613–615 (1973)
17. Li, P., Zdancewic, S.: Arrows for secure information flow. Theoretical Computer Science 411(19), 1974–1994 (2010)
18. Miller, M.S., Shapiro, J.S.: Paradigm Regained: Abstraction Mechanisms for Access Control. In: Saraswat, V.A. (ed.) ASIAN 2003. LNCS, vol. 2896, pp. 224–242. Springer, Heidelberg (2003)
19. Miller, M.S.: Robust Composition: Towards a Unified Approach to Access Control and Concurrency Control. PhD thesis, Johns Hopkins University, Baltimore, Maryland, USA (May 2006)
20. Myers, A., Liskov, B.: Complete, safe information flow with decentralized labels. In: IEEE Security and Privacy, pp. 186–197. IEEE (1998)
21. Myers, A.C., Liskov, B.: A decentralized model for information flow control. In: Proc. of the 16th ACM Symp. on Operating Systems Principles (1997)
22. Myers, A.C., Liskov, B.: Protecting privacy using the decentralized label model. ACM Trans. on Computer Systems 9(4), 410–442 (2000)
23. Papadimitriou, C.: Complexity Theory. Addison Wesley (1993)
24. Redell, D., Fabry, R.: Selective revocation of capabilities. In: Proceedings of the International Workshop on Protection in Operating Systems, pp. 192–209 (1974)
25. Sabelfeld, A., Sands, D.: Dimensions and principles of declassification. In: Proc. IEEE Computer Security Foundations Workshop, pp. 255–269 (June 2005)
26. Saltzer, J.H., Schroeder, M.D.: The protection of information in computer systems. Proc. of the IEEE 63(9), 1278–1308 (1975)
27. Sonnex, W., Drossopoulou, S., Eisenbach, S.: Zeno: A tool for the automatic verification of algebraic properties of functional programs. Technical report, Imperial College London (February 2011)
28. Stefan, D., Russo, A., Mitchell, J.C., Mazières, D.: Flexible dynamic information flow control in Haskell. In: Haskell Symposium, pp. 95–106. ACM SIGPLAN (September 2011)
29. Zdancewic, S., Myers, A.C.: Robust declassification. In: Proc. IEEE Computer Security Foundations Workshop, pp. 15–23 (June 2001)
30. Zeldovich, N., Boyd-Wickizer, S., Kohler, E., Mazières, D.: Making information flow explicit in HiStar. In: Proc. of the 7th Symp. on Operating Systems Design and Implementation, Seattle, WA, pp. 263–278 (November 2006)
31. Zeldovich, N., Boyd-Wickizer, S., Mazières, D.: Securing distributed systems with information flow control. In: Proc. of the 6th Symp. on Networked Systems Design and Implementation, San Francisco, CA, pp. 293–308 (April 2008)

Visualization Control for Event-Based Public Display Systems Used in a Hospital Setting

Inger Anne Tøndel

SINTEF ICT, Trondheim, Norway
inger.a.tondel@sintef.no

Abstract. This paper presents a solution for visualization control aimed at public displays used in a hospital setting. The solution controls what is displayed on a screen based on its location and the current time of day. In addition it makes risk/benefit trade-offs based on the quality and newness of the information, as well as its sensitivity and its importance for intended users. The solution can be realized by utilizing an existing publish/subscribe middleware solution.

1 Introduction

Big public displays are useful whenever there is a need to provide information to a group of people that is likely to be present at a given location. Examples of such systems are screens informing about incoming flights at an airport, or overviews of meeting room occupancy at hotels. In these example systems the information on the screen is unlikely to be sensitive, and thus there is no need to control information visualization. But imagine such information displays being used to inform users in emergency rooms [1] about waiting times and progress of patient treatment, or for coordination of peri-operative activities at a hospital [2,3]. In these situations, information that is presented in order to help health care personnel coordinate their work or to improve communication with patients and their next of kins, can constitute a privacy risk.

For public status displays, access control is a bit different than the traditional case where users request information and the access control solution accepts or denies the requests. There is no user requesting information. Instead information is put on the display based on what is likely to be useful for those that are present. The users of the system are those that at any time are in proximity of a screen, and commonly the system has no way of knowing who these users are.

In this paper we propose a visualization control[1] solution for public screens used in a health care setting. We use the term visualization control as our goal is not that much to control who accesses the system (i.e. looks at the screen) as controlling what is displayed in a given situation. The solution is based on the location of the screen, but also takes into account the current time. In addition, the solution performs risk/benefit trade-offs based on the data quality, data

---

[1] Note that though we use the term visualization we do not consider how information is presented in a user friendly way, but rather what is disseminated.

P. Laud (Ed.): NordSec 2011, LNCS 7161, pp. 240–255, 2012.
© Springer-Verlag Berlin Heidelberg 2012

newness and the sensitivity and importance of the information that is to be displayed. The information displayed is assumed to be status updates[2] generated automatically through catching events in underlying systems, and interpreting these events.

The rest of the paper is organised as follows: Section 2 introduces the domain we are addressing, and also provides an overview of existing access control approaches. Section 3 presents our solution, and Section 4 shows how this solution would work in an example setting. Section 5 explains how the solution can be realized through utilizing an existing security middleware solution for publish/subscribe systems. Then Section 6 discusses our contribution before Section 7 concludes the paper.

2 Visualization Control in a Hospital Setting

Hospital work is collaborative and problem-solving, involving several professions and expensive resources. Thus effective cooperation is a key to effective health care. Public status boards can play a role in facilitating better planning and cooperation in a hospital environment, by making health care workers more aware of the progress of care activities. [4]

Figure 1 gives an overview of a hospital setting in which public displays are used. Public displays are associated with a hospital department and are placed at a location. This location may be more or less public, and may or may not be protected by admission control mechanisms. Several individuals can be present at a given location, some of which may be health personnel and some patients. It is however important to be aware that the location can be available to other types of individuals as well, e.g. to maintenance personnel, cleaners and next-of-kins. The public displays provide status updates on the treatment of patients. These status updates come in form of events that may be of varying importance for the coordination of care activities, that may have different sensitivity, and also be of varying quality.

In the following we provide an overview the specific needs associated with visualization control in this context. Then we provide an overview of related work on access control, and explain to what extent they fit in this setting.

2.1 The Need for Visualization Control

Confidentiality. Health information is considered to be sensitive information, and is commonly protected by legislation. Though legislation, at least in Norway, allows some sharing of personal health information, e.g. to co-operating health personnel and to data processing expertise, it does not permit publishing such information in a way that makes it available to persons with no need for the data, such as *other* patients and their next of kins [5].

---

[2] We do not envision using public displays for displaying medical information, only status updates. Still the status information can reveal sensitive information regarding the type of treatment a patient is receiving.

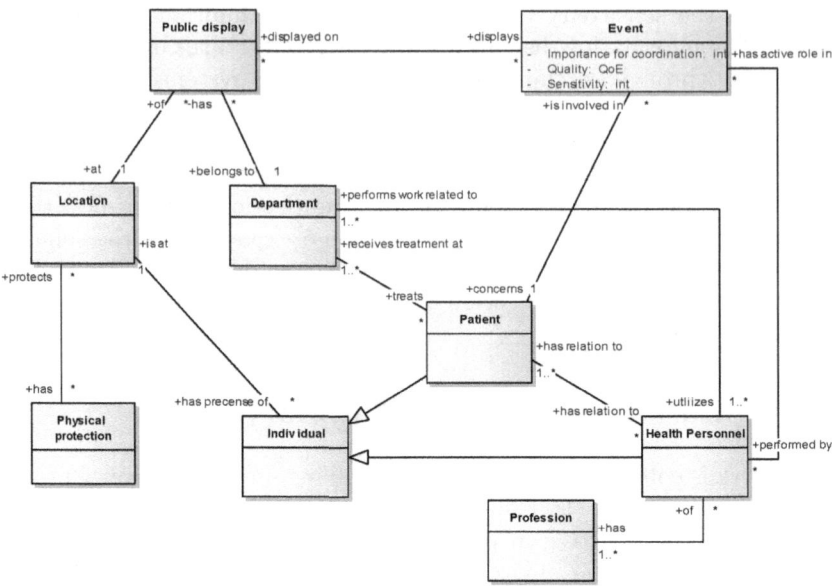

Fig. 1. Overview of a hospital setting in which public displays are used

One possible strategy in order to meet the legislative confidentiality requirements is the use of de-identification [5]. By removing or reducing the amount of
identifying data that is published, the information may no longer be considered
to be *personal* health data. As a consequence, the legislative requirements are
less strict. Gjære [6] provides an overview of de-identification techniques that
can be used for this purpose, and shows through user evaluations the potential of this approach. But in order to meet the strict legal requirements, the
de-identification must be at such a level that the health information cannot be
linked to a natural person. This requirement comes in conflict with usability requirements of health care personnel. They need to be able to guess which patient
is likely to be involved in a given status event.

As it may not be possible to meet the strict confidentiality requirements by de-
identification alone, other approaches also need to be investigated. This includes
smart ways to control what is displayed on a screen depending on the current
context. In pursue of such solutions, it is however also important to take into
account the employees and their privacy. Health care personnel are likely to
be reluctant to being tracked all the time at work, just to be able to perform
visualization control based on who is located close to a screen [7].

Availability. The success of public displays when it comes to improved cooperation and planning, depends on the information on the screen being useful
and easily available. This is in conflict with the confidentiality requirements, as
information is likely to be most useful if health care personnel are in no doubt
which patients the information displayed is concerning. In addition, usability

requirements make it difficult to utilize more traditional access control methods where users log on to get information. Studies have found that there are situations today where clinicians do not read documentation on the patients they are treating because they do not take the time to log in [8]. Requiring users to log in to public status boards would undermine the usefulness of such boards. Information should be available just by taking a quick look at the screen.

Integrity. In a risk analysis of an early version of a public display system intended used in a peri-operative hospital environment, *poor quality of data* was considered to be the main risk [7]. This shows a concern that the underlying system is not being able to catch and interpret events correctly. Researchers working on event contextualization in a decision support system intended to improve patient scheduling state that *"due to non-deterministic human behavior and with legacy medical equipment not designed for this purpose, it is impossible to assume a one-on-one mapping of system events onto patient assessment activities."* [9] Thus they have introduced a notion of event quality (QoE - Quality of Event) that measures how well events match real life activities.

Event quality should influence visualization decisions, as presenting information that is correct is important to assure integrity of the system.

Summary of visualization control needs. There is a need for solutions that make proper trade-offs between the risk of publishing information when it comes to confidentiality and the benefit of doing so in assuring availability of information. De-identification plays a crucial role in this respect, but is probably not enough in itself. There are a need for visualization control solutions that take into account the quality of the information that is to be presented, in order to ensure integrity. In addition, solutions should not require user interaction, to ensure usability.

2.2   Existing Access Control Approaches

At hospitals, current access control solutions are mainly based on Role Based Access Control [10] where users are granted access based on their profession [11][12]. Usually the department is also taken into account [13]. For these solutions to be useful for public displays (that may have any number of unknown individuals as users), access control decisions must be made based on the roles of the screens, rather than the roles of individuals, with e.g. one role for screens placed at public corridors and another for screens at locations that are protected with admission control mechanisms. Screens will however not request information the same way as individuals would, but instead display information as it is made available - as in the publish/subscribe communication paradigm. In this paradigm, applications publish events that are communicated to subscribers that have registered their interest for this particular type of events [14]. This leads to a need to control both who are allowed to publish and subscribe to events. Such functionality is offered by the solution of Bacon et al. [15] and Singh et al. [14]. In their approach RBAC is used to secure access to the communication service. In addition they support the use of transformation rules that extend the traditional binary access control decisions (accept/deny) with the possibility to modify data in transit and thereby change the sensitivity level of the information (similar to de-identification).

Though the work of Bacon et al. and Singh et al. utilize RBAC, they also allow specifying rules that are context sensitive, and support monitoring of context parameters in order to trigger re-evaluation of the rules should the conditions change. Such functionality is highly relevant in a health care environment, as previous research on access control in health care has suggested that there is a need for more context-aware solutions that are able to handle dynamic workflows and collaborations [13]. Parameters such as time, location, trust-level of authentication, relationship to patient, specialist area, emergency situation and presence of the patient have been pointed out as relevant context parameters [16,17]. For the public displays we envision, event quality should also be an important parameter.

Recognition of event quality as being important for visualization control leads to a need to deal with uncertainty; uncertainty in the events that are to be displayed and uncertainty in any events used to deduce the current context. With uncertainty comes risk, and thus an interest in including risk in the visualization control decisions. There are currently several access control solution that are based on risk. As examples, Dimmock [18,19] adds trust and risk to RBAC and Cheng et al. [20] adds risk to a Multi Level Security model. The models used to calculate risk related to access control decisions are to our experience quite complex, requiring detailed knowledge on e.g. all possible contexts, all possible outcomes of an actions, and the costs associated with these outcomes [21,18]. Providing such information is difficult at best, and there are high probabilities of mistakes. We have not been able to identify a risk-based access control solution that fits our domain and is not utterly complex. Still, we find that the notion of risk and the notion of benefit is important for visualization control.

Up till now we have only mentioned access control solutions not specifically addressing public displays. The need for controlling access to shared displays has however also received some attention from researchers, and proposed solutions include using special types of glasses to allow different people to see different types of information [22] and using visualization (e.g. colors) instead of text to present the most sensitive information [23] (similar to de-identification). In the health care sector, we are aware of a few public display systems in use [2,3]. As far as we understand, these systems control access by specifying for each screen what information should be displayed independent of the situation.

2.3   Relevance of Current Approaches

The usability requirements disallow any solutions that require use of special glasses or similar. Thus we do not consider tailoring information to individual users, but rather specify different visualizations for different types of screens (based on the screen's role). The publish/subscribe middleware solution described by Bacon et al. and Singh et al. seems promising and is able to offer

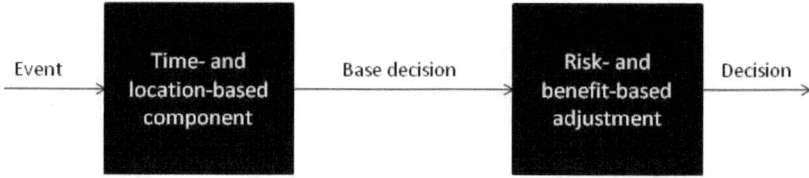

Fig. 2. Overview of solution

important features such as de-identification and context monitoring. Thus, it can be used for realization of a visualization control solution. Still there is a need for more directions on the types of policies to implement.

In our experience, current visualization control solutions for public displays used in health care offer little flexibility. Still their simplicity make them a viable alternative. In this work, we aim to extend simple location-based visualization control approaches with the possibility to take into account event quality and make simple trade-offs between the risk and benefit of publishing information.

3 Extending Location-Based Visualisation Control with Risk and Benefit Calculations

Figure 2 gives an overview of the visualization control solution we propose. The solution has two main parts; a *time- and location-based component* and a *risk- and benefit-based adjustment*. These are together used to decide what information to display and not, what level of de-identification should be used and whether users should be warned about problems with event quality. In the following we explain the workings of these two parts of our solution.

3.1 Time- and Location-Based Component

As have already been seen in Figure 1, screens can be placed at locations with varying degree of physical protection. Thus the different screens may have varying probability of being viewed by unauthorised individuals (unauthorised in the meaning that the individuals have no need or right for the information that is displayed). The likelihood that unauthorised individuals are present may be dependent on the time of day. Similarly, the likelihood that the *intended* viewers of the information are present may also vary. What is considered *typical* in this respect can be described beforehand, and be used to make a general recommendation on what to display.

The time- and location-based component gives the default visualization decision for any event at any location. This is done in two main ways: 1) By controlling which screens (in terms of their type of location) can subscribe to which types of events, and 2) by allowing screens the ability to customise the information they get through subscriptions. The type of location is considered to be a role and can be e.g. public corridor screen, access restricted corridor screen or coordinator room screen. It is also possible to take into account the screens department, so that screens only receive events concerning patients related to that department. Note that we assume access control on subscription, so that only a limited number of people is allowed to request subscriptions on behalf of screens.

For each screen role it can be specified what types of events they can subscribe to, and also the maximum identification level and the default identification level. Note that these may be the same ones. The default identification level represents a judgment of what level of identification would usually be appropriate for this type of location. By also having a maximum identification level, it becomes possible for individual screens to subscribe to events with a higher identification level if local considerations find this reasonable. The default identification level can be dependent on time of day, so that there e.g. are different policies for what to display at night-time compared to day-time, or increased identification offered during handover meetings.

When creating a subscription for a screen, it is possible to customise what events the screen is to receive (out of those that are allowed for the screen's role). If no identification level is specified for a subscription, the default identification level is used. It is possible to request different identification levels for different types of information, but with the limitation that some de-identification techniques are incompatible. This can be illustrated with an example. If a screen publishes two events, one concerning John Jackson born 1974 and another concerning JJ74, it is easy to deduce that both events concern the same patient. Thus there is no effect of the transformation into JJ74. In cases where screens subscribe to events with incompatible identification levels, the lowest of the incompatible levels will be used for all the involved events.

When an event is to be published, it will be considered for publication on all screens that subscribe to this event, using the identification level of the individual screen.

3.2 Risk- and Benefit-Based Adjustment

The time- and location-based component does not consider the differences in risk and benefit associated with individual events (e.g. when it comes to the quality of the event and its relevance). These are handled by the risk- and benefit-based adjustments component, and are added to the solution to assure the necessary flexibility in the visualization control solution.

The *benefit* of publishing an event is closely related to the quality of the event, and also its newness. If the event is not a close representation of a real world activity (low QoE) there is low benefit of publishing it. The same way, due to uncertainties in the event capturing and interpretation, newly detected events may concern activities that were performed some time in the past. The benefit of publishing information about activities performed quite some time ago is likely to be lower than for recent events. Different types of events may also be of varying importance for coordination.

The *risk* of publishing an event concerns both the sensitivity of the information and the probability that the information falls into the wrong hands [20]. Both these aspects are taken into account in the subscription rules associated with a given screen role, but sensitivity is also considered in the adjustments made to the base decision (as explained below).

In our approach, event quality is computed by using the QoE measure suggested by Wienhofen et al.[9]. A quality threshold is specified and used to determine whether or not the quality is acceptable. Newness is handled in two different ways. First, if the event concerns an activity that is older than all those currently displayed it is not displayed. Second, a configurable newness threshold is used to distinguish old and new events. This newness threshold can either be set to a time interval, e.g. an hour, or be set in reference to the number of newer events already displayed on the patient (based on the assumption that the newest events on a patient are more important for coordination). If the last option is used and the newness threshold is specified as "one step", the newness threshold of one patient is automatically set to the newness of the newest event concerning this patient.

When it comes to sensitivity and importance of events, any deviations from the normal can be specified. This means that events can be classified as highly sensitive or less sensitive, but if nothing is specified they are considered to be of medium sensitivity. The same way the events' importance for coordination can be classified as high, medium (default) or low. These are all transformed into numerical values, from 1-3, with 3 equaling "high". With three levels on each, it is straightforward to compute a sensitivity vs. importance measure,

$$si\_measure = importance - sensitivity \tag{1}$$

that is positive if importance is higher than the sensitivity, and negative if sensitivity is given more weight.

The quality threshold, the newness threshold and the si_measure is used the following way to adjust a base decision:

```
if newness < oldest.newness:
  do not publish
else:
  if QoE < quality_threshold:
    if newness > newness_threshold and si_measure > 0:
      publish according to base decision but with warning
    else:
      do not publish
  else:
    if newness < newness_threshold and si_measure < 0:
      publish with lowest identification level
    else:
      publish according to base decision
```

As a result, low quality events will still be published if they are new and important for coordination, while not being utterly sensitive (note that the si_measure will never be above zero if sensitivity is high, it will also never be above zero if it has not been classified as important for coordination or has low sensitivity). Low quality events will however be accompanied with a warning, e.g. being displayed with different colour or be associated with a warning symbol. Old events will be published with the lowest level of identification if they are of low importance or of high sensitivity.

3.3   Re-evaluation of Visualization Decisions

Due to imperfection in the way events are detected and interpreted, events or the quality measure of events that have been displayed can later be updated. These will be handled by the visualization control as any other event, only that the previous display of the event is deleted.

As the default identification level can be dependent on time of day, a trigger will be activated at any time that constitutes such a change in identification level in order to assure that all displayed events are according to the defined level. In this process, the adaptation will also be re-run. The newness threshold is also used as a trigger, so that all events below this newness threshold and with a si_measure below zero are at all times displayed with the lowest identification level.

3.4   Summary: Overview of Information Needed

To sum up, our solution requires the specification the following:

- *Screen roles* that are associated with *events* they are allowed to subscribe to. In addition each screen role has a *maximum identification level* and a *default identification level*. The default identification level may be dependent on time.
- Adjustments of *sensitivity* levels and *importance* levels of events.
- Rank of *de-identification techniques*, and specification of which techniques are *incompatible*.
- A *quality threshold* and a *newness threshold*.

4   An Example: Examination Day for Cardiac Patients

To illustrate the workings of our solution, we reuse the hospital example used by Wienhofen et al [9]. This example is taken from a Norwegian University Hospital and concerns pre-operative medical evaluation for cardiac patients. In this hospital all the pre-operative examination activities for cardiac patients are performed on one day, something that is convenient for the patients, but increases the need for coordination of the examinations.

Table 1. Example

Events	Locations	Identification
BloodTest(patient)	Open corridor	Full name
CardiologyOutpatientAssessment(patient)	Restricted corridor	Initials
RadiologyExamination(patient)	Meeting room	Pseudonym
PulmonaryAssessment(patient)	Coordination room	Anonymous
CardiologyAssessment(patient)	Examination room	
PhysiotherapyAssessment(patient)		
AnaesthesiaAssessment(patient)		
VascularSurgeonAssessment(patient)		

4.1   Description of the Examination Day

During the examination day, the patients have to undergo a number of standard tests: 1) Blood test, 2) Cardiology outpatient assessment, 3) Radiology examination, 4) Pulmonary assessment, 5) Cardiology assessment, 6) Physiotherapy assessment (not all patients), 7) Anaesthesia assessment, and 8) Assessment by vascular surgeon. For most patients, the examinations are performed in the above indicated order, but some deviations [9] are possible. The coordinating nurse is responsible for guiding the patients through all these examinations.

In order to ease the task of the coordinator, public displays can present information about the status of patient treatment. The screens would inform the coordinator of when patients are ready, what kind of examinations have been performed, and whether health care personnel are busy or available, and also inform the involved health care personnel about when their next patient is likely to be ready for the examination. In addition, patients could get some ideas on the status of the health care personnel they are to visit next and the patients' next of kins could get clues on when "their patient" is likely to be finished.

For the sake of this example we reuse the composite events from Wienhofen et al. [9] and add a number of screen locations. These are all listed in Table 1. This table also lists the identification levels considered in this example. We only focus on the department most involved in the information day, and do not include any screens at cooperating departments such as radiology.

4.2   Information Used as Input to Visualization Control

Table 2 shows the subscription rules used in this example and Table 3 shows any additional information included related to the sensitivity of the events, and also their importance for coordination[3]. The available identification levels were shown in Table 1 and are there listed with the highest identification level at the top (full name) and the lowest level at the bottom (anonymous). Note that (though not shown in the table) the identification levels "full name" and "initials" cannot be used together.

---

[3] Note that the values have been assigned for illustration purposes, and do not necessary reflect the actual sensitivity and importance of the information.

Table 2. Subscription rules

Locations	Events	Max ident.	Default ident.
Open corridor role	RadiologyExamination, AnaesthesiaAssessment, VascularSurgeonAssessment	Anonymous	Anonymous
Restricted corridor role	All	Initials	Day: Pseudonyms, Night: Initials
Meeting room role	All	Full name	Initials if it is the usual time for handover meetings, else anonymous
Coordination room role	All	Full name	Initials
Examination room role	All	Initials	Anonymous

Table 3. Events and their sensitivity and importance (note that an empty cell indicates that the default (medium) value is used)

Events	Sensitivity	Importance
BloodTest(patient)	low	low
CardiologyOutpatientAssessment(patient)		
RadiologyExamination(patient)		high
PulmonaryAssessment(patient)		high
CardiologyAssessment(patient)		
PhysiotherapyAssessment(patient)	high	
AnaesthesiaAssessment(patient)		
VascularSurgeonAssessment(patient)		low

In this example we use a quality threshold of 0.6 (value of QoE is between 0 and 1 [9]). The newness threshold is set to two hours.

4.3 Example Visualization Decisions

Example 1: New subscriptions. The department is getting a new screen that is to be placed at a restricted corridor, and subscriptions are set up for all available types of event. The default identification levels are used for all events except for the BloodTest-events. Instead the subscription specifically requests that blood tests are displayed using initials. This exception is allowed as it is within the accepted options (initials is the maximum level), and because this identification level is compatible with the other identification level in use (pseudonyms).

The department also wants to update the coordination room screen so that BloodTest-events are always displayed with full names. This change in subscription has however no effect, as the full name identification level is incompatible with the identification level used for the other events (initials). For this change to have had any effect, all the other subscribed events that use initials for identification would also have to be updated to full name. Alternatively, their identification level would need to be changed into a lower level that is compatible with full name (e.g. pseudonymous).

Example 2: Base decision is kept. A new BloodTest-event is available for a patient associated with the department. The event has a quality of 0.7 and the newness is 5 minutes. For the screen at the restricted corridor, the base decision is to publish this event with initials (because of the exception made in example 1). This suggestion is then subject to risk-and benefit-based adjustment. As the quality of the event is above the quality threshold and the newness is above the newness threshold, the event is displayed as initially suggested.

Example 3: Low quality event. A new CardiologyOutpatientAssessment-event is available for a patient associated with the department. The event has a quality of 0.3 and the newness is 8 minutes. For the screen at the restricted corridor, the base decision is to publish this event with pseudonyms as it is currently mid-day. This suggestion is then subject to risk-and benefit-based adjustment. The quality of the event is below the threshold, but the newness is above threshold. As the si_measure is 0 it is however not important enough to accept the low quality and the event is thus not published.

Example 4: Old event. A new PhysiotherapyAssessment-event is available for a patient associated with the department. The event has a quality of 0.85 and the newness is three hours. For the screen at the restricted corridor, the base decision is to publish this event with pseudonyms as it is currently mid-day. This suggestion is then subject to risk-and benefit-based adjustment. The quality of the event is above the threshold, but as the newness is below threshold and the si_measure is -1 it is published anonymously (the lowest identification level). It is however not excluded, as there are still older events at that is currently displayed.

5 Realization: Utilizing the Publish/Subscribe Security Middleware of Singh et al.

The work of Bacon et al. and Singh et al. on access control in publish/subscribe systems pose an excellent starting point for developing solutions for visualization control in event-based public display systems. It provides solutions for controlling who is allowed to publish and subscribe to the different types of events, allows more fine-grained access control decisions than accept/deny, and makes it possible to take the context into account in the access control decisions, and monitor context changes. We now describe how the publish/subscribe security middleware they have developed can be used to realize the type of visualization control suggested in this paper.

5.1   Overview of the Most Relevant Parts of the Publish/Subscribe Middleware

The publish/subscribe security middleware utilize databases for storing of policy, meaning that event types, credentials, functions and conditions are represented in relational tables. Policy can reference context, including system and environmental states, event content, subscriber specifics and stored data. Messages are transmitted in XML, and policy is also specified in XML.

ON SUBSCRIBE rules are evaluated by the broker whenever a subscription request is received. They have a name, a condition and a function. The function is called whenever the rule is executed, and returns the subscription registered in the system. Subscriptions can only be performed after proper authorisation. Subscriptions are only denied when no policy authorises access to the event type. Otherwise they are accepted with conditions imposed on event delivery (imposed conditions can be considered to be mandatory filters). It is also possible for subscribers to specify their own filters.

ON NOTIFY rules are evaluated by the broker whenever an event type matches a subscription. Similar to ON SUBSCRIBE rules, they have a name, a condition and a function, and the function returns the event that is delivered to the user (subject to any filters). Data transformations can be done on receipt or on notify and are performed through invocation of mapping functions.

It is possible to have several rules being activated by the same occurrence. The middleware allows conflicts to be detected and resolved by ordering the set of rules applicable in the current context.

5.2   Realization of the Time- and Location-Based Component

ON SUBSCRIBE rules can be used to specify which screens are allowed to subscribe to which events. The specifications of the maximum and default levels can be stored as data in the database, and be used by the function to generate the stored subscription. Subscriptions are then evaluated based on these rules. Imposed conditions can be used to assure the maximum identification levels are kept, while subscription filters can be used to specify individual identification levels for the different screens.

Transformation of events into different identification levels can be used by creating mapping functions for the different identification levels (e.g. one for initials, and another for pseudonyms).

5.3   Realization of the Risk- and Benefit-Based Adjustment

ON NOTIFY rules can be used to ensure acceptable quality and newness. The quality threshold, the newness threshold and the specifications on sensitivity levels and importance of events can be stored as data in the database, and be used as input.

6   Discussion

In this paper we have suggested a solution for visualization control aimed at public displays used in a hospital setting. The solution is based on screen location, but extended with the possibility to take into account time, and make risk/benefit trade-offs based on the quality, newness, sensitivity and importance of the information. It controls what information is published and not, but also the level of identification used. We have also explained how it can be realized through the use of an existing publish/subscribe middleware solution.

In our design we have made a trade-off between the complexity of the solution and the accuracy of the specified policies. Limiting complexity is important to assure ease of use and also reduce the chances of mistakes and unintended consequences of policy changes. The solutions in use today are quite simple, and it is our belief that simple solutions are more likely to be adopted. Still, the simple solutions are less able to take into account the varying risks of presenting information dependent on the situation. The solution we ended up with is less complex than most existing risk-based and context-aware access control solutions. Still, it takes into account context parameters like time of day and newness, and risk parameters such as the quality and the sensitivity of the information. Policies can be made quite simple; with no time-dependence, with only maximum identification levels specified and with no adjustment of sensitivity and importance levels of information. Still, the flexibility offered can be used to extend the simple rules offering more complex visualization control for some locations. The data quality and newness is however always taken into account, and this is highly important due to the imperfection of the event detection and interpretation mechanisms.

As outlined in Section 2, confidentiality and availability are both considered very important for the success of public displays within healthcare. Being able to make proper trade-offs between the benefits of publishing information and the risks of doing so is essential in order to come to solutions that will be both useful and legal. De-identification techniques offer one way of making such a trade-off, where information is published, but in less detail. With our suggestion, we aim to contribute with further abilities to make such trade-offs by offering the possibility to specify visualization control policies that take into account both the benefits and the risks of publishing information. Benefits and risks are directly addressed in the adjustments made to the base decisions, but should also influence the rules used as a basis for the time- and location-based component.

For further work, we plan to integrate the visualisation control approach presented here with Gjære's work on de-identification [6], and add the possibility for user interaction. Then we want to evaluate the usability of the visualization control approach in a hospital setting, either through trials or laboratory experiments in a usability lab.

7 Conclusion

We have suggested a visualization control solution useful for public displays in a hospital setting. The solution is able to take into account event quality and newness, and make simple risk/benefit trade-offs. Central to the solution is the ability to display information with different levels of identification. The solution can be realized by using an existing publish/subscribe middleware.

Acknowledgments. This work was supported by the Norwegian Research Council's VERDIKT program (grant no. 187854/S10). Thanks to all colleagues in the COSTT project, and especially to my colleagues Leendert Wienhofen, Maria B. Line and Erlend Andreas Gjære for discussions, comments and ideas. Thanks also to Arild Faxvaag for suggesting the term "visualization control".

References

1. O'Neill, E., Woodgate, D., Kostakos, V.: Easing the wait in the emergency room: building a theory of public information systems. In: Proceedings of the 5th Conference on Designing Interactive Systems: Processes, Practices, Methods, and Techniques, DIS 2004, pp. 17–25 (2004)
2. Bardram, J.E., Hansen, T.R., Soegaard, M.: Awaremedia: a shared interactive display supporting social, temporal, and spatial awareness in surgery. In: Proceedings of the 2006 20th Anniversary Conference on Computer Supported Cooperative Work, CSCW 2006, pp. 109–118 (2006)
3. Aronsky, D., Jones, I., Lanaghan, K., Slovis, C.M.: Supporting patient care in the emergency department with a computerized whiteboard system. Journal of the American Medical Informatics Association 15(2), 184–194 (2008)
4. Faxvaag, A., Røstad, L., Tøndel, I.A., Seim, A.R., Toussaint, P.J.: Visualizing patient trajectories on wall-mounted boards - information security challenges. In: Proceedings of MIE 2009. Studies in Health Technology and Informatics, pp. 715–719 (2009)
5. Gjære, E.A., Tøndel, I.A., Line, M.B., Andresen, H., Toussaint, P.: Personal health information on display: Balancing needs, usability and legislative requirements. In: Proceedings of MIE 2011. Studies in Health Technology and Informatics, vol. 169, pp. 606–610 (2011)
6. Gjære, E.A.: Sensitive Information on Display: Using flexible de-identification for protecting patient privacy in (semi-) public hospital environments, Master's thesis, Norwegian University of Science and Technology (2011)
7. Line, M.B., Tøndel, I.A., Gjære, E.A.: A Risk-Based Evaluation of Group Access Control Approaches in a Healthcare Setting. In: Tjoa, A.M., Quirchmayr, G., You, I., Xu, L. (eds.) ARES 2011. LNCS, vol. 6908, pp. 26–37. Springer, Heidelberg (2011)
8. Faxvaag, A., Johansen, T.S., Heimly, V., Melby, L., Grimsmo, A.: Healthcare professionals' experiences with ehr-system access control mechanisms. In: Proceedings of MIE 2011. Studies in Health Technology and Informatics, vol. 169, pp. 601–605 (2011)

9. Wienhofen, L.W.M., Preuveneers, D., Landmark, A.D., Toussaint, P.J., Berbers, Y.: A Notion of Event Quality for Contextualized Planning and Decision Support Systems. In: Beigl, M., Christiansen, H., Roth-Berghofer, T.R., Kofod-Petersen, A., Coventry, K.R., Schmidtke, H.R. (eds.) CONTEXT 2011. LNCS, vol. 6967, pp. 307–320. Springer, Heidelberg (2011)
10. ANSI, American National Standard for Information Technology - Role Based Access Control, ANSI INCITS 359-2004 (2004)
11. Appari, A., Johnson, M.E.: Information security and privacy in healthcare: Current state of research. Forthcoming: International J. Internet and Enterprise Management (2009)
12. Ferreira, A., Cruz-Correira, R., Antunes, L., Chadwick, D.: Access control: how can it improve patients' healthcare? Studies in Health Technology and Informatics, vol. 127, pp. 65–76 (2007)
13. Røstad, L., Edsberg, O.: A study of access control requirements for healthcare systems based on audit trails from access logs. In: ACSAC 2006: Proceedings of the 22nd Annual Computer Security Applications Conference, pp. 175–186 (2006)
14. Singh, J., Vargas, L., Bacon, J., Moody, K.: Policy-based information sharing in publish/subscribe middleware. In: IEEE International Workshop on Policies for Distributed Systems and Networks, pp. 137–144 (2008)
15. Bacon, J., Eyers, D.M., Singh, J., Pietzuch, P.R.: Access control in publish/subscribe systems. In: Proceedings of the Second International Conference on Distributed Event-Based Systems, DEBS 2008, pp. 23–34 (2008)
16. Hu, J., Weaver, A.: Dynamic, context-aware access control for distributed healthcare applications. In: Proceedings of the First Workshop on Pervasive Security, Privacy and Trust, PSPT (2004)
17. Alam, M., Hafner, M., Memon, M., Hung, P.: Modeling and enforcing advanced access control policies in healthcare systems with SECTET. In: 1st International Workshop on Model-Based Trustworthy Health Informaton Systems, MOTHIS 2007 (2007)
18. Dimmock, N., Belokosztolszki, A., Eyers, D., Bacon, J., Moody, K.: Using trust and risk in role-based access control policies. In: Proceedings of the Ninth ACM Symposium on Access Control Models and Technologies, SACMAT 2004, pp. 156–162 (2004)
19. Dimmock, N., Bacon, J., Ingram, D., Moody, K.: Risk Models for Trust-Based Access Control(TBAC). In: Herrmann, P., Issarny, V., Shiu, S.C.K. (eds.) iTrust 2005. LNCS, vol. 3477, pp. 364–371. Springer, Heidelberg (2005)
20. Cheng, P.-C., Fohatgi, P., Keser, C.: Fuzzy MLS: An Experiment on Quantified Risk-Adaptive Access Control, IBM Thomas J. Watson Research Center, Tech. Rep. (January 2007)
21. Diep, N.N., Hung, L.X., Zhung, Y., Lee, S., Lee, Y.-K., Lee, H.: Enforcing access control using risk assessment. In: European Conference on Universal Multiservice Networks, pp. 419–424 (2007)
22. Shoemaker, G.B.D., Inkpen, K.M.: Single display privacyware: augmenting public displays with private information. In: Proceedings of the SIGCHI Conference on Human Factors in Computing Systems, CHI 2001, pp. 522–529 (2001)
23. Tarasewich, P., Campbell, C.: What are you looking at. In: The First Symposium on Usable Privacy and Security, SOUPS 2005 (2005)

Exploring the Design Space of Prime Field vs. Binary Field ECC-Hardware Implementations

Erich Wenger and Michael Hutter

Institute for Applied Information Processing and Communications (IAIK),
Graz University of Technology, Inffeldgasse 16a, 8010 Graz, Austria
{Erich.Wenger,Michael.Hutter}@iaik.tugraz.at

Abstract. In this paper, we answer the question whether binary extension field or prime-field based processors doing multi-precision arithmetic are better in the terms of area, speed, power, and energy. This is done by implementing and optimizing two distinct custom-made 16-bit processor designs and comparing our solutions on different abstraction levels: finite-field arithmetic, elliptic-curve operations, and on protocol level by implementing the Elliptic Curve Digital Signature Algorithm (ECDSA). On the one hand, our $\mathbb{F}_{2^m}$ based processor outperforms the $\mathbb{F}_p$ based processor by 19.7 % in area, 69.6 % in runtime, 15.9 % in power, and 74.4 % in energy when performing a point multiplication. On the other hand, our $\mathbb{F}_p$ based processor (11.6 kGE, 41.4 μW, 1,313 kCycles, and 54.3 μJ) improves the state-of-the-art in $\mathbb{F}_{p_{192}}$ ECC hardware implementations regarding area, power, and energy results. After extending the designs for ECDSA (signature generation and verification), the area and power-consumption advantages of the $\mathbb{F}_{2^m}$ based processor vanish, but it still is 1.5-2.8 times better in terms of energy and runtime.

Keywords: Hardware Implementation, Elliptic Curve Cryptography, ECC, ECDSA, Binary-Extension Field, Prime Field.

1 Introduction

Elliptic Curve Cryptography (ECC) has been introduced in the 1980s and is used nowadays in a variety of different applications. Every application has its own design criteria and raises special requirements for hardware designs. While contact-less powered devices have to meet low-power constraints, battery-powered devices need energy-aware implementations that consume as little energy as possible to increase the life-time of the battery.

The most fundamental decision concerning future hardware designs is whether to use a binary-extension field or a prime field as basis of the used elliptic curve. Most related work in dedicated hardware designs has been done in implementing ECC over binary fields using full-precision arithmetic. Only a few papers compared binary and prime fields in hardware. Wolkerstorfer [36] and Satoh [32] used full-precision dual-field hardware with bit-serial multipliers. We however

P. Laud (Ed.): NordSec 2011, LNCS 7161, pp. 256–271, 2012.
© Springer-Verlag Berlin Heidelberg 2012

are interested in multi-precision designs, where the big integers are split and processed in small words. This design methodology has the advantage that the Central Processing Unit (CPU) can be reused to perform other work (*e.g.* protocol handling). In this paper we want to answer the following questions:

- What are the advantages and disadvantages of prime and binary-field processors in custom multi-precision hardware?
- How big are the differences when identical design methodologies and elliptic curves with similar security level are used?
- How does the performance of prime and binary-field processors scale in higher-level protocols?
- Does the speed advantage of carry-less operations makes up the additional need of prime-field arithmetics?

In this paper, we answer these questions by presenting two distinct custom 16-bit processors that leverage binary-field operations and prime-field operations and are based on [35] and [34]. Using a metric consisting of **area**, **speed**, **power**, and **energy**, we not only compare both designs in terms of finite-field operation and ECC point-multiplication performance, we also investigate a higher-level protocol. When performing an ECC-point-multiplication, the $\mathbb{F}_{2^m}$ based processor (9.3 kGE, 34.8 μW, 400 kCycles, and 13.9 μJ) is 3.3 times faster, 20 % smaller, uses 16 % less power, and needs 3.9 times less energy compared to the $\mathbb{F}_p$ based processor (11.6 kGE, 41.4 μW, 1,313 kCycles, and 54.3 μJ). Nevertheless our $\mathbb{F}_p$ based processor improves the state-of-the-art in area, power, and energy results for prime-field based ECC (doing point multiplication).

We further present two full hardware implementations of the Elliptic Curve Digital Signature Algorithm (ECDSA). It shows that the $\mathbb{F}_{2^m}$ based processor does not outperform the $\mathbb{F}_p$ based processor in every category of the metric. The $\mathbb{F}_{2^m}$ based processor is 4.4-5.5 % larger, needs up to 6.3 % more power, but still is 2.8 times faster and needs 2.8 times less energy when calculating a signature. The runtime and energy advantage drops down to a factor of 1.5 when the verification is done.

The paper is organized as follows. Section 2 discusses related work on ECC implementations. Section 3 gives an introduction to elliptic curve cryptography and introduces a metric. Whereas Section 4 gives a comparison, Section 5 thoroughly discusses all implementation results. Conclusions are given in Section 6.

2   Related Work on ECC-Hardware Implementations

There exist many hardware implementations of elliptic-curve cryptography. In the following, we consider only lightweight implementations that address embedded systems, wireless sensors, and contactless-powered applications. Most of the given implementations are based on either binary field, prime field, or dual-field arithmetic. A very tiny ECC processor over binary fields has been proposed by Y. K. Lee et al. [25] in 2008. They based their design on a compact architecture of a Modular Arithmetic Logic Unit (MALU) that has been first presented by the work of L. Batina et al. [4] in 2006. The processor performs (full-precision) operations in $\mathbb{F}_{2^{163}}$ and calculates a scalar multiplication between about 80 000 and 300 000 clock cycles (depending on the digit size of the hardware multiplier). The final architecture needs about 12-20 kGEs of area. Similar results have been also reported by S. Kumar and C. Paar [24] who presented a generic binary-field processor over $\mathbb{F}_{2^{113-193}}$. The run-time and area requirements of the proposed processor is similar, needing between 170 000 and 560 000 clock cycles and 10-19 kGEs. D. Hein et al. [15] reported a low-resource co-processor for passive Radio Frequency Identification (RFID) applications. In contrast to the previous work, they applied multi-precision arithmetic over $\mathbb{F}_{2^{163}}$. Their ECC design needs about 300 000 clock cycles for one scalar multiplication and consumes about 11 kGEs of chip area. In view of power consumption, all described designs need between 8 and 30 μWs of power at 100 kHz and are thus well applicable to the targeted applications.

Prime-field based processors have been reported by, for example, E. Öztürk et al. [31] in 2004. They presented an ECC architecture over the prime field $\mathbb{F}_{2^{(167+1)}/3}$. Their design needs 545 440 clock cycles for one scalar multiplication and requires about 30 kGEs of area. Similar results have also been reported by F. Fürbass and J. Wolkerstorfer [11] in 2007. Their $\mathbb{F}_{p_{192}}$ processor needs 502 000 clock cycles and about 23 kGEs of area. Recently, M. Hutter et al. [16] presented an ECC processor over the same prime field needing about 750 000 clock cycles for a scalar multiplication and about 19 kGEs of area. E. Wenger et al. [34] reduced the area requirements even further to only about 12 kGEs but their design needs about 1.4 million clock cycles. The power consumption of most of the reported prime-field processors is about 20 to several hundred μWs of power at 100 kHz.

By the given related work, it seems that binary-field processors benefit from a more efficient computation for application-specific hardware implementations. However, it is impossible to make a fair comparison since the authors used different design techniques, synthesis tools, bit/word sizes, and EC parameters. This renders a comparison largely unfeasible. Nevertheless, there exist only a few publications that reported dual-field processors for ECC that give detailed comparison results. A. Satoh and K. Takano [32] presented a processor over $\mathbb{F}_{2^m}$ and $\mathbb{F}_p$ supporting 160 to 256 bits. They show that the binary-field operations can be performed about six times faster than their prime-field opponents (1.21 ms vs. 0.19 ms for a 160-bit scalar multiplication). Furthermore, the area requirements for the prime-field controller is 1.47 times larger than the binary-field controller (6 606 GEs vs. 4 490 GEs for 8-bit word size and a 160-bit scalar). J. Wolkerstorfer [36] also presented a dual-field processor that supports 190 to 256 bits. One of his outcomes has been that binary-field operations can be performed about 1.58, 1.42, and 1.27 times faster than prime-field operations for 191/192, 233/224, and 283/256 bits respectively. However, he did not compare the hardware requirements of both types of supported fields and reported only the total area requirements of his processor which is between 24-31 kGEs.

In the following, we design both a binary and prime-field based ECC processor in order to compare them in a fair environment. In contrast to existing work, we consider not only scalar multiplication but evaluate and compare the performance also for higher-level protocols such as ECDSA. First of all, we give a brief introduction into ECC and define a metric to compare different criteria which is done in the next section.

3   Implementations of Elliptic-Curve Cryptography

Elliptic curves have been introduced by Koblitz [22] and Miller [28] in the 1980s and they have been thoroughly analyzed by the community throughout the last decades. They are based on the Weierstrass equation which can be written as

$$E : y^2 + a_1 xy + a_3 y = x^3 + a_2 x^2 + a_4 x + a_6 \tag{1}$$

with $a_{i=1,2,3,4,6}, x, y \in K$. K defines the finite field. A point $P = (x, y)$ is a valid point on the elliptic curve if it fulfills the Weierstrass equation, *i.e.* Equation (1). The basic operations performed on the elliptic curve are point addition and point doubling. Using those operations, a point multiplication (often referred as scalar multiplication) $Q = k \times P$ can be calculated. The Elliptic Curve Discrete Logarithm Problem (ECDLP) states that finding k is a mathematical hard problem if the points P and Q are given. For a more detailed introduction into elliptic curves and its properties we refer the reader to [3,5,13,23].

Figure 1 shows the hierarchy of ECC implementations. All ECC operations are based on finite-field arithmetics. Higher-level protocols make use of the underlying ECC operations to provide various cryptographic services such as authentication, data integrity, non-repudiation, or confidentiality. Note that most of these protocols (such as ECDSA) require different operations over finite fields such as prime-field addition or multiplication.

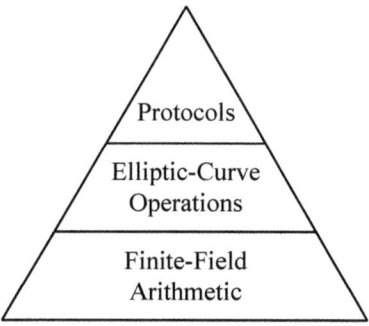

Among the most commonly used types of finite fields are prime fields $\mathbb{F}_p$ and binary-extension fields $\mathbb{F}_{2^m}$. These types have different characteristics so that the Weierstrass equation can be simplified and different formulas for point addition and point doubling

Fig. 1.   Hierarchy   of   ECC implementations

can be derived. Due to the differences of those fields, the performance of both software and hardware implementations can vary significantly.

In this paper, we compare two ECC implementations that are based on $\mathbb{F}_{2^{191}}$ and on $\mathbb{F}_{p_{192}}$. Both implementations use multi-precision arithmetic that means that all finite-field elements are split into smaller bit vectors of size W. Note that the one-bit difference does not have an impact in a relative comparison of ECC implementations since we use the same metric for both implementations. As elliptic curves, we decided to use the recommended NIST prime-field curve P-192 [30] and the ANSI X9.62 compliant binary-field curve B-191 [1], *i.e.* c2tnb191v1. This is because we would like to compare curves with nearly identical bit sizes (191 vs. 192 bits). The one-bit difference between those two fields can be considered as negligible.

Throughout the paper, we used the following notation. For prime fields with modulo p, $n = \lceil log_2(p) \rceil$ bits are required to represent a number. For binary fields with $f(z) = z^m + r(z)$ denoting an irreducible binary polynomial of degree m, a bit-vector with m entries can be used to represent any binary polynomial. Consequently the number of needed words to represent a $\mathbb{F}_p$ number is $N = \lceil n/W \rceil$ and number of needed words to represent a $\mathbb{F}_{2^m}$ polynomial is $M = \lceil m/W \rceil$.

3.1   Comparison Metric and Criteria

The efficiency of ECC-hardware implementations depends on different criteria. In order to make a fair comparison, we introduce the following metric consisting of four main attributes:

- The **area** requirement of a chip is important for any cost-sensitive application. This is because the area largely determines the chip costs at fabrication.
- Embedded systems require **low-power** and
- **low-energy** designs. This is an important issue especially in battery-powered environments.
- **Speed** of computation is important for many applications to be applicable in practice. The most neutral unit for measurement is the number of cycles it takes to perform a certain operation.

The maximum **frequency** that can be used to clock a design has a direct impact on the resulting execution time (speed) of any algorithm. But the previously mentioned applications heavily constrain the maximum frequency anyways, so we do not include the frequency measure into our metric.

Because the energy $W = Pt$ is defined as product of the electrical power P and time t, its properties are not handled explicitly within Section 4.

4   Comparing ECC-Hardware Designs over $\mathbb{F}_{2^m}$ and $\mathbb{F}_p$

In this section, we compare ECC hardware designs and the respective algorithms over $\mathbb{F}_{2^m}$ and over $\mathbb{F}_p$. We describe the differences of the finite-field operations, the respective elliptic-curve group operations, and compare the hardware designs of both types of fields regarding cryptographic protocols like ECDSA.

Algorithm 1. Prime-field addition	**Algorithm 2.** Binary-field addition
Require: Two integers $a, b \in [0, p-1]$ and modulus p.	**Require:** Binary polynomials $a(z), b(z)$ with maximum degree m-1.
Ensure: $c = (a + b) \pmod{p}$.	**Ensure:** $c(z) = a(z) + b(z)$.
1: $(\varepsilon, C[0]) \leftarrow A[0] + B[0]$.	1: **for** i from 0 to $M - 1$ **do**
2: **for** i from 1 to $N - 1$ **do**	2: $C[i] \leftarrow A[i] \oplus B[i]$.
3: $(\varepsilon, C[i]) \leftarrow A[i] + B[i] + \varepsilon$.	3: **end for**
4: **end for**	4: Return(c).
5: **if** $\varepsilon = 1$ or $c \geq p$ **then**	
6: $(\varepsilon, C[0]) \leftarrow C[0] - P[0]$.	
7: **for** i from 1 to $N - 1$ **do**	
8: $(\varepsilon, C[i]) \leftarrow C[i] - P[i] - \varepsilon$.	
9: **end for**	
10: **end if**	
11: Return(c).	

4.1 Finite-Field Arithmetics

Modular Addition and Subtraction. The most basic finite-field algorithms are addition and subtraction. Algorithm 1 and Algorithm 2 show modular-addition algorithms over $\mathbb{F}_p$ and $\mathbb{F}_{2^m}$. The major difference of those algorithms is the carry propagation ε. The polynomial addition is a simple XOR operation that does not incorporate a carry. A $\mathbb{F}_p$ addition, in contrast, needs up to three times more operations: the actual addition, a comparison of the result c with the prime p, and a modular reduction afterwards. By extending the range of the integers a, b, c form $[0, p - 1]$ to $[0, 2^{N*W} - 1]$, the comparison operation ($c \geq p$) can be avoided, which reduces the total number of arithmetic operations by about a third. Notice that for this partial reduction, all other operations handling a, b, c must be prepared for their extended range. A modular subtraction works similar as the modular addition.

Modular Multiplication. Modular multi-precision multiplications are usually realized by following an operand-scanning or product-scanning multiplication approach. A multiply-accumulate unit (cf. [12,15,16]) can be used to increase

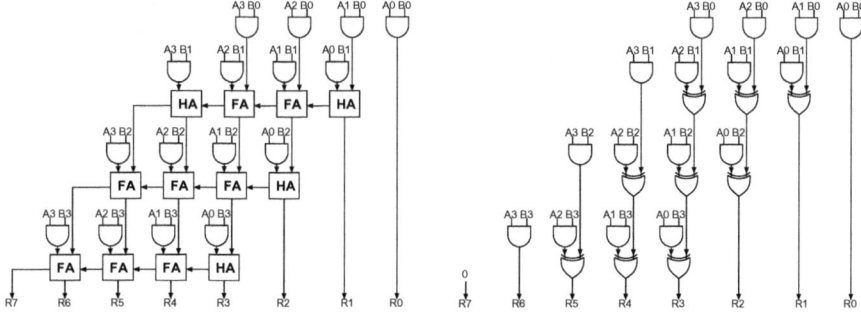

Fig. 2. 4-bit integer multiplier for $\mathbb{F}_p$ **Fig. 3.** 4-bit carry-less multiplier for $\mathbb{F}_{2^m}$

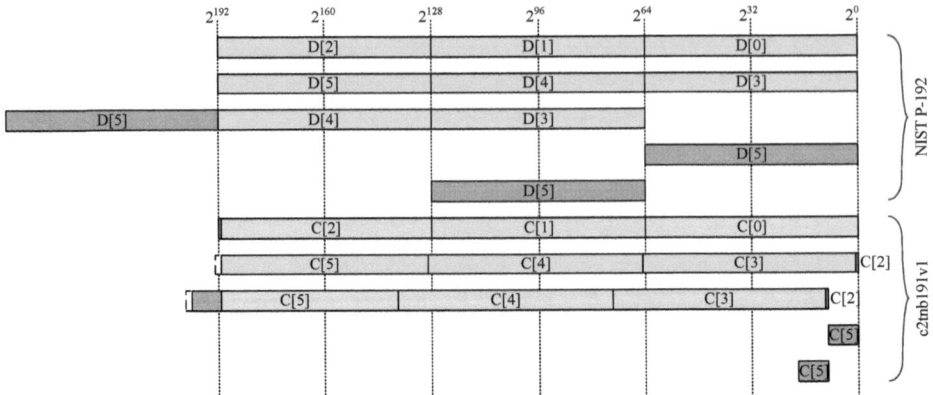

Fig. 4. Reduction using $p = 2^{192} - 2^{64} - 1$ on the top. Reduction using $f(z) = z^{191} + z^9 + 1$ on the bottom. In both cases, the product must be shifted and summed up.

the efficiency of the product-scanning method. Such a multiply-accumulate unit can be designed for $\mathbb{F}_p$ and $\mathbb{F}_{2^m}$. Figures 2 and 3 show the internal structure of 4-bit multipliers for integers and polynomials. The biggest advantage of the carry-less multiplier for $\mathbb{F}_{2^m}$ are the shorter critical path and the smaller area requirement (logical XOR cells are used instead of full-adder standard cells). Thus, the difference between a $\mathbb{F}_{2^m}$ and a $\mathbb{F}_p$ multiplication module can be up to 40 % in terms of area requirement. Also the power consumption for a multiplier designed out of XORs instead of full-adders is lower. However the execution times (in cycles) for an integer or binary-polynomial multiplication using the product-scanning method are equivalent.

A finite-field multiplication always needs a reduction. There exist many ways to realize modular reduction in hardware. One efficient way is to apply a (fast) reduction method using special primes, so called Mersenne-like primes, which are often used for recommended and standardized elliptic curves (e.g. the NIST recommended curves [30]). Figure 4 shows how intermediate multiplication results can be reduced using this fast reduction method for primes and polynomials over the curves NIST P-192: $p = 2^{192} - 2^{64} - 1$ and ANSI X9.62 c2tnb191v1: $f(z) = z^{191} + z^9 + 1$. The reduction can be performed with only shifts and additions. The for NIST P-192 necessary shift operations fit very well within the addressing scheme of 8-bit, 16-bit, or 32-bit architectures. The shift operations required by c2tnb191v1 do not fulfill this property. However, in cases where the shift operations are smaller than W, an additional hardcoded reduction logic can be used. In terms of area, this reduction logic is very cheap (about the size of a $\mathbb{F}_{2^m}$ addition).

Modular Squaring. Modular squaring is equivalent to a modular multiplication with two identical operands. Thus, an explicit implementation is often not necessary, especially in implementations where low area is a stringent requirement. However, if implemented it improves the performance since it is typically faster than modular multiplications [13].

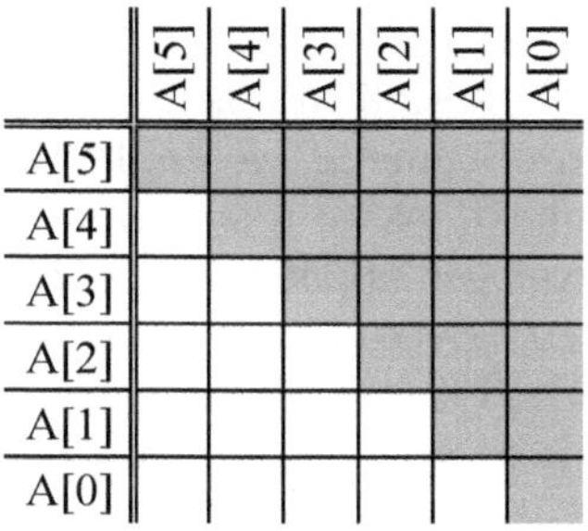

	A[5]	A[4]	A[3]	A[2]	A[1]	A[0]
A[5]	▓	▓	▓	▓	▓	▓
A[4]		▓	▓	▓	▓	▓
A[3]			▓	▓	▓	▓
A[2]				▓	▓	▓
A[1]					▓	▓
A[0]						▓

	A[5]	A[4]	A[3]	A[2]	A[1]	A[0]
A[5]	▓					
A[4]		▓				
A[3]			▓			
A[2]				▓		
A[1]					▓	
A[0]						▓

Fig. 5. Prime-field squaring operation. The necessary intermediate multiplications are shaded.

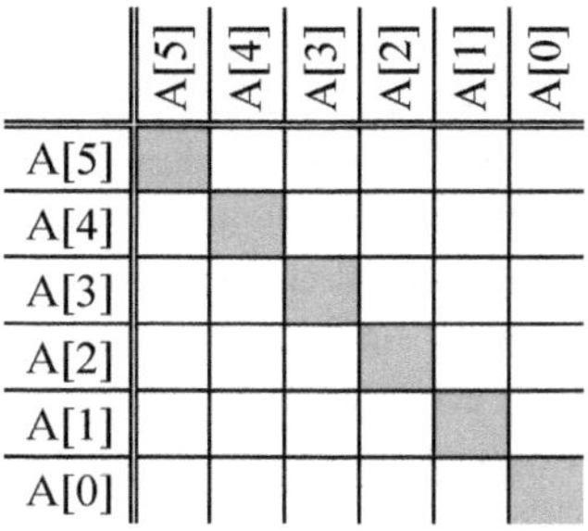

Fig. 6. Binary-field squaring operation. The necessary intermediate multiplications are shaded.

During a prime-field squaring operation, the two intermediate products $A[i] \times A[j]$ and $A[j] \times A[i]$, $\forall i \neq j \in [0, N-1]$, are identical. Figure 5 shows the operands of a 6-word squaring operation where only the necessary operations (multiplications) are shaded. Thus, the squaring operation can be up to two times faster than a multiplication.

Squarings over binary fields, as opposed, have the nice property that $a_i \times a_j + a_j \times a_i = 0$, $\forall i \neq j \in [0, m-1]$. If $a(z) = a_{m-1}z^{m-1} + \cdots + a_2 z^2 + a_1 z + a_0$, then $a(z)^2 = a_{m-1}z^{2m-2} + \cdots + a_2 z^4 + a_1 z^2 + a_0$. Thus, zero values are simply inserted between two consecutive bits a_i. Utilizing the binary multiplier from Figure 3, only M multiplications $A[i] \times A[i]$ are required to perform a binary-field squaring operation. As it can also be seen in Figure 6, the squaring operation is M times faster than a binary field multiplication. It can be performed with a similar runtime complexity as a modular addition.

In terms of runtime and lines-of-code, a $\mathbb{F}_{2^m}$ squaring can be up to $\frac{N^2}{2M}$ times faster than a $\mathbb{F}_p$ squaring.

Modular Inversion. What the inversion operations for prime and binary fields have in common is the very slow execution time. There are two common inversion methods. One is based on the extended Euclidean algorithm and one is based on Fermat's little theorem ($a = a^{2^m} \bmod f(z)\ \forall a \in \mathbb{F}_{2^m}$). For this paper the Montgomery inversion technique by Kalinski et al. [20] has been used for prime field inversion operations. Using Fermat's little theorem [18] for binary field inversions, with $a^{-1} \equiv a^{2^m-2} \bmod f(z)$, a field inversion can be performed by using $m-1$ squarings and several multiplications. In the case of c2tnb191v1, 190 squarings and 12 multiplications are necessary. Because of the fast squaring operations within binary fields, the runtime of this method exceeds any Euclidean-based algorithm. [14] gives a comparison of different algorithms for an inversion within the NIST B-163 field.

4.2   Elliptic-Curve Operations

The performance of EC-group operations over $\mathbb{F}_{2^m}$ and $\mathbb{F}_p$ differ significantly. We used formulae that reflect the state of the art in efficient ECC implementations.

For binary-field arithmetic, we applied the formulae proposed by J. López and R. Dahab [27]. Their formulae need six finite-field multiplications, five squarings, and three additions per key bit. For prime-field arithmetic, we applied the formulae of M. Hutter et al. [17] needing 12 multiplications, four squarings, and 16 additions (incl. subtractions). Both formulae have been applied within the Montgomery powering ladder scalar multiplication [19]. By comparing the formulae, it clearly shows that the binary formulae need 50 % less multiplications than the formulae over prime-field arithmetic. This is one of the most advantageous properties that encourages the use of $\mathbb{F}_{2^m}$ operations in ECC-hardware implementations. Note that both formulae use projective coordinates that means that no modular inversion is needed throughout the scalar multiplication[1].

4.3   Cryptographic Protocols

After the basic elliptic-curve operation of a scalar multiplication, we compare the performance of $\mathbb{F}_{2^m}$ and $\mathbb{F}_p$ processors in terms of higher-level protocols. In particular, we implemented ECDSA [30] on both types of (binary and prime-field based) processors. The main additional operations needed to support ECDSA is the SHA-1 [29] algorithm[2] to calculate the message digest of the message m and some prime-field operations, i.e. modular addition, multiplication, and inversion to calculate the digital signature $(r, s) = (k \times P, k^{-1}(\text{SHA-1}(m) + rd))$, where d represents the used private key.

For a more efficient ECDSA-verify algorithm, we additionally implemented a different methodology for calculating point multiplications. First, we applied Shamir's trick [8,9] to improve the performance of multiple point multiplication. Second, we used different formulae to perform the verification using Jacobian-projective coordinates [13] for the prime-field processor and López-Dahab coordinates [13,26] for the binary-field processor.

5   Comparison Results

For a fair comparison of binary field and prime-field ECC implementations, it is important to select a common controlling engine, common development tools, the same process technology, and elliptic curves of nearly the same bit size.

As a controller, we decided to use our own 16-bit microcontroller called Neptun [33,34,35] that is especially optimized for elliptic-curve cryptography. The processor comes with twelve special-purpose registers and uses a Harvard architecture with separated program and data memory. The usually area consuming data memory is made from a very area-efficient single-port RAM macro[3]. The program memory is a synthesized lookup table stored as Read-Only Memory

---

[1] Inversion is only needed after the calculation of $k \times P$ to convert the projective coordinates back to affine coordinates.

[2] Included in the design. 16-bit CPU is used to calculate the hash.

[3] All following area-related results would be different if latch or register-based RAM's are used.

Table 1. Prime-field vs. binary-field operations of our ECC-hardware architecture

	Cycles		Lines of Code		Operations/key-bit	
	$\mathbb{F}_{p_{192}}$	$\mathbb{F}_{2^{191}}$	$\mathbb{F}_{p_{192}}$	$\mathbb{F}_{2^{191}}$	$\mathbb{F}_{p_{192}}$ [17]	$\mathbb{F}_{2^{191}}$ [27]
Addition/Subtraction	64	38	64	38	16	3
Multiplication	329	265	329	265	12	6
Squaring	190	45	190	45	4	5
Inversion	46,560	14,611	397	117	-	-

(ROM). In fact, the area requirements of this lookup table is proportional to the number of lines-of-code (LOC) stored within the program memory. The central processing unit (CPU) is capable of the most basic arithmetic operations such as addition/subtraction, logic operations (AND, OR, XOR), and shift operations.

As target technology, we selected a 130nm low-leakage CMOS technology by UMC. This technology needs fewer power compared to larger 180 nm and 350 nm technologies and has a lower power leakage than smaller (*e.g.* 90 nm) technologies. The standard-cell library has been provided by Faraday Technology. The RAM-macro blocks have been generated using the Standard Memory Compiler FSA0A Memaker 200901.1.1 by the Faraday Technology Corporation [10]. For synthesis we used the Cadence RTL compiler [7] Version v08.10. For power-simulations we used Cadence First Encounter Version v08.10.

5.1   Finite-Field Arithmetic

The finite-field algorithms have been implemented as described in Section 4.1. All algorithms (except the algorithms for modular inverses) have been unrolled and optimized for our custom microcontroller instruction set (Assembler language). All results are summarized in Table 1.

It shows that our processor performs the binary-field addition about 40.6 % faster than the prime-field addition (the same holds for modular subtraction). Binary-field multiplication is 19.5 % faster than its prime-field counterpart because of the extra reduction logic provided to take advantage of the Mersenne-like irreducible polynomial. However, it shows that even when multi-precision arithmetic is used, the biggest advantage of binary-field operations is within the squaring operation. Its runtime is 4.2 times faster than the prime-field squaring operation. Finally, the two very distinct inversion techniques, discussed in Section 4.1, result in very different runtime and LOC results. The binary-field inversion implementation is 3.19 times faster and needs only 29.5 % LOC. It reuses the squaring and multiplication methods and subsequently only works for a single irreducible polynomial. The prime-field inversion, in contrast, works for any prime. The main reason for the higher code size are actually the additional utility functions (addition, subtraction, multiplication with 2, division by 2) that had to be implemented.

Table 2. Comparison of prime field vs. binary-field ECC implementations

Algorithm	$Q = k \times P$		ECDSA Sign		ECDSA Verify	
	$\mathbb{F}_{p_{192}}$	$\mathbb{F}_{2^{191}}$	$\mathbb{F}_{p_{192}}$	$\mathbb{F}_{2^{191}}$	$\mathbb{F}_{p_{192}}$	$\mathbb{F}_{2^{191}}$
Integer multiplier	required	–	required	required	required	required
Carry-less multiplier	–	required	–	required	–	required
Cycles	1,312,616	399,635	1,393,523	494,983	1,417,422	892,124
RAM entries	100	90	112	103	174	162
Program entries	1,207	699	1,662	1,689	1,519	1,875
Constants	61	60	100	129	100	141
Area requirements [GE]						
CPU	4,041	3,653	4,049	4,393	4,066	4,422
Program memory	4,494	2,683	7,203	7,432	7,589	8,031
Data memory	3,040	2,963	3,390	3,412	4,088	4,160
Total area	11,579	9,301	14,644	15,293	15,747	16,618
Power consumption @ 1 MHz [μW]						
CPU	20.40	19.99	18.36	18.48	17.93	20.38
Program memory	8.95	4.01	7.89	8.22	8.89	8.16
Data memory	10.59	8.92	11.91	10.86	11.80	12.52
Total power	41.37	34.78	39.54	39.47	40.55	43.12
Energy consumption [μJ]						
Energy	54.30	13.90	55.10	19.53	57.48	38.47

5.2 Elliptic-Curve Operations

Table 2 compares the absolute values and Table 3 compares the relative differences of the implemented prime-field and binary-field ECC implementations. The relative differences shown in Table 3 have been calculated using the Formula $\frac{Param(\mathbb{F}_{2^m})}{Param(\mathbb{F}_p)} - 1$. In the following, we separately consider point multiplication as well as signature generation and verification of the higher-level protocol of ECDSA.

In view of point multiplication, it shows that the binary-field based implementation is 3.28 times faster than the prime-field based opponent. The area requirement is 19.7 % better and the power consumption is 15.9 % lower for the binary-field processor. This results in an energy consumption which is 3.91 times lower than the calculation over prime fields. Note that the area difference mostly comes from the size of the program memory, the used multiplier within the CPU and the size of the necessary RAM macro. Even note that in both designs, about 50 % of the total power is consumed within the CPU.

Table 3. Relative difference between $\mathbb{F}_p$ and $\mathbb{F}_{2^m}$ based implementations

Algorithm	$Q = k \times P$	ECDSA Sign	ECDSA Verify
Runtime	−69.6 %	−64.5 %	−37.1 %
Area	−19.7 %	+4.4 %	+5.5 %
Power	−15.9 %	±0.0 %	+6.3 %
Energy	−74.4 %	−64.6 %	−33.1 %

Table 4. Comparison of different ECC implementation with related work

	ECC Curve	Area [GE]	Cycles [kCycles]	Power[a] μW	Energy μJ	VLSI technology
Auer 2009 [2]	$\mathbb{F}_{p_{192}}$	24,750	1,031	613.65	632.67	AMS C35
Fürbass 2007 [11]	$\mathbb{F}_{p_{192}}$	23,656	500	1,692.11	846.06	AMS C35
Wolkerstorfer 2005 [36]	$\mathbb{F}_{p_{192}}$	23,818	678	500.00	340.00	350nm
This work 2011	$\mathbb{F}_{p_{192}}$	**11,579**	**1,313**	**41.37**	**54.30**	**UMC L130**
Lee 2008 d=4 [25]	$\mathbb{F}_{2^{163}}$	15,356	79	37.39	2.95	UMC L130
Lee 2008 d=1 [25]	$\mathbb{F}_{2^{163}}$	12,506	276	32.42	8.95	UMC L130
Batina[b] 2006 d=4 [4]	$\mathbb{F}_{2^{163}}$	14,816	95	27.00	2.57	130nm
Batina[b] 2006 d=1 [4]	$\mathbb{F}_{2^{163}}$	13,104	354	27.00	9.56	130nm
Bock 2008 d=8 [6]	$\mathbb{F}_{2^{163}}$	16,247	47	148.76	6.99	INF SRF55V01P
Bock 2008 d=1 [6]	$\mathbb{F}_{2^{163}}$	10,392	280	54.31	15.21	INF SRF55V01P
Hein 2008 [15]	$\mathbb{F}_{2^{163}}$	11,904	296	101.87	30.15	UMC L180
Kumar 2006 [24]	$\mathbb{F}_{2^{163}}$	15,094	430	-	-	AMI C35
Kumar 2006 [24]	$\mathbb{F}_{2^{193}}$	17,723	565	-	-	AMI C35
Wolkerstorfer 2005 [36]	$\mathbb{F}_{2^{191}}$	23,818	426	500.00	213.00	350nm
This work 2011	$\mathbb{F}_{2^{191}}$	**9,301**	**399**	**34.78**	**13.90**	**UMC L130**

[a] All reference values were scaled to 1 MHz.
[b] RAM approximated with 4,890 GE. Power-consumption values do not include RAM.

5.3 Cryptographic Protocols

For ECDSA, only 455 lines of code (38 %) have to be added to the prime-field ECC processor to support all operations to sign data. This and the small increase of necessary RAM entries increased the total area requirement by 26.5 %. The execution time is increased by only 6.2 %. The differences in power and energy consumption are hardly noticeable. The changes to the binary-field ECC processor are much more significant. The CPU had to be extended with a small 8-bit integer multiply-accumulate unit, making it capable of prime and binary-field operations, increasing the area requirements of the CPU by 20 %. Adding all those algorithms increased the size of the program memory by 177 % and the total area of the processor by 64 %. Also the power and energy consumption increased by 13.5 % and 40.5 %. However, the runtime of the binary-field based ECDSA processor is still 2.82 times faster than the runtime of the prime-field based ECDSA processor. Even though the area and power consumption are approximately identical, the binary-field ECDSA processor needs 2.82 times less energy than the prime-field ECDSA processor.

The ECDSA verification needs one additional point multiplication compared to the ECDSA-signature generation algorithm which needs only one. Cause of Shamir's trick the runtime for the prime-field based algorithms differ by only 2 %. The area differs by 7.5 % and the power and energy results are almost identical. The ECDSA-signature verification algorithm over binary fields does not handle the two point multiplications as well. Whereas the area increased by only 8.7 %, the runtime increased by 80 %. This doubles the required energy needed for an ECDSA-signature verification compared to an ECDSA-signature generation.

Table 5. Comparison of our ECDSA implementations with related work

	ECC Curve	Area [GE]	Cycles [kCycles]	Power[a] μW	Energy μJ	VLSI technology
Kern 2010 [21]	$\mathbb{F}_{p_{160}}$	18,247	512	860.00	440.32	AMS C35
Hutter 2010 [16]	$\mathbb{F}_{p_{192}}$	19,115	859	1,507.79	1,295.19	AMS C35
Wenger[b] 2010 [34]	$\mathbb{F}_{p_{192}}$	11,686	1,377	113.86	156.79	UMC L180
This work[b] 2011	$\mathbb{F}_{p_{192}}$	**14,644**	**1,394**	**39.54**	**55.10**	UMC L130
This work 2011	$\mathbb{F}_{2^{191}}$	**15,293**	**495**	**39.47**	**19.53**	UMC L130

[a] All reference values have been scaled to 1 MHz.
[b] Nearly identical designs were used. The differences in area and power come from the different technologies and synthesizers used.

5.4 Comparison with Related Work

Table 4 gives a comparison with related work. All power results have been scaled to 1 MHz. The first five rows give related work over prime fields. The remaining rows contain related work over binary fields. Our $\mathbb{F}_p$ processor is 51 % smaller than the best related design by Wolkerstorfer [36]. In terms of cycles this processor is above average. Only the energy requirement by Öztürk [31] design is lower, but their design is not based on NIST P-192. The area results of the math processor are 10.4 % smaller than the smallest related implementation. Our speed, power, and energy results are larger than many other designs, but it should be noted that those designs have an advantage cause of the smaller elliptic curve used.

Table 5 summarizes related work regarding low-resource ECDSA-hardware implementations. In terms of power and energy consumption, we outperform existing solutions. The area requirements are lower than the work of Kern [21] and Hutter [16] but are higher than the work of Wenger [34].

6 Conclusion

In this paper, we compared the performance of two distinct ECC-hardware implementations that are based on prime-field (NIST P-192) and binary-field (ANSI c2tnb191v1) arithmetic. The comparison of the finite-field algorithms showed us the clear runtime advantage of the squaring (4.2 times) and addition (1.7 times) operations within the binary-extension field. When doing point multiplications, the $\mathbb{F}_{2^m}$ based processor outperforms the $\mathbb{F}_p$ based processor by 19.7 % in area, 69.6 % in runtime, 15.9 % in power, and 74.4 % in energy. In addition to these outcomes, we analyzed the impact of higher-level protocols on the finite-field processors. The implementation of both digital-signature generation and verification using ECDSA had led us to interesting findings. It was shown that the area and power advantages for the $\mathbb{F}_{2^m}$ based processor vanish while it still is 1.5-2.8 times faster and consequently more energy efficient than the $\mathbb{F}_p$ based processor.

These results can be applied to any future design of an ASIC ECC processor that is integrated in an area, power, or energy constrained device.

Acknowledgements. The work has been supported by the European Commission through the ICT program under contract ICT-SEC-2009-5-258754 (Tamper Resistant Sensor Node - TAMPRES) and by Austrian Science Fund (FWF) under grant number P22241-N23.

References

1. American National Standards Institute (ANSI). American National Standard X9.62-2005. Public Key Cryptography for the Financial Services Industry, The Elliptic Curve Digital Signature Algorithm (ECDSA) (2005)
2. Auer, A.: Scaling Hardware for Electronic Signatures to a Minimum. Master thesis, University of Technology Graz (October 2008)
3. Avanzi, R.M., Cohen, H., Doche, C., Frey, G., Lange, T., Nguyen, K., Vercauteren, F.: Handbook of Elliptic and Hyperelliptic Curve Cryptography. Chapman & Hall/CRC (2005)
4. Batina, L., Mentens, N., Sakiyama, K., Preneel, B., Verbauwhede, I.: Low-Cost Elliptic Curve Cryptography for Wireless Sensor Networks. In: Buttyán, L., Gligor, V.D., Westhoff, D. (eds.) ESAS 2006. LNCS, vol. 4357, pp. 6–17. Springer, Heidelberg (2006)
5. Blake, I.F., Seroussi, G., Smart, N.P.: Elliptic Curves in Cryptography. London Mathematical Society Lecture Notes Series, vol. 265. Cambridge University Press, Cambridge (1999)
6. Bock, H., Braun, M., Dichtl, M., Hess, E., Heyszl, J., Kargl, W., Koroschetz, H., Meyer, B., Seuschek, H.: A Milestone Towards RFID Products Offering Asymmetric Authentication Based on Elliptic Curve Cryptography. Invited talk at RFIDsec 2008 (July 2008)
7. Cadence Design Systems, Inc., San Jose, California, United States (2011). The Cadence Design Systems Website, http://www.cadence.com/
8. de Rooij, P.: Efficient Exponentiation Using Precomputation and Vector Addition Chains. In: De Santis, A. (ed.) EUROCRYPT 1994. LNCS, vol. 950, pp. 389–399. Springer, Heidelberg (1995)
9. El Gamal, T.: A Public Key Cryptosystem and a Signature Scheme Based on Discrete Logarithms. In: Blakely, G.R., Chaum, D. (eds.) CRYPTO 1984. LNCS, vol. 196, pp. 10–18. Springer, Heidelberg (1985)
10. Faraday Technology Corporation. Faraday FSA0A_C 0.13 μm ASIC Standard Cell Library (2004), http://www.faraday-tech.com
11. Fürbass, F., Wolkerstorfer, J.: ECC Processor with Low Die Size for RFID Applications. In: Proceedings of 2007 IEEE International Symposium on Circuits and Systems. IEEE (May 2007)
12. Großschädl, J., Savaş, E.: Instruction Set Extensions for Fast Arithmetic in Finite Fields GF(p) and GF(2^m). In: Joye, M., Quisquater, J.-J. (eds.) CHES 2004. LNCS, vol. 3156, pp. 133–147. Springer, Heidelberg (2004)
13. Hankerson, D., Menezes, A.J., Vanstone, S.: Guide to Elliptic Curve Cryptography. Springer, Heidelberg (2004)
14. Hein, D.: Elliptic Curve Cryptography ASIC for Radio Frequency Authentication. Master thesis, Technical University of Graz (April 2008)
15. Hein, D., Wolkerstorfer, J., Felber, N.: ECC Is Ready for RFID – A Proof in Silicon. In: Avanzi, R.M., Keliher, L., Sica, F. (eds.) SAC 2008. LNCS, vol. 5381, pp. 401–413. Springer, Heidelberg (2009)

16. Hutter, M., Feldhofer, M., Plos, T.: An ECDSA Processor for RFID Authentication. In: Ors Yalcin, S.B. (ed.) RFIDSec 2010. LNCS, vol. 6370, pp. 189–202. Springer, Heidelberg (2010)
17. Hutter, M., Joye, M., Sierra, Y.: Memory-Constrained Implementations of Elliptic Curve Cryptography in Co-Z Coordinate Representation. In: Nitaj, A., Pointcheval, D. (eds.) AFRICACRYPT 2011. LNCS, vol. 6737, pp. 170–187. Springer, Heidelberg (2011)
18. Itoh, T., Tsujii, S.: Effective recursive algorithm for computing multiplicative inverses in $GF(2^m)$. Electronic Letters 24(6), 334–335 (1988)
19. Joye, M., Yen, S.-M.: The Montgomery Powering Ladder. In: Kaliski Jr., B.S., Koç, Ç.K., Paar, C. (eds.) CHES 2002. LNCS, vol. 2523, pp. 291–302. Springer, Heidelberg (2003)
20. Kaliski, B.: The Montgomery Inverse and its Applications. IEEE Transactions on Computers 44(8), 1064–1065 (1995)
21. Kern, T., Feldhofer, M.: Low-Resource ECDSA Implementation for Passive RFID Tags. In: Proceedings of 17th IEEE International Conference on Electronics, Circuits and Systems (ICECS 2010), Athens, Greece, December 12-15, pp. 1236–1239. IEEE (2010)
22. Koblitz, N.: Elliptic Curve Cryptosystems. Mathematics of Computation 48, 203–209 (1987)
23. Koblitz, N.: A Course in Number Theory and Cryptography. Springer, Heidelberg (1994) ISBN 0-387-94293-9
24. Kumar, S.S., Paar, C.: Are standards compliant Elliptic Curve Cryptosystems feasible on RFID? In: Workshop on RFID Security (RFIDSec 2006), Graz, Austria, July 12-14 (2006)
25. Lee, Y.K., Sakiyama, K., Batina, L., Verbauwhede, I.: Elliptic-Curve-Based Security Processor for RFID. IEEE Transactions on Computers 57(11), 1514–1527 (2008)
26. López, J., Dahab, R.: Improved Algorithms for Elliptic Curve Arithmetic in $GF(2^n)$. In: Tavares, S., Meijer, H. (eds.) SAC 1998. LNCS, vol. 1556, pp. 201–212. Springer, Heidelberg (1999)
27. López, J., Dahab, R.: Fast Multiplication on Elliptic Curves over $GF(2^m)$. In: Koç, Ç.K., Paar, C. (eds.) CHES 1999. LNCS, vol. 1717, pp. 316–327. Springer, Heidelberg (1999)
28. Miller, V.S.: Use of Elliptic Curves in Cryptography. In: Williams, H.C. (ed.) CRYPTO 1985. LNCS, vol. 218, pp. 417–426. Springer, Heidelberg (1986)
29. National Institute of Standards and Technology (NIST). FIPS-180-3: Secure Hash Standard (October 2008), http://www.itl.nist.gov/fipspubs/
30. National Institute of Standards and Technology (NIST). FIPS-186-3: Digital Signature Standard (DSS) (2009), http://www.itl.nist.gov/fipspubs/
31. Öztürk, E., Sunar, B., Savaş, E.: Low-Power Elliptic Curve Cryptography Using Scaled Modular Arithmetic. In: Joye, M., Quisquater, J.-J. (eds.) CHES 2004. LNCS, vol. 3156, pp. 92–106. Springer, Heidelberg (2004)
32. Satoh, A., Takano, K.: A Scalable Dual-Field Elliptic Curve Cryptographic Processor. IEEE Transactions on Computers 52(4), 449–460 (2003)
33. Wenger, E., Feldhofer, M., Felber, N.: A 16-Bit Microprocessor Chip for Cryptographic Operations on Low-Resource Devices. In: Proceedings of Austrochip 2010, Villach, Austria, October 6, pp. 55–60 (2010) ISBN 978-3-200-01945-4
34. Wenger, E., Feldhofer, M., Felber, N.: Low-Resource Hardware Design of an Elliptic Curve Processor for Contactless Devices. In: Chung, Y., Yung, M. (eds.) WISA 2010. LNCS, vol. 6513, pp. 92–106. Springer, Heidelberg (2011)

35. Wenger, E., Hutter, M.: A Hardware Processor Supporting Elliptic Curve Cryptography for Less Than 9kGEs. In: Proceedings of the Tenth Smart Card Research and Advanced Application Conference, CARDIS 2011, Leuven, Belgium, September 15-16 (2011)
36. Wolkerstorfer, J.: Is Elliptic-Curve Cryptography Suitable for Small Devices? In: Workshop on RFID and Lightweight Crypto, Graz, Austria, July 13-15, pp. 78–91 (2005)

Author Index

GPSR Compliance

The European Union's (EU) General Product Safety Regulation (GPSR) is a set of rules that requires consumer products to be safe and our obligations to ensure this.

If you have any concerns about our products, you can contact us on ProductSafety@springernature.com

In case Publisher is established outside the EU, the EU authorized representative is:

Springer Nature Customer Service Center GmbH
Europaplatz 3
69115 Heidelberg, Germany

Batch number: 09474011

Printed by Printforce, the Netherlands